Carol J. Loomis is a senior editor-at-large at *Fortune*, where she has worked since 1954. She has been the magazine's expert on Warren Buffett since 1966 and has edited his annual letter to Berkshire Hathaway's shareholders since 1977. Her many honours include five lifetime achievement awards, including a Gerald Loeb Award for business journalism and Time Inc.'s first-ever Henry Luce Award. This is her first book. She lives in Westchester County.

# Tap Dancing to Work

WARREN BUFFETT

ON PRACTICALLY EVERYTHING, 1966–2013:

A *FORTUNE* MAGAZINE BOOK

· COLLECTED AND EXPANDED BY ·

**CAROL LOOMIS**

PORTFOLIO
PENGUIN

PORTFOLIO PENGUIN

Published by the Penguin Group
Penguin Books Ltd, 80 Strand, London WC2R 0RL, England
Penguin Group (USA) Inc., 375 Hudson Street, New York, New York 10014, USA
Penguin Group (Canada), 90 Eglinton Avenue East, Suite 700, Toronto, Ontario, Canada M4P 2Y3
(a division of Pearson Penguin Canada Inc.)
Penguin Ireland, 25 St Stephen's Green, Dublin 2, Ireland (a division of Penguin Books Ltd)
Penguin Group (Australia), 707 Collins Street, Melbourne, Victoria 3008, Australia
(a division of Pearson Australia Group Pty Ltd)
Penguin Books India Pvt Ltd, 11 Community Centre, Panchsheel Park, New Delhi – 110 017, India
Penguin Group (NZ), 67 Apollo Drive, Rosedale, Auckland 0632, New Zealand
(a division of Pearson New Zealand Ltd)
Penguin Books (South Africa) (Pty) Ltd, Block D, Rosebank Office Park,
181 Jan Smuts Avenue, Parktown North, Gauteng 2193, South Africa

Penguin Books Ltd, Registered Offices: 80 Strand, London WC2R 0RL, England

www.penguin.com

First published in the United States of America by Portfolio / Penguin,
a member of Penguin Group (USA) Inc. 2012
First published in Great Britain by Portfolio Penguin 2012
This paperback edition with new material published in the United States of America 2013
This edition published in Great Britain 2014
002

All of the articles (and excerpts from articles) in this book were first published
in *Fortune* magazine in the years 1966 through 2013

'Gates on Buffett' (originally titled 'What I Learned from Warren Buffett') by Bill Gates.
Copyright 1995 Microsoft Corp. Originally published by the *Harvard Business Review*
(January/February 1996 issue). Reprinted by permission of Microsoft Corp

'Letters from Chairman Buffett' by Andrew Tobias. Originally published in *Fortune* magazine,
issue of 22 August 1983. Reprinted by permission of the author

Printed in Great Britain by Clays Ltd, St Ives plc

ISBN: 978-0-670-92238-3

www.greenpenguin.co.uk

**MIX**
Paper from
responsible sources
FSC   **FSC® C018179**
www.fsc.org

Penguin Books is committed to a sustainable
future for our business, our readers and our planet.
This book is made from Forest Stewardship
Council™ certified paper.

# CONTENTS

# PREFACE

Because I have long been the chief writer about Warren Buffett at *Fortune*, which for decades has covered him more closely than any other business publication, I have often been asked whether I'm not going to branch out and write a Buffett biography. I have always said no, sure beyond a doubt that a writer who is a good friend of the subject does not make a good biographer. And I have indeed been a close friend of Warren's for more than forty years, a shareholder in his company, Berkshire Hathaway, for almost that long, and the pro bono editor of his annual letter to shareholders for thirty-five. All of those facts can be accommodated in my *Fortune* articles about Buffett, simply by my informing the reader that they exist. But they are not a firm base for a wide-ranging personal and professional biography, in which there should be considerable distance between writer and subject. Its absence in this case settled the question.

But then it dawned on me that the scores of Buffett articles we have published in *Fortune* are in themselves a *business* biography—and a perfect one for a book. Here you have it: *Tap Dancing to Work*, the description that Buffett has long applied to his love for running Berkshire. This book is a collection, arranged chronologically for the most part, of all our big articles about Warren (plus some shorter, lighter ones like "Are Jimmy and Warren Buffett Related?"). For each of the big stories I've written an introduction or commentary—about forty of them in total. These paragraphs explain, for example, what's particularly important about the story, what Warren forecast that did or didn't come true, what he thinks today about the story's main point. Overall, the book's material covers a large chunk of history—forty-seven years—an important span of time not only for Buffett but for the U.S. economy in which he has so successfully operated. ("Hmm, forty-seven years," Buffett would be inclined to say. "That's a long time—almost one-fifth of the years the U.S. has existed.")

The articles and excerpts in this book were for the most part written by me and about forty other *Fortune* journalists (including three, John Huey, Rik Kirkland, and Andy Serwer, who rose to managing editor, with John subsequently moving still higher to the post of Time Inc.'s editor-in-chief). But the authors also include Buffett himself, who wrote three important stories expressly for us and inserted think-piece sections into his annual letters that we lifted out and made into stories. Also represented is that well-known business writer Bill Gates.

In content as well as authors, this book is enormously diverse. We had the good sense along the way not to repeat ourselves too much, and when we did, I normally edited out the repetition. Actually, not repeating ourselves was pretty easy, because Warren kept doing new things.

When you finish this book, you will have seen the arc of Warren's business life. The first story in which we ever mentioned him was in 1966. He got one sentence then in an investing piece I wrote about another man (Alfred Winslow Jones) and in which I misspelled Buffett—giving it only one *t*. I will try, however weakly, to pardon myself for that by saying that outside Omaha (where a few investors knew Warren well because he was making them rich) he was in 1966 pretty much unknown. Jump to the early 1980s, and he hadn't gained much ground. When *Fortune* hired freelancer Andrew Tobias in 1983 to write a piece about Buffett's shareholder letters (see page 34), Tobias had never heard of this fellow. That means, alas, that Tobias had missed the big story about inflation that Warren wrote for us in 1977 (see page 9) and about which he still gets mail.

The middle part of the book, starting with my 1988 profile, "The Inside Story of Warren Buffett," describes his adding a second profession, business management, to his old one of investor—and next, of course, he made Berkshire Hathaway a huge force in corporate America. Few people recognize the insignificance from which that company has come. In 1965, when Warren took it over, Berkshire was a New England textile manufacturer far too small to have made the *Fortune 500* list. For 2012, in contrast, it was No. 5 on the *500*. That rank is for revenues, which is the *500*'s primary criterion. In market value, a higher accomplishment in Buffett's thinking, Berkshire was No. 4.

And all that has happened in one man's lifetime, which of course is not over.

The final years covered by the book complete the arc, so to speak, by taking Warren beyond investing and business to philanthropy. This step did not require him to invent a philosophy. He has never believed in large inheritances (see page 54) and almost all of his money has always been slated to go to philanthropy. But he had always assumed that his wife, Susie—two years younger—would outlive him and be the one who gave away his money. Susie then died of a stroke in 2004, and the philanthropy yoke settled back, none too lightly, on Warren. Thus came his announcement in 2006 that he would start to give away his money immediately, and his 2010 move, with Bill and Melinda Gates, to create the Giving Pledge. *Fortune* broke the news in each instance, in cover stories that appear toward the end of this book.

The final article in this paperback, "Warren Buffett Is Bullish . . . on Women," was written by Buffett himself and appeared in *Fortune* several months after the hardcover edition was released in late 2012. So the article is both new content in the book and the reason the publisher slightly adjusted its title to now take in 2013. The piece is also excellent reading, in which Buffett's distinctive voice is turned to a hot topic of the year—women in business.

This paperback also includes updated introductions that incorporate both Buffett/Berkshire events and stock price movements occurring since the hardcover edition was published.

For me, compiling this book has been a trek through my own career at *Fortune* (1954–still happening) and through endless warnings as well to put two *t*'s on Buffett. More significantly, it has been an extended and rewarding reminder of Buffett's investment and business genius, creativeness, and—not the least of these—consistency of thought.

A friend of well-known writer William Buckley made a statement about him that I will adapt here. *Fortune* and I were lucky to be standing alongside Warren Buffett as he was becoming Warren Buffett.

# The Jones Nobody Keeps Up With

## April 1966

### BY CAROL LOOMIS

*It may be odd to start a book about one man—Warren Buffett—with an article about another—Alfred Winslow Jones. But this 1966 piece about Jones deserves the lead-off position. To begin with, this is the first time that* Fortune *mentioned the name Buffett, except that we embarrassingly spelled it "Buffet," with only one t. I made that mistake: yours truly, Carol Loomis, the editor of this book and the author of many of the articles in it, including this one. Later my husband, John Loomis, then an institutional securities salesman, met Buffett, who shortly after called me up to kid me a bit about the misspelling. Further on, he and his wife, Susie, asked John and me to have lunch in New York, and they and we began a friendship that in time, you might say, led to this book.*

*A second point about the article is that it rather famously introduced A. W. Jones and his concept of a "hedged" fund to the world. Not that Jones was the first Wall Streeter to establish such a fund: Benjamin Graham, for one, had earlier run a partnership that used hedging strategies. But Jones's rocketing success was a revelation to most* Fortune *readers, and this article took on a life of its own, becoming an unofficial prospectus for many people who hastened to start "Jones-type" funds of their own. Histories of the hedge fund industry almost always refer to this article as a milestone in that world's development.*

*Close readers of the article may note the tentativeness of the first sentence: "There are reasons to believe . . ." is hardly a ringing declaration. The explanation, of course, is that though I had the record of private investor A. W. Jones & Co. and had discovered none better, my knowledge of how other private investors were doing was certainly not complete.*

*Had the record of Omaha's Buffett Partnership Ltd. then been in our hands, a matchup of Buffett and Jones would have been interesting but hardly conclusive. We had a ten-year record for A. W. Jones & Co., but Buffett Partnership kept its books on the calendar year and had only nine of those behind it. As for five years, Jones ended his 1965 fiscal year in May and for the period made 325 percent. Buffett's 1965 year ended in December, and he made 334 percent.*

*But all that was history and the paths of the two men soon diverged: As the next article discusses, Buffett closed down his partnership while Jones stayed on to struggle with a stock market grown—for the moment—very difficult for hedge funds.* —CL

There are reasons to believe that the best professional manager of investors' money these days is a quiet-spoken, seldom photographed man named Alfred Winslow Jones. Few businessmen have heard of him, although some with long memories may remember his articles in *Fortune*; he was a staff writer in the early 1940s. In any case, his performance in the stock market in recent years has made him one of the wonders of Wall Street—and made millionaires of several of his investors. On investments left with him during the five years ended last May 31 (when he closed his 1965 fiscal year), Jones made 325 percent. Fidelity Trend Fund, which had the best record of any mutual fund during those years, made "only" 225 percent. For the *ten*-year period ended in May, Jones made 670 percent; Dreyfus Fund, the leader among mutual funds that were in business all during that decade, had a 358 percent gain.

The vehicle through which Jones operates is not a mutual fund but a limited partnership. Jones runs two such partnerships, and they have slightly different investment objectives. In each case, however, the underlying investment strategy is the same: the fund's capital is both leveraged and "hedged." The leverage arises from the fact that the fund margins itself to the hilt; the hedge is provided by short positions—there are always some in the fund's portfolio. There are about sixty investors in each of the two funds, and their average investment now works out to about $460,000.

Jones's accomplishments have spawned a number of other "hedge funds." In the last two years, two of Jones's principal associates have left his organization and set up limited partnerships of their own. One is known as City Associates (it has capital of about $17,500,000), the other as Fairfield Partners ($14 million); both have had outstanding performance records.

This month a new partnership, Fleschner Becker Associates, will go into business as a hedge fund; its principals are Wall Street brokers who have done business with Jones over the last few years. Besides these partnerships, a number of other hedge funds are operating on a small scale.

In addition, a small brokerage firm named L. Hubshman & Co., which has also done business with Jones, has bypassed the partnership pattern and is setting up an open-end investment company (i.e., a mutual fund), the Hubshman Fund, which will invest on hedge-fund principles. It remains to be seen whether a regulated investment company can use Jones's techniques as effectively as a private partnership does. Meanwhile Hubshman's move opens the way for a large number of investors to buy themselves a stake in the hedge-fund idea.

For most of his life Jones, who is now sixty-five, was more interested in sociology and in writing than he was in the stock market. In 1938 he set out to get his Ph.D. in sociology at Columbia University. While working toward the degree, he served as director of Columbia's Institute for Applied Social Analysis and undertook for it a major project on class distinctions in the U.S. The project became the basis for his doctoral thesis, which was published under the title *Life, Liberty, and Property* (two years ago it was reprinted by Octagon Books, Inc.). *Fortune* asked Jones to condense the book into an article (February 1941) and hired him as a writer. Over the next five years (part of it spent with *Time*) he wrote articles on such non-financial subjects as Atlantic convoys, farm cooperatives, and boys' prep schools. He left Time Inc. in 1946, but in March 1949 he was back in the pages of *Fortune* with a free-lance article,

"Fashions in Forecasting," which reported on various "technical" approaches to the stock market.

His research for this story convinced him that he could make a living in the stock market, and early in 1949 he and four friends formed A. W. Jones & Co. as a general partnership. Their initial capital was $100,000, of which Jones himself put up $40,000. In its first year the partnership's gain on its capital came to a satisfactory 17.3 percent, but this was only a suggestion of things to come. Not quite all the original capital has been left in the partnership, but if it had been it would today be worth $4,920,789 (before any allowance for the partners' taxes).

In the early years Jones was experimenting with a number of investment approaches, including the "hedge" idea, which was essentially his own. Increasingly, he began to concentrate on refining and employing this new technique.

In effect, the hedge concept puts Jones in a position to make money on both rising and falling stocks, and also partially shelters him if he misjudges the general trend of the market. He assumes that a prudent investor wants to protect part of his capital from such misjudgments. Most investors would build their defenses around cash reserves or bonds, but Jones protects himself by selling short.

To those investors who regard short selling with suspicion, Jones would simply say that he is using "speculative techniques for conservative ends." As illustration, he is given to contrasting his methods with those of an investor who has, say, $100,000, and elects to invest $80,000 of it in stocks and the rest in "safe" bonds. Jones would use the $100,000 to borrow perhaps another $50,000. (Under the current margin requirements of 70 percent, he could not borrow that much to buy listed stocks; however, he could borrow even more than $50,000 for purchases of convertible bonds and unlisted stocks.) Of the $150,000 total, he might put $110,000 into stocks he likes and sell short $40,000 worth of stocks he thinks are overvalued. Thus he ends up with $40,000 of his long position hedged—i.e., offset by a short position—and the remaining $70,000 fully exposed.

This figure represents 70 percent of his original capital, and Jones therefore describes his "risk" as 70. (In practice, there is an added complication: Jones adjusts the dollar figures in a calculation that assumes some individual stocks to be more volatile, and therefore more risky, than others. Every stock in Jones's portfolio is assigned a "velocity" rating—e.g., Syntex's is 6.61, Kerr-McGee's 1.72—and the dollars invested are multiplied by these factors. The "adjusted" dollars are then used to figure the risk.) By Jones's method of measuring, the more conventional investor who put $20,000 into bonds, neither borrowing nor selling short, had a risk of 80. If the stock market goes down by 10 percent and all stocks in these two portfolios do likewise, Jones will break even on the hedged part of his portfolio and will lose less on his un-hedged position—$7,000 instead of $8,000—than the other investor. If the stocks all *rise* by 10 percent, Jones will make less than the other investor.

His problem, therefore, is to buy stocks that will rise more than the general market, and sell stocks short that will rise less than the averages (or will actually fall). If he succeeds in this effort, his rewards are multiplied because he is employing not just a portion of his capital but 150 percent of it. The main advantage of the hedge concept, then, is that the investor's short position enables him to operate on the long side with maximum aggressiveness.

Jones's record in forecasting the direction of the market seems to have been only fair. In the early part of 1962 he had his investors in a high risk position of 140. As the market declined, he gradually increased his short position, but not as quickly as he should have. His losses that spring were heavy, and his investors ended up with a small loss for the fiscal year (this is the only losing year in Jones's history). After the break, furthermore, he turned bearish and so did not at first benefit from the market's recovery. Last year, as it happened, Jones remained quite bullish through the May–June decline, and then got bearish just about the time the big rally began. As prices rose in August, Jones actually moved to a minus 18 risk—i.e., his short positions exceeded his longs, with the unhedged short position amounting to 18 percent of the partnership capital.

Despite these miscalculations about the direction of the market, Jones's selections of individual stocks have generally been brilliant. When he finally did turn bullish in the fall, he was long on a lot of the "right" stocks—e.g., Syntex, National Video, Fairchild Camera, the airlines. By the end of February he had racked up gains for the fiscal year of 38 percent in one fund, 31 percent in the other, compared to an increase (including dividends) of 6 percent for the Dow-Jones industrials.

Any hedge-fund operator will explain that although the hedge concept is essential—"I need it to sleep nights," says one of them—the real secret of his success is his ability to get good information about stocks and to be able to act on it quickly. The partnership form of organization is helpful in both respects, and it is worth examining Jones's arrangements closely.

Jones changed his firm from a general to a limited partnership in 1952 in order to accommodate several friends who were by then eager to have him handle their money. The new partners were let in on the understanding that they could withdraw their money from the partnership, or put new money into it, only at the end of each fiscal year. This agreement still exists. Moreover, Jones and the other general partners are to receive as compensation 20 percent of any realized profits (after deduction of realized losses) made on the limited partners' money. This arrangement is common to all the hedge funds, and the idea was not original with Jones. Benjamin Graham, for one, had once run a limited partnership along the same lines. There are also some mutual funds today—e.g., Oppenheimer Fund, Equity Fund, Leon B. Allen Fund—whose managers are paid on the basis of profits, although less liberally than Jones; the Hubshman Fund will have a similar arrangement.

The limited partners would seem to have no cause for complaint about the huge profits realized by Jones. Those sensational comparative performance figures reflect the limited partners' results *after* deduction of the general partners' share of their profits. In other words, the figures understate Jones's actual superiority over Fidelity Trend and Dreyfus in portfolio performance.

It is small wonder, then, that as the years have gone by a lot of investors have sought to get into Jones's partnerships. But since they are organized as private, unregistered funds, Jones took in only a few additional partners each year, primarily investors who were relatives or close friends of existing partners.

By now, however, the partners have got to be a diverse group. The largest limited partnership interest belongs to Louis E. Stephens, a Mexico City businessman (he is the retired general manager of General Products S.A., a chemical company), who had $2,260,000 in one Jones partnership at the start of this fiscal year. Another large stake is held by A. Arlie Sinaiko, a physician turned professional sculptor, who, together with his family, has about $2 million invested with Jones; most of this amount represents portfolio appreciation. Several of the Richardsons associated with Richardson-Merrell, including the company's chairman, Smith Richardson Jr., have money in the partnerships. So does Louis Fischer, author of *The Life of Lenin* and other books, and Samuel Stayman, the bridge expert. Stayman, whose wealth comes primarily from a woolen business, also has money in the two other big hedge funds, City Associates and Fairfield Partners, and in Buffet [sic] Partnership Ltd., a $45 million Omaha operation that uses hedge principles to some extent but that has mainly, and very successfully, concentrated on long-term investment. Other prominent businessmen in the hedge funds are Laurence Tisch, president of Loew's Theatres, and Maurice Perlstein, ex-president of Kellwood Co.

All told, Jones's limited partners had an investment with him of $44,898,000 as of June 1. Of this amount, about $5 million represented investments by the immediate families of the ten general partners. In addition, the general partners themselves, who have agreed to keep all of their investment funds in the partnership, had another $5 million invested. Of this about $2 million is Jones's own. (His two children, both of them limited partners, have another $2,500,000 together.) In total, including the gains he has made so far this fiscal year, Jones is managing close to $70 million of capital. Even with the borrowed money added in, this makes his operation no bigger than a medium-sized mutual fund.

But the weight Jones swings on Wall Street is many times magnified by the fact that, like all hedge-fund operators, he is a prodigious producer of commissions. Since short sales can never result in anything but short-term gains or losses, the hedge operator moves in and out of them freely. Similarly, when he has losses on the short sales, he also finds it easier to take offsetting short-term gains on long positions. In general, the hedge funds have a high portfolio turnover.

One big reason the hedge funds find it natural to move in and out of stocks a lot is that, far more than most other funds, they have a special ability to get a flow of good, fresh ideas about stocks from brokers—and get them early. Most mutual funds are virtually compelled to channel a large proportion (perhaps as much as 90 percent) of the commissions they generate to brokers who sell the shares of their fund to the public. They have very little commission business left over for any firms that are unimportant in mutual-fund sales but that are strong on research. The partnership funds, on the other hand, have no shares to sell and thus can afford to "pay" a generous portion of their commissions for research. In Jones's case, the payments take a round-about form. The brokerage firm of Neuberger & Berman executes practically all Jones's orders, but keeps only about 50 percent of the commissions generated; it sends the remaining 50 percent, in the form of "give-up" checks, to brokers designated by Jones. A brokerage firm that Jones relies on heavily for research may get possibly $50,000 in give-ups a year, of which a third or more might go to the salesman who was covering the account and supplying those good ideas. That salesman is therefore likely to be very cooperative about keeping Jones informed.

The Jones organization is set up so that decisions about purchases and sales can be made immediately, without committee consultation. There are five portfolio managers, all general partners, each of whom has discretion over a percentage of the partnership capital; in addition, several outside "advisers," one of them an investment counselor, the rest brokerage-house analysts or salesmen, have been given blocks of capital to manage. Either Jones or his No. 2 man, Donald Woodward, sees each order before it is executed, but they interfere only when it seems to them that the partnership is getting overloaded with a given stock—e.g., if several of the portfolio managers are being sold on the stock at the same time—or is maneuvering itself into an undesirable "risk" position.

The portfolio managers will tell you that, given the long-term trend of the market upward, their most difficult job is picking good short sales. Wall Street's analysts typically concentrate on discovering bullish corporate situations, and only rarely have promising shorts to bring to Jones. As a result, he and the other hedge-fund managers normally consider themselves lucky to break even on their short portfolios. Early last month Jones was short about sixty different stocks, including Korvette, Bristol-Myers, Admiral, and Du Pont. *All* of the big hedge funds were short Control Data.

Recently Jones has devoted more and more time to traveling and to philanthropic projects, many of them financed by his own Foundation for Voluntary Service. He has made some field trips for the Peace Corps, and his own foundation is currently supporting the activities in this country of five young social workers from India, as a sort of "Reverse Peace Corps." He is also thinking of writing another book—on what to do about poverty in the U.S.

# From "Hard Times Come to the Hedge Funds"

January 1970

*An excerpt from an article by Carol Loomis*

*After years of extravagant profits, many gained in the wildly speculative market of 1968, the fledgling hedge fund industry was hammered in 1969 by a rough bear market. The hedging strategies that were supposed to protect the funds largely failed. Most funds showed losses, some suffered large withdrawals of capital, and a few folded.*

*In contrast, Buffett Partnership—the subject of a short section in this article—made money in 1969, adding to its unbroken string of profits. The fund had meanwhile grown big, to $100 million in assets (versus the $160 million divided between two funds that A. W. Jones ran).*

*But Warren Buffett, then thirty-nine, was hardly happy with this world. He regarded the speculative excesses of 1968 as insane. "This is a market I don't understand," he said. He also suspected that making money in stocks was going to become harder to do. So he announced in 1969 that, after thirteen years of operation, he would close Buffett Partnership at the end of the year.*

*That point starts off the article's two paragraphs about Buffett, which we reprint here. This excerpt also reports the outstanding returns that Buffett delivered his limited partners: a compounded annual return for the thirteen years of 23.8 percent. The fund's "gross" record—that is, before Buffett took his incentive compensation—was naturally still more stunning: a compounded annual return of 29.5 percent, against a comparable total return for the Dow of 7.4 percent. Buffett himself accumulated a fortune of about $25 million from running the partnership.*

*Buffett's reasoning as to why he should close the partnership turned out to be less on the money. True, over the near term the stock market ran into tough times, particularly in 1973 and 1974. But stocks, of course, proceeded over the decades to reward investors handsomely. Fortunately for Buffett—and for the investors who followed him—he stayed in the market as chief executive of Berkshire Hathaway and master investor of its excess cash.*

*Buffett's other stated reason for closing up shop—that it was time to stop amassing money and get on to other things—simply faded into unreality. It wasn't the money that drove him on. To this day, he leads an unostentatious life. But building wealth has to him been an endlessly fascinating game. One inning of that game ended as he closed the partnership. The others commenced as he settled back to running Berkshire. —CL*

The arrival of 1970 will mark not only the demise of certain unsuccessful hedge funds and the constriction of still others, but will also bring the liquidation of one of the country's oldest, largest, and most successful investment partnerships, Buffett Partnership Ltd. of Omaha. To call the Buffett operation a hedge fund is accurate only in the sense that Warren E. Buffett, 39, the general partner, shares in the profits of the limited partners. (Under his quite unusual arrangement, the limited partners keep all of the annual gains up to 6%; above that level Buffett takes a one-quarter cut.) Otherwise he is set apart from the regular hedge funds by the fact that he has invested almost exclusively in long-term "value" situations. Buffett's record has been extraordinarily good. In his thirteen years of operation, all of them (including 1969) profitable, he compounded his investors' money at a 24% annual rate.

But now, to the immense regret of his limited partners, Buffett is quitting the game. His reasons for doing so are several, and include a strong feeling that his time and money (he is a millionaire many times over) should now be directed toward other goals than simply the making of more money. But he also suspects that some of the juice has gone out of the stock market and that sizable gains are in the future going to be very hard to come by. Consequently, he has suggested to his investors that they may want to take the "passive" way out, investing their partnership money not in the stock market but rather municipal bonds.

*The full text of "Hard Times Come to the Hedge Funds" is available at fortune .com/buffettbook.*

# How Inflation Swindles the Equity Investor

May 1977

## BY WARREN BUFFETT

*This book contains thirteen articles authored by Warren Buffett. Three are pieces that he wrote expressly for* Fortune, *the first of which follows. The others are two major speeches of his that we turned into articles; an important letter he sent to a congressman; his philanthropic pledge; and six excerpts from his annual Berkshire letter.*

*For this article, the inaugural piece of the twelve, a senior and very talented* Fortune *editor, Dan Seligman, made a trip to Omaha to negotiate with Buffett about revisions to his first draft. Seligman found this $1-an-article writer generally resistant to shortening the piece and not too amenable to changes of any kind. At one point, a frustrated Seligman called* Fortune's *managing editor, Bob Lubar, to suggest that perhaps the magazine should not publish the article at all. But Lubar said he thought the article was worthwhile and should not be abandoned.*

*The article that emerged—no doubt reflecting at least some Seligman edits— was an early example of Buffett's extraordinary talent for thinking through complicated problems. To this day, the article is remembered for its erudition. Both Buffett and* Fortune *still get letters about it, commenting on one aspect or another.*

*Nevertheless, the piece turned out to be wrong in several ways. First, Buffett (along with the business world in general) thought high inflation rates were here to stay and would plague investors. What he could not foresee was the genius and resolve of Paul Volcker, who took over as Fed chairman in 1979 and broke the back of inflation.*

*Second, Buffett misjudged the course of corporate tax rates, which he thought were "unlikely" to fall. In reality, a succession of tax cuts beginning in 1979 brought the marginal rate down from the 48 percent prevailing when the article was written to 35 percent today.*

*That helps explain why Buffett also erred in believing that the return on equity of major corporations would continue to be stuck around 12 percent. By 1981 I was writing an article titled "Profitability Breaks Through a Ceiling," which reported that the median return for the* Fortune *500 over the previous five years had—despite high rates of inflation—leaped to an average of 14.8 percent. The article attributed the jump to corporations' increasing their leverage a bit, enjoying reduced tax rates, and managing to raise their pretax profit margins.*

*Today, Buffett says that had capitalism worked perfectly, competition would have kept profit margins down. Nonetheless, he adds, "You can't get around it—I was wrong in my assumptions, particularly about tax rates."*

*He remains convinced, however, that high rates of inflation are sure to swindle the equity investor, and he cites evidence from the years when inflation was out of control. Until Volcker pushed inflation below 8 percent in 1982, Buffett recalls, investors who bought stocks in 1977 had suffered a clear-cut loss in purchasing power.* —CL

I t is no longer a secret that stocks, like bonds, do poorly in an inflationary environment. We have been in such an environment for most of the past decade, and it has indeed been a time of troubles for stocks. But the reasons for the stock market's problems in this period are still imperfectly understood.

There is no mystery at all about the problems of bondholders in an era of inflation. When the value of the dollar deteriorates month after month, a security with income and principal payments denominated in those dollars isn't going to be a big winner. You hardly need a Ph.D. in economics to figure that one out.

It was long assumed that stocks were something else. For many years, the conventional wisdom insisted that stocks were a hedge against inflation. The proposition was rooted in the fact that stocks are not claims against dollars, as bonds are, but represent ownership of companies with productive facilities. These, investors believed, would retain their value in real terms, let the politicians print money as they might.

And why didn't it turn out that way? The main reason, I believe, is that stocks, in economic substance, are really very similar to bonds.

I know that this belief will seem eccentric to many investors. They will immediately observe that the return on a bond (the coupon) is fixed, while the return on an equity investment (the company's earnings) can vary substantially from one year to another. True enough. But anyone who examines the aggregate returns that have been earned by companies during the postwar years will discover something extraordinary: the returns on equity have in fact not varied much at all.

In the first ten years after the war—the decade ending in 1955—the Dow Jones industrials had an average annual return on year-end equity of 12.8 percent. In the second decade, the figure was 10.1 percent. In the third decade it was 10.9 percent. Data for a larger universe, the *Fortune* 500 (whose history goes back only to the mid-1950s), indicate somewhat similar results: 11.2 percent in the decade ending in 1965, 11.8 percent in the decade through 1975. The figures for a few exceptional years have been substantially higher (the high for the 500 was 14.1 percent in 1974) or lower (9.5 percent in 1958 and 1970), but over the years, and in the aggregate, the return on book value tends to keep coming back to a level around 12 percent. It shows no signs of exceeding that level significantly in inflationary years (or in years of stable prices, for that matter).

For the moment, let's think of those companies, not as listed stocks, but as productive enterprises. Let's also assume that the owners of those enterprises had acquired them at book value. In that case, their own return would have been around 12 percent too. And because the return has been so consistent, it seems reasonable to think of it as an "equity coupon."

In the real world, of course, investors in stocks don't just buy and hold. Instead, many try to outwit their fellow investors in order to maximize their own proportions of corporate earnings. This thrashing about, obviously fruitless in aggregate, has no impact on the equity coupon but reduces the investor's portion of it, because he incurs substantial frictional costs, such as advisory fees and brokerage charges. Throw in an active options market, which adds nothing to the productivity of American enterprise but requires a cast of thousands to man the casino, and frictional costs rise further.

It is also true that in the real world investors in stocks don't usually get to buy at book value. Sometimes they have been able to buy in below book; usually, however, they've had to pay more than book, and when that happens there is further pressure on that 12 percent. I'll talk more about these relationships later. Meanwhile, let's focus on the main point: *as inflation has increased, the return on equity capital has not.* Essentially, those who buy equities receive securities with an underlying fixed return—just like those who buy bonds.

Of course, there are some important differences between the bond and stock forms. For openers, bonds eventually come due. It may require a long wait, but eventually the bond investor gets to renegotiate the terms of his contract. If current and prospective rates of inflation make his old coupon look inadequate, he can refuse to play further unless coupons currently being offered rekindle his interest. Something of this sort has been going on in recent years.

Stocks, on the other hand, are perpetual. They have a maturity date of infinity. Investors in stocks are stuck with whatever return corporate America happens to earn. If corporate America is destined to earn 12 percent, then that is the level investors must learn to live with. As a group, stock investors can neither opt out nor renegotiate. In the aggregate, their commitment is actually increasing. Individual companies can be sold or liquidated and corporations can repurchase their own shares; on balance, however, new equity flotations and retained earnings guarantee that the equity capital locked up in the corporate system will increase.

So, score one for the bond form. Bond coupons eventually will be renegotiated; equity "coupons" won't. It is true, of course, that for a long time a 12 percent coupon did not appear in need of a whole lot of correction.

There is another major difference between the garden variety of bond and our new exotic 12 percent "equity bond" that comes to the Wall Street costume ball dressed in a stock certificate.

In the usual case, a bond investor receives his entire coupon in cash and is left to reinvest it as best he can. Our stock investor's equity coupon, in contrast, is partially retained by the company and is reinvested at whatever rates the company happens to be earning. In other words, going back to our corporate universe, part of the 12 percent earned annually is paid out in dividends and the balance is put right back into the universe to earn 12 percent also.

This characteristic of stocks—the reinvestment of part of the coupon—can be good or bad news, depending on the relative attractiveness of that 12 percent. The news was very good indeed in the 1950's and early 1960's. With bonds yielding only 3 or 4 percent, the right to reinvest automatically a portion of the equity coupon at 12 percent was of enormous value. Note that investors could not just invest their own money and get that 12 percent return. Stock prices in this period ranged far above book value, and investors were prevented by the premium prices they had to pay from directly extracting out of the underlying corporate universe whatever rate that universe was earning. You can't pay far above par for a 12 percent bond and earn 12 percent for yourself.

But on their retained earnings, investors *could* earn 12 percent. In effect, earnings retention allowed investors to buy at book value part of an enterprise that, in the economic environment then existing, was worth a great deal more than book value.

It was a situation that left very little to be said for cash dividends and a lot to be said for earnings retention. Indeed, the more money that investors thought likely to be reinvested at the 12 percent rate, the more valuable they considered their reinvestment privilege, and the more they were willing to pay for it. In the early 1960's, investors eagerly paid top-scale prices for electric utilities situated in growth areas, knowing that these companies had the ability to reinvest very large proportions of their earnings. Utilities whose operating environment dictated a larger cash payout rated lower prices.

If, during this period, a high-grade, noncallable, long-term bond with a 12 percent coupon had existed, it would have sold far above par. And if it were a bond with a further unusual characteristic—which was that most of the coupon payments could be automatically reinvested at par in similar bonds—the issue would have commanded an even greater premium. In essence, growth stocks retaining most of their earnings represented just such a security. When their reinvestment rate on the added equity capital was 12 percent while interest rates generally were around 4 percent, investors became very happy—and, of course, they paid happy prices.

Looking back, stock investors can think of themselves in the 1946-66 period as having been ladled a truly bountiful triple dip. First, they were the beneficiaries of an underlying corporate return on equity that was far above prevailing interest rates. Second, a significant portion of that return was reinvested for them at rates that were otherwise unattainable. And third, they were afforded an escalating appraisal of underlying equity capital as the first two benefits became widely recognized. This third dip meant that, on top of the basic 12 percent or so earned by corporations on their equity capital, investors were receiving a bonus as the Dow Jones industrials increased in price from 133 percent of book value in 1946 to 220 percent in 1966. Such a marking-up process temporarily allowed investors to achieve a return that exceeded the inherent earning power of the enterprises in which they had invested.

This heaven-on-earth situation finally was "discovered" in the mid-1960's by many major investing institutions. But just as these financial elephants began trampling on one another in their rush to equities, we entered an era of accelerating inflation and higher interest rates. Quite logically, the marking-up process began to reverse itself. Rising interest rates ruthlessly reduced the value of all existing fixed-coupon investments. And as long-term corporate bond rates began moving up (eventually reaching the 10 percent area), both the equity return of 12 percent and the reinvestment "privilege" began to look different.

Stocks are quite properly thought of as riskier than bonds. While that equity coupon is more or less fixed over periods of time, it does fluctuate somewhat from year to year. Investors' attitudes about the future can be affected substantially, although frequently erroneously, by those yearly changes. Stocks are also riskier because they come equipped with infinite maturities. (Even your friendly broker wouldn't have the nerve to peddle a 100-year bond, if he had any available, as "safe.") Because of the additional risk, the natural reaction of investors is to expect an equity return that is comfortably above the bond return—and 12 percent on equity versus, say, 10 percent on bonds issued by the same corporate universe does not seem to qualify as comfortable. As the spread narrows, equity investors start looking for the exits.

But, of course, as a group they can't get out. All they can achieve is a lot of movement, substantial frictional costs, and a new, much lower level of valuation, reflecting the lessened attractiveness of the 12 percent equity coupon under inflationary conditions. Bond investors have had a succession of shocks over the past decade in the course of discovering that there is no magic attached to any given coupon level: at 6 percent, or 8 percent, or 10 percent, bonds can still collapse in price. Stock investors, who are in general not aware that they too have a "coupon," are still receiving their education on this point.

Must we really view that 12 percent equity coupon as immutable? Is there any law that says the corporate return on equity capital cannot adjust itself upward in response to a permanently higher average rate of inflation?

There is no such law, of course. On the other hand, corporate America cannot increase earnings by desire or decree. To raise that return on equity, corporations would need at least one of the following: (1) an increase in turnover, i.e., in the ratio between sales and total assets employed in the business; (2) cheaper leverage; (3) more leverage; (4) lower income taxes; (5) wider operating margins on sales.

And that's it. There simply are no other ways to increase returns on common equity. Let's see what can be done with these.

We'll begin with *turnover*. The three major categories of assets we have to think about for this exercise are accounts receivable, inventories, and fixed assets such as plants and machinery.

Accounts receivable go up proportionally as sales go up, whether the increase in dollar sales is produced by more physical volume or by inflation. No room for improvement here.

With inventories, the situation is not quite so simple. Over the long term, the trend in unit inventories may be expected to follow the trend in unit sales. Over the short term, however, the physical turnover rate may bob around because of special influences—e.g., cost expectations, or bottlenecks.

The use of last-in, first-out (LIFO) inventory-valuation methods serves to increase the reported turnover rate during inflationary times. When dollar sales are rising because of inflation, inventory valuations of a LIFO company either will remain level (if unit sales are not rising) or will trail the rise in dollar sales (if unit sales are rising). In either case, dollar turnover will increase.

During the early 1970's, there was a pronounced swing by corporations toward LIFO accounting (which has the effect of lowering a company's reported earnings and tax bills). The trend now seems to have slowed. Still, the existence of a lot of LIFO companies, plus the likelihood that some others will join the crowd, ensures some further increase in the reported turnover of inventory.

In the case of fixed assets, any rise in the inflation rate, assuming it affects all products equally, will initially have the effect of increasing turnover. That is true because sales will immediately reflect the new price level, while the fixed asset account will reflect the change only gradually, i.e., as existing assets are retired and replaced at the new prices. Obviously, the more slowly a company goes about this replacement process, the more the turnover ratio will rise. The action stops, however, when a replacement cycle is completed. Assuming a constant rate of inflation, sales and fixed assets will then begin to rise in concert at the rate of inflation.

To sum up, inflation will produce some gains in turnover ratios. Some improvement would be certain because of LIFO, and some would be possible (if inflation accelerates) because of sales rising more rapidly than fixed assets. But the gains are apt to be modest and not of a magnitude to produce substantial improvement in returns on equity capital. During the decade ending in 1975, despite generally accelerating inflation and the extensive use of LIFO accounting, the turnover ratio of the *Fortune* 500 went only from 1.18/1 to 1.29/1.

*Cheaper leverage?* Not likely. High rates of inflation generally cause borrowing to become dearer, not cheaper. Galloping rates of inflation create galloping capital needs; and lenders, as they become increasingly distrustful of long term contracts, become more demanding. But even if there is no further rise in interest rates, leverage will be getting more expensive because the average cost of the debt now on corporate books is less than would be the cost of replacing it. And replacement will be required as the existing debt matures. Overall, then, future changes in the cost of leverage seem likely to have a mildly depressing effect on the return on equity.

*More leverage?* American business already has fired many, if not most, of the more-leverage bullets once available to it. Proof of that proposition can be seen in some other *Fortune* 500 statistics: in the twenty years ending in 1975, stockholders' equity as a percentage of total assets declined for the 500 from 63 percent to just under 50 percent. In other words, each dollar of equity capital now is leveraged much more heavily than it used to be.

An irony of inflation-induced financial requirements is that the highly profitable companies—generally the best credits—require relatively little debt capital. But the laggards in profitability never can get enough. Lenders understand this problem much better than they did a decade ago—and are correspondingly less willing to let capital-hungry, low-profitability enterprises leverage themselves to the sky.

Nevertheless, given inflationary conditions, many corporations seem sure in the future to turn to still more leverage as a means of shoring up equity returns. Their managements will make that move because they will need enormous amounts of capital—often merely to do the same physical volume of business—and will wish to get it without cutting dividends or making equity offerings that, because of inflation, are not apt to shape up as attractive. Their natural response will be to heap on debt, almost regardless of cost. They will tend to behave like those utility companies that argued over an eighth of a point in the 1960's and were grateful to find 12 percent debt financing in 1974.

Added debt at present interest rates, however, will do less for equity returns than did added debt at 4 percent rates in the early 1960's. There is also the problem that higher debt ratios cause credit ratings to be lowered, creating a further rise in interest costs.

So that is another way, to be added to those already discussed, in which the cost of leverage will be rising. In total, the higher costs of leverage are likely to offset the benefits of greater leverage.

Besides, there is already far more debt in corporate America than is conveyed by conventional balance sheets. Many companies have massive pension obligations geared to whatever pay levels will be in effect when present workers retire. At the low inflation rates of 1955-65, the liabilities arising from such plans were reasonably predictable. Today, nobody can really know the company's ultimate obligation. But if the inflation rate averages 7 percent in the future, a twenty-five-year-old employee who is now earning $12,000, and whose raises do no more than match increases in living costs, will be making $180,000 when he retires at sixty-five.

Of course, there is a marvelously precise figure in many annual reports each year, purporting to be the unfunded pension liability. If that figure were really believable, a corporation could simply ante up that sum, add to it the existing pension-fund assets, turn the total amount over to an insurance company, and have it assume all the corporation's present pension liabilities. In the real world, alas, it is impossible to find an insurance company willing even to listen to such a deal.

Virtually every corporate treasurer in America would recoil at the idea of issuing a "cost-of-living" bond—a noncallable obligation with coupons tied to a price index. But through the private pension system, corporate America has in fact taken on a fantastic amount of debt that is the equivalent of such a bond.

More leverage, whether through conventional debt or unbooked and indexed "pension debt," should be viewed with skepticism by shareholders. A 12 percent return from an enterprise that is debt-free is far superior to the same return achieved by a business hocked to its eyeballs. Which means that today's 12 percent equity returns may well be less valuable than the 12 percent returns of twenty years ago.

*Lower corporate income taxes* seem unlikely. Investors in American corporations already own what might be thought of as a Class D stock. The Class A, B, and C stocks are represented by the income-tax claims of the federal, state, and municipal governments. It is true that these "investors" have no claim on the corporation's assets; however, they get a major share of the earnings, including earnings generated by the equity buildup resulting from retention of part of the earnings owned by the Class D shareholders.

A further charming characteristic of these wonderful Class A, B, and C stocks is that their share of the corporation's earnings can be increased immediately, abundantly, and without payment by the unilateral vote of anyone of the "stockholder" classes, e.g., by congressional action in the case of the Class A. To add to the fun, one of the classes will sometimes vote to increase its ownership share in the business retroactively—as companies operating in New York discovered to their dismay in 1975. Whenever the Class A, B, or C "stockholders" vote themselves a larger share of the business, the portion remaining for Class D—that's the one held by the ordinary investor—declines.

Looking ahead, it seems unwise to assume that those who control the A, B, and C shares will vote to reduce their own take over the long run. The Class D shares probably will have to struggle to hold their own.

The last of our five possible sources of increased returns on equity is *wider operating margins on sales.* Here is where some optimists would hope to achieve major gains. There is no proof that they are wrong. But there are only 100 cents in the sales dollar and a lot of demands on that dollar before we get down to the residual, pretax profits. The major claimants are labor, raw materials, energy, and various non-income taxes. The relative importance of these costs hardly seems likely to decline during an age of inflation.

Recent statistical evidence, furthermore, does not inspire confidence in the proposition that margins will widen in a period of inflation. In the decade ending in 1965, a period of relatively low inflation, the universe of manufacturing companies reported on quarterly by the Federal Trade Commission had an average annual pretax margin on sales of 8.6 percent. In the decade ending in 1975, the average margin was 8 percent. Margins were down, in other words, despite a very considerable increase in the inflation rate.

If business was able to base its prices on replacement costs, margins would widen in inflationary periods. But the simple fact is that most large businesses, despite a widespread belief in their market power, just don't manage to pull it off. Replacement cost accounting almost always shows that corporate earnings have declined significantly in the past decade. If such major industries as oil, steel, and aluminum really have the oligopolistic muscle imputed to them, one can only conclude that their pricing policies have been remarkably restrained.

There you have the complete lineup: five factors that can improve returns on common equity, none of which, by my analysis, are likely to take us very far in that direction in periods of high inflation. You may have emerged from this exercise more optimistic than I am. But remember, returns in the 12 percent area have been with us a long time.

Even if you agree that the 12 percent equity coupon is more or less immutable, you still may hope to do well with it in the years ahead. It's conceivable that you will. After all, a lot of investors did well with it for a long time. But your future results will be governed by three variables: the relationship between book value and market value, the tax rate, and the inflation rate.

Let's wade through a little arithmetic about book and market value. When stocks consistently sell at book value, it's all very simple. If a stock has a book value of $100 and also an average market value of $100, 12 percent earnings by business will produce a 12 percent return for the investor (less those frictional costs, which we'll ignore for the moment). If the payout ratio is 50 percent, our investor will get $6 via dividends and a further $6 from the increase in the book value of the business, which will, of course, be reflected in the market value of his holdings.

If the stock sold at 150 percent of book value, the picture would change. The investor would receive the same $6 cash dividend, but it would now represent only a 4 percent return on his $150 cost. The book value of the business would still increase by 6 percent (to $106) and the market value of the investor's holdings, valued consistently at 150 percent of book value, would similarly increase by 6 percent (to $159). But the investor's total return, i.e., from appreciation plus dividends, would be only 10 percent versus the underlying 12 percent earned by the business.

When the investor buys in below book value, the process is reversed. For example, if the stock sells at 80 percent of book value, the same earnings and payout assumptions would yield 7.5 percent from dividends ($6 on an $80 price) and 6 percent from appreciation—a total return of 13.5 percent. In other words, you do better by buying at a discount rather than a premium, just as common sense would suggest.

During the postwar years, the market value of the Dow Jones industrials has been as low as 84 percent of book value (in 1974) and as high as 232 percent (in 1965); most of the time the ratio has been well over 100 percent. (Early this spring, it was around 110 percent.) Let's assume that in the future the ratio will be something close to 100 percent meaning that investors in stocks could earn the full 12 percent. At least, they could earn that figure before taxes and before inflation.

How large a bite might taxes take out of the 12 percent? For individual investors, it seems reasonable to assume that federal, state, and local income taxes will average perhaps 50 percent on dividends and 30 percent on capital gains. A majority of investors may have marginal rates somewhat below these, but many with larger holdings will experience substantially higher rates. Under the new tax law, a high-income investor in a heavily taxed city could have a marginal rate on capital gains as high as 56 percent.

So let's use 50 percent and 30 percent as representative for individual investors. Let's also assume, in line with recent experience, that corporations earning 12 percent on equity pay out 5 percent in cash dividends (2.5 percent after tax) and retain 7 percent, with those retained earnings producing a corresponding market-value growth (4.9 percent after the 30 percent tax). The after-tax return, then, would be 7.4 percent. Probably this should be rounded down to about 7 percent to allow for frictional costs. To push our stocks-disguised-as-bonds thesis one notch further, then, stocks might be regarded as the equivalent, for individuals, of 7 percent tax-exempt perpetual bonds.

Which brings us to the crucial question—the inflation rate. No one knows the answer on this one including the politicians, economists, and Establishment pundits, who felt, a few years back, that with slight nudges here and there unemployment and inflation rates would respond like trained seals.

But many signs seem negative for stable prices: the fact that inflation is now worldwide; the propensity of major groups in our society to utilize their electoral muscle to shift, rather than solve, economic problems; the demonstrated unwillingness to tackle even the most vital problems (e.g., energy and nuclear proliferation) if they can be postponed; and a political system that rewards legislators with reelection if their actions appear to produce short-term benefits even though their ultimate imprint will be to compound long-term pain.

Most of those in political office, quite understandably, are firmly against inflation and firmly in favor of policies producing it. (This schizophrenia hasn't caused them to lose touch with reality, however; Congressmen have made sure that *their* pensions—unlike practically all granted in the private sector—are indexed to cost-of-living changes *after* retirement.)

Discussions regarding future inflation rates usually probe the subtleties of monetary and fiscal policies. These are important variables in determining the outcome of any specific inflationary equation. But, at the source, peacetime inflation is a political problem, not an economic problem. Human behavior, not monetary behavior, is the key. And when very human politicians choose between the next election and the next generation, it's clear what usually happens.

Such broad generalizations do not produce precise numbers. However, it seems quite possible to me that inflation rates will average 7 percent in future years. I hope this forecast proves to be wrong. And it may well be. Forecasts usually tell us more of the forecaster than of the future. You are free to factor your own inflation rate into the investor's equation. But if you foresee a rate averaging 2 percent or 3 percent, you are wearing different glasses than I am.

So there we are: 12 percent before taxes and inflation; 7 percent after taxes and before inflation; and maybe zero percent after taxes and inflation. It hardly sounds like a formula that will keep all those cattle stampeding on TV.

As a common stockholder you will have more dollars, but you may have no more purchasing power. Out with Ben Franklin ("a penny saved is a penny earned") and in with Milton Friedman ("a man might as well consume his capital as invest it").

The arithmetic makes it plain that inflation is a far more devastating tax than anything that has been enacted by our legislatures. The inflation tax has a fantastic ability to simply consume capital. It makes no difference to a widow with her savings in a 5 percent passbook account whether she pays 100 percent income tax on her interest income during a period of zero inflation, or pays *no* income taxes during years of 5 percent inflation. Either way, she is "taxed" in a manner that leaves her no real income whatsoever. Any money she spends comes right out of capital. She would find outrageous a 120 percent income tax, but doesn't seem to notice that 6 percent inflation is the economic equivalent.

If my inflation assumption is close to correct, disappointing results will occur not because the market falls, but in spite of the fact that the market rises. At around 920 early last month, the Dow was up fifty-five points from where it was ten years ago. But adjusted for inflation, the Dow is down almost 345 points—from 865 to 520. And about half of the earnings of the Dow had to be withheld from their owners and reinvested in order to achieve even that result.

In the next ten years, the Dow would be doubled just by a combination of the 12 percent equity coupon, a 40 percent payout ratio, and the present 110 percent ratio of market to book value. And with 7 percent inflation, investors who sold at 1800 would still be considerably worse off than they are today after paying their capital-gains taxes.

I can almost hear the reaction of some investors to these downbeat thoughts. It will be to assume that, whatever the difficulties presented by the new investment era, they will somehow contrive to turn in superior results for themselves. Their success is most unlikely. And in aggregate, of course, impossible. If you feel you can dance in and out of securities in a way that defeats the inflation tax, I would like to be your broker—but not your partner.

Even the so-called tax-exempt investors, such as pension funds and college endowment funds, do not escape the inflation tax. If my assumption of a 7 percent inflation rate is correct, a college treasurer should regard the first 7 percent earned each year merely as a replenishment of purchasing power. Endowment funds are earning nothing until they have outpaced the inflation treadmill. At 7 percent inflation and, say, overall investment returns of 8 percent, these institutions, which believe they are tax-exempt, are in fact paying "income taxes" of 87 1/2 percent.

Unfortunately, the major problems from high inflation rates flow not to investors but to society as a whole. Investment income is a small portion of national income, and if per capita real income could grow at a healthy rate alongside zero real investment returns, social justice might well be advanced.

A market economy creates some lopsided payoffs to participants. The right endowment of vocal chords, anatomical structure, physical strength, or mental powers can produce enormous piles of claim checks (stocks, bonds, and other forms of capital) on future national output. Proper selection of ancestors similarly can result in lifetime supplies of such tickets upon birth. If zero real investment returns diverted a bit greater portion of the national output from such stockholders to equally worthy and hardworking citizens lacking jackpot-producing talents, it would seem unlikely to pose such an insult to an equitable world as to risk Divine Intervention.

But the potential for real improvement in the welfare of workers at the expense of affluent stockholders is not significant. Employee compensation already totals twenty-eight times the amount paid out in dividends, and a lot of those dividends now go to pension funds, nonprofit institutions such as universities, and individual stockholders who are not affluent. Under these circumstances, if we now shifted *all* dividends of wealthy stockholders into wages—something we could do only once, like killing a cow (or, if you prefer, a pig)—we would increase real wages by less than we used to obtain from one year's growth of the economy.

Therefore, diminishment of the affluent, through the impact of inflation on their investments, will not even provide material *short-term* aid to those who are not affluent. Their economic well-being will rise or fall with the general effects of inflation on the economy. And those effects are not likely to be good.

Large gains in real capital, invested in modern production facilities, are required to produce large gains in economic well-being. Great labor availability, great consumer wants, and great government promises will lead to nothing but great frustration without continuous creation and employment of expensive new capital assets throughout industry. That's an equation understood by Russians as well as Rockefellers. And it's one that has been applied with stunning success in West Germany and Japan. High capital-accumulation rates have enabled those countries to achieve gains in living standards at rates far exceeding ours, even though we have enjoyed much the superior position in energy.

To understand the impact of inflation upon real capital accumulation, a little math is required. Come back for a moment to that 12 percent return on equity capital. Such earnings are stated after depreciation, which presumably will allow replacement of present productive capacity—*if* that plant and equipment can be purchased in the future at prices similar to their original cost.

Let's assume that about half of earnings are paid out in dividends, leaving 6 percent of equity capital available to finance future growth. If inflation is low—say, 2 percent—a large portion of that growth can be real growth in physical output. For under these conditions, 2 percent more will have to be invested in receivables, inventories, and fixed assets next year just to duplicate this year's physical output—leaving 4 percent for investment in assets to produce more physical goods. The 2 percent finances illusory dollar growth reflecting inflation and the remaining 4 percent finances real growth. If population growth is 1 percent, the 4 percent gain in real output translates into a 3 percent gain in real per capita net income. That, very roughly, is what used to happen in our economy.

Now move the inflation rate to 7 percent and compute what is left for real growth after the financing of the mandatory inflation component. The answer is nothing—if dividend policies and leverage ratios remain unchanged. After half of the 12 percent earnings are paid out, the same 6 percent is left, but it is all conscripted to provide the added dollars needed to transact last year's physical volume of business.

Many companies, faced with no real retained earnings with which to finance physical expansion after normal dividend payments, will improvise. How, they will ask themselves, can we stop or reduce dividends without risking stockholder wrath? I have good news for them: a ready-made set of blueprints is available.

In recent years the electric-utility industry has had little or no dividend-paying capacity. Or, rather, it has had the power to pay dividends *if* investors agree to buy stock from them. In 1975 electric utilities paid common dividends of $3.3 billion and asked investors to return $3.4 billion. Of course, they mixed in a little solicit-Peter-to-pay-Paul technique so as not to acquire a Con Ed reputation. Con Ed, you will remember, was unwise enough in 1974 to simply tell its shareholders it didn't have the money to pay the dividend. Candor was rewarded with calamity in the marketplace.

The more sophisticated utility maintains—perhaps increases—the quarterly dividend and then asks shareholders (either old or new) to mail back the money. In other words, the company issues new stock. This procedure diverts massive amounts of capital to the tax collector and substantial sums to underwriters. Everyone, however, seems to remain in good spirits (particularly the underwriters).

Encouraged by such success, some utilities have devised a further shortcut. In this case, the company declares the dividend, the shareholder pays the tax, and—presto—more shares are issued. No cash changes hands, although the IRS, spoilsport as always, persists in treating the transaction as if it had.

A.T. &T., for example, instituted a dividend-reinvestment program in 1973. This company, in fairness, must be described as very stockholder-minded, and its adoption of this program, considering the folkways of finance, must be regarded as totally understandable. But the substance of the program is out of *Alice in Wonderland*.

In 1976, A.T. &T. paid $2.3 billion in cash dividends to about 2.9 million owners of its common stock. At the end of the year, 648,000 holders (up from 601,000 the previous year) reinvested $432 million (up from $327 million) in additional shares supplied directly by the company.

Just for fun, let's assume that all A.T. & T. shareholders ultimately sign up for this program. In that case, no cash at all would be mailed to shareholders just as when Con Ed passed a dividend. However, each of the 2.9 million owners would be notified that he should pay income taxes on his share of the retained earnings that had that year been called a "dividend." Assuming that "dividends" totaled $2.3 billion, as in 1976, and that shareholders paid an average tax of 30 percent on these, they would end up, courtesy of this marvelous plan, paying nearly $700 million to the IRS. Imagine the joy of shareholders, in such circumstances, if the directors were then to double the dividend.

We can expect to see more use of disguised payout reductions as business struggles with the problem of real capital accumulation. But throttling back shareholders somewhat will not entirely solve the problem. A combination of 7 percent inflation and 12 percent returns will reduce the stream of corporate capital available to finance real growth.

And so, as conventional private capital-accumulation methods falter under inflation, our government will increasingly attempt to influence capital flows to industry, either unsuccessfully as in England or successfully as in Japan. The necessary cultural and historical underpinning for a Japanese-style enthusiastic partnership of government, business, and labor seems lacking here. If we are lucky, we will avoid following the English path, where all segments fight over division of the pie rather than pool their energies to enlarge it.

On balance, however, it seems likely that we will hear a great deal more as the years unfold about underinvestment, stagflation, and the failures of the private sector to fulfill needs.

*Addendum: A sidebar explaining who Buffett was—that's how unfamous he was in 1977—accompanied this article. Most of the details included there are now widely familiar and we will not repeat them here. But we will report that Buffett's Berkshire holdings were then worth $35 million and his Blue Chip Stamps stake almost $10 million—and both of those companies were active investors as well. So why, the last paragraph of the sidebar sensibly asked, does a man so gloomy about stocks own so much of them? "Partly it's habit," Buffett answered. "Partly, it's that stocks mean business, and owning businesses is much more interesting than owning gold or farmland. Besides, stocks are probably still the best of all the poor alternatives in an era of inflation—at least they are if you buy in at appropriate prices." —CL*

# A Small College Scores Big in the Investment Game

December 18, 1978

**BY LEE SMITH**

*Grinnell College's remarkable, Buffett-aided success with its endowment fund was a story not known nationally until* Fortune *published this article. The story describes an important component of this success, Grinnell's unorthodox purchase in 1976 of a television station in Dayton, and ends with Buffett's thought that it might be "one hell of an asset" to keep holding. But prices for stations continued to rise, and a short time later Buffett was ready for Grinnell to exit. The station, bought only four years earlier for $12.9 million (only $2 million of that cash, the rest a nonrecourse loan), was sold to Hearst in 1980 for $50 million.*

*Joe Rosenfield, who persuaded Buffett to join the Grinnell board, stayed close to the college, an institution he loved, until his death in 2000. Buffett remained an active trustee until 1987 and a lifetime trustee until 2011.*

*He meanwhile harbored some doubts about his board experience. What bothered him the most was that the outsized gains he and Rosenfield attained for Grinnell's endowment—multiplying it more than sixty times—seemed otherwise not to lead to much. Today Buffett says, "It was a fine school with twelve hundred students when it had an $8 million endowment, and it was a fine school with twelve hundred students when it had a $500 million endowment."*

*To bring Grinnell up-to-date: In its 2012-13 year, it had about sixteen hundred students and its endowment was around $1.4 billion. —CL*

Grinnell College has always been a little bit improbable. Its 90-acre campus sits on the edge of a typical mid-Iowa farm community, where the tallest structure in town is the grain elevator, and where a college might be expected to emphasize the animal husbandry and go easy on the humanities. Not Grinnell. It offers its 1200 or so students a rigorous, traditional curriculum, based on such staples as American colonial history, the poetry of John Milton, and an introduction to quantum theory. It has thus earned a reputation as one of America's fine liberal-arts colleges.

These days Grinnell is surprising for quite another reason. The little school in the Cornbelt has managed its endowment fund so adroitly that the fund has doubled in the past five years to $37.5 million, and that appraisal is conservative. If all of its assets were marked up to their true market value, the total would be closer to $60 million. New contributions to the endowment have amounted to only about $5.4 million. The fund has grown mainly because of the stunning appreciation of its assets. Even using the conservative valuation, appreciation—along with income—has yielded for the fund an average total return of 16.2 percent annually over the last five years.

During that same period college and university endowments in general have fared dismally. The median return for the 150 endowment funds tracked by A.G. Becker in that five-year period has been a meager 1.7 percent annually....

To accomplish what it did, Grinnell employed investment strategies and ventured into enterprises that educational institutions normally shun. For example, rather than tuck its eggs cautiously into a variety of conventional baskets in the equity and bond markets, Grinnell has not hesitated to stash a lot of eggs in one or two baskets or to take a flier on a speculative issue. Its most unusual and dramatic move was to buy a commercial television station for $12.9 million....

The trustees of Grinnell, unlike those of many other schools, have not relinquished day-to-day control of the endowment to a bank or an outside portfolio manager or even to a professional in-house manager. They have deliberately kept it in their own hands; or, more precisely, they have entrusted it to their finance committee—principally to two members of the committee who had demonstrated their fitness for the job by having previously accumulated considerable fortunes for themselves. One is Joseph F. Rosenfield of Des Moines, a retired attorney and active investor, who was once chairman of Younkers Brothers, a prosperous department-store chain operating in five midwestern states.

The second key member of the committee is Warren E. Buffett. Buffett achieved considerable fame as the Omaha investor who parlayed a small stake from family and friends into an investment partnership that grew at a phenomenal average annual rate of 29.5 percent over a thirteen-year period, and was worth $100 million by the time he liquidated it and distributed the profits in 1969. Through his own holdings, he still controls a substantial number of companies, including financial institutions and newspapers.

When Rosenfield, class of '25, joined the board in 1941, the endowment was worth only about $1 million; it included a few farms the school had inherited and $250,000 in securities. The first windfall came in the early 1950's when the school was left about $5 million in assets from the estate of oilman Fred Darby. A second boost followed in the early Sixties when the Ford Foundation promised that if Grinnell could raise $4 million on its own, Ford would contribute $2 million. Grinnell raised the money, with $400,000 coming directly from the pocket of Joe Rosenfield.

Rosenfield has continued to contribute to the school, and most of his donations have been placed in a special kitty within the endowment that has come to be known as the J.F.Rosenfield Fund. It is into this fund that he and Warren Buffett have dipped to take some limited risks with small amounts of money that would not have yielded very much if they had been left in the traditional blue-chip stocks and bonds. The two investors have been strikingly successful. A hypothetical "share" in the fund would have increased about eighteenfold in the past fifteen years....

The Rosenfield Fund made its first spectacularly successful investment ten years ago. Robert N. Noyce, one of the founders of Fairchild Semiconductor, was a Grinnell trustee and alumnus (having been a somewhat mischievous student who was once suspended for stealing a farmer's pig for a midnight barbecue). Rosenfield and another trustee, Chicago attorney Samuel R. Rosenthal, were far-sighted enough to recognize that Noyce's genius could be put to work for the college. "We told Bob that when he went into his own business the college wanted part of it," Rosenfield recalls. And so when Noyce left Fairchild in 1968 to form Intel, a company that would make tiny semiconductor memory chips for computers, he gave the college the opportunity to buy $300,000 worth of Intel convertible bonds. Rosenthal and Rosenfield each contributed $100,000; the final third came from the Rosenfield Fund. As Intel flourished, the school's investment increased in value about forty-six times. The endowment fund converted the bonds and over the years has sold off most of its Intel stock at a profit of close to $12 million; it holds on to some 37,000 shares with a market value of about $2 million. . . .

Buffett is not a Grinnell alumnus. He attended the Wharton School and the University of Nebraska as an undergraduate and later got a master's degree in economics from the Columbia University Graduate School of Business. He was persuaded to become a Grinnell trustee only because of Rosenfield, whom he had met through mutual friends. Although they are a generation apart—Rosenfield is seventy-four and Buffett is forty-eight—the two are very close. And so in 1968, at Rosenfield's request, Buffett joined the board. "Joe is not the kind of guy you can say no to," muses Buffett. "For one thing, he's the one guy I know who actually seems to take his net worth down with his contributions. Others just give to the limit of what's tax-deductible." The two men consult frequently with one another, sometimes with other members of the finance committee—especially the chairman, thirty-eight-year-old Tom Hutchison, a wealthy Des Moines investment counselor—but rarely with the entire thirty-two-member board. Buffett in particular is a loner, restless at the daylong board meetings that are held three times a year at the Grinnell Library and impatient with committee proceedings.

Buffett's and Rosenfield's investment strategies are similar, but one may be more enthusiastic about an idea than the other. During the Intel purchase, for example, Buffett stood quietly on the sidelines. "I wasn't against it," he explains. "It's just that I don't understand the semiconductor business, and I don't go into businesses that I can't understand, that my sister can't understand."

Buffett is at heart a disciple of Benjamin Graham, under whom he studied at Columbia, and as such he believes in seeking out an undervalued company and investing in it heavily. Buffett, in fact, carries the Graham philosophy even further than Graham himself, for Graham was willing to sell out when the price of the stock rose to what he considered its true value. Buffett prefers to buy stocks that he will want to hold indefinitely. These days, his notion of an ideal opportunity is to buy into a business for $1 million when it is really worth $2 million and will be worth $4 million in five years. Such situations, he acknowledges, are not easy to find. "We don't have a lot of good ideas," he says, "and therefore we don't do a lot of things."

Buffett found Grinnell's main chance, almost by accident, in 1976. During a conference on newspaper economics in New Orleans, Thomas S. Murphy, chairman of Capital Cities Communications and a friend of Buffett's, mentioned to him over breakfast that Avco Corp. was selling its television stations. Buffett would have been interested in buying a station for himself or Berkshire Hathaway, a company he controls, were it not for a possible conflict of interest. Berkshire Hathaway owns 12 percent of the Washington Post Co. Any one owner is limited to five television stations (seven, if at least two are the less desirable UHF stations). The Post company already owns four VHF stations. It was conceivable that, even though Berkshire's stock in the Post is not voting stock, the government would count a purchase of an Avco station by either Buffett or Berkshire in the Post's column, using up the Post's last bullet, so to speak. He was about to forget about the idea when, during a telephone conversation with Rosenfield, it suddenly occurred to him that a television station might be just the thing for Grinnell. Because of cash problems, Avco was willing to dispose of the stations, and so Grinnell was likely to acquire just the sort of solid undervalued asset Buffett prizes. It was not unheard of for a college to own a television station. (The leading commercial television station in New Orleans is a division of Loyola University). But it was extraordinary for a college to go out into the market and bid on one.

The board went along, but there was so much delay while they discussed how they were going to finance the purchase that Grinnell lost out on its first choice, Avco's Cincinnati station, which Multimedia Inc. bought for $16 million. (Grinnell managed to salve its disappointment by quickly purchasing $315,000 worth of Multimedia stock, which has since tripled in value.) In the second attempt, aimed at Avco's Dayton station, Buffett decided simply to plunge ahead and worry about the financing later. He offered $12.9 million for station WLWD-TV 2, an NBC affiliate, a price that represented about two-and-one-half times the station's gross revenues—not overly generous in view of the fact that stations often sell for at least three times revenues. But Avco accepted.

The station, housed in a converted roller-skating rink just outside the Dayton city limits, in Moraine, Ohio, is the No. 2 station in a three-station market. Grinnell changed the call letters to WDTN and formed a separate company, Grinnell Communications, to run it. (The company pays corporate income taxes on its earnings, just as it would if it were owned by an organization run for profit rather than education.) Grinnell Communications invested about $1.3 million in capital improvements, including $750,000 to double the height of its broadcast tower and thereby expand its audience. Running the station has presented little problem so far. Ray W. Colie, general manager of the station under Avco, has stayed on to operate it under Grinnell, and although the company's six-member board is dominated by Grinnell trustees, they leave Colie and his staff pretty much alone.

As the station was ultimately financed, the Rosenfield Fund supplied $2 million in equity and Grinnell borrowed the other $11 million, half from outside lenders and half from the endowment fund itself. The truly noteworthy aspect of the investment has been its impressive appreciation. Television stations in the top fifty markets (Dayton is No. 46) have sold recently for as much as four times revenues. WDTN expects revenues of about $9 million this year, which means it likely has a market value in the neighborhood of $35 million—more than two and one-half times what the school paid for it.

The value of the station is understated considerably on Grinnell's books. The original $2 million equity investment is shown at cost, along with about $5 million in debt still owed the endowment. (Some of the debt has been paid off). That $7 million would rise dramatically if WDTN were accounted for realistically—at its market value less the $4.7-million debt still owed to outsiders. The value of the endowment would then be closer to $60 million than the $37.5 million at which Grinnell appraises it. . . .

Buffett believes there is no reason why even large schools with immense endowments cannot adopt the same strategy that he has applied at Grinnell, limiting the portfolio to relatively few areas. That certainly leads to some fascinating possibilities. What if Harvard had been able to acquire control of American Broadcasting Co. at the start of 1978, when the market value of the stock was about $700 million—half the size of Harvard's endowment. As fanciful as the idea is, a $700-million investment in ABC would have given Harvard a commitment to broadcasting roughly proportional to Grinnell's.

It seems highly unlikely that any large school is going to move quite as boldly as Grinnell. In fact, even some of Grinnell's trustees are beginning to worry about the imbalance of their portfolio. Paradoxically, the more WDTN appreciates in value, the more uneasy they get. Their discomfort is understandable enough. The station now accounts for somewhere around half of the real wealth of the endowment, and there is a question as to whether it is prudent for a fiduciary to permit such a concentration. "I can envision a situation in which the value of the station goes down," says one Grinnell trustee, "and a student brings a class action against us, claiming that his tuition would have been lower if we had sold the station."

Buffett says that, of course, if the trustees want to sell the station eventually, it is their right to do so. Clearly, however, he would be reluctant to vote in favor of such a sale, at least for now. "I'm always reevaluating things," he says, and pauses. "But that's one hell of an asset." When Buffett looks into the future he focuses not on the chance of a lawsuit but on another possibility. He sees a school that owns perhaps a cluster of businesses worth twenty times more than the amount of the operating budget. With a 5 percent real return on that investment, the school could be perpetually funded by its endowment: a school, in short, with no tuition at all.

# BERKSHIRE'S SHAREHOLDER CONTRIBUTIONS

DEPARTING FROM OUR LARGELY *chronological format in this book, we pair two articles that are related. The first, from 1981, describes a Buffett innovation through which Berkshire shareholders were able to designate charities to which the company made gifts. The second, published twenty-two years later, reports Buffett's decision to close down the program because it had angered the opponents of abortion, who believed it favored pro-choice charities.*

Their ire was certainly not based on the range of charities that received contributions: Among the designees in 2002, for example, were 790 schools and 437 churches and synagogues. Reporting those numbers in his chairman's letter, Buffett also addressed the abortion issue and said he thought Berkshire's shareholders were probably on both sides of it in roughly the same proportion as the American population. But both Buffett and his late first wife, Susie, and also Berkshire's vice chairman, Charlie Munger, another very large shareholder, were known to be pro-choice in their thinking. So the pro-life forces assumed that charities they didn't wish to see flourish—such as Planned Parenthood—were getting a disproportionate share of the total contributions. (The Buffetts' contributions to, say, Planned Parenthood, would have flowed through their foundation, of which I am a director.)

The pro-life opposition did not sway Buffett when the anger was aimed mainly at him and Munger. But it then began to be focused on a Berkshire subsidiary, Pampered Chef, and the independent "consultants"—mostly housewives—who sold its kitchen goods. It seemed unfair to Buffett that these women should lose their livelihood because of the Berkshire contributions program, so he closed it down.

Over its twenty-two-year history, the program—a sort of "charitable dividend"—had dispensed $197 million and pleased many a shareholder. With the program's end, many Berkshire holders no doubt increased their personal gifts to charity. It seems likely, though, that these increases did not entirely offset the disappearance of Berkshire's contributions and that total shareholder giving therefore declined. —CL

# Shareholders Get to Vote on Charity

November 30, 1981

**BY LEE SMITH**

Unconscionable as it may seem, large corporations usually deprive their shareholders of the right to vote on which charities the companies give money to. Management decides where most of the dough will go. Employees get their say by using increasingly popular matching-gift plans. But owners, for the most part, remain disenfranchised.

That inequity for the people who hold equity has long bothered Warren E. Buffett, a noted investor and chairman of Berkshire Hathaway Inc. So last month Buffett gave Berkshire Hathaway's shareholders the right to distribute about $2 million to the colleges, churches, museums, social agencies, and other nonprofit organizations they believe in.

"I wouldn't want shareholders to write checks on my bank account for charities of their choice," he says. "So I feel it inappropriate to write checks on their corporate bank account for charities of my choice." As Buffett sees it, most corporate managers give reflexively to whatever causes their peers support.

Buffett, 51, is one manager who goes his own way. Barely out of college, he formed a partnership with friends and relatives and raised $100,000. Adding new capital from time to time, he ultimately parlayed the fund into $100 million in the stock market. In 1965 he took over and reorganized Berkshire Hathaway, which controls, among other things, See's Candies, Blue Chip Stamps, and a dozen insurance companies. It also owns 5% of General Foods and 13% of the Washington Post Co. Earnings are sizable—$53 million, or $51.72 a share, last year. The stock currently sells over the counter for around $500 a share. Berkshire Hathaway hasn't paid a dividend since 1967, but net worth has grown an average of 20% a year. Despite its wealth, the company has given relatively little to charity—$200,000 or so a year. That's little more than 0.2% of 1980's pretax profits, vs. contributions averaging 1% for U.S. companies in general.

Buffett was tightfisted because he didn't know how to improve on the methods other big corporations used to choose recipients. His new scheme, he thinks, is both fair and practical. It imitates closely held corporations that poll shareholders on their preferences. But instead of polling a dozen or so shareholders, Buffett is contacting 1,500.

The ballots go in the mail this month. With some one million shares outstanding, each share gives its owner the right to allocate $2 to charity. A shareholder with 1,000 shares, in other words, can instruct the company to send out $2,000. The most important shareholders by far will not have to be polled. Buffett and his wife own 47% of the company and will be able to assign $935,000 to their favorite charities. The money will go initially to the Buffett Foundation, established 15 years ago, and then to organizations promoting birth control.

Buffett's plan has tax advantages. Berkshire Hathaway could pay shareholders dividends, which they in turn could pass along to charity. But before profits are distributed to shareholders, they are taxed. Corporate charitable contributions, on the other hand, are treated as business expenses and are not taxed. So for every dollar that leaves Berkshire Hathaway's coffers, more goes to charity and less to the tax man.

At first glance, Buffett seems to be inviting a blizzard of paperwork that will bury the five-member staff at his four-room corporate office in Omaha. Buffett's shareholders will send in forms giving the names and addresses of up to three charities to receive contributions. If a designated recipient is not obviously tax-exempt under Internal Revenue Service rules, Buffett's staff will ask for proof. (What's obviously a charity to a widow in Winnetka might not be so obvious to Buffett.)

The staff will also have to verify the number of shares owned, make out the checks, and mail them, along with notes explaining that the gifts are being sent at the shareholder's request. Each shareholder must swear that the gift fulfills no other pledge he has made, or the IRS could treat the money as a dividend and increase Berkshire Hathaway's taxes accordingly. Despite these complications, Buffett says the paperwork shouldn't amount to much more than the minor storm of proxy votes for an annual meeting. "If I'm wrong," he says, "I'll be down here working Saturdays and Sundays."

The contributions made in shareholders' names could reduce Berkshire Hathaway's net income by $1 million or more. (Assuming a 46% tax rate, the effect of giving away $2 million is to cut after-tax profits by $1,080,000.) But not all the charity money will be spoken for. Stock held in street names for customers by brokerage houses and other institutions can't be voted, and some individuals won't bother to vote or may prefer that the money not go to charity. Unallocated funds will be returned to corporate earnings.

After sizing up the immediate reaction, Buffett estimates that as many as 85% of the shareholders will respond. "There's a lot of enthusiasm," he says. "I know of one elderly woman who is very religious but doesn't have much income and can give only $5 a month to her church. She has quite a bit of our stock, so she'll now be able to give $60 or $70 a month."

Buffett's plan is similar to but less problematical than a proposal by Robert A. Sproull, president of the University of Rochester, who has come up with a scheme by which a shareholder could send a gift to charity nearly double the size of his dividend at no additional cost to anyone—except the U.S. Treasury. The shareholder would tell the company that he would forgo, say, his $100 third-quarter dividend if the company would send that amount, plus whatever income tax would have been paid on those earnings, to the American Red Cross, the University of Rochester, or some other charity. As Sproull reckons it, a corporation paying 46% of its earnings in taxes shouldn't care whether it sent $185 before taxes to charity or a $100 dividend to a shareholder and $85 to the government.

Ingenious though it is, Sproull's plan is illegal. Senator Daniel Patrick Moynihan is trying to persuade Congress to legalize the plan, but he isn't likely to have much success, given current concern about the deficit. Corporations, moreover, seem lukewarm to the idea. AT&T, for one, is concerned that it might compete with a system under which its shareholders may automatically reinvest their dividends in stock. In 1980 alone, Ma Bell raised almost $1 billion through dividend reinvestment.

Whether Buffett's plan will be imitated remains to be seen. Many corporations have far more shareholders than Berkshire Hathaway, but they also presumably have larger staffs to handle the paperwork. Several corporations to which *Fortune* explained the idea thought it imaginative but had reservations. One contributions manager feared a shareholder backlash against giving corporate money to religious organizations, where much of Berkshire Hathaway's is almost certain to wind up under Buffett's plan. (Churches receive over half of all contributions made by individuals.) To avoid controversy most corporations give only to secular organizations.

In at least one significant sense Berkshire Hathaway is an unusual company for which Buffett's plan is particularly appropriate. Buffett says it has no important corporate goals that could be advanced by directing $2 million to charities of the management's rather than the shareholders' choice. Other corporations do have such goals. Companies that hire engineers give money to engineering schools, hoping to stimulate research and attract graduates. Oil companies contribute to public television partly to persuade people in general and legislators in particular that they are responsible citizens and not simply collectors of "obscene" profits.

Still, many companies might well follow Berkshire Hathaway's example— especially those with strong profits, few public relations problems, and a charitable impulse. Buffett has had good ideas about philanthropy before. Several years ago he advised Grinnell College in Iowa to invest some of its endowment in a TV station, an unconventional choice for a school. Grinnell bought a station in Dayton for $12.9 million and sold it for $50 million two months ago. So when Buffett wanders off on his own, it makes sense to watch where he's going.

# Berkshire Gives Up on Giving

August 11, 2003

## BY NICHOLAS VARCHAVER

Warren Buffett has drawn criticism in the past for supporting pro-choice causes, but it never affected Berkshire Hathaway's charitable giving—that is, until Cindy Coughlon, a 34-year-old stay-at-home mom in Peoria, Ariz., came along. Now, as a result of her campaign against pro-choice donations, the most powerful man in business has terminated Berkshire's entire contribution program, which distributed nearly $200 million over the past two decades to institutions ranging from schools to groups on either side of the abortion debate.

The unusual program—call it a charitable dividend—allowed Berkshire shareholders to designate $18 per share annually for up to three charities of their choosing. Some shareholders, including Buffett via his foundation, used the mechanism to give to pro-choice causes such as Planned Parenthood. (*Fortune* editor-at-large Carol Loomis is a director of the Buffett Foundation.)

The events were set in motion this winter by Coughlon, a mother of three who wanted to earn some money by selling for the Pampered Chef, a recent Berkshire acquisition with $740 million in revenues. Some 70,000 freelance "consultants" sell kitchen wares through Tupperware-style parties in people's homes. Coughlon says she was drawn to the Pampered Chef because she felt it shares her Christian, pro-family values. The company's mission statement, for example, encourages people to "develop their God-given talents."

But Coughlon was dismayed to learn that Berkshire's purchase of the Pampered Chef meant that some portion of the profits she'd generate could fund pro-choice groups. She e-mailed a petition, which asked Berkshire and Buffett to end donations to such organizations, to 100 friends and family in January. Pro-life organizations such as Life Decisions International began publicizing it.

Pampered Chef chairman Doris Christopher initially told consultants in an April e-mail that though "my personal views on some issues differ from Warren Buffett's . . . it is not my place to ask or to judge." But her message didn't quell the furor. Consultants were resigning, says Coughlon, and customers complaining. (Coughlon numbers the petitioners at "less than a thousand.") By late June the pressure had become intolerable, and Christopher "went to Warren with a heavy heart," according to an e-mail she wrote to consultants. "It troubled him deeply that charitable donations from Berkshire Hathaway were causing you difficulty." On July 3, Berkshire announced the end of the charity program.

Before this year, Berkshire seemed impervious to such pressures. Pro-life activists had picketed its annual meetings and boycotted it for years. Last year a shareholder resolution to cancel the charity program was soundly defeated, with 97% of shares voted against it. And Buffett defended the program in Berkshire's 2001 annual report, saying Berkshire makes "no contributions except those designated by shareholders," who "are probably on both sides of the abortion issue in roughly the same proportion as the American population."

So why did Berkshire abandon the program now? The company's announcement said that "its ownership is now harming" not only a subsidiary, but also individuals. The board was willing to accept some damage from boycotts in the past because the cost was diffused across a giant corporation, but this was affecting Pampered Chef consultants, who had nothing to do with Berkshire's policy.

For her part, Coughlon is "just delighted with the decision." But she says she won't be satisfied until the man she deferentially refers to as "Mr. Buffett" stops donating to pro-choice causes. "Now," she says, "the focus is on him."

# Letters from Chairman Buffett

August 22, 1983

## BY ANDREW TOBIAS

*Buffett has written the chairman's letter in the Berkshire Hathaway annual report since 1966. But ten years later, he served on a Securities and Exchange Commission panel studying how companies could improve their shareholder communications, and by the 1977 annual report he was ready to renovate his own annual letter. The changes he made were gradual. By the early 1980s, though, his letters stood out for their intellectual content, humor, and individuality, and they began to attract wide attention.*

*Fortune* then determined to do a story—visualized as a kind of book re-view—about the letters. I was not a logical candidate to be the writer, because as the date drew near for the 1977 annual report, Buffett, then a friend of mine for around ten years, asked me to weigh in with suggestions for his largely finished letter. My memory is that I advised changing a "the" to an "a." Since that time, I have been his pro bono, but attentive, editor. I will admit to inten-sifying my suggestions a lot since the 1977 letter, but the drill has never changed: He writes, I edit (and, alas, sometimes lose arguments about how a sentence should go).

*With my opting out of doing the 1983 article,* Fortune *turned to an outside writer, Andrew Tobias, who had almost come to work for the magazine several years earlier (our loss that he didn't) but who had instead embarked on a brilliant career of writing books (*The Only Investment Guide You'll Ever Need*) and free-lance articles. Tobias says that when a* Fortune *editor called him about doing this piece, he had never heard of this guy Buffett, who was said to have "an almost cult following." Tobias then proceeded to do an article—far more than a book review—displaying his own humor and individuality.*

*And did he next buy Berkshire stock, then selling around $1,000 a share (ver-sus almost $170,000 recently)? Tobias answers: "I tell people endlessly that Berk-shire was the worst investment I ever made—for not making it. If I'd just taken the $1,500 that I remember* Fortune *paying me for the article, added a few dol-lars, and bought two shares—well . . ." Tobias had the view back then, he says, that the stock was a little ahead of itself and that when it dropped back a bit, he'd buy. He recalls thinking the same thing when the stock was $10,000 and $30,000.*

*A redeeming fact is that Tobias and Buffett became good friends, drawn to-gether not only by their conversations about this article but also their mutual interest in supporting Democratic candidates. —CL*

Berkshire Hathaway shareholders have come to expect two things of their an-nual report: good news (book value has increased from $19 to $737 per share in the last 18 years) and the unorthodox letter of their chairman, Warren Buffett (who took over 18 years ago). Indeed, the chairman's letter practically *is* the Berkshire Hathaway annual report.

Shareholders get no photographs, no colored inks or foil embossing, no bar charts or graphs—not even a logo. It looks like the kind of annual you see from a company whose bubble has finally burst, only Berkshire Hathaway, an insurer with major holdings in several other industries, is no bubble; and at $955 a share, up from $85 six years ago, it shows no signs of bursting.

The conventional wisdom in reading annual reports is to glance at the auditor's opinion, then check the financial results and the footnotes. The chairman's letter? Save your time. Yet of such interest are Warren Buffett's letters that they have drawn a sophisticated following. Requests for reprints even! The company has assembled a compendium of the past five to meet the demand.

"They're wonderful," says Leon Levy of Odyssey Partners, no minor Wall Street legend himself, whereupon he recounts the passage in the last letter that most amused him—the one in which Buffett says he wouldn't have wanted any part of the acquisitions most others were making in 1982. "For in many of these acquisitions," Buffett writes, "managerial intellect wilted in competition with managerial adrenaline. The thrill of the chase blinded pursuers to the consequences of the catch. Pascal's observation seems apt: 'It has struck me that all men's misfortunes spring from the single cause that they are unable to stay quietly in one room.' (Your chairman left the room once too often last year and almost starred in the Acquisition Follies of 1982. In retrospect our major accomplishment of the year was that a very large purchase to which we had firmly committed [fell through] for reasons totally beyond our control. Had it come off, this transaction would have consumed extraordinary amounts of time and energy, all for a most uncertain payoff. If we were to introduce graphics to this report, illustrating favorable business developments of the past year, two blank pages depicting this blown deal would be the appropriate centerfold.)"

"I love that," beams Levy.

Buffett himself says he tries to talk to shareholders as if they were his partners. "I assume I've got a very intelligent partner who has been away for a year and needs to be filled in on all that's happened." He also assumes little turnover among his 2,000 shareholders. "Rather than repeat the same things each year," he says, "I take up topics that further their education." It is an exercise he seems clearly to enjoy—the letters, currently running around 12 printed pages, get longer every year. (The other extreme may have been reached last year by Wisconsin banker Jack Puelicher, another iconoclastic C.E.O., whose letter to Marshall & Ilsley shareholders read, in its entirety: "Your company had a very good year in 1982. Some of it was due to luck; some of it was due to good planning and management. We hope you enjoy the numbers and the pictures.")

Buffett's attention to his letters was sharpened by his service on an SEC panel formed in 1976 to study disclosure practices. (The committee issued a 1,200-page document that concluded the disclosure system was basically sound.) Former

SEC Commissioner A. A. Sommer Jr., who chaired the committee—himself a Berkshire Hathaway shareholder—says the group felt such letters were very important. Even so, he adds, "Warren's letters are unique. Damn few C.E.O.s are as smart in as many ways as Warren. It would be awfully hard to require that kind of discussion from all C.E.O.s."

Does Buffett ever take on unorthodox subjects in his letters? Yes, he responds, he discusses his mistakes.

"The textile business again had a very poor year," he reported in 1977. (When Buffett first took over Berkshire Hathaway in 1965, that's *all* it was—a New Bedford, Massachusetts, textile manufacturer.) "We have mistakenly predicted better results in each of the last two years. Many difficulties experienced [have been] due primarily to industry conditions, but some of the problems have been of our own making."

"We continue to look for ways to expand our insurance operation," he wrote his shareholders in 1979, "but your reaction to this intent should not be unrestrained joy. Some of our expansion efforts—largely initiated by your chairman—have been lackluster, others have been expensive failures."

Buffett downplays the excellence of his own efforts but, like a proud coach, highlights it in his players. Berkshire Hathaway owns a big chunk of GEICO, the auto insurer, and of that company's brass he writes: "Jack Byrne and Bill Snyder are achieving the most elusive of human goals—keeping things simple and remembering what you set out to do."

And of an 81-year-old subsidiary chief, since deceased: "Our experience has been that the manager of an already high-cost operation frequently is uncommonly resourceful in finding new ways to add overhead, while the manager of a tightly run operation usually continues to find additional methods to curtail costs, even when his costs are already well below those of his competitors. No one has demonstrated this latter ability better than Gene Abegg."

Here and there notes of sentimentality pop up, but if Buffett wants to say something a little silly about the Washington Post Co., for which he delivered papers at the age of 13, or GEICO, which first caught his eye at 20, it should be remembered that Berkshire's holdings in the one have risen in value from $11 million to $103 million and in the other from $47 million to $310 million, both in under a decade. So he can say what he likes.

Happily, he says it with a sense of humor. "In a characteristically rash move," he writes, "we have expanded World Headquarters by 252 square feet (17%), coincidental with the signing of a new five-year lease." World Headquarters—in Omaha—houses, in addition to Buffett, five other people. ("A compact organization lets all of us spend our time managing the business rather than managing each other.")

Most chairmen's letters describe how well everything went, under the circumstances, hoping the shareholders will buy it. Buffett's stress the negative, knowing that they won't.

In the most recent report, immediately after observing that Berkshire Hathaway's 18-year rise in book value represents a 22% compound annual rate of growth, he adds: "You can be certain that this percentage will diminish in the future. Geometric progressions eventually forge their own anchors." (He's right, of course. Maintaining that rate for another 18 years would mean growing in book value to $22 billion and, after 18 years more, to nearly $1 million per share.) Even when stating the paper gains in the Berkshire Hathaway portfolio—up 40% in 1982—he is careful first to subtract the taxes that would be paid if those gains were taken.

To be sure, it's easy to be candid and self deprecatory when any fool can see that you're terrific. What may be a tad galling to some of his peers is that Buffett's letters review not only his own performance and mistakes but those of the rest of the nation's managers as well. "There are indications," he writes, "that several large insurers opted in 1982 for obscure accounting and reserving maneuvers that masked significant deterioration in their underlying businesses. In insurance, as elsewhere, the reaction of weak managements to weak operations is often weak accounting." His recurring theme: the rights of shareholders, as trampled on by so many other managers.

Well-known are the corporate managers who fight heroically to fend off generous tender offers. Less sharply perceived are the managers who pay too much to grow by acquisition. "Managers who want to expand their domain at the expense of owners," Buffett chides wryly, "might better consider a career in government."

It's even worse, in his view, when the acquisition is made with stock, because the acquirer's stock so often sells in the market for a discount to its true value. "The acquirer who nevertheless barges ahead is using an undervalued currency [his stock] to pay for a fully valued property . . . Friendly investment bankers will reassure him as to the soundness of his actions. (Don't ask the barber whether you need a haircut.)"

In light of the enormous premium required to buy *all* of a company, Buffett's strategy has been one of partial acquisition. Where another company will bid $48 a share for all of a company whose shares were yesterday selling at $25, Buffett is content to buy quietly at $25. "What really makes us dance," he admits, is to buy 100% of a business at a good price, but that is awfully hard to do. And so it is that at year's end Berkshire Hathaway, owned, among other holdings, chunks of Blue Chip Stamps (60%), GEICO (35%), General Foods (4%), precious metals fabricator Handy & Harman (17%), R.J. Reynolds (2.7%), Interpublic (15%), Ogilvy & Mather (9%), Time Inc., publisher of *Fortune* (2.7%), and the Washington Post Co. (13%).

Berkshire Hathaway's reported earnings include its share of the earnings at Blue Chip Stamps—which it is merging with—but only the dividend income from the other companies in its investment portfolio. So Buffett must each year remind shareholders that reported profits exclude a large portion of true earning power. "This is not a criticism of accounting procedures," he hastens to add.

"We would not like to have the job of designing a better system. It's simply to say that managers and investors alike must understand that accounting numbers are the beginning, not the end, of business valuation."

Lamenting the complexities of accounting, he reveals that "the Yanomamö Indians employ only three numbers: one, two, and more than two. Maybe their time will come."

Because of the growing importance of the company's nonconsolidated holdings, Buffett argues, it's no longer appropriate for shareholders to gauge Berkshire's performance by the ratio of reported earnings to equity, as until recently he had been advising they should. But then he adds: "You should be suspicious of such an assertion. Yardsticks seldom are discarded while yielding favorable readings. But when results deteriorate, most managers favor disposition of the yardstick rather than disposition of the manager. To managers faced with such deterioration, a more flexible measurement system often suggests itself: just shoot the arrow of business performance into a blank canvas and then carefully draw the bull's-eye around the implanted arrow. We generally believe in preset, long-lived, and small bull's-eyes."

One of the bull's-eyes he considers notably unimpressive is the widely trumpeted achievement of "record earnings." "After all," he explains, "even a totally dormant savings account will produce steadily rising interest earnings each year because of compounding."

It's no surprise that Buffett would champion shareholders' rights; at 52, he has long been a professional shareholder himself. He and his wife own shares in Berkshire Hathaway recently worth $460 million, and Berkshire Hathaway is itself largely in the business of owning shares.

Author Jerry Goodman, in *Supermoney*, labels Buffett "easily the outstanding money manager of the generation," noting that a partnership he began in 1956—and had the consummate foresight to close down in 1969—achieved a compound annual growth of 31%. "What was more remarkable," writes Goodman, "was that he did it with the philosophy of another generation . . . just pure Benjamin Graham, applied with absolute consistency." The late Benjamin Graham, of course, authored *The Intelligent Investor*, in print almost continuously since 1949. Buffett chose Graham as a mentor (and, years later, Graham chose Buffett to help revise his book).

Although Graham and Buffett did not agree in all things, their common perception was to buy assets so cheaply that, over time, they could hardly fail to profit. This approach calls for a level head and hard work. "The market, like the Lord," Buffett writes, "helps those who help themselves. But, unlike the Lord, the market does not forgive those who know not what they do."

Buffett's strategy of partial acquisition makes sense when companies are selling in the marketplace at a substantial discount to their true value as ongoing businesses, but not when the market, as it periodically does, jumps over the moon. In 1972, with Avon and the rest selling at 60 times earnings, Berkshire had only 15% of its portfolio in equities, vs. 80% at the end of 1982.

"There were as many good businesses around in 1972 as in 1982," he writes, "but the prices the stock market placed upon those businesses in 1972 looked absurd." Should the stock market keep climbing, he warns, Berkshire's "ability to utilize capital effectively in partial-ownership positions will be reduced or eliminated. We currently are seeing early traces of this problem." (Damn—another bull market.)

One problem all Buffett's letters address is the state of the property/casualty insurance industry—his core business. "For much of this century," he writes, "a large portion of the industry worked, in effect, within a legal quasi-administered pricing system fostered by insurance regulators. While price competition existed, it was not pervasive among the larger companies." That gentlemanly day, says Buffett, is gone. "Although parts of the old structure remain . . . the new capacity is not reluctant to use price as a prime competitive weapon. Indeed, it relishes that use. In the process, customers have learned that insurance is no longer a one-price business. They won't forget."

It is Buffett's plan to live with low volume while he waits for the shakeout that will cause prices to firm.

He is less confident, letter after letter, of the prospects for the textile industry—a capital-intensive commodity business in which periods of tight supply, and hence decent prices, come around only rarely (and then last only "the better part of a morning"). Out of loyalty to his employees, however, and perhaps out of a certain nostalgia for Berkshire's roots, Buffett steadfastly refuses to abandon his business. Such behavior might seem to flout the interests of Berkshire shareholders—only, with 47% of the company stock, Buffett is able to summon a majority vote for this policy, or any other, practically all by himself. Even so, he assures his shareholders, it's not the kind of business he is eager to enter in the future.

Among the final notes in Buffett's letters is a virtual BUSINESSES WANTED classified. It tells a lot about how Warren Buffett operates. Berkshire Hathaway, Buffett writes, is looking for large, simple businesses ("if there's lots of technology, we won't understand it") with consistent earning power, little debt, management in place ("we can't supply it"), and an offering price ("we don't want to waste our time or that of the seller by talking, even preliminarily, when price is unknown"). "We will not engage in unfriendly transactions. We can promise complete confidentiality and a very fast answer as to possible interest—customarily within five minutes."

To write an interesting chairman's letter, it helps if you are a chairman with interesting ideas. Buffett's is a refreshing style in business as in prose.

# From "Can You Beat the Stock Market?"

December 26, 1983

*An excerpt and a sidebar from an article by Daniel Seligman*

*The efficient market hypothesis (EMH), as this article incisively says, holds that "the stock market cannot be beaten by mere mortals." To all those believing in EMH, therefore, Buffett's long record in successfully picking stocks was, at the very least, discordant. The usual reaction of the believers was to describe Buffett as just lucky—extraordinarily, damnably lucky.*

*As Buffett's fame grew, however, he came to be viewed as an "anomaly," an investor whose superb record just could not be explained away by chance. This development did not thrill Fortune's Dan Seligman, who wrote this article. A mentor and close friend of mine, Seligman was intellectually drawn to EMH—a leaning he discloses in the article—and much preferred that it be proved right. But his honesty and news sense told him there was a fine, unreported story here, and he proceeded to write it.*

*We have not reprinted the entire article, only its beginning and a core section and an accompanying sidebar that describes Buffett and three of his longtime friends, Charlie Munger, the late Bill Ruane, and the late Walter Schloss. The full story is available online (see below); but beware that it basically describes a relic, since EMH has largely been assigned to the dustbin.*

*There was an important postscript to the article: a May 1984 debate about EMH, staged by Columbia University and pitting Buffett against a well-known business school academic, University of Rochester finance professor Michael Jensen. Speaking first, Jensen expressed his strong belief in EMH, gave his reasons cogently, and then ended with a specific reference to Fortune's article—an "excellent review" of EMH, he said. But it would be wrong, he contended, to think that the standout investment records of Buffett and the other three men were undeniably attributable to skill. Statistically, he said, citing coin-flipping probabilities, the records could just as easily have been compiled by luck.*

*Not so, said Buffett, realizing he'd been given a liftoff into the very argument he had planned to make. To himself and the three other investors named above, Buffett added five more "coin flippers," calling this group of nine The Superinvestors of Graham-and-Doddsville. All nine, he explained, describing each, had a common "intellectual father," famed investor and author Ben Graham, who believed that investors should search for discrepancies between the value of a business and the price of small pieces of that business in the market.*

*These nine investors, however, said Buffett, had produced their records in widely different ways, with very few stocks duplicated among their portfolios. In other words, they were residents of the same "intellectual village," but varied in how they plied their trade. To call their superior records "luck," said Buffett, would be absurd.*

*Attending that debate, I felt that Buffett had decisively bested Jensen, a conclusion that indeed became the consensus about the event. Buffett himself feels that of all the written and oral presentations he has given, this one was the most logically reasoned and therefore the best. ("The Superinvestors of Graham-and-Doddsville" can be accessed on the Internet.)* —CL

**M**ost people interested in the stock market fall into one of three categories: (1) academic scholars who doubt anybody really knows how to beat the market; (2) professional investors who indignantly reject this view of the matter; and (3) amateur investors who also believe that you can beat the market but don't realize how controversial this assumption is. I have long been a partisan of the first group, and until the last year or so had assumed that its case was airtight.

The professors seemed to have built an overwhelming case for the so-called efficient market hypothesis (EMH). If you think of the hypothesis as a literal description of the real world, the stock market cannot be beaten by mere mortals. Question: how close to reality is EMH? Having now resurveyed the basic case made for it in the business schools and also looked at some recent findings that seem inconsistent with it, I find myself answering that EMH is extremely useful for understanding the stock market—but doubting that it's as close to reality as I had previously assumed. It seems fairly clear that some superior investors are out there beating the market systematically. . . .

Like many other EMH fans, I have been shaken by the proliferation of "anomalies"—this being the professors' preferred term for stock market news that seems to confound the hypothesis. . . .

One disturbing anomaly centers on the extraordinary records compiled by certain high-visibility investors. The records of one tightly knit group of investors, of whom Warren Buffett is the best known, are laid out below. Buffett . . . is very much aware of the extent to which his investment record constitutes a challenge to the efficient market hypothesis. He believes that there are exploitable "pockets of inefficiency" in the market, and he has at several times argued his case in appearances at the Stanford business school, on whose advisory council he serves. Speaking to the council, Professor William F. Sharpe of Stanford, one of the school's academic stars and the author of a popular textbook solidly endorsing EMH, once referred to Buffett as a "five-sigma event." In business school lingo, this superlative signifies that you should think of his investment performance as being five standard deviations above the mean; if literally true—no one claims that it is—this would tell us that there is only about one chance in 3.5 million of compiling an investment record like Buffett's by chance.

## YOU ONLY SWING ON 3 AND 0

### A Sidebar by Daniel Seligman

In principle, says the efficient market hypothesis, no one can systematically beat the stock market. In applying EMH to Warren Buffett, Charles Munger, William Ruane, and Walter Schloss, you would have three difficulties:(1) all have outperformed the market over long periods; (2) they have generally done so in both bullish and bearish environments, so it's hard to argue that their higher returns simply reflect greater risk-taking; and (3) all are pursuing strategies that reflect the ideas of the late Benjamin Graham, so it's hard to view their performance as a random event. Buffett, Ruane, and Schloss all studied under Graham, and all four have been influenced by his classic *Security Analysis,* written with David L. Dodd and first published in 1934. Graham's core idea: look for companies that for some reason are undervalued and hold the stocks for as long as it takes the market to see the values. Obviously such companies are hard to find. Says Buffett, "You wait for the 3 and 0 pitch." Prize example of what you get by waiting: the Washington Post Co. in 1974, when its market value was $80 million and its TV stations alone were worth more than that. Now its market value is about $1 billion, and Buffett's Berkshire Hathaway owns 13%.

Buffett himself has not formally been in the money management business since 1969, when he dissolved the Buffett Partnership Ltd. after nearly 14 years of operation. One reason for the dissolution: Buffett had stopped finding undervalued securities. During its lifetime the partnership had an annual average return of 29.5%, vs. 8.2% for the S & P 500. (Like the figures below, these assume annual reinvestment of dividends.)

Charles Munger's partnership (Wheeler Munger & Co.) operated from 1962 to 1975. It had an average return of 19.8%, vs. 5.3% for the S & P 500. Bill Ruane runs the immensely successful Sequoia Fund, which was first offered to the public in July 1970 and since then has had an average return of 18.6% vs. 10.6% for the S & P. Sequoia now has $333 million of assets and has suspended sales to new investors because, says Ruane, "the money was coming in faster than I had ideas."

The private partnership run by Walter Schloss [since 1956] has had an average return of 21.3%, vs. 8.7% for the S & P. In a recent sentimental letter to his partners, Schloss saluted Graham and *Security Analysis,* which "helped many of us along a rocky road."

*The full text of "Can You Beat the Stock Market?" is available at fortune.com/buffettbook.*

# BUFFETT AND CAPITAL CITIES/ABC

THE ACQUISITION OF AMERICAN *Broadcasting Cos. by Capital Cities Communications in 1985, and Berkshire's involvement in the deal, was a combination and investment that Buffett liked from the beginning, particularly because it put him into business with his longtime friend, Cap Cities chairman Thomas S. Murphy. The deal did not disappoint: Cap Cities/ABC flourished and in 1996 was bought by Walt Disney Co., with Berkshire more than quadrupling its original investment. Here are four* Fortune *excerpts that describe key moments along the way.* —CL

## From "Capital Cities Capital Coup"

April 15, 1985

*An excerpt from an article by Stratford Sherman*

**B**uffett says of Murphy: "I think he is the top manager in the U.S." No slouch as a manager himself, Buffett has placed a substantial part of his future in Murphy's hands. Buffett helped bring off the friendly acquisition by agreeing to buy about 18% of the merged company, Capital Cities/ABC Inc., for $518 million. . . . More extraordinary, Buffett agreed to vote with management for 11 years—on condition that either Murphy or [President Daniel] Burke be in charge—and accepted severe limitations on his freedom to buy and sell the stock.

# From "Merger Fees That Bend the Mind"

January 20, 1986

**BY PETER PETRE**

Faced with towering [investment banker] fees, some corporate chieftains play do-it-yourself. . . . Successful do-it-yourselfers tend to be financiers with extraordinary talent for sizing up a transaction. . . . [One of these] faced down two of Wall Street's most famous gun-slingers. Warren Buffett stepped in last March on behalf of Capital Cities Communications in its effort to acquire American Broadcasting Cos. [He] went into negotiations assisted by merger lawyer Martin Lipton of the law firm Wachtell Lipton Rosen & Katz. Across the table were Bruce Wasserstein, co-director of First Boston's mergers and acquisitions department, and takeover specialist Joseph Flom of the law firm Skadden Arps Slate Meagher & Flom.

As the two sides neared an agreement, the professional dealmakers held out for more. "Buffett is so smart," remembers Wasserstein, "that you had to be careful to avoid being picked." As the dealmaker tells it, he and Flom demanded that Cap Cities sweeten its cash offer for ABC with stock; but Buffett, who was not to be pushed far, finally closed by throwing in some small change—a thin veneer of warrants that raised the deal's value by perhaps 3%. Buffett has declined to comment.

# From "The Inside Story of Time Warner"

November 20, 1989

**BY BILL SAPORITO**

In the mid-eighties [Time Inc. CEO J. Richard Munro saw a way to attack] all of his big problems: Hook up through acquisition or merger with another media giant. . . .

In the fall of 1988, Warren Buffett came by with his friends from Capital Cities/ABC, in which he was a major investor. Munro and [Time Inc. president Nicholas J. "Nick" Nicholas Jr.] met with Buffett and Cap Cities CEO Thomas Murphy and President Daniel Burke. The meetings continued into December until, according to Nicholas, Murphy mentioned that in any deal there should be one or two more Cap Cities directors than Time directors. Munro says he told Murphy, a good friend, thank you very much but Time Inc. is not for sale. A Cap Cities source says the two men couldn't agree on who would be boss.

Time had rebuffed Buffett before. In 1984 he had asked Munro informally about acquiring up to 10% of Time Inc.'s stock, enough to frighten a raider. Buffett's practice with other large stockholdings is to hang on to them for years or decades and become a trusted board member and adviser. But when Munro took Buffett's feeler to the Time Inc. board, the directors—to Munro's regret—discouraged him from pursuing it.

## From "Buffett to Disney: All Thumbs Up"

<hr>

April 1, 1996

<hr>

### BY CAROL LOOMIS

Just in from Omaha and making a do-it-yourself delivery, Berkshire Hathaway chairman Warren Buffett strolled into the downtown Manhattan offices of Harris Trust on March 5 and handed two envelopes to a Harris officer. In Envelope No. 1 was stock worth, gulp, $2.5 billion, Berkshire's 20 million shares of Capital Cities/ABC, being delivered to the company's purchaser, Walt Disney Co.

In Envelope No. 2, sealed and marked "Do not open until 4:30 P.M. on March 7," were Buffett's wishes—kept secret from even the managements of Disney and Cap Cities—as to how he wanted Berkshire to be paid for the contents of Envelope No. 1. Like any ordinary Cap Cities stockholder, Buffett had the option of taking the standard package, which was Disney stock plus cash, or requesting all stock, or all cash.

And the envelope, please? Giving Disney a huge thumbs-up, Buffett asked for stock only. Talking to Disney CEO Michael Eisner late on the 7th, Buffett said he had paid the company and its boss his ultimate compliment by entrusting them with Berkshire's money. Eisner assured Buffett he'd work to make the decision right. . . .

In Berkshire's 1995 annual report, due out momentarily, Buffett will acknowledge that he is returning to the scene of an investing crime. Attracted to Disney in 1966 by its film library, its burgeoning theme park business, and its peanut-gallery stock price—the market capitalization of the entire company was less than $90 million—Buffett invested a large chunk of Buffett Partnership money in the stock at a split-adjusted price of 31 cents a share. The stock recently sold for $65—but did Buffett hang around for the ride? No. He sold out in 1967 at 48 cents a share. "Oh, well," says Buffett, with surely a wince, "it's nice to be back."

*Editor's note: Back, yes, but not for long. For a time, true, Buffett liked Disney, even adding shares to the large Disney stake that Berkshire received when the*

*deal closed. But then Disney went through a period of management turmoil—*
*Frank Wells died, Michael Ovitz failed as a manager—and Buffett turned thumbs*
*down on the investment. By 1999, Berkshire was completely out of Disney.*

*The full text of the four Cap Cities articles excerpted is available at fortune.com/*
*buffettbook*

# From "Beating the Market by Buying Back Stock"

April 29, 1985

*An excerpt from an article by Carol Loomis*

*Making a groundbreaking study of stock buybacks,* Fortune *found that, on average, large benefits accrued to the stockholders of companies buying in significant quantities of their own stock.*

*This article also presented many pro and con opinions, some of them Buffett's, about repurchases. Buffett was then, as now, a fan of managements who bought in stock for the right reason—because they knew their stocks to be undervalued. Conversely, he has always disdained managers who buy because they are trying to prop their stock or counteract the effects of stock options, which tend to shovel new shares into the market. "The only reason for a company to repurchase its stock," Buffett has often said, "is because it is selling for less than it's worth."*

*Buffett's views about repurchases sometimes have drawn perplexed, or even indignant, questions at Berkshire annual meetings because he has not appeared to be practicing what he preaches. Why, shareholders would ask, had not Berkshire itself repurchased shares when they were undervalued? In 2009, in fact, one questioner virtually quoted from this article, reminding Buffett that he has said the stock market will discount the prices of companies that should be buying back their stock and don't.*

*Over the years, Buffett has responded in several ways. In Internet bubble days, when Berkshire was thought antediluvian and its shares were sinking toward $40,000, Buffett conceded that in the past he had sometimes "erred" in not making repurchases. "My appraisal of Berkshire's value," he wrote in the 1999 annual report letter, "was then too conservative or I was too enthused about some alternative use of funds." He then used the letter to open the door to repurchases. He said that after shareholders had a chance to read his discussion and understand the issues, Berkshire would entertain the offers of shareholders who wished to sell stock.*

*And what happened? Nothing that led to Berkshire buying shares. Buffett says that the very few offers that came in were asking for prices that he was unwilling to pay.*

*After that nonevent, Buffett said on more than one occasion that a move by Berkshire to buy in shares would be self-defeating. That is, the mere announcement by the company that it would repurchase stock (a disclosure that would be required, he said) would send up the price and make the shares no longer attractive to buy. In other words—these are my words, definitely not his—if Warren Buffett, a genius at identifying undervalued stocks, were to indicate that Berkshire was so cheap it should be bought, it would immediately rise to a price not cheap.*

*An acid test of this proposition came on September 26, 2011, when book value of Berkshire A stock was about $96,900 and the stock had on some days dipped* *below $100,000. Buffett announced then that Berkshire's board had authorized the company to buy shares—A or B—at a price no higher than 10 percent above book value. Within the day, the stock jumped to a price over Buffett's limit, and by all rights Berkshire should not have been able to buy any shares. But a few shareholders nevertheless made offers within Buffett's range. Berkshire bought in 98 shares of A stock and 802,000 of B for about $67 million in total—pocket change for a company that could have, and probably would have, paid billions to buy.*

*To Buffett's 110 percent declaration there came a fairly prompt amendment: In December 2012 Berkshire announced that it had paid 120 percent of book—that was a price of $131,000 per share—to acquire 9,200 A shares from the estate of a longtime shareholder (later rumored to be Al Ueltschi, former CEO of Berkshire subsidiary Flight Safety International, who had died two months earlier). The total cost was $1.2 billion. Berkshire said that its board, in authorizing this purchase, also set 120 percent of book as the new limit at which it might purchase other shares. Through June 2013, no further shares had been repurchased.  —CL*

"**[O**ne]** buyback enthusiast is Warren E. Buffett, the noted Omaha investor. The company he controls is due to acquire 18% of Capital Cities in the ABC deal [in which Cap Cities acquired ABC], and that will become his biggest investment. But right now his four largest common-stock holdings are in corporations that have [as Cap Cities has] repurchased substantial amounts of stock: GEICO, General Foods, Exxon, and Washington Post. The Exxon investment is new, built up only after the company started acquiring its shares in 1983. "A big reason I got in," Buffett says, "is that the company has recognized the values in its stock and been smart enough and pro-shareholder enough to repurchase it." On the other hand, Buffett has sold the stocks of certain companies because they would *not* make repurchases.

He is convinced, in fact, that the market discounts the prices of companies that should be making repurchases and don't, instead frittering their money away on acquisitions or other investments of far less value. The corollary, he says, is a markup in prices for companies that do repurchase shares, because investors identify the buybacks as a sign that management will be consistently inclined to act in the interests of shareholders. "All managements *say* they're acting in the shareholders' interests," he observes. "What you'd like to do as an investor is hook them up to a machine and run a polygraph to see whether it's true. Short of a polygraph, the best sign of a shareholder-oriented management—assuming its stock is undervalued—is repurchases. A polygraph proxy, that's what it is."

*The full text of "Beating the Market by Buying Back Stock" is available at fortune.com/buffettbook.*

# Guess Who's Bought Whoops Bonds

April 29, 1985

## BY KENNETH LABICH

*By the mid-1980s Buffett's reputation had grown to the point that every invest-
ment move he made was news—and in early 1985, the revelation was Berkshire's
purchase of that frequent butt of investment jokes, "Whoops" bonds.*

*In his chairman's letter in Berkshire's 1985 annual report, published days before
this article came out, Buffett took pains to explain both this off-the-wall investment
and the prosaic considerations (beware inflation, for example) that go into buying
bonds generally. Investors, Buffett stressed, need to think about the prices of securities—or more precisely, the mispricing that an investor hopes to identify and exploit. Said the letter, "Charlie [Munger] and I judged the risks at the time we
purchased the bonds and at the prices Berkshire paid (much lower than present
prices) to be considerably more than compensated for by prospects of profit."*

*In that letter, Buffett also stated his opinions—laid out in many of his annual
reports—about buying businesses, in their entirety or in the "pieces" that stocks
(and occasionally bonds) represent. He wrote, "We feel that if we can buy small
pieces of businesses with satisfactory underlying economics at a fraction of the
per-share value of the entire business, something good is likely to happen to us."*

*It did in the Whoops case. In the aggregate, Berkshire bought $260 million of
the bonds, holding varying quantities from 1983 into the early 1990s. On this
investment, Berkshire reaped tax-free interest of $263 million and in time, upon
disposing of the bonds, recorded capital gains of $68 million. —CL*

In building his reputation as one of America's most astute investors, Warren
Buffett has often startled Wall Street with bold, unexpected moves. Lately,
he's been springing them fortnightly. Having just played a big part in Capital
Cities Communications' deal to take over American Broadcasting Cos., the
54-year-old chairman of Omaha-based Berkshire Hathaway Inc. has come up
with another stunner. Buffett revealed in the Berkshire Hathaway annual report that he has spent $139 million to buy long-term bonds issued by the Wash-
ington Public Power Supply System (WPPSS)—the notorious nuclear
construction agency in Washington state that defaulted on $2.25 billion of
bonds in 1983 and has come to be known as Whoops.

A municipal corporation composed of towns and utility districts, WPPSS
began construction of five huge nuclear power plants in the 1970s. Buffett didn't
buy the defaulted bonds issued to finance nuclear generating units 4 and 5.
WPPSS scrapped these two plants during the early stages of construction after
costs ran way over budget and evidence emerged that the region had overesti-
mated its power needs. Buffett's bonds are tied to units 1, 2, and 3. They have
continued to pay interest because, unlike the bonds for units 4 and 5, they are
backed by a regional federal power agency.

So far Buffett seems to have triumphed again. Because he started buying the bonds not long after the well-publicized default brought a plunge in all WPPSS bonds, he locked in an attractive 16.3% tax-free current yield—a $22.7-million annual return on his investment. In addition, his 1, 2, and 3 bonds appreciated by about 13% by the end of 1984.

Still, the WPPSS venture is a departure for Buffett. Though Berkshire Hathaway, an insurance, retail, and publishing conglomerate, holds large amounts of bonds, Buffett's forte is buying shares in companies whose values he believes have been underestimated by the stock market. His WPPSS purchases are a dicier proposition, as he is quick to admit. Only one of the three nuclear reactors financed by the bonds has gone on line; work on the other two has been suspended because their output won't be needed until the mid-1990s. The mothballing calls into question WPPSS's long-term financial stability. Investors holding the defaulted bonds and other parties have filed dozens of lawsuits against WPPSS, and interest payments could be interrupted. Buffett even warns shareholders of "a very slight risk that the 'business' could be worth nothing within a year or two."

Buffett doesn't seem concerned about such an outcome. Neither does he judge himself, or expect to be judged by others, on the basis of one investment decision; it's the overall record that counts. Buffett's record has been astounding. Owner of 41% of Berkshire Hathaway, he currently manages more than $1.7 billion in company investments. Berkshire Hathaway shares that were selling for $40 ten years ago now command well over $1,800.

Slumped on a couch in his modest office, the genial Nebraskan compares the WPPSS investment to other unconventional moves he has made over the years—most notably his plunge into American Express stock right after a 1963 contretemps involving master swindler Tino De Angelis. The case, which became known as the salad oil scandal, involved an obscure American Express warehousing subsidiary that issued receipts for large quantities of cottonseed and soybean oil that proved nonexistent. Though many on Wall Street feared the affair would bankrupt American Express, Buffett and some partners took a chance and bought 5% of the company's shares at fire-sale prices. In the end, American Express's liability turned out to be far less than originally suspected, the stock skyrocketed and Buffett's contrariety triumphed. "Things aren't right just because they are unpopular," Buffett says with a chuckle, "but it is a good pond in which to fish. You pay a lot on Wall Street for a cheery consensus."

WPPSS is a contrarian's paradise. Bondholders in units 1, 2, and 3 have just survived a hair-raising legal challenge. They get their interest payments because the federal government's Bonneville Power Administration, which sells hydroelectric power to towns and utilities throughout the Northwest, has earmarked some of its revenues to pay the 1, 2, and 3 bondholders. The town of Springfield, Oregon, which had contracted to buy power from the WPPSS nuclear projects, asked the courts to look into this setup because ratepayers had questioned its legality. In February a U.S. appeals court in San Francisco allowed the arrangement to stand.

More litigation on this issue is possible, and other worries abound. To meet the interest payments, Bonneville must have a reliable cash flow, which partly depends on adequate rainfall for the dams whose power it sells. Nor can it count on selling all the kilowatts. Aluminum smelters, the major industrial customers in the region, have been hurt by foreign competition, and Bonneville has had to lower rates to keep them going. Another fear for 1, 2, and 3 bondholders is that a court will decide that 4 and 5 bondholders are entitled to part of the revenues now being sluiced through Bonneville to 1, 2, and 3. WPPSS watchers call the current partition between the two classes of bondholders the Chinese wall. Most dangerous of all for 1, 2, and 3 bondholders is the possibility that WPPSS might declare bankruptcy. Since no public agency of this size has gone bankrupt in the U.S., no one is quite sure how 1, 2, and 3 bonds might fare.

Given all these imponderables, many municipal bond specialists have advised clients to stay away from WPPSS. A West Coast bond expert compares a WPPSS investment to troop convoys crossing the North Atlantic during World War II. "You're pretty sure some torpedoes will be aimed at you," he says. "But you don't know if you're going to get hit." The two major bond-rating agencies on Wall Street, Moody's and Standard & Poor's, have both refused to rate WPPSS 1, 2, and 3 bonds.

Yet other bond experts share Buffett's enthusiasm for the high WPPSS yields. Says Robert Adler, vice president of the municipal bond department at Shearson Lehman Brothers: "They're not investment-grade, quality bonds, but they could work for a high net worth individual who understands the risks." (Apparently, American Express, which owns Shearson Lehman, is less bullish. In 1984 an American Express insurance subsidiary unloaded WPPSS 1, 2, and 3 bonds worth $76 million.) Howard Sitzer, director of municipal bond research at Thomson McKinnon Securities, recommends WPPSS 1, 2, and 3. He argues that Bonneville, which had gross revenues of $2.7 billion in 1984, can cover its $570 million or so in WPPSS interest obligations for some time. Sitzer also sees little possibility of a WPPSS bankruptcy.

Buffett maintains that his decision to buy WPPSS, like all his other investment decisions, followed a hardheaded analysis of the underlying values. He points out, for example, that the after-tax earnings on his bonds would normally require an investment at least twice as big. Before pushing ahead, Buffett says, he carefully surveyed the hazards. "We don't make judgments based on ratings," he adds. "If we wanted Moody's and Standard & Poor's to run our money, we'd give it to them." Buffett adds, rather proudly, that his Omaha headquarters has no computers and that his analyses are based on no electronic data. Says he: "We read—that's about it."

Buffett won't say whether he has bought more WPPSS bonds or has lightened his holdings since the end of last year. His commitment to invest $517.5 million in ABC won't necessarily force him to sell the WPPSS bonds to raise money. He can tap his company's cash flow and liquid assets or resort to his considerable borrowing power. Berkshire Hathaway also holds large blocks of communications stocks, including 4% of Time Inc., publisher of *Fortune*— some of which the Federal Communications Commission may force him to sell as a condition for investing in ABC.

Buffett says that occasions to buy bonds in the future are likely to be few. He is concerned that the federal budget deficit will lead to substantially higher inflation and surging interest rates—a disastrous situation for bondholders. "In runaway inflation," says Buffett, "what you've bought is wallpaper."

While Buffett has been making news lately, he doesn't make a lot of investments. "My problem is I don't get 50 great ideas a year;" he says. "I'm lucky if I get one or two." But when he does decide to plunge, he bets big. In the latest annual report, Buffett warns shareholders that betting heavily on a few ideas is bound to produce a bad year once in a while. That may be, but so far the shareholders have had plenty to whoop about.

# From "Now Hear This"

April 28, 1986

"Our gain in net worth during the year was $613.6 million, or 48.2 percent. It is fitting that the visit of Halley's comet coincided with this percentage gain; neither will be seen again in my lifetime."

—Warren E. Buffett, 55, chairman of Berkshire Hathaway, in the company's 1985 annual report.

*Editor's note: Actually, Buffett was wrong: The gain thirteen years later, in 1998, was a peg higher, 48.3 percent, with no accompanying Halley's comet. But in his 1998 letter Buffett dismissed the accomplishment, saying that most of the gain was simply the effect of Berkshire's issuing shares during the year to make acquisitions (principally NetJets and General Re) at a time when its stock was selling at a large premium over book value.*

*It was no accident, of course, that Buffett was issuing Berkshire stock in a year when its price related to a more important indicator, intrinsic value, was also high. He would regard it as sinful to hand out Berkshire shares when they are the opposite—"cheap," so to speak.*

# From "Should You Leave It All to the Children?"

September 29, 1986

### *Excerpts from an article by Richard I. Kirkland Jr.*

*This story put Warren Buffett on the cover of* Fortune *for the first time (though certainly not the last). Still, Buffett was only the principal actor in a long story that also included a large supporting cast, all of its members rich. So we have simply excerpted the Buffett paragraphs, including those opening the article.*

Buffett's strongly negative views about large inheritances—opinions known to me—prompted this story. But there was definitely no shortage of other rich people willing to talk, remembers writer Rik Kirkland (who later became For- tune's *managing editor). His piece proceeded to hit a nerve with readers as well. Said Fed Chairman Paul Volcker upon spotting a* Fortune *editor at a Washing- ton party: "Everyone is talking about your story." Even today, a quarter century after the article was published, Buffett gets questions about it—as if, he says, readers had cut it out and saved it. His daughter, Susie (the oldest of three Buf- fett children, the others sons Howard and Peter) probably fields questions still more often because of one anecdote included in the story. Susie says that people she meets still ask her incredulously, "He wouldn't give you money to fix up your kitchen?".*

Buffett thought then that "a few hundred thousand dollars" might be appro- priate for a child to inherit. Even now, he remains in the parsimonious camp. But as the years passed, inflation and his own reflections changed his opinions about what his children should get and led him to revise—upwardly—those early thoughts about "a few hundred thousand dollars."

For many years, he did not publicly disclose where his thinking had taken him. But at a 2010 dinner in New York, amid a small group of people loaded with money, Buffett made news by spelling out for the first time what his children had up to then received and would further receive at his death. He said that when his first wife, Susie, died in 2004, her will had left each of the three children $10 mil- lion, and that his will, which he happened to have just rewritten, provided that each would receive $15 million.

For Buffett's three children, therefore, that's a total of $75 million, as in million with an m. His fortune as he spoke was close to $50 billion, with a b. Obviously, he still believes that, no, you shouldn't leave it all to the children.

Neither does he expect to hand the management of Berkshire Hathaway down to his children, though that matter is nuanced. Believing that a member of his family could best preserve the company's culture, Buffett has said that he hopes his older son, Howard, will succeed him as Berkshire's chairman when the need arises. But the active management of the company is to be taken over by non- family members.

To all of this there is an implied codicil, relating to philanthropy. In 1999, well before Susie Buffett's death, she and Warren had encouraged their children to *move into philanthropy by giving each of them $10 million for the establishment of their own foundations. Later, additional gifts, some bestowed by Susie's will, raised each of the foundations to more than $100 million in size. Then came what son and author Peter Buffett (see page 316 for an article about him) has called "the Big Bang." This was Warren Buffett's stunning 2006 announcement (made by means of a* Fortune *article) that he would gradually give away most of his fortune to five foundations, the three run by his children among them. Since then, each of those three foundations has received shares worth close to $400 million at the dates of the gifts.*

*The stakes were upped still more on August 30, 2012, as Buffett—celebrating his 82nd birthday that day—announced that he would henceforth double the shares of stock he will give the foundations run by his children. The price of Berkshire stock over the years will determine the amount bestowed. But it is easy to imagine that the total gift emanating from the original Big Bang, and its 2012 variation, will reach $2 billion for each foundation and perhaps a good deal more. (The* Fortune *article that disclosed Buffett's huge gift begins on page 256 of this book.)* —CL

## As the article begins:

Warren Buffett, 56, the chairman and guiding genius of Berkshire Hathaway, the phenomenally successful holding company, is worth at least $1.5 billion. But don't bother being jealous of his three children. Buffett does not believe that it is wise to bequeath great wealth and plans to give most of his money to his charitable foundation. Having put his daughter and two sons through college, the Omaha investor contents himself with giving them several thousand dollars each at Christmas. Beyond that, says daughter Susan, 33, "If I write my dad a check for $20, he cashes it."

Buffett is not cutting his children out of the family fortune because they're wastrels or wantons or refuse to go into the family business—the traditional reasons rich parents withhold money. Says he: "My kids are going to carve out their place in this world, and they know I'm for them whatever they want to do." But he believes that setting up his heirs with "a lifetime supply of food stamps just because they came out of the right womb" can be "harmful" for them and is "an antisocial act." To him the perfect amount to leave children is "enough money so they would feel they could do anything, but not so much that they could do nothing." For a college graduate, Buffett reckons "a few hundred thousand dollars" sounds about right.

How much should you leave the kids? Agonizing over that question is a peculiarly American obsession. In much of the world, custom and law dictate that children, unless they have committed some particularly heinous crime, automatically receive most of the parents' wealth when they die. Only Britain and her colonies—common-law countries all—give property owners the right to leave their children whatever they want.

### As the article continues midway:

Some rich individuals argue that not giving money to the children can cause problems, too. Says one: "If you're the child and you see your father with all this dough and you get some but not much, I just can't help thinking resentment will enter in." Susan Buffett, who works in Washington as an administrative assistant to the editor of *U.S. News & World Report* and is married to a public interest lawyer, admits her father's position is tough to live with. "My dad is one of the most honest, principled, good guys I know," she says, "And I basically agree with him. But it's sort of strange when you know most parents want to buy things for their kids and all you need is a small sum of money—to fix up the kitchen, not to go to the beach for six months. He won't give it to us on principle. All my life my father has been teaching us. Well, I feel I've learned the lesson. At a certain point you can stop."

### And further along:

Warren Buffett argues that most proprietors should forget trying to keep the management of their beloved companies in the family; he assumes current non-family management will continue running Berkshire after he is gone. He grants that occasionally an heir may be the most suitable candidate to manage a company but believes the odds are against it. Says Buffett, "Would anyone say the best way to pick a championship Olympic team is to select the sons and daughters of those who won 20 years ago? Giving someone a favored position just because his old man accomplished something is a crazy way for a society to compete."

*The full text of "Should You Leave It All to the Children?" is available at fortune .com/buffettbook.*

# Dial B-U-F-F-E-T-T for Merger

December 22, 1986

### *From Newstrends Section*

In one of the most unusual want ads the *Wall Street Journal* has ever run, Warren E. Buffett, 56, the chairman of Berkshire Hathaway Inc., announced that he was looking to buy businesses worth $100 million or more before December 31, 1986. "We have the money," reads the $47,000, nearly full-page ad, "and we can act with extraordinary speed . . . If you have any possible interest, call promptly."

The reason to act fast is the tax law that takes effect January 1. While the jump in the federal capital gains tax rate for individuals from 20% to 28% is alarming enough, Buffett warns that business owners could pay the equivalent of a 52.5% capital gains tax if they wait until after December 31 to sell. He comes up with that figure by considering the new 34% capital gains tax that corporations must pay on the sale of a business and the 28% that shareholders owe on the remaining capital gain. Says Buffett: "Many companies have a reason to beat the clock."

Before you rush to your telephone, however, be warned that not just any potential acquisition will do. The company must have "at least $10 million of after-tax earnings and preferably much more" according to the ad, and must also boast good return on equity, little or no debt, and a management in place. It should also be in a simple business: "If there's lots of technology, we won't understand it."

*Editor's note: Buffett got no takers.*

# Early Fears about Index Futures

December 7, 1987

*A warning letter sent by Warren Buffett to Congressman John Dingell Jr.*

*In mid-October of 1987, a week of vicious selling in the stock market culminated on Black Monday, the nineteenth, when the Dow Industrials average dropped by 22.6 percent. As the causes of the crash came under intense investigation, attention focused on the role played by a derivative, S&P index futures, in which trading had been permitted for only a few years. In particular, institutional investors following a "portfolio insurance" strategy had repeatedly shorted S&P index futures, with their trading drawing in other institutional investors who did the same, thereby magnifying the market panic.*

*Suddenly, there was a remarkable timeliness to—and a strong reason for Fortune to—publish a letter that Buffett had written years earlier, in 1982, to Congressman John Dingell Jr. (D-Michigan), then chairman of the subcommittee on oversight and investigations. Congress was in that year debating whether to allow the Chicago Mercantile Exchange to begin trading futures contracts tied to the level of stock indexes. Dingell was opposed to that plan and so, he learned, was Buffett. The two men knew each other a little because many years before their fathers, both congressmen, had been friends, though Howard Buffett (R-Nebraska) was an archconservative and John Dingell the senior (D-Michigan) was the polar opposite. Against that background, the younger Dingell asked the younger Buffett to explain in a letter why he thought trading in stock index futures was a bad idea. Said Buffett, as he wound up his carefully reasoned letter: "We do not need more people gambling in nonessential instruments identified with the stock market in this country, nor brokers who encourage them to do so."*

*Dingell and Buffett were, of course, on the losing side of this argument. Trading in S&P futures began on the Merc in April 1982 and, notwithstanding crises like the one in 1987, mushroomed. The contract was then eclipsed twenty-five years later by its electronic offspring, S&P E-mini futures, which speculators could trade in for relatively small amounts and which quickly became the king of contracts. When the Flash Crash of May 2010 occurred, terrifying many investors, E-mini contracts accounted for a huge portion of the volume.*

*Below is the letter that Buffett sent to Congressman Dingell in 1982. —CL*

This letter is to comment upon the likely sources for trading activity that will develop any futures market involving stock indexes. My background for this commentary is some 30 years of practice in various aspects of the investment business, including several years as a securities salesman. The last 25 years have been spent as a financial analyst, and I currently have the sole responsibility for an equity portfolio that totals over $600 million.

It is impossible to predict precisely what will develop in investment or speculative markets, and you should be wary of any who claim precision. I think the following represents a reasonable expectancy:

1. A role can be performed by the stock index future contract in aiding the risk-reducing efforts of the true investor. An investor may quite logically conclude that he can identify undervalued securities, but also conclude that he has no ability whatsoever to predict the short-term movements of the stock market. This is the view I maintain in my own efforts in investment management. Such an investor may wish to "zero out" market fluctuations, and the continual shorting of a representative index offers him the chance to do just that. Presumably, an investor with $10 million of undervalued equities and a constant short position of $10 million in the index will achieve the net rewards or penalties attributable solely to his skill in selection of specific securities—and have no worries that these results will be swamped—or even influenced—by the fluctuations of the general market. Because there are costs involved—and because most investors believe that, over the long term, stock prices in general will advance—I think there are relatively few investment professionals who will operate in such a constantly hedged manner. But I also believe that it is a rational way to behave and that a few professionals, who wish always to be "market neutral" in their attitude and behavior, will do so.

2. As previously stated, I see a logical risk-reducing strategy that involves shorting the futures contract. I see no corresponding investment or hedging strategy whatsoever on the long side. By definition, therefore, a very maximum of 50% of the futures transactions can be entered into with the expectancy of risk reduction, and not less than 50% (the long side) must act in a risk-accentuating or gambling manner.

3. The actual balance would be enormously different from this maximum fifty-fifty division between risk reducers and risk accentuators. The propensity to gamble is always increased by a large prize vs. a small entry fee, no matter how poor the true odds may be. That's why Las Vegas casinos advertise big jackpots and why state lotteries headline big prizes. In securities, the unintelligent are seduced by the same approach in various ways, including: (a) "penny stocks," which are "manufactured" by promoters precisely because they snare the gullible—creating dreams of enormous payoffs but with an actual group result of disaster, and (b) low margin requirements through which

financial experience attributable to a large investment is achieved by committing a relatively small stake.

4. We have had many earlier experiences in our history in which the high total commitment/low down payment phenomenon has led to trouble. The most familiar, of course, is the stock market boom in the late Twenties, which was accompanied and accentuated by 10% margins. Saner heads subsequently decided that there was nothing pro-social about such thin-margined speculation, and that rather than aiding capital markets, in the long run it hurt them. Accordingly, margin regulations were introduced and made a permanent part of the investing scene. The ability to speculate in stock indexes with 10% down payments, of course, is simply a way around the margin requirements and will be immediately perceived as such by gamblers throughout the country.

5. Brokers, of course, favor new trading vehicles. Their enthusiasm tends to be in direct proportion to the amount of activity they expect. And the more the activity, the greater the cost to the public and the greater the amount of money that will be left behind by them to be spread among the brokerage industry. As each contract dies, the only business involved is that the loser pays the winner. Since the casino (the futures market and its supporting cast of brokers) gets paid a toll each time one of these transactions takes place, you can be sure that it will have a great interest in providing very large numbers of losers and winners. But it must be remembered that for the players it is the most clear sort of a "negative sum game." Losses and gains cancel out before expenses; after expenses the net loss is substantial. In fact, unless such losses are quite substantial, the casino will terminate operations since the players' net losses compose the casino's sole source of revenue. This "negative sum" aspect is in direct contrast to common stock investment generally, which has been a very substantial "positive sum game" over the years simply because the underlying companies, on balance, have earned substantial sums of money that eventually benefit their owners, the stockholders.

6. In my judgment, a very high percentage—probably at least 95% and more likely much higher—of the activity generated by these contracts will be strictly gambling in nature. You will have people wagering as to the short-term movements of the stock market and able to make fairly large wagers with fairly small sums. They will be encouraged to do so by brokers who will see rapid turnover of customers' capital—the best thing that can happen to a broker in terms of his immediate income. A

great deal of money will be left behind by these 95% as the casino takes its bite from each transaction.

7. In the long run, gambling-dominated activities that are identified with traditional capital markets, and that leave a very high percentage of those exposed to the activity burned, are not going to be good for capital markets. Even though people participating in such gambling activity are not investors and what they are buying really are not stocks, they still will feel that they have had a bad experience with the stock market. And after having been exposed to the worst face of capital markets, they understandably may, in the future, take a dim view of capital markets generally. Certainly that has been the experience after previous waves of speculation. You might ask if the brokerage industry is not wise enough to look after its own long-term interests. History shows brokers to be myopic (witness the late Sixties); they often have been happiest when behavior was at its silliest. And many brokers are far more concerned with how much they gross this month than whether their clients—or, for that matter, the securities industry—prosper in the long run.

We do not need more people gambling in nonessential instruments identified with the stock market in this country, nor brokers who encourage them to do so. What we need are investors and advisers who look at the long-term prospects for an enterprise and invest accordingly. We need the intelligent commitment of investment capital, not leveraged market wagers. The propensity to operate in the intelligent, pro-social sector of capital markets is deterred, not enhanced, by an active and exciting casino operating in somewhat the same arena, utilizing somewhat similar language and serviced by the same work force.

In addition, low-margined activity in stock equivalents is inconsistent with expressed public policy as embodied in margin requirements. Although index futures have slight benefits to the investment professional wishing to "hedge out" the market, the net effect of high-volume futures markets in stock indexes is likely to be overwhelmingly detrimental to the security-buying public and, therefore, in the long run to capital markets generally.

# The Inside Story of Warren Buffett

April 11, 1988

## BY CAROL LOOMIS

*This story has a little more history than most. In the first twenty years after I became a friend of Warren Buffett's and soon after a Berkshire Hathaway stockholder and still later the pro bono editor of his annual letter to stockholders, I wrote no more than a few paragraphs about him in* Fortune. *True, as his reputation grew exponentially, I suggested some Buffett stories—the Grinnell and Whoops articles, for example. But other members of the magazine's staff wrote them, and that suited me fine.*

*In early 1988, however,* Fortune's *managing editor, Marshall Loeb, called me into his office and gave me a fish-or-cut-bait choice. He said it was time we did a full profile about Buffett. "You can write it," he said to me, knowing that I knew Warren well, "or I'll assign someone else to do it."*

*My decision, made after a hard day's thought, was to write the story myself. I knew that was the right choice for the readers of* Fortune, *who would get a true "inside story" from me because I understood Buffett's world so well. But naturally they needed to know also that I was a friend of Buffett's, a shareholder of Berkshire, and editor of his annual letter. All of those facts were reported in the article and have since become regulars in other pieces I have written about Buffett.*

*Marshall's timing for the profile was excellent. My article told an important story that had up until then stayed below the radar: how Buffett the extraordinary investor had also come to be Buffett the extraordinary businessman and manager. At his side, playing a critical advisory role, was his brilliant friend Charlie Munger. To an extent recognized by outsiders hardly at all, the two had put Berkshire on the path to becoming a very big and successful business.* —CL

Warren Buffett, chairman of Berkshire Hathaway, calls the conglomerate his "canvas," and shortly, when its annual report comes out, the world will learn precisely what kind of picture this legendary investor painted in the tumultuous year of 1987. A preview: As a work of art, the year was not a minor Buffett. Berkshire—whose shareholders, I wish to say quickly and happily, have long included me—chalked up a $464 million gain in net worth, an advance of no less than 19.5%. That is somewhat below the 23.1% annual average that Buffett has recorded since taking over the company 23 years ago. But in a year in which many professional investors had their heads handed to them, this latest example of Buffett brushwork has to rank as one more masterpiece.

The annual report, which readers always comb for Buffett's once-a-year revelations about what he has been doing in the securities markets, will carry two special pieces of news. First, Buffett, who bought $700 million of Salomon Inc. redeemable convertible preferred stock for Berkshire just before the October crash, makes it clear in his chairman's letter that he is solidly behind the investment bank's chairman, John Gutfreund. That should put an end to the persistent rumors about divisions between the two men. Second, Buffett reveals that Berkshire began buying short-term Texaco bonds last year after the company went into bankruptcy, at a point when many other investors were bailing out of the bonds. At year-end Berkshire had an unrealized profit in the Texaco securities. But both that holding and the Salomon preferred (which Buffett figures to have been worth about $685 million at year-end) are carried at cost on Berkshire's books and were nonevents as far as the company's 1987 record is concerned.

Behind that record—behind Buffett, in fact—is a double-barreled story, which in all the words that have been written about him has usually been told as single-bore only. Most of the business world knows about Warren Buffett the investor. The Wizard of Omaha; the stock-picking genius who turned $9,800, most of it saved from paper routes, into a personal net worth that is today more than $1.6 billion; the man whose superlative, long-running investment performance has become ever more difficult for the efficient-market camp to explain away as luck.

That Buffett was certainly abroad in the land in 1987. Having said for more than two years that he could not find reasonably priced stocks to buy for Berkshire, Buffett came into October 19 wearing heavy armor, owning almost no common equities besides those of three companies that he thinks of as "permanent" parts of Berkshire's portfolio. All three, though they fell substantially in the crash, were standouts for the entire year: GEICO, the auto insurance company, was up by 12%; Washington Post by 20%; Capital Cities/ABC by 29%.

Not bad for Buffett the investor. But the other craftsman at work in Berkshire is Buffett the businessman, a buyer and manager of companies and a fellow whose skill is not understood widely at all. In effect, this guy grinds out the yardage, while Buffett the investor throws bombs. In 1987 the Berkshire offense was nicely balanced: The investor produced $249 million (after allowances for taxes) in realized and unrealized gains; the businessman generated $215 million in after-tax operating earnings from Berkshire's stable of businesses, for that total of $464 million. The operating earnings were more than the net income of Dow Jones, or Pillsbury, or Corning Glass Works.

The vehicle through which all this got done, Berkshire, had a stock price of around $12 in 1965 when Buffett took control. It rose to a high of $4,200 in 1987 and was recently about $3,100. Buffett, a witty, straightforward man of 57, owns 42% of the company; his wife, Susan, 55, another 3%. Berkshire had more than $2 billion in revenues in 1987, will probably rank around 30th in *Fortune*'s annual list of the largest diversified services companies, and is powerfully strange in its makeup.

At Berkshire's heart is a large property-and-casualty insurance operation composed of several unfamous companies (such as National Indemnity), which generates "float" that Buffett invests. Beyond insurance, Berkshire owns a set of sizable businesses that Buffett bought, one by one, and that he calls his Sainted Seven. They are the Buffalo *News*; Fechheimer Brothers, a Cincinnati manufacturer and distributor of uniforms; the Nebraska Furniture Mart, an Omaha retailer that sells more home furnishings than any other store in the country; See's Candies, the dominant producer and retailer of candy in California; and three operations that Buffett took into the fold when Berkshire bought Scott & Fetzer of Cleveland in 1986: *World Book*, Kirby vacuum cleaners, and a diversified manufacturing operation that makes industrial products such as compressors and burners.

A motley crew, yes—but in his 1987 annual report, Buffett the businessman comes out of the closet to point out just how good these enterprises and their managers are. Had the Sainted Seven operated as a single business in 1987, he says, they would have employed $175 million in equity capital, paid only a net $2 million in interest, and earned, after taxes, $100 million. That's a return on equity of 57%, and it is exceptional. As Buffett says, "You'll seldom see such a percentage anywhere, let alone at large, diversified companies with nominal leverage."

A business school professor trying gamely a few years ago to reconcile the efficient-market hypothesis with Buffett's success at investing called him "a five-sigma event," a statistical aberration so rare it practically never happens. In the buying and managing of whole companies, he may well be a phenomenon equally uncommon. He brings to buying the same acuity and discipline he brings to investing. As a manager he disregards form and convention and sticks to business principles that he calls "simple, old, and few."

The Berkshire companies, for example, never lose sight of what they're trying to do. Says Buffett: "If we get on the main line, New York to Chicago, we don't get off at Altoona and take side trips. We also have a reverence for logic around here. But what we do is not beyond anybody else's competence. I feel the same way about managing that I do about investing: It's just not necessary to do extraordinary things to get extraordinary results."

My credentials for writing about both Buffetts, the investor and the businessman, are unusual. Besides having been a staff member of this magazine for more than 30 years, I have been a friend of Buffett's for more than 20. I do some editing of his annual report, which is why I know what it's going to say. I am an admirer of Buffett's. In this article, because it has been written by a friend, you can expect two things: an inside look at how Warren Buffett operates and something less than total objectivity.

But here is an incontestable fact: Buffett brings an immense mental brilliance to everything he does. Michael Goldberg, 41, who runs Berkshire's insurance operations and occupies the office next to Buffett's in Omaha, thinks that he saw people as smart at the Bronx High School of Science, "but they all went into math and physics." Buffett's intellectual power is totally focused on business, which he loves and knows incredible amounts about. Says Goldberg: "He is constantly examining all that he hears: 'Is it consistent and plausible? Is it wrong?' He has a model in his head of the whole world. The computer there compares every new fact with all that he's ever experienced and knows about— and says, 'What does this mean for us?'" For Berkshire, that is. Buffett owns a few stocks personally but spends little time thinking about them. Says he: "My ego is wrapped up with Berkshire. No question about that."

Meeting him, most people would see little evidence of ego at all. Buffett is down-to-earth, ordinary looking in a pleasant, solid Midwestern way—as a private eye, for example, he could blend into any crowd—and in matters of dress not snappy. He likes McDonald's and cherry Cokes and dislikes large parties and small talk. But in the right setting he can be highly gregarious and even a ham: This winter, at a Cap Cities management meeting, he donned a Salvation Army uniform, tooted away on a horn, and serenaded the company's chairman, Thomas Murphy, by singing, "What a friend I have in Murphy," featuring lyrics he had written.

Sometimes, and particularly on intellectual subjects, Buffett talks with great intensity and speed, trying to keep up with the gyrator in his mind. When he was young, he was terrified of public speaking. So he forced himself to take a Dale Carnegie course, filled, he says, "with other people equally pitiful." Today he gives speeches with ease, drawing them entirely from an outline in his head—no written speech, no notes—and lacing them with an inexhaustible supply of quips, examples, and analogies (for which a professional writer would kill).

In his work Buffett has not let the complexities of his thinking prevent him from forming a very simple view of life. The key point about the two Buffetts, the investor and the businessman, is that they look at the ownership of businesses in exactly same way. The investor sees the chance to buy *portions* of a business in the stock market at a price below intrinsic value—that is, below what a rational buyer would pay to own the entire establishment. The manager sees the chance to buy the *whole* business at no more than that intrinsic value.

The kind of merchandise that Buffett wants is simply described also: "good businesses." To him that essentially means operations with strong franchises, above-average returns on equity, a relatively small need for capital investment, and the capacity therefore to throw off cash. That list may sound like motherhood and apple pie. But finding and buying such businesses isn't easy; Buffett likens the hunt to bagging "rare and fast-moving elephants." He has avoided straying from his strict criteria. The Sainted Seven all possess the characteristics of a good business. So do the companies in which Buffett owns stock, such as GEICO, Washington Post, and Cap Cities.

In his annual reports Buffett regularly extols the managers of all these companies, most of whom rival him—if anyone can—in their conviction that working is fun. He devoutly wishes to keep them fanatics. "Wonderful businesses run by wonderful people" is his description of the scene he wants to look down on as a chief executive.

But he believes that over the years his largest mistakes in investing have been the failure to buy certain "good business" stocks just because he couldn't stomach the quality of management. "I'd have been better off trusting the businesses," he says. So in the stocks he has sometimes held, though not in the businesses he owns directly, he has on occasion gritted his teeth and tolerated a fair amount of management inanity. A few years ago, when he owned many more stocks than now, he complained to a friend about the absurdities of an annual report he had just read, describing the content as misleading and self-serving of management and "enough to make you throw up." The friend said, "And yet you're in the stock." Yes, was his answer: "I want to be in businesses so good that even a dummy can make money."

Naturally, good businesses do not come cheap, particularly not today when the whole world has caught on to their attributes. But Buffett has been consistently shrewd as a buyer—he simply will not overpay—and patient in waiting for opportunities. He regularly puts an "ad" in his annual report explaining what kind of businesses he'd like to buy. "For the right business—and the right people—we can provide a good home," he says. Some folks of the right sort, by the name of Heldman, read that ad and brought him their uniform business, Fechheimer, in 1986. The business had only about $6 million in profits, which is an operation smaller than Buffett thinks ideal. But the Heldmans seemed so completely the kind of managers he looks for—"likable, talented, honest, and goal-driven" is his description—that he made the acquisition and is delighted he did.

In buying at least one business, the Buffalo *News*, Buffett was particularly farseeing. Both the Washington Post Co. and Chicago's Tribune Co. turned it down when it came up for sale in 1977, perhaps discouraged because it was an evening paper, a dwindling breed. The *News* was also a six-day publisher, with no Sunday edition and revenue stream, competing against a seven-day publisher, the *Courier-Express*. But the *News* was the stronger of the two during the week, and Buffett concluded the paper had the makings to do well if it could establish a Sunday edition.

Buying the paper for $32.5 million, he immediately started to publish on Sunday. The *News*'s special introductory offers to subscribers and advertisers prompted the *Courier-Express* to bring an antitrust suit, which he defeated. Both papers went for years losing money—and then, in 1982, the *Courier-Express* gave up and closed down. Last year the *News*, as a flourishing monopoly paper, made $39 million in pretax operating profits and certainly did not do it by stinting on editorial copy. The paper delivers one page of news for every page of advertising, a proportion not matched by any other prosperous paper of its size or larger. Because Buffett loves journalism—he says that if he had not been an investor, he might well have picked journalism as a career—the *News* is probably his favorite property.

The oddity of Buffett's intense focus on good businesses is that he came late to that philosophy, after a couple of decades of mucking around and making prodigious amounts of money anyway. As a kid in Omaha, he was precocious and fascinated by anything having to do with numbers and money. His father, Howard Buffett, a stockbroker whom the son adored, affectionately called him

"Fireball." He virtually memorized a library book, *One Thousand Ways to Make $1000*, fantasizing in particular about penny weighing machines. He pictured himself starting with a single machine, pyramiding his take into thousands more, and turning himself into the world's youngest millionaire. In Presbyterian church he calculated the life spans of the composers of hymns, investigating whether their religious calling had rewarded them with extra years of life (his conclusion: no). At age 11 he and a friend moved into more secular pursuits, putting out a horse-racing handicapping sheet under the name *Stable-Boy Selections*.

Through it all he thought about stocks. He got his first books on the market when he was 8, bought his first stock (Cities Service preferred) at 11, and went on to experiment with all manner of trading methodologies. He was a teenage stock "chartist" for a while, and later a market timer. His base from 1943 on was Washington, where his family moved upon Howard Buffett's election to Congress. Deeply homesick for Omaha, young Warren once ran away from home and also got disastrous grades for a while in junior high, even in the math at which he was naturally gifted. Only when his father threatened to make Warren give up his lucrative and much-loved paper routes did his grades improve. Graduating from high school at 16, Buffett went through two years at the University of Pennsylvania and then transferred to the University of Nebraska. There, in early 1950, while a senior, he read Benjamin Graham's newly published book, *The Intelligent Investor*. The book encouraged the reader to pay attention to the intrinsic value of companies and to invest with a "margin of safety," and to Buffett it all made enormous sense. To this day there is a Graham flavor to Buffett's only articulated rules of investment: "The first rule is not to lose. The second rule is not to forget the first rule."

In the summer of 1950, having applied to Harvard business school, Buffett took the train to Chicago and was interviewed by a local alum. What this representative of higher learning surveyed, Buffett says, was "a scrawny 19-year-old who looked 16 and had the social poise of a 12-year-old." After ten minutes the interview was over, and so were Buffett's prospects of going to Harvard. The rejection stung. But Buffett now considers it the luckiest thing ever to have happened to him, because upon returning to Omaha he chanced to learn that Ben Graham was teaching at Columbia's business school, and immediately—and this time successfully—applied. Another student in Graham's class was William Ruane, who today runs the top-performing Sequoia Fund and is one of Buffett's closest friends. Ruane says that a kind of intellectual electricity coursed between Graham and Buffett from the start and that the rest of the class was mainly an audience.

At the end of the school year Buffett offered to work for Graham's investment company, Graham-Newman, for nothing—"but Ben," says Buffett, "made his customary calculation of value to price and said no." Buffett did not succeed in getting a job offer from Graham until 1954, when he started at Graham-Newman as jack-of-all-trades and student of his mentor's mechanistic, value-based investment techniques. Basically, Graham looked for "bargains," which he rigidly defined as stocks that could be bought at no more than two-thirds of their net working capital. Most companies, he figured, could be liquidated for at least their net working capital; so in buying for still less, he saw himself building in the necessary margin of safety. Today few stocks would meet Graham's standards; in the early 1950s, many did.

Buffett returned to Omaha in 1956 at age 25, imbued with Graham's theories and ready to embark upon the course that was to make him rich and famous. Assembling $105,000 in limited partnership funds from a few family members and friends, he started Buffett Partnership Ltd. The economics of the partnership were simple: The limited partners earned 6% on their funds and got 75% of all profits made in addition; Buffett, as general partner, got the remaining 25%. The partnership earned impressive profits from the start, and as word spread about this young man's abilities, new partners climbed aboard, bearing money.

When Buffett decided in 1969 to disband the partnership, having grown disenchanted with a market that had turned wildly speculative, he had $100 million under management, of which $25 million was his own—most of it the fruits of his share of the profits. Over the 13 years of the partnership, he had compounded its funds at an average annual rate of 29.5%. That record is the forerunner of his performance with Berkshire: 23.1%. The drama of his Berkshire record is that he has scored colossal gains on the company's capital while retaining 100% of its earnings—Berkshire pays no dividends. This means that he has had to find investment outlets for a vigorously expanding amount of money. The company's equity at year-end was $2.8 billion, an impressive figure to be compounding at superlative rates.

Despite the outstanding record of the partnership, Buffett feels today that he managed its money with only part of his senses at work. In his 1987 annual report Buffett laments 20 misspent years, a period including all of the partnership days, during which he searched for "bargains"—and, alas, "had the misfortune to find some." His punishment, he says, was "an education in the economics of short-line farm implement manufacturers, third-place department stores, and New England textile manufacturers." The farm implement company was Dempster Mill Manufacturing of Nebraska; the department store was Hochschild Kohn of Baltimore; and the textile manufacturer was Berkshire Hathaway itself.

The Buffett partnership got in and out of Dempster and Hochschild Kohn quickly during the 1960s. Berkshire Hathaway, the textile business, of which the partnership bought control for around $11 million, was a more lasting problem. Buffett nursed the business for 20 years while deploring the benightedness that had taken him into such industrial bogs as men's suit linings, in which he was just another commodity operator with no edge of any kind. Periodically Buffett would explain in his annual report why he stayed in an operation with such poor economics. The business, he said, was a major employer in New Bedford, Massachusetts; the operation's managers had been straightforward with him and as able as the managers of his successful businesses; the unions had been reasonable. But finally, in 1985, Buffett closed the operation, unwilling to make the capital investments that would have been necessary if he was even to subsist in this deeply discouraging business.

A few years earlier, for his annual report, Buffett wrote a line that has become famous: "With few exceptions, when a manager with a reputation for brilliance tackles a business with a reputation for poor fundamental economics, it is the reputation of the business that remains intact." As a requiem for Buffett's textile experience, the sentiment will do nicely. In his own mind, also, this is not just a case of a relatively small investment gone bad. Calculating what Berkshire might have earned if he had not made the bet on textiles, he thinks of the opportunity cost as being around $500 million.

Occasionally during his misspent years, Buffett would be drawn toward a good business and, as if startled into unusual action, would plunge abnormal amounts into the opportunity. In 1951, then investing only his own money and mainly gravitating toward such "bargains" as Timely Clothes and Des Moines Railway, Buffett became fascinated by GEICO, whose low distribution costs and ability to sign up a better set of policyholders than other insurers gave it a crucial advantage. Though the company did not begin to meet Ben Graham's mathematical tests, Buffett put $10,000—around two-thirds of his net worth—into GEICO stock.

He sold a year later at a 50% profit and did not again own the company until 1976. By then GEICO was magnitudes larger but near bankruptcy because it had miscalculated its claim costs and was underpricing. Buffett thought, however, that the company's competitive advantage was intact and that a newly named chief executive, John J. Byrne, could probably restore the company's health. Over five years Buffett invested $45 million in GEICO. Byrne did the job, becoming a close friend of Buffett's and often seeking his advice. GEICO is today an industry star, and Berkshire's stake is worth $800 million.

On another occasion, in 1964, while running the partnership, Buffett barreled into American Express stock at the time of the so-called salad oil scandal. An Amexco subsidiary that issued warehouse receipts was found to have certified the existence of mountainous quantities of oil that did not exist. On a worst-case basis American Express might have emerged from that crisis with no net worth. The company's stock plunged. Ben Graham would have scorned the stock because, by his definitions, it offered no margin of safety. But Buffett assessed the franchises embodied in the company's charge card and traveler's checks businesses and concluded these were assets that could carry Amexco through almost any storm. Buffett had an unwritten rule at the time that he would not put more than 25% of the partnership's money into one security. He broke the rule for American Express, committing 40%, which was $13 million. Some two years later he sold out at a $20 million profit.

Buffett considers himself to have been nudged, prodded, and shoved toward a steady, rather than intermittent, appreciation of good businesses by Charles T.

Munger, 64, vice chairman of Berkshire and the "Charlie" of Buffett's annual reports. In the U.S. corporate system, vice chairmen have a way of often not being important. That is decidedly not the case at Berkshire Hathaway.

Munger's mental ability is probably up to Buffett's, and the two can talk as equals. They differ, however, in political views—Munger is a traditional Republican, Buffett a fiscally conservative Democrat—and in demeanor. Though sometimes cutting in his annual report, Buffett employs great tact when doling out criticism in person. Munger can be incisively frank. Last year, chairing the annual meeting of Wesco, a California savings and loan 80% owned by Berkshire, Munger delivered a self-appraisal: "In my whole life nobody has ever accused me of being humble. Although humility is a trait I much admire, I don't think I quite got my full share."

Like Buffett, Munger is a native of Omaha, but as boys the two did not know each other. After getting the equivalent of a college degree in the Army Air Force and graduating from Harvard law school, Munger went to Los Angeles, where he started the law firm now known as Munger Tolles & Olson. On a visit back to Omaha in 1959, Munger attended a dinner party that also included Buffett. Munger had heard tales of this 29-year-old who was remaking the Omaha investment scene and was prepared to be unimpressed. Instead, he was bowled over by Buffett's intellect. "I would have to say," says Munger, "that I recognized almost instantly what a remarkable person Warren is."

Buffett's reaction was that of a proselytizer. Convinced that the law was a slow boat to wealth, he began arguing that Munger should give up his practice and start his own investment partnership. Finally, in 1962, Munger made the move, though he hedged his bets by also keeping a hand in the law. His partnership was much smaller than Buffett's, more highly concentrated, and much more volatile. Nonetheless, in the partnership's 13-year history, extending through 1975, Munger achieved an annual average gain, compounded, of 19.8%. His wealth expanded as Buffett expected: Among other holdings, he owns nearly 2% of Berkshire, recently worth about $70 million.

When he met Buffett, Munger had already formed strong opinions about the chasms between good businesses and bad. He served as a director of an International Harvester dealership in Bakersfield and saw how difficult it was to fix up an intrinsically mediocre business; as an Angeleno, he observed the splendid prosperity of the Los Angeles *Times*; in his head he did not carry a creed about "bargains" that had to be unlearned. So in conversations with Buffett over the years he preached the virtues of good businesses, and in time Buffett totally accepted the logic of the case. By 1972, Blue Chip Stamps, a Berkshire affiliate that has since been merged into the parent, was paying three times book value to buy See's Candies, and the good-business era was launched. "I have been shaped tremendously by Charlie," says Buffett. "Boy, if I had listened only to Ben, would I ever be a lot poorer."

Last year at a Los Angeles party, Munger's dinner partner turned to him and coolly asked, "Tell me, what one quality most accounts for your enormous success?" Recalling this delicious moment later, Munger said, "Can you imagine such a wonderful question? And so I looked at this marvelous creature—whom I certainly hope to sit by at every dinner party—and said, 'I'm rational. That's the answer. I'm rational.'" The anecdote has a particular relevance because rationality is also the quality that Buffett thinks distinguishes the style with which he runs Berkshire—and the quality he often finds lacking at other corporations.

Essentially, Buffett, as chief executive officer, does the jobs for which he judges himself to have special competence: capital allocation, pricing in certain instances, and analysis of the numbers coming out of the operating divisions. "Warren would die if he didn't get the monthly figures," says Munger. As long as the numbers are looking as they should, though, Buffett does not poke into operations, but rather leaves his managers free to run their businesses as their intelligence tells them to. When he talks about the kind of companies he wishes to buy, Buffett always stipulates that they must come in the door with their own good management because, he says, "We can't supply management, and won't." He is solicitous of the talent working for him. Most of the people heading his operations are rich and could retire. In what he writes and says, Buffett never lets them forget that he regards their continued hard work as one of the great rewards of his life.

Buffett sets the pay of the top man in an operating company but plays no role in compensation beyond that. All the top people are paid through incentive plans that Buffett carefully tailors to achieve whatever objectives fit—higher profit margins in a business, for example, or reductions in the capital it employs, or improved underwriting results for the insurance operation and more "float" for Buffett to invest. The incentives do not have ceilings. And so it is that Mike Goldberg, of the insurance business, earned $2.6 million in 1986 and $3.1 million last year. On the other hand, in 1983 and 1984, when the insurance business was rotten, he earned his base salary, which is roughly $100,000. Looking ahead, and running an insurance business that is souring rapidly, Goldberg thinks he could be back at base pay again by 1990. Buffett earns base pay by all definitions: $100,000 per year.

At the price he offers undoubtedly the best-value consulting business around. His operating managers can call him whenever they wish with whatever concerns they have, and none pass up the opportunity to draw on his encyclopedic knowledge of the way businesses work. Stanford Lipsey, publisher of the Buffalo *News*, tends to talk to Buffett once or twice a week, usually at night. Ralph Schey, chairman of Scott Fetzer, says he saves up his questions, checking in with Buffett every week or two. With the family Buffett usually refers to as "the amazing Blumkins," who run the Nebraska Furniture Mart, the drill is dinner, held every few weeks at an Omaha restaurant. The Blumkins attending usually include Louie, 68, and his sons: Ron, 39; Irv, 35; and Steve, 33.

The matriarch of the family and chairman of the Furniture Mart is Rose Blumkin, who emigrated from Russia as a young woman, started a tiny furniture store that offered rock-bottom prices—her motto is "Sell cheap and tell the truth"—and built it into a business that last year did $140 million in sales. At age 94, she still works seven days a week in the carpet department. Buffett says in his new annual report that she is clearly gathering speed and "may well reach her full potential in another five or ten years. Therefore, I've persuaded the Board to scrap our mandatory-retirement-at-100 policy." And it's about time, he adds: "With every passing year, this policy has seemed sillier to me."

He jests, true, but Buffett simply does not regard age as having any bearing on how able a manager is. Perhaps because he has tended to buy good managements and stick with them, he has worked over the years with an unusually large number of older executives and treasured their abilities. "My God," he says, "good managers are so scarce I can't afford the luxury of letting them go just because they've added a year to their age." Louis Vincenti, chairman of Wesco until shortly before he died at age 79, used to periodically question whether he should not be training a successor. Buffett would turn him off with a big smile: "Say, Louie, how's your mother feeling these days?"

The Berkshire companies do not in any way practice togetherness. There are no company-wide management meetings and most of the operating heads do not know one another, or at most have exchanged a few words. Buffett has never visited Fechheimer in Cincinnati. Charles "Chuck" Huggins, president of See's for the 16 years Berkshire has owned it, has never been to Omaha.

Naturally, Buffett does not impose any systems of management on the heads of the operating companies, who are free to be as loose or structured as they wish. Schey, 63, the chief executive of Scott Fetzer (1987 sales: $740 million), is a graduate of Harvard business school and uses the full panoply of management tools: detailed budgets, strategic plans, annual conclaves of his executives. A few hundred miles away at Fechheimer (1987 sales: $75 million), Robert Heldman, 69, and brother George, 67, sit down every morning in a cluttered conference room and go through all the mail that comes into headquarters. "Somebody slits it open for us, though," says Bob Heldman, not wanting to be thought an extremist.

As the latest businesses to be acquired by Berkshire, Scott Fetzer and Fechheimer have been getting accustomed to dealing with this unusual boss in Omaha. A few years ago, before selling to Berkshire, Schey had attempted to lead a management buyout that would have taken Scott Fetzer, a listed company, private. But Ivan Boesky meddled in the deal, the company's fate grew uncertain, and in time Buffett wrote Schey an exploratory letter. Buffett and Munger met with Schey on a Tuesday in Chicago, made an offer on the spot, and waived the "due diligence" rigmarole that acquirers usually demand. One week later Scott Fetzer's board approved the sale.

Schey regards that episode as illustrative of the lack of bureaucracy he encounters in working with Buffett. "If I couldn't own Scott Fetzer myself, this is the next best thing"—better, he feels, than being a public company. In that life he had institutional investors on his neck and a board that tended to be ultra-cautious about authorizing major moves. Schey's prize example is his current intention to decentralize the World Book organization, which has been hunkered down at Chicago's Merchandise Mart forever. Schey's old board, he says, would probably have resisted the risk of restructuring; Buffett waved him ahead. Schey says, with a grin, that Buffett has also solved the recurring problems that Scott Fetzer had finding a use for all the cash its very good businesses throw off. "Now," says Schey, "I just ship the money to Warren."

The Heldmans at Fechheimer sold 80% of their company in 1981 to a venture capital group and, on the advice of an investment counselor, put part of the proceeds into Berkshire Hathaway stock. When the venture group decided in 1985 to get out, Bob Heldman recalled Buffett's annual report pitch for acquisitions and negotiated his way into the Berkshire fold. Though their relationship with the venture capitalists was pleasant, the Heldmans thoroughly disliked six New York board meetings they had to attend every year and also the lavish expense of those meetings. Buffett, says Bob Heldman, is "terrific." Is there anything that you wish he would do differently? "Well," says Heldman, "he never second-guesses us. Maybe he should do more of that." Buffett roars upon learning of this complaint: "Believe me, if they needed second-guessing—which they definitely don't—they'd get it."

Buffett can actually be very tough. He recalls landing on one of the operating divisions a few years ago when it put in new "labor saving" data-processing equipment and nonetheless let its head count in the accounting department go from 16 1/2 to 22 1/2. For all of his laid-back management style, Buffett knows about numbers like that and deplores them. There is a right-size staff for any operation, he thinks, whether business is good or bad, and he is totally impatient with unnecessary costs and managers who allow them to materialize. He says: "Whenever I read about some company undertaking a cost-cutting program, I know it's not a company that really knows what costs are all about. Spurts don't work in this area. The really good manager does not wake up in the morning and say, 'This is the day I'm going to cut costs,' any more than he wakes up and decides to practice breathing."

When they criticize him, which they do only mildly, Buffett's operating managers tend to think him too rational and demanding about numbers. No one can quite imagine him paying up for a small "seed" business with a possible future but no present. Buffett and Munger are not in the least suffused with animal spirits, and they do not even consider making discretionary capital expenditures—say for flashy offices—that aren't going to do them any economic good. Neither are they inventors. Says Buffett: "We don't have the skill to be. Above all, I guess you'd say we have a strong sense of our own limitations."

They are not timid, though, about prices. Buffett works with the heads of both See's and the Buffalo *News* in setting prices once a year, and he has tended to be aggressive. A chief executive, he says, can bring a perspective to pricing that a divisional manager cannot: "The manager has just one business. His equation tells him that if he prices a little too low, it's not that serious. But if he prices too high, he sees himself screwing up the only thing in his life. And no one knows what raising prices will do. For the manager, it's all Russian roulette. For the chief executive, with more than one thing in his life, it really isn't. So I would argue that someone with wide experience and distance from the scene should set prices in certain cases."

Buffett extends his own experience to one other kind of pricing: the setting of premium rates for large-risk insurance policies, such as product liability coverage. That game is one of seven- and eight-figure premiums, probabilities, and years of "float." It is a game made to order for Buffett, who tends to do a few calculations in his head and come up with a bid. He does not own a calculator—"or a computer or abacus," he says—and would never see himself as needing any kind of mathematical crutch. Though the point is hardly provable, he must be the only billionaire who still does his own income tax.

At his office in Omaha, in fact, he does what he pleases, leading an unhurried, unhassled, largely unscheduled life. Counting the boss, headquarters includes only 11 people, and that's a shade too many, Buffett thinks. The place is kept efficient by his assistant, Gladys Kaiser, 59, who has worked for him 20 years and for whom he wishes perpetual life. "If Gladys can't have it," Buffett says, "I'm not sure I want it either."

He spends hours at a stretch in his office, reading, talking on the phone, and, in the December to March period, agonizing over his annual report, whose fame is one of the profound satisfactions of his life. He is not in the least moody. "When I talk to him," says Chuck Huggins of See's, "he's always up, always positive." But in general he is something of a loner in his office, apt there to be less communicative and gracious than when talking on the phone to friends or the operating managers. Munger thinks it would not work for the managers to be physically in the same place as Buffett. "He's so damn smart and quick that people who are around him all the time feel a constant mental pressure from trying to keep up. You'd need a strong ego to survive in headquarters." Goldberg, whose ego has been put to the test, says it's not easy. "I've had a chance to see someone in action who can't be believed. The negative is: How do you ever think much of your own abilities after being around Warren Buffett?"

When Buffett is buying stocks, he often interrupts other phone conversations to talk on three direct lines that connect him with brokers. But he will say in the new annual report that he has not found much to do in stocks lately. "During the break in October," he writes, "a few stocks fell to prices that interested us, but we were unable to make meaningful purchases before they rebounded." At year-end Berkshire held no stock positions worth more than $50 million, other than its "permanent" holdings and a short-term $78 million arbitrage position in Allegis, which is radically restructuring.

The friends that Buffett talks to on the phone and often sees include a few other chief executives, among them the Washington Post's Katharine Graham and Cap Cities' Murphy. Graham has leaned on him for advice for years. As she says, "I'm working on my degree from the Buffett school of business." Buffett thinks Murphy the finest executive in the country, but Murphy tunes in for advice also. "I talk to him about all the important aspects of my business," says Murphy. "He's never negative and always supportive. He's got such a massive mind and such a remarkable ability to absorb information. You know, we're supposed to be pretty good managers around here, but his newspaper outdoes ours."

Buffett himself thinks that his investing abilities have been helped by his business experiences, and vice versa. "Investing," he says, "gives you this wide exposure that you just can't get directly. As an investor, you learn where the surprises are—in retailing, for example, where business can just evaporate. And if you're a really good investor you go back and pick up 50 years of vicarious experience. You also learn capital allocation. Instead of putting water in just one bucket, you learn what other buckets have to offer."

"On the other hand," he goes on, "could you really explain to a fish what it's like to walk on land? One day on land is worth a thousand years of talking about it, and one day running a business has exactly the same kind of value. Running a business really makes you feel down to your toes what it's like." His summary judgment: It's been awfully good to have a foot in both camps.

# BUFFETT AND SALOMON

NO ONE MADE A MOVIE *out of Buffett's experience at Salomon Brothers. They could have. They could even have called it* Too Big to Fail, *though its ending would have been far different from the one in that 2011 movie.*

*Buffett himself, commenting in Berkshire's 1997 annual report about Salomon's sale to Travelers (which was soon to be reconstituted as Citigroup), ended with one of his stand-up comic bits: "Looking back, I think of my Salomon experience as having been both fascinating and instructional, though for a time in 1991–1992 I felt like the drama critic who wrote, 'I would have enjoyed the play except that I had an unfortunate seat. It faced the stage.'"*

*In case you don't notice the dates as you start to read the two Salomon articles that follow, please note that the two were published nine years apart. The first of these, "The Wisdom of Salomon?," was a sidebar contained in "The Inside Story of Warren Buffett," which you have just read. This short piece describes the beginning of the Salomon tale: the out-of-the-ordinary $700 million investment in the company that Berkshire made in 1987.*

*What no one could then have dreamed, of course, was that within a very few years—specifically, in the 1991–1992 period that Buffett referred to in the quotation above—Salomon would a) get into terrible trouble for illegal trading in Treasury securities and b) Buffett would be forced to parachute in to try to save it. Those events are spelled out in "Warren Buffett's Wild Ride at Salomon." But that article, for unusual reasons, did not see the light of day until a string of years had passed. The story itself, in its opening paragraphs, explains the delay in publication.*

*To read the 1997 story today and to realize how close Salomon came to bankruptcy in 1991—at least as Buffett saw it—is inevitably to think about Lehman Brothers, which many years later did go bankrupt. In the Salomon article is a one-sentence description of the chaos that an emotional Buffett warned Washington would ensue if the firm failed. Said the sentence: "He predicted that a Salomon bankruptcy would be calamitous, having domino effects that would reach worldwide and play havoc with a financial system that subsists on the expectation of prompt payments."*

*We'll never know about Salomon, because Buffett's pleas saved it. But that is an all too perfect description of what happened in 2008 when Lehman went down. —CL*

# The Wisdom of Salomon?

### April 11, 1988

### BY CAROL LOOMIS

"**W**e have no special insights regarding the direction or future profitability of investment banking," says Warren Buffett in the forthcoming Berkshire Hathaway annual report for 1987. "What we do have a strong feeling about is the ability and integrity of John Gutfreund, CEO of Salomon Inc." With that declaration, Buffett takes a hatchet to the rumors that have been sweeping Wall Street for months, in which he is typically presented as wanting (a) Gutfreund out and (b) someone like William Simon in.

Since Buffett has a policy of not making hostile moves against the managements of companies he invests in, the rumors were always a reach. But the timing of Buffett's push into Salomon last year almost guaranteed that stories would begin to fly. On October 1 he put $700 million of Berkshire's money, his biggest investment ever, into Salomon redeemable convertible preferred. The stock pays 9%, is convertible after three years into Salomon common at $38, and if not converted will be redeemed over five years beginning in 1995. The rub is the $38. Salomon stock was around $33 when Buffett made the deal. After October 19 it sank to almost $16 and was recently about $23.

The crash transformed the Street's perception of Buffett's move. He was originally thought to have bought a dream security, worth more than he paid. Salomon, it was said, had panicked at the prospect that raider Ronald Perelman might try a takeover and had allowed Buffett his own bit of banditry. The post-crash reading, which takes into account many defections and much turmoil at Salomon, is that Buffett has bought a bummer and that his whole credibility as an investor is at stake.

Buffett notes in his annual report that the economics of investment banking are far less predictable than those of most businesses in which he has major commitments. He says that's one reason he went for a convertible preferred. But he also sounds serene in outlook: "We believe there is a reasonable likelihood that a leading, high-quality capital-raising and market-making operation can average good returns on equity. If so, our conversion right will eventually prove valuable." By the way, he adds, he'd like to buy more convertible preferreds of the Salomon variety, which sounds like serenity squared.

The most fascinating aspect of Buffett's Salomon investment is that it puts him in bed with Wall Streeters, whose general greed he has scored in the past. In his 1982 annual report he derided the inclination of investment bankers to provide whatever advice would bring in the most income. "Don't ask your barber whether you need a haircut," he said. But this year's report suggests he finds Gutfreund's barbering a cut above: In dealings with Gutfreund, Buffett says, he has seen him advise clients not to take steps they were itching to take, even though that caused Salomon to miss out on large fees.

Note that Buffett's description of Salomon's business does not include those Wall Street buzzwords "merchant banking." To Buffett, the bridge loans that are the current merchant-banking fad and that grease the way for many leveraged buyouts all too often look like dangerous commitments—debt so junior that it is almost equity. He and his associate, Charles Munger, are directors of Salomon and may well argue that the firm should avoid making bridge loans. But, says Buffett, "If John Gutfreund ends up thinking he wants to do them, we will support him. We don't go into companies with the thought of effecting a lot of change. That doesn't work any better in investments than it does in marriages."

# Warren Buffett's Wild Ride at Salomon

October 27, 1997

## BY CAROL LOOMIS

*A harrowing, bizarre tale of misdeeds and mistakes that pushed Salomon to the brink and produced the "most important day" in Warren Buffett's life.*

As Sanford I. Weill, 64, the dealmaking CEO of Travelers Group, steps up to his biggest acquisition ever—the purchase of Salomon Inc. for $9 billion—a famous Wall Street figure, Warren E. Buffett, 67, steps out of Salomon. His days there began almost precisely a decade ago, in the early fall of 1987, when his company, Berkshire Hathaway, became Salomon's largest shareholder and he moved in as a director. But that was training-wheels stuff, nothing to the high-wire unicycle act that came later: Buffett was physically, emotionally, and *really* at Salomon for nine months in 1991 and 1992, when the firm's trading illegalities created a giant sucking sound that brought him in to run the place.

Though much has been written about Buffett and Salomon, a lot of what you will read here will be new. I have been a friend of Buffett's for about 30 years and have long been a shareholder of Berkshire (though never a shareholder of Salomon). As a friend, I do some editing every year on Buffett's well-known annual report, and we have for eons talked about collaborating on a book about his business life. All this has given me many opportunities to learn Buffett's thinking. Some of what I've gleaned has ended up in *Fortune* stories that I wrote, most especially in an April 11, 1988, article, "The Inside Story of Warren Buffett," and in an accompanying box, "The Wisdom of Salomon?" But much of what I learned about Buffett's experiences at Salomon in 1991 was confidential, embargoed by him because Salomon was both struggling to regain its footing and dealing with big legal problems. Later on, though those emergencies eased and the embargo might have been lifted, there was no immediate reason to print the story. Now, with the Travelers deal, there is. To that reason, add another: This drama of 1991 sends a powerful message about the hazards lurking in a financial system that every day grows more complex.

This tale should begin with the thought that the ten months Buffett spent at Salomon were a profound break in the rhythm of his life. Warren Buffett is an executive accustomed to making maybe one big investment decision a year, but Salomon left him dealing with 25 operating decisions a day. At the center of this experience was a single day—what he has called "the most important day of my life," Sunday, Aug. 18, 1991—in which the U.S. Treasury first banned Salomon from bidding in government securities auctions and then, because of Buffett's efforts, rescinded the ban. In the four hours of suspense between the two actions, Buffett struggled passionately to ward off a tragedy he saw threatening to unfold. In Buffett's opinion, the ban put Salomon, this company now being priced at $9 billion, in sure danger of having immediately to file for bankruptcy. Even more important, he believed on that day, as he does now, that the collapse of Salomon would have shaken the world's financial system to its core.

That Sunday in August was a far cry from the commercialism of another Sunday, Sept. 27, 1987, when Buffett and John Gutfreund, then Salomon's chairman and CEO, agreed that Berkshire Hathaway would buy $700 million of Salomon convertible preferred stock, which equated to a 12% stake in the company. The deal allowed Gutfreund to stave off takeover artist Ronald Perelman, who seemed poised to buy a large block of Salomon common stock from certain South African investors wanting to sell. With Berkshire's $700 million, Gutfreund was able to strike a deal that allowed Salomon itself to buy the South African stock—and with that, Perelman was dispatched.

It was easy to see why Gutfreund welcomed Warren Buffett, White Knight. It was less easy to see why Buffett wanted to hook up with Salomon, much less trust it with this mint, $700 million—the largest amount he'd ever invested in a single company. Over the years, Buffett had derided investment bankers, deploring their enthusiasm for deals that provided huge fees but that were turkeys for their clients. He has also spoken often of wanting to work only with people he likes. So here he was, handing over mountains of Berkshire's carefully accumulated and husbanded cash to the high-living, cigar-chomping, corner-cutting crowd soon to be made infamous in *Liar's Poker*?

Several reasons explain the move, none of them really good enough in the light of what followed. One is that Buffett had been having trouble for a couple of years finding stocks he thought reasonably priced and was looking for fixed-income alternatives. A second is that the Salomon proposal came from John Gutfreund, whom Buffett had seen do principled, non-greedy, client-friendly work for GEICO, in which Berkshire was then a major stockholder (and which is now owned 100% by Berkshire). Buffett liked Gutfreund—still does, in fact.

A third explanation was simply that Buffett thought the terms of the deal worth accepting. In effect, convertible preferreds are fixed-income investments with lottery tickets attached. In this case, the security was to pay 9% and be convertible after three years into Salomon common stock at $38 a share—against the $30 for which the stock had been selling. If Buffett did not convert the stock, it was to be redeemed over five years beginning in 1995. To Buffett, it looked like a decent proposition. "It's not 'a triple,' which is what you'd like to have," he said to me in 1987, "but it could work out okay."

To some of the brainy, mathematical types at Salomon, that appraisal would have qualified as the understatement of the year. From Day One, they thought—and let it be known to the press—that Buffett had exploited Gutfreund's fear of Perelman and had secured a dream security, with a too-high dividend or a too-low conversion price or some combination thereof. Over the next few years, this opinion did not die at Salomon, and more than once executives of the firm (though never Gutfreund) came to Buffett with propositions for deep-sixing the preferred.

It's fair to say that Buffett might have taken those offers more seriously had he known that ahead lay the business-wrecking, profit-shredding scandal that broke in August 1991—and that turned the world upside down for both Salomon and him.

A little stage setting here: Before the crisis hit, Salomon was on its way to an excellent business year, marred only by a Treasury investigation into a May T-bill auction in which Salomon was thought perhaps to have engineered a short squeeze. Despite that sticky matter, Salomon's stock had climbed to $37 a share, a price very near Buffett's conversion point of $38.

For the story of what then happened, we may begin with Buffett in Reno. Yes, Reno, which was the spot two executives of a Berkshire subsidiary had picked for an annual getaway with Buffett. Arriving in Reno on the afternoon of Thursday, Aug. 8, Buffett checked with his office and found that John Gutfreund, en route at that moment from London to New York, wanted to talk to him that evening. Gutfreund's office said he'd then be at Salomon's principal law firm, Wachtell Lipton Rosen & Katz, and Buffett agreed to call him there at 10:30 P.M. New York time.

Mulling this over, Buffett concluded that it couldn't be bad news, because Gutfreund hadn't been in New York to attend to it. Maybe, he thought, Gutfreund had made a deal to sell Salomon and needed a quick okay from the directors. Heading out to dinner in Lake Tahoe, Buffett actually told his group that he might be hearing "good news" before the evening was out—a characterization indicating Buffett was ready to bail from this supposedly plummy deal he'd got into four years earlier.

At the appointed time, breaking from dinner, Buffett stood at a pay phone to make his call. After a delay, he was put through to Salomon's president, Tom Strauss, and its inside lawyer, Donald Feuerstein, who told him that because Gutfreund's plane had been held up, they would instead brief Buffett on "a problem" that had arisen. Speaking calmly, they said that a Wachtell Lipton investigation commissioned by Salomon had discovered that two of its government securities traders, including the top gun, managing director Paul Mozer (a name Buffett didn't know), had broken the Treasury's bidding rules on more than one occasion in 1990 and 1991.

Mozer and his colleague, said Strauss and Feuerstein, had been suspended, and the firm was now moving to notify its regulators and put out a press release. Feuerstein then read a draft of the release to Buffett and added that earlier in the day he had talked at some length to Salomon director Charles T. Munger, Berkshire's vice-chairman and Buffett's sidekick in everything important.

The release contained only a few details about Mozer's sins. But a fuller account dribbled out over the next few days, depicting a man at war with the Treasury over bidding rules that he despised. A new rule, promulgated in 1990 to prevent such behemoths as Salomon from cornering the market, said that a single firm could not bid for more than 35% of the Treasury securities being offered in a given auction. In December 1990 and again in February 1991, Mozer simply made hash of this rule by, first, bidding for Salomon's allowable of 35%; second, submitting, without authorization, separate bids for certain customers; and, third, simply stuffing the securities that these bidders won into Salomon's own account, never telling the customers a word about the whole exercise. From all this, Salomon emerged with more than 35% of the auctioned securities and with increased power to swing its weight around.

On that Thursday night, with other pay-phoners chattering all around him, Buffett did not hear nearly that much detail nor detect, in Strauss and Feuerstein's matter-of-fact tones, any reason to be particularly alarmed. So he went back to dinner.

Only on Saturday, when he reached Munger, then vacationing on a northern Minnesota island, did Buffett get a sense of real trouble. Munger, a lawyer by training, had stopped Feuerstein's recital two days earlier to explore what Feuerstein meant by saying—to use the words that were on a sheet of "talking points" drawn up by lawyers for these calls—that "one part of the problem has been known since late April." In writer-speak, that is the "passive voice," and it raises an obvious question: "Who knew?"

Munger bore down on that question and found out that Mozer, believing that he was about to be unmasked, had disclosed the February bidding infractions to his boss, John Meriwether, in late April. Calling Mozer's behavior "career-threatening," Meriwether immediately went to Strauss with the news and, days later, met with Strauss, Gutfreund, and Feuerstein to decide what to do.

Feuerstein advised the others that Mozer's act was probably "criminal," and the group concluded that the New York Federal Reserve must be told what had happened. But then no one did a thing about telling—neither in April nor in May, June, or July. That was the inaction that Buffett later said was "inexplicable and inexcusable," and that pushed the crisis to its limits.

Talking to Buffett on that Saturday, Munger called management's extended failure to act "thumb sucking," which is a term Buffett thinks he heard repeated when he himself was talking to Strauss and Feuerstein. But he does not otherwise think the two men made any effort to clearly inform him about top management's part in this mess. Some of Salomon's regulators later voiced a similar complaint, saying they were told about top management's dereliction, but in soft, shrouded words that failed to get the point across.

Even so, that left them better off than the public, which in the Aug. 9 press release learned absolutely nothing about management's having known anything, at any time. In his phone conversation with Feuerstein, Munger sharply challenged the omission. But Feuerstein said that management and its lawyers worried that too much disclosure would threaten the firm's "funding"—its ability to roll over the billions of dollars of short-term debt that became due every day. So Salomon's plan was to tell its directors and regulators that management had known of Mozer's misconduct, but to avoid saying this publicly. Munger didn't like it, finding this behavior neither candid nor smart. But not considering himself an expert on "funding," he subsided.

When he and Buffett talked on Saturday, however—with the Salomon story played big on the front page of the *New York Times*—they resolved to insist on prompt disclosure of the full facts. On Monday, Munger delivered their strong opinions to Gutfreund's close friend and adviser, Martin Lipton of Wachtell Lipton, and was told that the matter would be discussed at a telephone board meeting scheduled for Wednesday afternoon. Buffett, meanwhile, was talking to Gutfreund, who allowed that just about all the affair meant was "a few points on the stock."

At the Wednesday board meeting, the directors heard a reading of a second press release, which included three pages of details and a straightforward admission that top management had learned of Mozer's February transgression back in April. But a sentence that followed sent the directors into a telephonic uproar. It said that management had then failed to go to the regulators because of the "press of other business." Buffett, listening in Omaha, remembers calling this impossibly lame excuse "ridiculous." The explanation in the press release was later changed to incorporate the words "due to a lack of sufficient attention to the matter, this determination was not implemented promptly," another passive-voice specimen slightly less lame but unflinching in its refusal to assign any blame.

The real offense of that Wednesday directors meeting, though, was not language but a flagrant omission: Gutfreund's failure to tell the board that he had the day before received a letter from the Federal Reserve Bank of New York that contained some doomsday words. The letter was signed by an executive vice president of the bank, but anyone reading it would have known that behind it stood 6 feet 4 inches of Irish force and temper, Gerald Corrigan, the bank's president. Corrigan by then knew enough to have become incensed by these doings on his watch. The letter said that Salomon's bidding "irregularities" called into question its "continuing business relationship" with the Fed and pronounced the Fed "deeply troubled" by the failure of Salomon's management to make a timely disclosure of what it had learned about Mozer. It asked for a comprehensive report within ten days of all "irregularities, violations, and oversights" Salomon knew to have occurred.

Buffett learned later that Corrigan expected the letter to be promptly given to Salomon's directors, whom he believed would just as promptly recognize that top management had to be changed. When the directors didn't act, Corrigan thought they were being defiant—but instead, of course, they were simply in the dark. Buffett did not hear about any Fed letter until later in the week, when he spoke to Corrigan, and even then Buffett assumed the Fed had only sent a request for information. Buffett did not actually see the letter until more than a month later, after he heard Corrigan refer pointedly to it in congressional hearings.

In Buffett's opinion, the Fed's belief that its letter had been ignored stoked the fury with which the regulators came down on Salomon a few days later. There is no shortage, Buffett says, of "vital matters" that Gutfreund, Strauss, and Feuerstein kept from the directors in the previous months, all the while acting as if things were perfectly normal. But not conveying the Fed letter to the board was in his thinking "the atom bomb." Or maybe, he says, a more earthy description fits: "Understandably, the Fed felt at this point that the directors had joined with management in spitting in its face."

You may reasonably ask what was going on in Salomon's stock while all of this was transpiring. It was emphatically down, from above $36 per share on Friday to under $27 on Thursday, when the second press release rocked the market. But the stock was only the facade for a much graver matter, a corporate financial structure that by Thursday was beginning to crack because confidence in Salomon was eroding. It is not good for any securities firm to lose the world's confidence. But if the firm is "credit dependent," as Salomon was to an extreme, it cannot tolerate a negative change in perceptions. Buffett likens Salomon's need for confidence to a mortal's need for air: When the required good is present, it's never noticed. When it's missing, that's all that's noticed.

Unfortunately, the erosion of confidence was occurring in a company grown enormous. Salomon in August of 1991 had bulged up to $150 billion in assets (not counting, of course, huge off-balance-sheet items) and was among the five largest financial institutions in the U.S. Propping the company on the right-hand side of the balance sheet was—are you ready?—only $4 billion in equity capital, and above that was about $16 billion in medium-term notes, bank debt, and commercial paper. This total of about $20 billion was the capital base that supported the remaining $130 billion in liabilities, most of these short-term, due to run off in one day to six months.

The paramount fact about those liabilities is that short-term lenders have their track shoes on at all times: They have absolutely no enthusiasm for earning an extra fraction of a percentage point in interest if they perceive that their capital is even slightly at risk. Just waving a premium rate in front of them is in fact counterproductive, since it makes them suspect there is hidden danger. Moreover, unlike commercial banks, whose creditors can look to the FDIC or to the "too big to fail" doctrine, securities firms have no declared "Big Daddy" whose mere presence is a deterrent to runs.

So on that Thursday, Salomon began to experience a run. It materialized out of left field in the form of investors who wished to sell this big-league trader and market maker, Salomon, its own debt securities—specifically, the medium-term notes that the company had outstanding. Salomon had always made a market in these securities, but that was ordinarily a yawn, since nobody wanted to sell. But now the sellers poured in. Salomon's traders responded by lowering their bids, trying to deter the traffic—dying to do that, in fact, because every repurchase of notes they made melted down the capital base that was holding up the whole Salomon structure. Finally, after the traders had bought about $700 million of the notes, Salomon did the unthinkable: It stopped trading in its own securities. That called a halt on the rest of the Street too. If Salomon wasn't going to buy its own paper, it's for sure nobody else would.

That Thursday evening, as newspapers cranked out their stories of the day's extraordinary events at Salomon—when the teller's window slams down, there's no keeping it secret—John Gutfreund and Tom Strauss talked by phone to Gerry Corrigan. Trouble was all around, and in the conversation Gutfreund and Strauss questioned their ability to keep leading Salomon.

The next morning, at 6:45 A.M. Omaha time, Buffett was awakened by a phone call. On the line were Gutfreund, Strauss, and Marty Lipton. Gutfreund said that he and Strauss were resigning, and the question of who was going to take over sort of hung there. Gutfreund later said he asked Buffett to take the job. Buffett thinks he volunteered. He did not in any case nail down anything while at home, but instead said he would call the New Yorkers when he got to his office, five minutes away. Once there, he looked at a just-arrived fax of that day's *New York Times* story, whose front-page headlines said: WALL STREET SEES A SERIOUS THREAT TO SALOMON BROS.; HIGH-LEVEL RESIGNATIONS AND CLIENT DEFECTIONS FEARED. And at 7:45 A.M. Omaha time, he called the Salomon group back and said he would take on the job until things got straightened out.

To this day, newspapers report that he went in to protect Berkshire's $700 million, but that seems awfully simplistic. Sure, he wished for the safety of that investment. But beyond that, he was a director of a company in deep trouble and, in a way that few directors do, he felt an obligation to all of its shareholders. In addition, he had a job—CEO of Berkshire—that he could for a while run with one hand while picking up trouble in the other, and for the $1 a year he earned at Salomon, he didn't need to waste time working out an employment contract. Okay, he knew he was changing his life, and not for the better. "But somebody had to take this job," he said then and has said since, "and I was the logical person."

On that Friday morning, Buffett made immediate plans to fly to New York. But the group from Salomon had asked him to stay at his office to await a call from Corrigan, and it was slow in coming. While Buffett waited, the stock market opened—but trading in Salomon stock did not. Then came the call from Corrigan. It was short and contained word that he was willing to let up a little on "the ten-day schedule" now that Buffett was entering the picture. Not having seen the Fed's letter, Buffett didn't have a clue what Corrigan was talking about, but grasped from the context that the Fed must be asking for information. When the conversation ended, Buffett flew to New York, arriving there around 4 P.M. By that time, Salomon had released the news that he was becoming interim chairman, and the New York Stock Exchange had opened up trading in the stock. In its brief exposure to the light, the stock traded heavily and moved up a dollar, closing just under $28.

Buffett's own exposure that day included an evening meeting with Corrigan at the Fed's office. Gutfreund and Strauss went too, and the three men stepped into a session totally devoid of the cordiality that normally greets Buffett. Corrigan said soberly that he hadn't found that interim chairmanships worked well; warned Buffett that he should not attempt to get around Corrigan by seeking help from "Washington friends"; and, in a dire but mysterious comment, told Buffett to prepare for "any eventuality."

Then he asked Buffett to step out while he talked privately to Gutfreund and Strauss, two men who had long been—past tense needed here—friends of his. When the two emerged, Gutfreund told Buffett that Corrigan had emotionally expressed his personal regrets about the part he was playing in ending their careers. Gutfreund, iron tough to the end, angrily dismissed the incident when talking to Buffett, saying he wasn't about to grant Corrigan "absolution." Today, Buffett, recalling those strange moments, remembers also that George Washington cried as he signed the death warrant of Major Andre, a British spy. But like Corrigan, he signed.

For Buffett, the rest of Friday and all of Saturday were given over to crucial operating decisions. One obliged him to address the fate of John Meriwether, who had sped to tell his bosses about Mozer's misdeeds when he learned of them but then had willingly or unwillingly got caught up in the web of nondisclosure. Marty Lipton, terribly visible in these crisis days, wanted Meriwether fired, and so did a good many members of the management committee, who were clawing for anything that might save the firm.

But Buffett, unclear that it was fair to fire Meriwether, kept searching for more understanding of what had truly happened after April. He gained some knowledge on Saturday, when two Wachtell Lipton lawyers spent more than an hour telling Buffett and the surviving members of Salomon's management committee what they had learned in their investigation, which had begun in early July. Then, late on Saturday, the Meriwether question became moot, because he himself decided it was best that he resign.

The still bigger decision facing Buffett was determining which member of Salomon Brothers' executive group would become the new head of the securities operation, now losing its two bosses, Gutfreund and Strauss. So on Saturday, at Wachtell Lipton's offices, Buffett talked serially to about ten members of Salomon's management committee, asking each man whom, among this group, he thought most qualified to run the business. The great majority said Deryck Maughan, then 43, who had recently returned from running Salomon's Tokyo office and been made co-head of investment banking. Maughan himself had a subtle answer: "I think that when you ask many of the others whom they want, you'll find it's me." Buffett knew also that Gutfreund thought the choice should be Maughan. So Buffett identified his man that day. But he held off telling both Maughan and the world because the Salomon board—ready to meet in emergency session at 10 A.M. on Sunday, Aug. 18—needed to ratify the decision and indeed to elect Buffett himself.

Had the whole regulatory establishment slept through that weekend, the board meeting would still have been a landmark event. But as it was, on Saturday Salomon's regulators were putting the finishing touches on a guided missile. It hit Salomon's offices in downtown Manhattan just before 10 A.M. on Sunday, by way of a phone call from the Treasury saying that in a few minutes it would announce that Salomon was to be barred from bidding at Treasury auctions, both for its own account and for customers.

Buffett got the message in a small room where he was talking with a handful of people, including two, Gutfreund and Strauss, who were set to offer their resignations at the meeting. The three men immediately concluded that the news would put Salomon out of business—not because of the economic loss that would be sustained because of the Treasury's lockout, but because the world would interpret the news as "Treasury to Salomon: drop dead." Furthermore, this blow would fall on a company already staggered by credit problems and just barely hanging on.

Nor was there time to maneuver: Word had already gone out that Buffett would appear at a 2:30 P.M. press conference, and a crowd of journalists was expected. Worse than that, the tyranny of a worldwide market was bearing down on the firm. The Japanese market would be opening in the late afternoon, and then London, and then New York. Bad news would cascade from one market to the other and center on just one thought: Salomon's credit is shot. In a firm dependent on credit, other thoughts didn't matter anyway. This one alone would destroy the company.

In the small room where they got the news, Buffett and the others huddled to consider their options. They saw three possible courses of action. First, get the Treasury to rescind or at least modify the ban. Second, put on a brave face, spout confident statements, and hope that the world would buy the act—or, in other words, lie. Third, liquidate by declaring bankruptcy, hoping thereby to fail honorably, minimize the damage, and spread its effects equitably among Salomon's creditors.

The second strategy got ditched almost before it was articulated. The other two lived and were pursued simultaneously. That meant bankruptcy lawyers needed to be called in. A team was summoned from Wachtell Lipton and put to work investigating how a mammoth international securities firm goes bankrupt, on a Sunday, possibly needing some judge, yanked from watching baseball and eating popcorn, who might suspect that a careless typist had added an extra zero to that figure of $150 billion, and who would in any case probably never have heard of a derivative or repos or fails to deliver. In short, the bankruptcy filing, if things came to that end, was going to be a nightmare.

In a personal sense, it would have been that for Buffett also. His job description was on the verge of drastic changes that would leave him no reason for being there: He had come to save Salomon, not to escort it through the endless process of bankruptcy. All manner of people could do that job, he told himself.

So early on that Sunday, Buffett concluded that he would refuse election if bankruptcy ensued. He did not, however, kid himself about the furor that would follow, since he knew that his exit would be viewed as the abandonment of a sinking ship or, worse yet, as the very cause of its going down. Buffett had long told his three children that it takes a lifetime to build a reputation but only five minutes to tear it down. As he moved along through Sunday, he told himself he might be edging up on the five minutes.

But that did not short-circuit a ton of energy he was putting into Plan A: getting a reversal of the ban. Buffett assigned himself to calling the Treasury and also talked once that day to Fed Chairman Alan Greenspan. Gutfreund and Strauss were put on the job of finding Corrigan, who proved hard to reach. Meriwether, lending help, was told to track down Richard Breeden, chairman of the SEC. That thrust turned out to be a total nonwinner. Breeden, once Meriwether got him, said he had participated in the Treasury's decision, pronounced Salomon "rotten to the core," and said it would get no help from him.

On the Treasury front, logistics dealt an early blow. When Buffett tried almost immediately to call back the Treasury official who had delivered the awful message, the line was busy. The phone company agreed to interrupt the call, but there was confusion and error and delay. By the time Buffett actually got through to the Treasury spokesman, the announcement of the Treasury ban had hit the wires and gone flashing around the world.

The Treasury spokesman then got Secretary of the Treasury Nicholas Brady, at that moment visiting Saratoga Springs, N.Y., for the horseraces, to call Buffett. The two men had been friendly acquaintances over the years but could hardly have imagined they would be facing off on this Sunday morning. His voice cracking with emotion and strain, Buffett made his case, telling the Secretary that Salomon could not cope with the Treasury ban and that it was bringing in bankruptcy experts to prepare for a possible filing. Buffett stressed Salomon's gargantuan size and the worldwide nature of its business. He predicted that a Salomon bankruptcy would be calamitous, having domino effects that would reach worldwide and play havoc with a financial system that subsists on the idea of prompt payments.

Doomsday scenarios are not easy to get across. Responding, Brady was friendly and empathetic but inclined to think this talk of bankruptcy and financial meltdowns was far-fetched. He could not imagine Buffett refusing to take the job or failing in its execution. Brady was also highly aware of where things stood: The announcement had gone out, and reversing it would be an enormous problem.

But to Buffett's enormous relief, Brady did not cut off the dialogue. Instead, he went off to make some calls and then kept getting back to Buffett. In one of the stranger details of the day, Buffett talked on Salomon phones that had been programmed not to ring but instead flashed a tiny green light when someone was calling. For longer than he cares to remember, Buffett stared at the telephone, waiting for the Secretary of the Treasury to create light.

With each call, Buffett tried to make Brady realize the seriousness of the situation and his sense that they were rocketing along on a train that had to be stopped—but that *could* be, once everybody realized that this was an accident that mustn't be allowed to happen. At one point in the Brady conversations, all of Buffett's anguish and sense of futility got jammed into a single sentence: "Nick, this is the most important day of my life."

Brady said, "Don't worry, Warren, we'll get through this." But that didn't mean at all that he had changed his opinions.

It took Corrigan's entrance into the telephone calls in the afternoon to make a difference. This was the man who told Buffett to prepare for "any eventuality" and defined his term by endorsing the ban. But Corrigan now listened hard and seemed to assign credence to Buffett's talk of bankruptcy and of his personal plans to leave were a filing to come. Said Corrigan to Brady and another regulator on the phone with them: "We better talk among ourselves."

Buffett went back into the boardroom and waited with the other directors. Six floors below, over 100 reporters and photographers, this author among them, were gathering for the 2:30 press conference. Directly outside the boardroom, some of the managing directors that Buffett had interviewed on Saturday were milling around, summoned because one of their number was to be named operating head of Salomon.

And then, just at 2:30, Jerome Powell, an Assistant Secretary of the Treasury, called Buffett to read a statement the Treasury was ready to go with. It was effectively half a loaf, or maybe two-thirds, saying that the ban on Salomon's bidding for its own account was lifted while the ban on bidding for customers' accounts remained. "Will that do?" asked Powell. "I think it will," answered

Buffett. The board then raced through electing Buffett as interim chairman of Salomon Inc. and Deryck Maughan as a director and operating head of Salomon Brothers. Buffett found Maughan and said, "You're tapped," and the two went down to the press conference, entering at 2:45.

The start was abrupt: "I'm Warren Buffett, and I was this afternoon elected interim chairman of Salomon Inc." A few minutes later he was into the just-released Treasury announcement, which he read aloud. When he finished, there were muffled cheers from the back of the auditorium and a scrambling of feet as employees ran with the lifesaving news. Buffett then moved into more than two hours of questions. "How will you handle needing to be both here and in Omaha?" he was asked, and the answer popped right back: "My mother has sewn my name in my underwear, so it'll be okay."

On Monday, the headlines didn't say drop dead; they took in the reversal as well as the ban. Salomon's stock opened on time and traded in orderly fashion, falling about a point and a half.

Pointing out a paradox, Buffett says today that the whole Treasury episode, excruciating though it was at the time, probably gave Salomon a boost that it could not have got any other way. The reversal, coming along at 2:30 P.M., sent a message to the market that this almighty regulator, the Treasury, thought Salomon was okay. Had not that endorsement materialized, Monday's debt markets would have been forced to make their own determination about Salomon's creditworthiness, and who knows what kind of thoughts they would have pulled from the ether.

As it was, Salomon emerged from that weekend with just enough stamina to limp through some exceedingly tough months, in which the interim CEO reduced leverage by vastly shrinking the balance sheet, haggled with banks about money Salomon badly needed, and hoped above all else that Mozer's wrongdoing (which cost him nearly four months in prison after he pleaded guilty to lying to the Fed) would not entrap Salomon itself in criminal charges. In the end, the company settled for $290 million, an outcome mainly reflecting the extraordinary cooperation Buffett decreed should be given both regulators and the law in getting things cleaned up.

A big broom in this cleanup was a California lawyer who had worked often for Berkshire, Robert Denham, and whom Buffett pulled into Salomon full-time. When May of 1992 rolled around, with many of Salomon's biggest problems under control, Buffett went back to Omaha, and Denham stepped into his place as chairman of Salomon Inc. and overseer of the shareholders' interests. Having now overseen these folk into $9 billion of Travelers stock, Denham will be stepping on to something else.

And Berkshire's part of the $9 billion? It's about $1.7 billion, though some of the Travelers stock Berkshire will receive is committed to holders of a Berkshire convertible bond. About that complication you do not wish to know more, nor do you wish to deeply analyze other acrobatics that Buffett has carried out with

Salomon stock. Just note this: a share of Salomon is right now worth about $81 in Travelers stock. Against that, Berkshire owns some Salomon stock that it bought in 1987 at an effective price of $38, and it owns other Salomon shares purchased later at an average price of about $48.

In short, Buffett said in 1987 that Salomon wouldn't be "a triple," and it hasn't been. On the other hand, this record hardly equates to a strikeout. "I'd say we hit a scratch single," says Buffett, "but not before the count got to 0 and 2."

And then inching oh-so-slightly toward a philosophical summary of Salomon, he hauls out one of his favorite expressions: All's well that ends.

## From "Now Hear This"

### January 10, 1994

*Buffett's wry comment 2½ years after the Salomon crisis broke*

**W**arren Buffett, 63, chairman of Berkshire Hathaway, a big investor in Salomon Inc., on the fine and jail sentence laid on Paul Mozer, who precipitated the firm's Treasury-auction scandal: "Mozer's paying $30,000 and is sentenced to prison for four months. Salomon's shareholders—including me—paid $290 million, and I got sentenced to ten months as CEO."

# Nebraska Special

September 26, 1988

**BY TERENCE PARÉ**

Warren E. Buffett, the Omaha investor who prides himself on producing extraordinary results by doing ordinary things, has now done an extraordinary thing to produce an ordinary result. In a letter to shareholders of Berkshire Hathaway, his hometown conglomerate, Buffett, 58, announced plans to move trading in the firm's shares from the over-the-counter market to the New York Stock Exchange.

That's extraordinary because the exchange demands that companies applying for a listing have at least 2,000 stockholders who own at least one "round lot" of 100 shares. Berkshire doesn't. With shares selling for around $4,300 each, not many people can afford a round lot, and Berkshire has relatively few shares outstanding—less than 3% of the average number among companies listed on the Big Board. Buffett has always refused to split the stock—in part to discourage speculators—and instead waited for the exchange to change the rule, which it recently did. It will allow Berkshire Hathaway to trade in round lots of ten shares. As soon as the SEC approves, Buffett will apply for a listing.

The move is not intended to boost that astronomical stock price. Indeed, Buffett wrote to his investors, "Berkshire should sell, and we hope will sell, on the NYSE at prices similar to those it would have commanded in the over-the-counter market, given similar economic circumstances." His goal is less exciting. Because the market maker's spread is generally narrower on the New York Exchange, it is a little cheaper to trade securities listed there.

# A Warm Tip from Warren Buffett: It's Time to Buy Freddie Macs

December 19, 1988

### BY BRETT DUVAL FROMSON

*This article delivered a true rarity: a stock tip from Buffett. The reason those so seldom materialize is that Buffett will not normally discuss stocks he is buying or selling. But, as a photo caption in this article explained, he made an exception in this case because Berkshire—the owner of a savings and loan company that had the right to buy in early—had reached the maximum number of shares it could own in Freddie Mac.*

*So how good was the stock tip? It was superlative. An investor who bought Freddie Mac in early December 1988 (when the December 19 issue of* Fortune *would have reached subscribers) would have paid a split-adjusted price of about $4 a share. If the investor had then held ten years—until December 1998—he could have sold at prices around $60. Investors looking for cues from Buffett might in fact have held on that long, because Berkshire retained almost all of its Freddie Mac stock—roughly 60 million shares—through the 1990s.*

*But as the decade ended, Buffett was ready to sell. In 2000, a year in which Freddie's stock price ranged from $37 to $70, Berkshire unloaded more than 95 percent of its position, registering a big capital gain of around $3 billion. The sales were made out of the public eye, because Berkshire had secured the SEC's permission to keep its sales confidential—that is, the company was allowed to omit any mention of Freddie in what are called 13-F filings—until they were completed. Once they were, Berkshire amended its 13-Fs, and Buffett disclosed in the 2000 annual report that Freddie was largely gone. He added no details, though, as to why the sales had been made.*

*The reasons were eventually to come out, however, because of Freddie Mac's own theatrics. In 2003, the news flashed that Freddie had regularly misreported its earnings and would have to restate them. By 2007, Freddie's regulator, the Office of Federal Housing Enterprise Oversight (OFHEO), was trying to force Leland Brendsel, who'd been dumped as CEO of Freddie, to relinquish a large chunk of his compensation. Buffett was then called as a witness by the regulators, who expected him—correctly—to testify that he had sold Berkshire's stock in 2000 because he had lost respect for Freddie's management.*

*Elaborating, Buffett testified that he'd met with Brendsel several times and found him unwisely striving for double-digit earnings gains—of, say, 15 percent. Gains like that don't come naturally for financial companies, Buffett said, and managements reaching for them can "start making up the numbers." Freddie had also made a big, unorthodox investment that Buffett didn't like, and he wondered what else bad it was doing that he didn't know about. "There's never just one cockroach in the kitchen," Buffett said. The regulators won the case, and Brendsel was fined and penalized a total of $16 million.*

*Turns out that Buffett could have taken his time about selling Berkshire's Freddie stock. A winner during the housing bubble, Freddie sailed along in the stock market—surviving Berkshire's sales, the earnings scandal, and management upheaval—until October 2007. Then its stock collapsed, becoming a central casualty of the financial crisis. Once a penny stock selling around 25 cents per share, Freddie was recently at $1.55—pushed to that price by speculators hoping that the government's revamping of the company will bestow some value on its common stock.* —CL

Great investment opportunities come around when excellent companies are surrounded by unusual circumstances that cause the stock to be misappraised.

Thus saith the prophet Warren Buffett, chairman of Berkshire Hathaway and stock picker supreme. In his opinion, Federal Home Loan Mortgage Corp., otherwise known as Freddie Mac, is just such an opportunity. A quasi-public corporation like its older cousin Fannie Mae (the Federal National Mortgage Association), it earns an impressive 23% return on equity and sells for less than eight times estimated 1988 earnings. "Freddie Mac is a triple dip," says Buffett. "You've got a low price/earnings ratio on a company with a terrific record. You've got growing earnings. And you have a stock that is bound to become much better known to equity investors."

Berkshire Hathaway's savings and loan subsidiary owns or has contracted to buy about $108 million of Freddie Mac stock—the maximum allowed. Lots of Buffett's friends and associates have invested too—including Louis Simpson, vice chairman of GEICO, and William Ruane, chairman of the Sequoia Fund. Should the ordinary investor consider joining the Buffett gang? In a word, yes.

Freddie Mac helps make the American dream of owning a house a reality. Chartered by Congress in 1970, the company buys residential mortgages from lenders, guarantees the mortgages against default, packages them as securities, and sells them to investors, including many S&Ls. From 1970 through 1987, the market for conventional residential mortgages grew at a compound annual rate of more than 13% and never at less than 5.5% a year. Not bad, but what makes the business outstanding is the paucity of competition. Fannie Mae is the only other major player; the chief difference between them is that Freddie resells virtually all its mortgages, while Fannie holds onto a substantial amount of them.

Together, Freddie and Fannie control 90% of the market. Says Buffett: "It's the next best thing to a monopoly." The future of the Freddie-Fannie family duopoly looks encouraging. The market could expand for years to come. So far only 33% of conventional residential mortgages are securitized, leaving plenty of room for growth. Moreover, savings institutions will soon have another powerful incentive to buy more mortgage-backed securities. In 1990 savings banks and S&Ls holding ordinary mortgages will be required to maintain bigger reserves against loan losses than if they owned a diversified portfolio of securitized mortgages.

Of the two, Freddie may be the better bet. Over the past decade, its return on equity has averaged more than twice Fannie's. Because Freddie's managers buy only top-quality mortgages, Freddie's delinquency rate for conventional fixed-rate single-family mortgages is a mere 0.4% of its $230 billion portfolio. With holdings of similar size, Fannie has 1.1% delinquencies. President Leland Brendsel and the other Freddie Mac managers minimize their exposure to interest rate spikes, which hurt mortgage bankers by raising their cost of money while lowering the price of mortgages in the secondary market. Brendsel keeps only $15 billion worth of mortgages on the balance sheet, vs. Fannie Mae's $102 billion.

Freddie's lower exposure to rising interest rates may be one reason Berkshire Hathaway sold shares in Fannie not long ago and bought more of Freddie. Says Berkshire Hathaway vice chairman Charles Munger: "I can't think of a more tangible compliment to the stock than to buy every damn share we are allowed to." By law, no one may own more than 4% of Freddie Mac's outstanding shares.

Shares in Freddie Mac have a few peculiarities. First, the stock is properly called "participating preferred." Preferred shareholders normally get fixed dividend payments, but Freddie's get the first $10 million a year in dividends and are guaranteed 90% of any further distributions. The second wrinkle for the would-be investor is that Freddie trades over the counter on a "when-issued" basis until January 3, when it will be listed on the New York Stock Exchange. Heretofore, Federal Home Loan Bank Board rules allowed only its member institutions to own the participating preferred because they provided Freddie's seed money. The board decided to end that restriction because the resulting illiquidity kept the stock price far below what it would command in a free market. The change should raise some $2 billion for capital-starved S& Ls.

Freddie's when-issued stock began trading in October. Most institutional investors have yet to discover its charms or have not bought it because their rules preclude owning when-issued shares; mutual funds and insurance companies rarely hold them. The pros may seem to rule the equity markets, but with Freddie Macs, for once the edge goes to the individual investor. And there's a bonus. Because you cannot take delivery of when-issued shares right away, you can put up 30% now and pay the rest later. In this case, you don't have to settle the bill until January 10.

# WHAT HAPPENED AT THE BRIDGE TABLE

## A Very Full Deck

June 5, 1989

**BY JULIA LIEBLICH**

Inspired by a *Fortune* cover story that featured billionaire and bridge player Warren Buffett, the American Contract Bridge League put together a match that pitted Buffett and five other big moneymakers against a team made up of elected politicians. The result: Businessmen 54, Politicians 39. An audience paid $100 a head to watch the Washington match. The money goes to the league's educational foundation and the Reading is Fundamental program. "Everyone played well," said CBS chief executive Laurence Tisch, who skippered the winning team. His teammates, in addition to Buffett, were Alan Greenberg, chairman of Bear Stearns, the brokerage house, and Jimmy Cayne, its president; Malcolm Forbes, chairman of *Forbes* magazine; and George Gillespie III, partner in the high-powered law firm Cravath Swaine & Moore. Said Congressman Arlan Stangeland (R-Minnesota), the legislators' captain, of the final score: "It was the pits."

## Raising Cayne

January 15, 1990

**BY ALAN DEUTSCHMAN**

Bear Stearns president James Cayne has won national tournaments in bridge, but when a men's magazine interviewed him about his passion for the game, the blunt Wall Streeter didn't know when to pass. *M* asked him about his teammates—his boss, Bear Stearns CEO and amateur magician Alan Greenberg plus [Tisch, Forbes, Gillespie, and Buffett, as mentioned above]—who compete as Corporate America's Six Honchos (CASH). Cayne not only criticized his partners ("they don't know what a good bridge player looks like") but went on to claim that women lack the emotional cool to be top bridge players—or stock traders. Under intense pressure, said Cayne, 52, a woman "will probably have to go to the ladies' room and dab her eyes." Those words won't help Bear Stearns defend itself against two sex-discrimination claims, including one from a female trader.

Cayne says the *M* quotes were fabricated, distorted, or taken out of context. In a letter to Bear Stearns employees, he wrote, "I sincerely apologize to everyone for the totally false impression given by the article and assure you I disagree with its contents." The writer, Duncan Christy, says the quotes—transcribed from a tape—were "meticulously accurate."

What could have possessed Cayne? Lawyer George Gillespie gallantly "pleads guilty" to being a less skillful player than his teammate. But Cayne knows at least one top-notch bridge player who is a woman—his coach, grand master Judi Radin, 39. Her view: "Maybe Jimmy got carried away. He's a great guy, but he's just too intense. Before the article came out he said I wasn't going to like it." Radin now has to prep her crew for the upcoming match against a team from the British Parliament. Prime Minister Margaret Thatcher isn't expected to play.

*Editor's note: The Americans beat the British House of Commons team, but lost to the House of Lords.*

# From "How to Live with a Billion"

September 11, 1989

### *Excerpts from an article by Alan Farnham*

Says Warren Buffett, who still puts in ten-hour days despite his $3.6 billion: "I'm doing what I would most like to be doing in the world, and I have been since I was 20." What keeps him going, he says, is the admiration he holds for his business colleagues. "I choose to work with every single person I work with. That ends up being the most important factor. I don't interact with people I don't like or admire. That's the key. It's like marrying." . . .

When it comes to personal giving, Buffett feels that picking causes is harder than picking stocks. "In stocks, you're looking for things that are obvious and easy to do. You try to identify the one-foot bars you can step over. But when you get in the charitable arena, you are attacking problems that have been the most intractable and resistant to solution throughout history. The most important ones are all seven-foot bars." Population control and diffusing the nuclear threat, the two causes Buffett's foundation supports, "are bars so high up that I can't see 'em. Real lulus."

Though Buffett has spent only $10 million to $15 million on these causes so far, he intends to give much more. Waldemar Nielsen [an expert on foundations and author of *The Golden Donors*], thinks Buffett hasn't even warmed up yet: "He's one of those very rare guys who is not only one hell of an entrepreneur in business, but one hell of an entrepreneur in the philanthropic field. We haven't had one in a long time."

The Buffett Foundation will get almost all of Buffett's stock when he dies. And he doesn't think giving its trustees a narrow charter would be wise: "That's like telling them what to invest in ten years after I die. I would rather have a smart, well-intentioned, high-grade person looking at the problems of the day through eyes that are open, not through my eyes that are in a coffin. I found in running businesses that the best results come from letting high-grade people work unencumbered. Stick around. If you're young enough, you'll see how it all works out."

*Editor's note: As described in "Warren Buffett Gives It Away" (see page 256), Buffett changed his mind about giving most of his money to the Buffett Foundation after his first wife, Susie, for whom the foundation is now named, died in 2004. He is instead gradually giving most of it to the Bill and Melinda Gates Foundation.*

*The complete text of "How to Live with a Billion" is available at fortune.com/ buffettbook.*

# From "Now Hear This"

## October 23, 1989

**W**arren Buffett, 59, billionaire investor and chairman of Berkshire Hatha-way, on why he borrowed $400 million and put the cash into Treasuries: "The best time to buy assets may be when it is hardest to raise money."

# NEW WARREN BUFFETTS?
# AND THE OLD ONE

CARRYING A HEADLINE ALMOST *impossible to resist, the first article in this 1989 combo contained a few words of wisdom from Buffett and descriptions of twelve young money managers the story's writer, Brett Fromson, had identified as possibly having investing talents comparable to Buffett's.*

*Fromson, it turned out, had a great eye. More than twenty years after the article's publication, nine of the twelve profiled are still well known in the investment world: Jim Chanos; Jim and Karen Cramer (who were then married and are now divorced); Glenn Greenberg, with his then partner John Shapiro (they split in 2009); Seth Klarman; Eddie Lampert; Richard Perry; and Michael Price. Of the others, John Constable runs a successful money management firm in suburban Philadelphia; Randy Updyke, a lone wolf whom Fromson plucked from obscurity to write about, manages an investment partnership in Sun Valley; and Tom Sweeney, a fund manager at Fidelity when the article was published, has retired from investing money professionally.*

*This book is about Buffett, so we are only excerpting his part of the story, not reprinting the profiles of the twelve money managers. But the complete article is available at fortune.com and is also accessible via a Google search, where it appears under the name of almost every person included in the article.*

*The second piece, "And Now, a Look at the Old One," begins with the engaging tale of how Homer Dodge, a physics professor, went to Omaha and persuaded Buffett to manage his money. To that incident we will add a postscript, about Homer's son, Norton, who died in November 2011 at the age of eighty-four. Norton got a long obituary in the New York Times, its length perhaps surprising for a man who was himself an unheralded professor (of economics). But a paragraph in the obit identified Norton Dodge as the son of an early Buffett-spotter and went on to explain what Norton did with a big part of his inheritance. He became an avid collector of nonconformist Soviet art, meaning works created by dissidents clandestinely protesting the Kremlin's oppressive acts. In time, he gave much of his highly valuable collection to Rutgers University. His sister, Alice, was also throughout her life a major giver to education.*

*And therein lies my point: Though Buffett himself has never been the least interested in giving to cultural or educational institutions, other Berkshire shareholders have been—generously. A few instances: Polytechnic Institute of Brooklyn (now part of New York University) benefitted significantly from the $750 million estates left by one of its professors, Nebraska native Donald Othmer, and his wife, Mildred; Kansas City's new performing arts center has its Helzberg Hall, given by Barnett and Shirley Helzberg, whose jewelry retailing company was bought by Berkshire; and in Omaha—of course—there's the Holland Performing Arts Center, named for Richard and Mary Holland, and the Sorrell Center for Health Science Education at the University of Nebraska Medical School, to which the lead donors were Bill and Ruth Scott. Both the Hollands and the Scotts began investing with Buffett in his partnership days (when Bill Scott was working as well for Buffett as a securities buyer).*

*As of early 2012, Berkshire had a market value of $202 billion, the ninth highest market cap in the Fortune 500. Buffett's huge portion of that—more than $40 billion, with many billions already given away—has been committed almost entirely to philanthropy. Nobody can know how many other Berkshire holders will be big givers as well, but they seem likely to become a crowd.* —CL

## From "Are These the New Warren Buffetts?"

October 30, 1989

*An excerpt from an article by Brett Duval Fromson*

Wouldn't you like to become partners with someone who would double your money every three to four years ad infinitum? To put it another way, wouldn't you like to invest with the next Warren Buffett? Riches come to investors who, early in their lives, find great money managers. Buffett is certifiably one of the greatest. His early clients are now worth tens of millions of dollars. He achieved that by compounding money consistently and reliably at about 25% per annum. The young investors you will meet here show comparable signs of talent. But even if they can return only 20% a year—most have done at least that well so far—$10,000 invested with them today would be worth $5.9 million in the year 2025.

What reveals their potential? Strong investment performance, of course. But that is not conclusive, especially among young managers who generally lack a ten-year record. More important are certain character traits. Buffett himself starts with "high-grade ethics. The investment manager must put the client first in everything he does." At the very least, the manager should have his net worth invested alongside of his clients to avoid potential conflicts of interest. Those profiled here have put the bulk of their assets with their customers. Buffett says he would invest only with someone who handled his mother's money too (as he did).

Brains help, but above a certain level they are not the salient distinction among investment managers. Says Buffett, "You don't need a rocket scientist. Investing is not a game where the 160 IQ guy beats the guy with the 130 IQ." The size of the investor's brain is less important than his ability to detach the brain from the emotions. "Rationality is essential when others are making decisions based on short-term greed or fear," says Buffett. "That is when the money is made."

*The full text of "Are These the New Warren Buffetts?" is available at fortune.com/buffettbook.*

## And Now a Look at the Old One

October 30, 1989

### BY BRETT DUVAL FROMSON

In the muggy summer of 1956 a 67-year-old physics professor from Vermont pulled his Jeep to a stop on a tree-lined street in Omaha. Looking for the man he thought would be one of the next great American investors, Homer Dodge had driven 1,500 miles alone in hopes of persuading 25-year-old Warren Buffett to manage his family's savings. The perspicacious Dodge had been a client of Buffett's former boss, Benjamin Graham, the father of modern financial analysis, but Graham had recently liquidated his investment company.

Recalls Buffett: "Homer told me, 'I'd like you to handle my money.' I said, 'The only thing I'm doing is a partnership with my family.' He said, 'Well, I'd like one with you.' So I set one up with Homer, his wife, children, and grandchildren." The Dodges placed $100,000 with Buffett. When Homer Dodge died in 1983, that sum had multiplied into the tens of millions.

What did Dodge spot that most people missed? Says his son, Norton: "My father saw immediately that Warren was brilliant at financial analysis. But it was more than that." The senior Dodge recognized a uniquely talented craftsman who loved the process of investing and who had mastered all the tools.

The Dodges passed the word to friends, and by the early 1960s a small choir of limited partners was singing Buffett's praises. One man was so taken with the music he heard that he wrote the young wizard a check for $300,000 without even having met him. The man simply enclosed a business card on which he had written, "Include me in." The trusting soul? Future billionaire Larry Tisch. "Warren's reputation was excellent. He was a believer in value and a man of integrity," says Tisch. "I didn't do it casually—$300,000 was a lot more money then, especially to me."

Buffett was ably prepared for the craft of stock picking. He had a sound approach on which to ground his investing—buying securities on the basis of value, not popularity. His hometown offered everything he needed—family, friends, good hamburgers (of which Buffett is inordinately fond), and very few distractions. Lastly, Buffett possessed a superior intellect. Says his longtime associate, Charles Munger, now vice chairman of Buffett's conglomerate, Berkshire Hathaway: "There were a thousand people in my Harvard law school class. I knew all the top students. There was no one as able as Warren. His brain is a superbly rational mechanism. And since he's articulate, you can see the damn brain working."

Buffett structured his partnerships to minimize unnecessary interruptions from the backers. Says he: "I told them, 'What I'll do is form a partnership where I'll manage the portfolio and have my money in there with you. I'll guarantee you a 6% return, and I get 20% of all profits after that. And I won't tell you what we own because that's distracting. All I want to do is hand in a scorecard when I come off the golf course. I don't want you following me around and watching me shank a three-iron on this hole and leave a putt short on the next one." His partners accepted the conditions because they knew he was totally committed to investing. Says Omaha investment banker Charles Heider: "I told my family, 'Look, Warren is going to think about how to invest our money seven days a week.'"

Buffett dug for information where other investment managers hardly pawed. Take, for instance, his work on American Express in 1963 during the Salad Oil Affair. The company's stock had tanked after it was discovered that a subsidiary might be liable for tens of millions of dollars in damage claims arising from the sale of salad oil that did not exist. Buffett and his people determined by visiting retailers that the core business of the credit cards and traveler's checks was as profitable as ever. That convinced him he should load up on the battered stock. It quintupled in five years.

Like all master craftsmen, Buffett prizes consistency. Marshall Weinberg of the brokerage firm Gruntal & Co. recalls going to dinner with him in Manhattan. "He had an exceptional ham-and-cheese sandwich. A few days later, we were going out again. He said, 'Let's go back to that restaurant.' I said, 'But we were just there.' He said, 'Precisely. Why take a risk with another place? We know exactly what we're going to get.' And that," says Weinberg, "is what Warren looks for in stocks too. He only invests in companies where the odds are great that they will not disappoint."

# How I Goofed

April 9, 1990

*An excerpt from Buffett's letter to shareholders in the
1989 Berkshire Hathaway annual report*

*Typically, around 80 percent of Warren Buffett's annual chairman's letter is
Berkshire-specific. The remainder is op-ed, Buffett-style. It turns out that excerpts from either portion may work nicely as a Fortune article, and we proved
that over the years by turning six varied excerpts from the letters into articles,
with this one the first. In Berkshire's annual report, we will note, the excerpt
printed here had a different title. Referring implicitly to Buffett's quarter century
at the helm of Berkshire, it was called "Mistakes of the First 25 Years (A Con-
densed Version)." Our title instead summed things up as "How I Goofed."*

*The content of the piece—a CEO pointing out his errors—was obviously un-
usual, extraordinarily so for an annual report. Of course, it is relatively easy to
engage in a confessional when you run a company whose stock has risen more
than four hundred times in the twenty-five years at issue (going from about $18
per share to $7,450). Even so, Buffett says in this piece that the record could have
been even better—had he just not been so dumb in certain instances.*

*As this book is published, in 2013, we are only two years away from the fifty-
year managerial mark for Buffett, at which point he has promised to once again
catalog his mistakes. "I will not lack for material," he told me recently. —CL*

To quote Robert Benchley, "Having a dog teaches a boy fidelity, perseverance,
and to turn around three times before lying down." Such are the shortcomings of experience. Nevertheless, it's a good idea to review past mistakes before
committing new ones. So let's take a quick look at the last 25 years.

My first mistake, of course, was in buying control of Berkshire. Though I
knew its business—textile manufacturing—to be unpromising, I was enticed to
buy because the price looked cheap. Stock purchases of that kind had proved
reasonably rewarding in my early years, though by the time Berkshire came
along in 1965 I was becoming aware that the strategy was not ideal.

If you buy a stock at a sufficiently low price, there will usually be some hic-
cup in the fortunes of the business that gives you a chance to unload at a decent
profit, even though the long-term performance of the business may be terrible.
I call this the "cigar butt" approach to investing. A cigar butt found on the street
that has only one puff left in it may not offer much of a smoke, but the "bargain
purchase" will make that puff all profit.

Unless you are a liquidator, that kind of approach to buying businesses is
foolish. First, the original "bargain" price probably will not turn out to be such
a steal after all. In a difficult business, no sooner is one problem solved than
another surfaces—never is there just one cockroach in the kitchen. Second, any

initial advantage you secure will be quickly eroded by the low return that the business earns. For example, if you buy a business for $8 million that can be sold or liquidated for $10 million and promptly take either course, you can realize a high return. But the investment will disappoint if the business is sold for $10 million in ten years and in the interim has annually earned and distributed only a few percent on cost. Time is the friend of the wonderful business, the enemy of the mediocre.

You might think this principle is obvious, but I had to learn it the hard way—in fact, I had to learn it several times over. Shortly after purchasing Berkshire, I acquired a Baltimore department store, Hochschild Kohn, buying through a company called Diversified Retailing that later merged with Berkshire. I bought at a substantial discount from book value, the people were first-class, and the deal included some extras—unrecorded real estate values and a significant LIFO inventory cushion. How could I miss? So-o-o—three years later I was lucky to sell the business for about what I had paid. After ending our corporate marriage to Hochschild Kohn, I had memories like those of the husband in the country song "My Wife Ran Away With My Best Friend and I Still Miss Him a Lot."

I could give you other personal examples of "bargain purchase" folly but I'm sure you get the picture: It's far better to buy a wonderful company at a fair price than a fair company at a wonderful price. Charlie [Munger] understood this early; I was a slow learner. But now, when buying companies or common stock, we look for first-class businesses accompanied by first-class managements.

That leads right into a related lesson: Good jockeys will do well on good horses, but not on broken-down nags. Both Berkshire's textile business and Hochschild Kohn had able and honest people running them. The same managers employed in a business with good economic characteristics would have achieved fine records. But they were never going to make any progress while running in quicksand.

I've said many times that when a management with a reputation for brilliance tackles a business with a reputation for bad economics, it is the reputation of the business that remains intact. I just wish I hadn't been so energetic in creating examples. My behavior has matched that admitted by Mae West: "I was Snow White, but I drifted."

A further related lesson: Easy does it. After 25 years of buying and supervising a great variety of businesses, Charlie and I have not learned how to solve difficult business problems. What we have learned is to avoid them. To the extent we have been successful, it is because we concentrated on identifying one-foot hurdles that we could step over rather than because we acquired any ability to clear seven-footers.

The finding may seem unfair, but in both business and investments it is usually far more profitable to simply stick with the easy and obvious than it is to resolve the difficult. On occasion, tough problems must be tackled, as was the case when we started our Sunday paper in Buffalo [thereby challenging an established competitor]. In other instances, a great investment opportunity occurs when a marvelous business encounters a one-time huge, but solvable, problem as was the case many years back at both American Express and GEICO. . . . Overall, however, we've done better by avoiding dragons than by slaying them.

My most surprising discovery: the overwhelming importance in business of an unseen force that we might call "the institutional imperative." In business school, I was given no hint of the imperative's existence and I did not intuitively understand it when I entered the business world. I thought then that decent, intelligent, and experienced managers would automatically make rational business decisions. But I learned over time that isn't so. Instead, rationality frequently wilts when the institutional imperative comes into play.

For example: (1) As if governed by Newton's first law of motion, an institution will resist any change in its current direction; (2) Just as work expands to fill available time, corporate projects or acquisitions will materialize to soak up available funds; (3) Any business craving of the leader, however foolish, will be quickly supported by detailed rate-of-return and strategic studies prepared by his troops; and (4) The behavior of peer companies, whether they are expanding, acquiring, setting compensation, or whatever, will be mindlessly imitated.

Institutional dynamics, not venality or stupidity, set businesses on these courses, which are too often misguided. After making some expensive mistakes because I ignored the power of the imperative, I have tried to organize and manage Berkshire in ways that minimize its influence. Furthermore, Charlie and I have attempted to concentrate our investments in companies that appear alert to the problem.

After some other mistakes, I learned to go into business only with people whom I like, trust, and admire. As I noted before, this policy of itself will not ensure success: A second-class textile or department-store company won't prosper simply because its managers are men that you would be pleased to see your daughter marry. However, an owner—or investor—can accomplish wonders if he manages to associate himself with such people in businesses that possess decent economic characteristics. Conversely, we do not wish to join with managers who lack admirable qualities, no matter how attractive the prospects of their business. We've never succeeded in making a good deal with a bad person.

Some of my worst mistakes were not publicly visible. These were stock and business purchases whose virtues I understood and yet didn't make. It's no sin to miss a great opportunity outside one's area of competence. But I have passed on a couple of really big purchases that were served up to me on a platter and that I was fully capable of understanding. For Berkshire's shareholders, myself included, the cost of this thumb-sucking has been huge.

Our consistently conservative financial policies may appear to have been a mistake, but in my view were not. In retrospect, it is clear that significantly higher, though still conventional, leverage ratios at Berkshire would have produced considerably better returns on equity than the 23.8% we have actually averaged. Even in 1965, perhaps we could have judged there to be a 99% probability that higher leverage would lead to nothing but good. Correspondingly, we might have seen only a 1% chance that some shock factor, external or internal, would cause a conventional debt ratio to produce a result falling somewhere between temporary anguish and default.

We wouldn't have liked those 99:1 odds—and never will. A small chance of distress or disgrace cannot, in our view, be offset by a large chance of extra returns. If your actions are sensible, you are certain to get good results; in most such cases, leverage just moves things along faster. Charlie and I have never been in a big hurry: We enjoy the process far more than the proceeds—though we have learned to live with those also.

We hope in another 25 years to report on the mistakes of the first 50. If we are around in 2015 to do that, you can count on this [confession] occupying many more pages than it does here.

# From "The Children of the Rich and Famous"

September 10, 1990

***Excerpts from an article by Alan Farnham***

Not spendthrifts, sots, nor simps, these billionheirs and billionheiresses
are working hard—even though they don't have to.

They're exotic. Some neurotic. They're billionaire children—saplings bent by
a green money wind. . . .

. . . Some inheritors learn to use their wealth to good effect, like a tool. They
escape the pitfalls of their class and lead full, productive lives, accomplishing
what they have set out to do. How do they succeed? What motivates them? The
reasons range from personal pride to a pining for adventure. Much depends on
how they were raised. Telling children early and bluntly whether they will inherit makes for a good start . . .

Warren Buffett's son Howard knows that dad intends to use his Berkshire
Hathaway lucre to curb population growth. Yet Howard, 35, has not wasted
time complaining. He farms corn and soybeans just outside of Omaha, and in
1989 he was elected commissioner of Douglas County, Nebraska . . .

Having to measure up to one's family name can be daunting. His famous
dad is the reason Howard Buffett never had a lemonade stand as a kid. "I felt
discouraged from trying. It seemed nothing I could do would be as successful
as what he did. And what I did might reflect badly on him." The shadow of the
elder Buffett's success stretches across the imagination of his 6-year-old grand-
child. Says Howard, "Little Howie owns ten shares of Coke stock that he bought
with money he saved. One day my wife was explaining that there's a first time
for everything, and he said, 'I don't think there'll ever be a first time I can afford
to buy a share of Berkshire Hathaway.'" . . .

All rich kids suffer from a form of discrimination that [one] calls
"wealthism." . . . Howard Buffett is philosophical: "There are jerks with money
and jerks without." He regularly suffers from the public's assumption that anyone named Buffett must be rich. "One night at a restaurant," he recalls, "I pulled
out my checkbook to pay the bill, and some guy says, 'Gee, I wish I had *that*
checkbook!' I didn't have the patience to tell him, 'No, buddy, you really don't.'"
Though he tries to behave as if his father's wealth didn't exist, doing so for very
long is almost impossible. "When I get back to the office this afternoon, there
will be nine messages," he says. "Eight of them will be from someone wanting
something from my dad." . . .

Howard Buffett says, "There are certain things you need to do with kids,
whether you have money or not. My mom and dad taught me responsibility:
Clean out the gutters and mow the lawn. When you do wrong, pay the consequences." Teaching his own son Howie how to live with privilege has not been
easy. When basketball hero Michael Jordan visited Omaha, Howie wanted to sit

at the head table with the other dignitaries. Howard senior had to explain to him that he wasn't automatically entitled to. . . .

Almost all billionaires' children really want to work . . . [They] understand that by starting a career or business they will increase their self-esteem and gain independence from their parents. But where parents are bankrolling the experiment, gains can prove ephemeral.

Howard Buffett farms 406 acres and loves the work: "I've been farming nine years. It's a very independent form of activity—everything's up to you. It teaches you a value system, and gives you an instrument to achieve that." So far, so good.

Except for one thing. "Dad owns the land. I pay him a percentage of the gross income as rent. I probably shouldn't tell you this, but the rent is based upon my weight. I'm 5 foot 8, and I weigh about 200 pounds. He thinks I weigh too much—that I should weigh 182.5. If I'm over, my weight is 26% of gross income. If I'm under, 22%. It's the Buffett family version of going to Weight Watchers. I don't mind it, really. He's showing he's concerned about my health. But what I do mind is that, even at 22%, he's getting a bigger paycheck than almost anybody around. Somehow he always manages to control the circumstances."

*The full text of "The Children of the Rich and Famous" is available at fortune .com/buffettbook*

# The Midas Touch at a Discount

November 5, 1990

**BY EDMUND FALTERMAYER**

Turbulence and trouble occasionally make for good bargains. Consider Berkshire Hathaway, akin to a juggernaut that unaccountably takes a backward step. Already stumbling before Saddam Hussein and recession worries cannonaded the market, the Omaha company's stock has fallen 36% this year to $5,550 a share, more than twice the descent of Standard & Poor's 500-stock index. For CEO Warren Buffett, 60, the investing wizard who owns 42% of Berkshire stock, that translates into a paper loss of $1.5 billion—or $215,450 an hour. It also spells a buying opportunity for others.

Says Michael Price, who runs the $3.1 billion Mutual Shares fund and is no investing slouch himself: "It's a way for the defensive growth investor to be in stocks." Other money managers recommend the stock, including John Tilson, who runs the high-performing $63 million Pasadena Growth Fund for Roger Engemann Associates. He has been buying Berkshire stock.

Buffett himself displays no erosion of confidence, not even on the matter of his paper losses. Says he: "I have not cut back from double hamburgers to single hamburgers." How about the corporate jet, dubbed *The Indefensible*? "That'll be the last thing to go," he jokes.

Buffett took over Berkshire Hathaway in 1965, and by the time the stock reached its peak in late 1989 it had advanced 741-fold, from $12 a share to $8,900. But a down year is not a new experience for Buffett: Berkshire's stock fell 55% in 1974. A unique creature that leads three lives, the company is a property and casualty insurance company that doubles as Buffett's investing vehicle; it also owns a collection of manufacturing, publishing, and retailing operations. In 1989 these companies—which include the publisher of *World Book* encyclopedia—collectively earned an astounding 57% on average equity.

One possible explanation for this year's slide in Berkshire's stock price: Some of its biggest holdings are in broadcasting, publishing, and insurance, industries whose shares have been especially hard hit in recent months.

The Buffett name may also have lost some of its magic, which previously helped push the stock price to a lofty premium over book value per share. A few money managers carp at his so-called white squire deals with Salomon Inc., Gillette, USAir, and Champion International. In part to help these companies deter raiders, Buffett bought preferred stock that can be converted into big blocks of common. Portfolio manager John Neff of Vanguard's Windsor Fund says he sees "some negatives there" because the deals helped to insulate the management of each company. Buffett has said that Berkshire will ultimately achieve satisfactory returns on these preferreds only if the companies' common stocks do well.

Says Pasadena's Tilson: "The market could be saying to Buffett, 'You've lost it, pal.' But I don't think so." Using a computer model, Tilson's firm calculated that Berkshire's stock recently sold for $510 less than it's really worth. "Because of the discount," reasons Tilson, "you're buying Warren Buffett's abilities for nothing." For investors, that's an inviting price.

# Buffett Buys Junk

April 22, 1991

**BY JENNIFER REESE**

Wall Street has long wondered if star investors would find bargains in the disarray of the junk bond market. Enter Warren Buffett. In the 1990 annual report of Berkshire Hathaway, the billionaire CEO discloses that Berkshire has put $440 million into RJR Nabisco's high-yield bonds. Buffett, who last year made an intensive study of the junk market, says in an interview, "There was even more carnage than I'd thought."

He concluded that the RJR bonds were a better value than anything else he saw in the field because the company is well-run and its credit better than commonly perceived. Buffett estimates that the market value of his RJR bonds is now some $175 million above his cost.

Does he wish he'd bought more? Says he, "There are a lot of things I wish I'd done in hindsight. But I don't think much of hindsight generally in terms of investment decisions. You only get paid for what you do."

# From "Now Hear This"

April 5, 1993

**W**arren E. Buffett, 62, billionaire CEO of Berkshire Hathaway, on why the cost of executive stock options should be recognized on companies' income statements:

"If options aren't a form of compensation, what are they? If compensation isn't an expense, what is it? And if expenses shouldn't go into the calculation of earnings, where in the world should they go?"

# BUFFETT AND COCA-COLA

TWENTY-FIVE YEARS AGO, *in 1988, the then president of Coca-Cola, Donald Keough, called his long-term friend and onetime Omaha neighbor, Warren Buffett, with a question: "Warren, the trading in Coke stock suggests that someone is buying a lot of it. Could that possibly be you?" Said Buffett, "Well, keep it quiet between you and Roberto. But, yep, it's me." Keough, delighted, hung up to tell his boss, CEO Roberto Goizueta, while Buffett went back to buying.*

*The market crash of 1987 had hammered Coke, and Buffett picked up huge amounts of the stock in 1988 and 1989, adhering to his own famous advice: "Be greedy when others are fearful." He finished his buying in 1994, having accumulated the nice, round number of 400 million (split-adjusted) Coke shares. The position, which in 1994 gave Berkshire 7.8 percent ownership of Coke, cost nearly $1.3 billion, for an average of just under $3.25 a share.*

*That was the start of a great relationship—overall. But Buffett, who served as a Coke director from 1989 until 2007, used his power on one occasion to unseat a Coke CEO and, on another, to kill a management decision he thought bad for the company. Here are three excerpts from* Fortune *articles, the first published in the salubrious early days of the Buffett/Coke relationship, the others during times of controversy.*

## From "The World's Best Brand"

### May 31, 1993

*Excerpts from an article by John Huey*

S ays Buffett: "If you run across one good idea for a business in your lifetime, you're lucky, and fundamentally this is the best large business in the world. [Its product] sells for an extremely moderate price. It's universally liked—the per capita consumption goes up almost every year in almost every country. There isn't any other product like it." . . .

On Goizueta and Keough: "If you have the 1927 Yankees, all you wish for is their immortality," Buffett says . . . "As long as we have the kind of people who are as focused as they are, I don't worry about the business. If you gave me $100 billion and said take away the soft-drink leadership of Coca-Cola in the world, I'd give it back to you and say it can't be done."

*Goizueta died in 1997, Keough retired, and the new CEO, Douglas Ivester, looked more like a batboy at the plate than a Ruth or Gehrig. In early 2000, Fortune published an exclusive story whose opening paragraphs follow:*

## From "What Really Happened at Coke"

January 10, 2000

### BY BETSY MORRIS AND PATRICIA SELLERS

First of all, let's clear up the mystery about why Doug Ivester—at age 52 and after only a little more than two years on the job—suddenly resigned as chairman and CEO of Coca-Cola. He was pushed. Hard.

Sure, he was beleaguered by a string of setbacks in his short, unhappy tenure. But aides who worked with him every day—and who were as shocked as anyone when the dogged executive threw in the towel—report that everything was business as usual on the first day of December, a Wednesday, when Ivester flew from Atlanta to Chicago for a routine meeting with McDonald's executives.

Upon his return, everything seemed to have changed. What hasn't come to light until now is that while Ivester was in Chicago he attended another, very private meeting—this one called by Coke's two most powerful directors, Warren Buffett and Herbert Allen. At that meeting the two directors informed Ivester that they had lost confidence in his leadership.

For most of the past year Buffett had remained in the wings, while Allen had had numerous conversations with Ivester about his cramped management style. This time it was different, according to well-placed sources close to the situation. Together, Buffett and Allen, the board's two 800-pound gorillas, told Ivester that they had reached an irreversible conclusion: He was no longer the man who should be running Coke. It was time for a change.

The meeting was nonconfrontational—even sympathetic—and it apparently ended without a conclusion as to the next step. Conceivably Ivester could have decided to fight. But it's also conceivable that Buffett and Allen could have decided to force the issue, perhaps as early as the next board meeting, scheduled for two weeks later. Their leadership as directors is outsized, considering that Buffett's Berkshire Hathaway (of which he owns 31%) controls about 200 million shares, or 8.1%, of Coke, while Allen owns or controls about nine million shares.

Whatever they were all thinking when they left the meeting, Ivester returned to Atlanta and called an emergency board meeting for that Sunday, at which he quit. His announcement stunned executives, directors, employees, and Wall Street—even the man who was named to replace him: Doug Daft, a 56-year-old Australian whose experience has mostly been running Coke's businesses in Asia.

*Daft came in believing that Coke needed to diversify into non-cola drinks. Months after taking over in early 2000, he championed a $15.7 billion merger with Quaker Oats, which owned Gatorade. The deal was to be done with Coke stock, and that ran into Buffett's strong conviction that using stock in a merger often causes the acquirer to give up more value than it gets. A five-hour Coke board meeting followed in which Buffett led the way in arguing against the deal. Here is my account of the Coke debate (part of a sidebar in a 2001 article).*

## A Sidebar from "The Value Machine"

February 19, 2001

### BY CAROL LOOMIS

**B**uffett was a true gorilla, though by no means the only director opposed, in persuading Coke to drop its plan to buy Quaker Oats. Buffett will hold his tongue in a board meeting if a proposal up for discussion just nibbles at shareholder value. But if a monster bite is to be taken, he won't stay quiet—and in this case he thought the price Coke was proposing to pay, all of it in stock, was just too much. The terms would have left Coke giving up more than 10% of its very valuable self for assets that, even assuming some synergies, did not strike Buffett as granting Coke's shareholders an acceptable payoff, even over the long-term. By the time Buffett got through presenting his argument, the plan to buy Quaker was effectively dead. Debating Buffett about price is not, for most people, a rewarding experience. He is simply too logical and smart to be sent to defeat.

*Under Daft and his successor as CEO, Neville Isdell, Coke's growth stalled and its stock languished. The next CEO, Muhtar Kent, took over in 2008, just in time for the credit crisis. But he has presided over good growth in the last couple of years, and as of mid-2013 Coke stock was selling at $40 per share (versus the all-time high of $41, set in the bubble year of 1998).*

*Berkshire still owns all of its 400 million shares. Against their cost basis of about $1.3 billion, they were valued at $16 billion in midyear 2013. Coke's repurchases of stock have raised Berkshire's holding to 9 percent of what Buffett still thinks (well, leaving aside Berkshire) is the best large business in the world. —CL*

*The full text of the three Coke articles excerpted here is available at fortune.com/buffettbook.*

# How Buffett Views Risk

April 4, 1994

*An excerpt from Buffett's letter to shareholders in the*
*1993 Berkshire Hathaway annual report*

The strategy we've adopted precludes our following standard diversification dogma. Many pundits would therefore say the standard must be riskier than that employed by more conventional investors. We disagree. We believe that a policy of portfolio concentration may well *decrease* risk if it raises, as it should, both the intensity with which an investor thinks about a business and the comfort level he must feel with its economic characteristics before buying into it. In stating this opinion, we define risk, using dictionary terms, as the possibility of loss or injury.

Academics, however, like to define investment "risk" differently, averring that it is the relative volatility of a stock or a portfolio of stocks—that is, their volatility as compared to that of a large universe of stocks. Employing data bases and statistical skills, these academics compute with precision the "beta" of a stock—its relative volatility in the past—and then build arcane capital investment and capital allocation theories around this calculation. In their hunger for a single statistic to measure risk, however, they forget a fundamental principle: It is better to be approximately right than precisely wrong.

For owners of a business—and that's the way we think of shareowners—the academic's definition of risk is far off the mark, so much so that it produces absurdities. For example, under beta-based theory, a stock that has dropped very sharply compared to the market—as had Washington Post when we bought it in 1973—becomes "riskier" at the lower price than it was at the higher price. Would that description have then made *any* sense to someone who was offered the entire company at a vastly reduced price?

In fact, the true investor *welcomes* volatility . . . because a wildly fluctuating market means that irrationally low prices will periodically be attached to solid businesses. It is impossible to see how the availability of such prices can be thought of as increasing the hazards for an investor who is totally free to either ignore the market or exploit its folly.

# Buffett Hits $200 Million Downdraft

## November 17, 1994

### BY COLIN LEINSTER

**Q**uick: What's the fastest way to become a millionaire in the airline business? Answer: Start with a billion. So goes a joke from Warren Buffett, who, by *Fortune*'s estimate, is sitting on a paper loss of about $200 million on his $358 million investment in the embattled USAir Group.

But behind the scenes, Buffett is obviously talking tougher. USAir's 1994 proxy contains what amounts to a warning. He and Charles Munger, vice-chairman of Berkshire Hathaway, Buffett's company and investing arm, will quit as USAir directors if the company doesn't win cost-cutting concessions from its union. USAir has the highest costs among domestic carriers and aims to slice $1 billion out of its overhead, with $500 million coming from labor.

Like other insiders, Buffett declines to comment on where USAir is headed. But the September 8 crash near Pittsburgh, which killed 132 people, made a cloudy future even murkier. Observers at first hoped the disaster would encourage pilots, machinists, and flight attendants to agree to bigger cuts. But that optimism soon faded. Says Robert Flocke, a spokesman for the Air Line Pilots Association: "Every time before when the company has been in trouble, it has come to the pilots and then squandered what it got."

Analyst John Pincavage of the Transportation Group points out that money-losing, cash-strapped USAir has no control over other big costs such as fuel prices. Says he: "There's not a lot of room for anything to go wrong, no barrier between USAir and sailing into the sunset."

USAir spokeswoman Andrea Butler insists that anything like going into Chapter 11 "is a last resort. Management is more focused on working out productive labor agreements." The airline may well have to add profit-sharing and board representation to its current offer. Such sweeteners were part of how Northwest and TWA settled their union differences.

*Editor's note: Buffett's misstep into USAir in the early 1990s drew so much public attention—and no doubt produced so many chuckles—that many people think to this day that the investment was a painful loser for Berkshire. But in 1996, a new CEO, Stephen Wolf, took over the company and engineered what Buffett described in Berkshire's 1997 annual report as a "resuscitation" bordering on the "miraculous." USAir's stock went from a low of $4 a share to $75 a share—and the conversion rights in Berkshire's USAir convertible preferreds therefore shot up in value. Dividends on the preferred that had not been paid were made up and were also, because of their lateness, accompanied by compensatory payments. With the preferred to be called for redemption in 1998, Buffett said in the 1997 annual report: "It is now almost certain that our US Airways share will* *produce a decent profit—that is, if my cost for Maalox is excluded—and the gain could even be indecent." The dollar gain was never reported. But much later, in the 2007 annual report, Buffett called it "hefty." He also noted what had happened in the intervening years to USAir: "The company went bankrupt. Twice."*

# BUFFETT AND GATES

WE'VE PUT THESE TWO articles together because they appeared sequentially and have the shared virtue of dipping into the friendship—the surprising friendship—between Buffett and Bill Gates in its early days. What we have here, after all, is not only an age difference of twenty-five years, but also a yawning gap then (if less exclusively so now) between what the two were obsessively interested in: investments for Buffett and technology for Gates.

In 1991, nonetheless, a mutual friend of the two titans, Meg Greenfield, editor of the Washington Post editorial page and a longtime friend of Gates's mother brought them together. Greenfield, in fact, was intrigued by her idea: "I was not unaware," Greenfield told Fortune in the mid-1990s, "that this was an interesting pairing."

The site of their meeting was the country home, outside Seattle, of Mary and Bill Gates, the other Bill's parents. Greenfield, who grew up in Seattle and kept a house there, brought her houseguests, Buffett and Washington Post Co. CEO Katharine Graham. They came to the gathering in Greenfield's ancient, cramped Subaru. Bill and his girlfriend (soon to be wife), Melinda French, arrived more grandly, in a helicopter. Bill hoped, even upon landing, to escape early: He hadn't wanted to come, but had given in to his mother's wishes that he be there.

His view changed immediately as he began talking to Buffett. Their minds connected, as if each man had quickly realized that, for once, the playing field for brilliance had leveled out. That was the start of a close friendship that lasts to this day—and that, in particular, has gone on to create philanthropic history.

Back to the nature of the two articles that follow. The first was a box within a long piece about Gates. The second piece, by Gates himself, is ostensibly his review of a new Buffett book by Roger Lowenstein. But more than half the article is simply Gates presenting, in a wide-ranging way, his impressions of Buffett.

The second piece is also, to my knowledge, unique in Fortune's history, being probably the only article in our more than eighty years to have been first published in another business magazine, specifically Harvard Business Review. The article, nonetheless, seemed so interesting to Fortune's editors—one billionaire talking about the other—that we secured permission from Bill Gates to republish it verbatim. Thanks to the author, once again. —CL

# The Billionaire Buddies

January 16, 1995

## BY BRENT SCHLENDER

Who says you can't put a value on friendship? When the pals are Bill Gates and Warren Buffett, the total comes to nearly $19 billion, give or take a few hundred million.

For four years now, America's two richest men—at the moment, Buffett is No. 1—have cultivated an intriguing cross-generational friendship in which their wealth is probably their biggest similarity. "We're sort of the odd couple, aren't we?" says Buffett, the chairman of Berkshire Hathaway Inc. and self-professed technophobe. Buffett, 64, is the epitome of the Industrial Age investor, spinning billions from holdings in the most basic of businesses—companies that make things like shoes, soda pop, and razor blades. Gates, on the other hand, is the Midas of the Information Age, who made his billions selling pure thought stuff.

The two were introduced by mutual friend Meg Greenfield, a *Washington Post* editorial page editor who, like Gates, is a native of Seattle. The billionaires avail each other of free advice from time to time. For years Gates tried in vain to convince Buffett that he ought to at least think about buying a personal computer. (Buffett finally bought one at the behest of another friend so he could play online bridge. Among his playing partners is Bill Gates' dad.) And Buffett, who flies around the country in a used jet he calls *The Indefensible*, has offered Gates some sage advice about such corporate status symbols. Says Buffett: "I told him that I didn't get mine until I was 55, and that maybe he ought to save something for his old age too."

Buffett also helped Gates find a cut-rate deal on a diamond ring when he got engaged a couple of years ago. Gates cooked up a scheme to surprise his wife-to-be, Melinda French, with a trip to Omaha to pick out a ring at Borsheim's, the famous jewelry store owned by Berkshire Hathaway. Gates chuckles as he recalls: "Warren had them open up the store on a Sunday especially for us. On the way there, he told me that when he first got engaged, he spent 6% of his net worth on the ring, and that as a sign of true loyalty, I should do the same for Melinda."

The two occasionally tease each other about who is richer. Knowing that Gates is an inveterate gambler, Buffett once brought a pair of what he calls "tricky" dice to a get-together. Says Buffett: "I was trying to put him in second place permanently, but Bill immediately caught on, of course." Buffett also jokes that "if I had known that it was Bill that I was bidding against for Leonardo da Vinci's notebook, I would have bid the price up even higher."

What does Gates enjoy most about Buffett? The conversation. Says he: "Warren is so humble and yet so good at describing complicated things. At the surface level it's funny for him to quote, say, Mae West when talking about his investment philosophy, but of course he is really saying something much deeper. He's like that all the time, so I'm always learning something about him."

# Gates on Buffett

February 5, 1996

## BY BILL GATES

R oger Lowenstein begins his biography of Warren Buffett with a disclaimer. He reveals that he is a longtime investor in Berkshire Hathaway, the company that under Buffett's guidance has seen its share price rise in 33 years from $7.60 to approximately $30,000.

In reviewing Lowenstein's book, I must begin with a disclaimer too. I can't be neutral or dispassionate about Warren Buffett, because we're close friends. We recently vacationed together in China with our wives. I think his jokes are all funny. I think his dietary practices—lots of burgers and Cokes—are excellent. In short, I'm a fan.

It's easy to be a fan of Warren's, and doubtless many readers of *Buffett: The Making of an American Capitalist* (Random House, 1995) will join the growing ranks. Lowenstein's book is a straightforward account of Buffett's remarkable life. It doesn't fully convey what a fun, humble, charming guy Warren is, but his uniqueness comes across. No one is likely to come away from it saying, "Oh, I'm like that guy."

The broad outlines of Warren's career are well known, and the book offers enjoyable detail. Lowenstein traces Warren's life from his birth in Omaha in 1930 to his first stock purchase at age 11, and from his study of the securities profession under Columbia University's legendary Benjamin Graham to his founding of the Buffett Partnership at age 25. The author describes Buffett's secretiveness about the stocks he picked for the partnership, and his contrasting openness about his guiding principle, which is to buy stocks at bargain basement prices and hold them patiently. As Warren once explained in a letter to his partners, "This is the cornerstone of our investment philosophy: Never count on making a good sale. Have the purchase price be so attractive that even a mediocre sale gives good results."

Lowenstein describes how Warren took control of Berkshire Hathaway and cash-cowed its dying textile business in order to purchase stock in other companies. The book traces how Berkshire evolved into a holding company and how its investment philosophy evolved as Warren learned to look beyond financial data and recognize the economic potential of unique franchises like dominant newspapers. Today Berkshire owns companies such as See's Candies, the Buffalo News, and World Book, as well as major positions in companies such as American Express, Capital Cities/ABC (about to be Disney), Coca-Cola, Gannett, Gillette, and the Washington Post Co.

Readers are likely to come away from the book feeling better educated about investing and business, but whether those lessons will translate into great investment results is less than certain. Warren's gift is being able to think ahead of the crowd, and it requires more than taking his aphorisms to heart to accomplish that—although Warren is full of aphorisms well worth taking to heart.

For example, Warren likes to say that there are no called strikes in investing. Strikes occur only when you swing and miss. When you're at bat, you shouldn't concern yourself with every pitch, nor should you regret good pitches that you don't swing at. In other words, you don't have to have an opinion about every stock or other investment opportunity, nor should you feel bad if a stock you didn't pick goes up dramatically. Warren says that in your lifetime you should swing at only a couple dozen pitches, and he advises doing careful homework so that the few swings you do take are hits.

His penchant for long-term investments is reflected in another aphorism: "You should invest in a business that even a fool can run, because someday a fool will." He doesn't believe in businesses that rely for their success on every employee being excellent. Nor does he believe that great people help all that much when the fundamentals of a business are bad. He says that when good management is brought into a fundamentally bad business, it's the reputation of the business that remains intact.

Warren installs strong managers in the companies Berkshire owns, and tends to leave them pretty much alone. His basic proposition to managers is that to the degree that a company spins off cash, which good businesses do, the managers can trust Warren to invest it wisely. He doesn't encourage managers to diversify. Managers are expected to concentrate on the businesses they know well so that Warren is free to concentrate on what he does well: invest.

My reaction upon meeting Warren took me by surprise. Whenever somebody says to me, "You've got to meet my friend so-and-so; he's the smartest guy ever," my defenses go up. Most people are quick to conclude that someone or something they encounter personally is exceptional. This is just human nature. Everybody wants to know someone or something superlative. As a result, people overestimate the merit of that to which they've been exposed. So the fact that people called Warren Buffett unique didn't impress me much.

In fact, I was extremely skeptical when my mother suggested I take a day away from work to meet him on July 5, 1991. What were he and I supposed to talk about, P/E ratios? I mean, spend all day with a guy who just picks stocks? Especially when there's lots of work to do? Are you kidding?

I said to my mom, "I'm working on July 5. We're really busy. I am sorry."

She said, "Kay Graham will be there."

Now, that caught my attention. I had never met Graham, but I was impressed with how well she had run the Washington Post Co. and by her newspaper's role in political history. As it happened, Kay and Warren had been great friends for years, and one of Warren's shrewdest investments was in Post stock. Kay, Warren, and a couple of prominent journalists happened to be in the Seattle area together, and owing to an unusual circumstance they all squeezed into a little car that morning for a long drive to my family's weekend home, which is a couple of hours outside the city. Some of the people in the car were as skeptical as I was. "We're going to spend the whole day at these people's house?" someone in the cramped car asked. "What are we going to do all day?"

My mom was really hard-core that I come. "I'll stay a couple of hours, and then I'm going back," I told her.

When I arrived, Warren and I began talking about how the newspaper business was being changed by the arrival of retailers who did less advertising. Then he started asking me about IBM: "If you were building IBM from scratch, how would it look different? What are the growth businesses for IBM? What has changed for them?"

He asked good questions and told educational stories. There's nothing I like so much as learning, and I had never met anyone who thought about business in such a clear way. On that first day, he introduced me to an intriguing analytic exercise that he does. He'll choose a year—say, 1970—and examine the ten highest market-capitalization companies from around then. Then he'll go forward to 1990 and look at how those companies fared. His enthusiasm for the exercise was contagious. I stayed the whole day, and before he drove off with his friends, I even agreed to fly out to Nebraska to watch a football game with him.

When you are with Warren, you can tell how much he loves his work. It comes across in many ways. When he explains stuff, it's never "Hey, I'm smart about this, and I'm going to impress you." It's more like "This is so interesting, and it's actually very simple. I'll just explain it to you, and you'll realize how dumb it was that it took me a long time to figure it out." And when he shares it with you, using his keen sense of humor to help make the point, it does seem simple.

Warren and I have the most fun when we're taking the same data that everybody else has and coming up with new ways of looking at them that are both novel and, in a sense, obvious. Each of us tries to do this all the time for our respective companies, but it's particularly enjoyable and stimulating to discuss these insights with each other.

We are quite candid and not at all adversarial. Our business interests don't overlap much, although his printed World Book Encyclopedia competes with my electronic Microsoft Encarta. Warren stays away from technology companies because he likes investments in which he can predict winners a decade in advance—an almost impossible feat when it comes to technology. Unfortunately for Warren, the world of technology knows no boundaries. Over time, most business assets will be affected by technology's broad reach—although Gillette, Coca-Cola, and See's should be safe.

One area in which we do joust now and then is mathematics. Once Warren presented me with four unusual dice, each with a unique combination of numbers (from 0 to 12) on its sides. He proposed that we each choose one of the dice, discard the third and fourth, and wager on who would roll the highest number most often. He graciously offered to let me choose first. Then he said, "Okay, because you get to pick first, what kind of odds will you give me?"

I knew something was up. "Let me look at those dice," I said.

After studying the numbers on their faces for a moment, I said, "This is a losing proposition. You choose first."

Once he chose a die, it took me a couple of minutes to figure out which of the three remaining dice to choose in response. Because of the careful selection of the numbers on each die, they were nontransitive. Each of the four dice could be beaten by one of the others: die A would tend to beat die B, die B would tend to beat die C, die C would tend to beat die D, and die D would tend to beat die A. This meant that there was no winning first choice of a die, only a winning second choice. It was counterintuitive, like a lot of things in the business world.

Warren is great with numbers, and I love math too. But being good with numbers doesn't necessarily correlate with being a good investor. Warren doesn't outperform other investors because he computes odds better. That's not it at all. Warren never makes an investment where the difference between doing it and not doing it relies on the second digit of computation. He doesn't invest—take a swing of the bat—unless the opportunity appears unbelievably good.

One habit of Warren's that I admire is that he keeps his schedule free of meetings. He's good at saying no to things. He knows what he likes to do—and what he does, he does unbelievably well. He likes to sit in his office and read and think. There are a few things he'll do beyond that, but not many. One point that Lowenstein makes that is absolutely true is that Warren is a creature of habit. He grew up in Omaha, and he wants to stay in Omaha. He has gotten to know a certain set of people, and he'd like to spend time with those people. He's not a person who seeks out exotic new things. Warren, who just turned 65, still lives in the Omaha house he bought for himself at age 25. His affinity for routine extends to his investment practices too. Warren sticks to companies that he is comfortable with. He doesn't do much investing outside the U.S.

There are a few companies that he has decided are great long-term investments. And despite the self-evident mathematics that there must be a price that fully anticipates all the good work that those companies will do in the future, he just won't sell their stock no matter what the price is. I think his reluctance to sell is more philosophical than optimization-driven, but who am I to second-guess the world's most successful investor? Warren's reluctance to sell fits in with his other tendencies.

Warren and I share certain values. We both feel lucky that we were born into an era in which our skills have turned out to be so remunerative. Had we been born at a different time, our skills might not have had much value. Since we don't plan on spending much of what we have accumulated, we can make sure our wealth benefits society. In a sense, we're both working for charity. In any case, our heirs will get only a small portion of what we accumulate, because we both believe that passing on huge wealth to children isn't in their or society's interest. Warren likes to say that he wants to give his children enough money for them to do anything but not enough for them to do nothing. I thought about this before I met Warren, and hearing him articulate it crystallized my feelings.

Lowenstein is a good collector of facts, and *Buffett: The Making of an American Capitalist* is competently written. Warren has told me that the book is in most respects accurate. He says he is going to write his own book someday, but given how much he loves to work and how hard it is to write a book (based on my own personal experience), I think it will be a number of years before he does it. When it comes out, I'm sure it will be one of the most valuable business books ever.

Already, Warren's letters to shareholders in the Berkshire Hathaway annual reports are among the best of business literature. Much of Lowenstein's analysis comes from those letters, as it should. If, after reading *Buffett*, you're intrigued by the man and his methods, I strongly commend to you the annual reports—even ones from ten or 15 years ago. They are available in many libraries.

Other books have been written about Warren Buffett and his investment strategy, but until Warren writes his own book, this is the one to read.

Originally titled "What I Learned from Warren Buffett" by Bill Gates. Copyright 1995 Microsoft Corp. Originally published by the *Harvard Business Review* (January/February 1996 issue). Reprinted by permission of Microsoft Corp.

# From "Untangling the Derivatives Mess"

March 20, 1995

*An excerpt from an article by Carol Loomis*

*Here are the last two paragraphs of this article:*

Given the range of complications that derivatives present, outside directors cannot possibly achieve close communion with the contracts their companies hold. Most chief executives won't master the game, either. In the end, the choice of what risks to hedge, what derivatives to employ in doing it, and how to draw the bright line between risk management and speculation will be largely left to financial people down the corridor—some of whom, recent train wrecks notwithstanding, may think of themselves as running a profit center. And on the other end of their phones will be derivatives salespeople trying to sell the latest innovation, which assuredly will not be a plain-vanilla hedge.

It's not a particularly cheerful picture—not for a problem as big as derivatives. So maybe what we need is new thinking, a fresh approach, a suggestion so radical it goes off the page. Here's one: Warren E. Buffett, chairman of Berkshire Hathaway, says he'd deal with derivatives by requiring every CEO to affirm in his annual report that he understands each derivatives contract his company has entered into. Says Buffett: "Put that in, and I suspect you'll fix up just about every problem that exists." In a market that seems to thrive on complexity and obfuscation, such a solution won't happen. It's too simple. But he's right.

# Two Items from "Now Hear This"

**W**arren E. Buffett, 64, chairman of Berkshire Hathaway, which sells its candy, shoes, and other products at the annual meeting:

"Though we'd like to think of the meeting as a spiritual experience, we must remember that even the saintliest of religions includes the ritual of the collection plate."

**C**harles T. Munger, 71, vice-chairman of Berkshire Hathaway, referring to litigation involving the company:

"They subpoenaed our staffing papers. Not only didn't we have any staffing papers, we didn't have any staff."

# From "Why Warren Buffett's Betting Big on American Express"

<hr>

October 30, 1995

<hr>

### *Excerpts and a sidebar from an article by Linda Grant*

*When Buffett is accumulating a stock, he doesn't want it known. When the news gets out—usually because of an SEC filing—and Buffett figures he still might buy more of the stock, he won't say much about why he likes it. That was the case with American Express in 1995. The business press, including* Fortune, *was calling, but Buffett wasn't talking.*

*So we wrote our story anyway, even flagging it on the cover with a title more skeptical than the inside title above. The cover read, "Why Is Warren Buffett Betting Billions on This House of Cards?" The reality is that the* Fortune *writer and editors working on this story didn't like Amex's prospects at all, but had to deal with the annoying fact that Buffett apparently did.*

*Our approach to this problem was to write a long article beginning and ending with Buffett, and also including a sidebar about him, but that otherwise dealt at length with the difficulties facing Harvey Golub, the company's new CEO. Golub had come from consulting firm McKinsey.* Fortune *took the view that a consultant's talents—cost-cutting and selling divisions, in particular—might not be ideal for restoring the prestige that Amex had lost in the early 1990s.*

*Here is what* Fortune *had to say about Buffett in several paragraphs and the sidebar. At the end we will report what he eventually had to say about the subject himself.* —CL

## The story's beginning:

Warren Buffett loves to tell a parable about the stock market's irrationality. It was 1963, and a scandal involving fake inventories of salad oil at a small subsidiary of American Express drove down the price of Amex shares. How bad a problem was this? To find out, Buffett spent an evening with the cashier at Ross's Steak House in Omaha seeing if people would stop using their green cards. The scandal didn't seem to give any of the diners indigestion, so Buffett seized the opportunity to buy 5% of the company for $13 million. He later sold his holding for a $20 million profit.

Now Buffett hopes to relive the story—with much larger numbers. Over the past few years the CEO of Berkshire Hathaway has accumulated more than 49 million shares of American Express, a 10.1% stake. Its value, about $2.2 billion, makes it one of Buffett's largest investments, along with Coca-Cola, Gillette, and Capital Cities/ ABC. Once again he thinks Wall Street is irrationally down on Amex stock. The trouble this time is not salad oil but a long and well-publicized catalogue of strife: A nearly dysfunctional management team led by James Robinson III damaged the brand in the early 1990s; his grand strategy to build a financial supermarket fell like a house of cards, with Amex's Shearson

Lehman brokerage subsidiary eating up $4 billion in capital before being sold last year. More recently the tarnished American Express card has been losing market share to Visa and MasterCard as Amex's principal consumer benefit—prestige—becomes a tougher sell. And the company's international business, say analysts, is in the doldrums.

Always the patient investor, Buffett—worth $14.2 billion at last count—believes the latest troubles are little more than a distraction. What he likes is exactly what has made him rich before: a mighty brand coupled with a healthy cash flow. After all, American Express, according to London marketing group Interbrand, is still one of the ten most-recognized brands in the world. Buffett believes the name remains "synonymous with financial integrity and money substitutes around the world." As he explained to Berkshire Hathaway shareholders at last spring's annual meeting: "By far the most important factor in [Amex's] future for a great many years to come will be the credit card. We think American Express's management thinks well about . . . how to keep the card special." Buffett probably isn't particularly concerned about the company's loss of market share. More likely, he's gambling that Amex, even if it fails to grow dramatically, will become a very profitable niche player in the card market.

But if American Express is to fulfill Buffett's expectations, it will have to breathe new life into its brand—no easy task. . . .

### And at the story's end:

No matter how tough the challenges that lie ahead for Amex, it's rarely wise to bet against Warren Buffett. After all, he has wagered on strong brands like Coke and Gillette and made a bundle. He also invested successfully in auto insurer GEICO, which, like Amex, has a strong cash flow. When Buffett comes up aces, it's usually because he's backing a strong management hand. What's hard to see this time around is how a bunch of consultants can rake in the pot in a truly cutthroat game.

## HOW BUFFETT RATED AMEX A BUY
## OCTOBER 30, 1995

### A Sidebar by Linda Grant

Just about everyone knows that Warren Buffett is a zealous disciple of value investing, the approach championed by Wall Street legend Benjamin Graham in the 1930s and 1940s. Value investors buy stocks only when they believe the market is temporarily—and irrationally—valuing a company at far below what they call its intrinsic value.

continued on next page

continued from previous page

But many are mystified by Buffett's purchase of roughly $2 billion of American Express shares. Wall Street has shunned the stock in recent years as Amex began losing market share and suffered from problems at its former brokerage subsidiary, Shearson Lehman. But maybe it's all the bad news that attracted Buffett in the first place. After all, a primary Graham tenet is to think for yourself and understand the difference between price and value. He also counseled followers to rake the market for bargains.

Value investor Robert G. Hagstrom Jr., author of *The Warren Buffett Way* and portfolio manager of Philadelphia's Focus Trust, points out that to understand any Buffett investment, investors must start with his philosophy, stated in his 1989 letter to shareholders of Berkshire Hathaway. Buffett wrote that the value of any business today is "calculated by taking all future cash flows—in and out—and discounting them at prevailing interest rates. So valued, all businesses, from manufacturers of buggy whips to operators of cellular telephones, become economic equals."

In other words, Hagstrom believes that Buffett determines a stock's value as if it were a bond. He starts with "net owner earnings," which is reported earnings plus depreciation and amortization minus capital investments. For Amex this was $1.4 billion last year, the same amount the company reported as its earnings, although that's not always the case. Then he asks: If Amex were a bond with annual coupons of $1.4 billion, how much would the coupon grow, and what would the bond be worth ten years out?

"It's difficult to determine a company's coupon," says Hagstrom, "because you have to make best-guess estimates about a rate of growth."

This is very basic financial theory, but of course the secret is in the doing. So far no one has cracked the Buffett valuation code, but Hagstrom has tried. His model calculates Amex's intrinsic value per share at $86.77. The spread between $86.77 and Amex's recent market price of about $44 represents a margin of safety. "It is a big buffer," says Hagstrom, "that will protect investors even if Amex loses money in a bad year." Liking the equation, Hagstrom himself decided to buy some 8,000 Amex shares for his own account.

*All that is what* Fortune *had to say in its October 30, 1995, issue about Buffett and American Express. And when Buffett finally began talking about the subject himself—that was not until his 1997 annual shareholder letter—did he also lay out a set of deeply analytical reasons as to why he had bought Amex stock? Absolutely not. Instead, he admitted getting a tip on the golf course.*

*The background of the tip is that in 1991 Berkshire had bought $300 million of American Express Percs, a security that was essentially a common stock and that in its first three years featured a trade-off. Specifically, Berkshire got extra dividend* *payments in those years, but was also capped in the price appreciation it could realize. In August 1994, the Percs were due to convert into common, and earlier that summer Buffett was trying to decide whether to keep Amex stock or sell.*

The facts pushed him in two directions, Buffett wrote in his 1997 letter: He thought Amex CEO Harvey Golub was outstanding and would realize the company's full potential; he was worried, though, about the relentless competition that Amex was getting from other card companies, especially Visa. "Weighing the arguments," Buffett said, "I leaned toward sale."

But then he played golf one 1994 day in Prouts Neck, Maine, with Frank Olson, CEO of Hertz. Wrote Buffett in his letter: "Frank is a brilliant manager, with intimate knowledge of the card business. So from the first tee on I was quizzing him about the industry. By the time we reached the second green, Frank had convinced me that Amex's corporate card was a terrific franchise, and I had decided not to sell. On the back nine I turned buyer, and in a few months Berkshire owned 10% of the company."

Since the end of 1994, a midway point in Buffett's buying of American Express common, Berkshire has realized, through mid-2013, an average annual compounded total return of almost 14 percent. (Included in that calculation is the value, at the distribution date, of a company that Amex spun off in 2005, Ameriprise; the distribution was treated as a special Amex dividend, which—like all dividends—went into the calculation of total return.) At mid-2013, Berkshire's Amex stock had a cost basis of $1.3 billion and a market value of $11.3 billion.

Nice, but that is not to say Berkshire has lacked for drama while holding Amex. Between July 2007 and March 2009, as financial stocks got shellacked, Amex dropped from $65 a share to $10, before it began to climb back. Naturally, Buffett just patiently watched. By the middle of 2013, Amex stock was in new-high territory, rising to nearly $80. Amex has meanwhile bought in large quantities of its own stock, to the degree that Berkshire now owns 13 percent of the company. —CL

*The full text of "Why Buffett's Betting Big on American Express" is available at fortune.com/buffettbook.*

# Gift That Gives—A Bit O' Buffett

March 18, 1996

**BY BETHANY MCLEAN**

The $32,800 pricetag on Berkshire Hathaway has thwarted both owners who wanted to give (even one share would trigger gift taxes) and little outsiders who wanted to own Warren Buffett's hot stock. On May 6, shareholders will vote on Buffett's plan to sell at least $100 million of new Class B shares for a mere $1,000 or so each. Current shares, to be renamed Class A, can convert to B's at any time. "We just want to attract those who are attracted to us," Buffett says. To deter a slew of converts, he advises that the B's are "a tiny bit inferior" to the existing A's: They have fewer voting rights and lack the A's input on corporate donations. But for gift givers and little guys, these baby B's buy you real Buffett.

# The Bill and Warren Show

July 20, 1998

### EDITED BY BRENT SCHLENDER

*This was Bill Gates and Warren Buffett on a University of Washington stage, lecturing, so to speak, but mostly doing it by answering questions. For an introduction, I will simply reprint (with small edits) the excellent Brent Schlender paragraphs with which* Fortune *led off this historic, duopoly event.* —CL

*The queue of students stretched through the lobby and out the door of the University of Washington's Husky Union Building in Seattle on a balmy Friday afternoon in late May. You could tell by the abundance of pressed chinos and dress shirts (and the shortage of nose rings) that this wasn't the ticket line for a Phish concert. Instead, the well-groomed group was staking out prime seats for, of all things, a lecture—albeit a very special lecture. The students and a few lucky guests were to be treated to a rare, public dialogue between the two richest businessmen in the solar system: Bill Gates and Warren Buffett.*

*The billionaire buddies conceived the event to coincide with Buffett's weekend visit to Gates' home, following Microsoft's annual summit meeting for CEOs. The superinvestor and the cybertycoon asked some 350 business school students to participate in the session and invited the Public Broadcasting System and Fortune to document the affair.*

*While the students milled downstairs, Gates and Buffett bantered with their wives and a small group of friends that included, among others, Katharine Graham, the former CEO of the Washington Post Co., and Bill's dad and sister. They noshed on fresh fruit in a makeshift greenroom while a makeup artist powdered Bill's nose and trimmed Warren's unruly eyebrows, much to Susie Buffett's amusement. At one point the Oracle of Omaha entertained the group with a goofy imitation of Richard Nixon's "V for victory" sign.*

*As showtime approached, the two gamely posed for photos and traded barbs like old college roomies. The other guests' main concern was that the titans not be too long-winded, so everyone could get back to Gates' house in time to play bridge. It felt like a convivial family reunion—granted, of one very high-powered family.*

*For a guest in that greenroom, perhaps the most lasting impression was the cross-generational affection between America's best-known billionaires. (For the record, on that day the 42-year-old Gates' net worth hovered around $48 billion, compared with Buffett's $36 billion. Buffett, who only a few years ago was considerably richer than Gates, has managed to remain 25 years older, though.) Buffett's presence seemed to calm Gates, who acted loose and gregarious despite Microsoft's legal fisticuffs with federal trustbusters and the stress of hosting several dozen prominent CEOs for the previous two days. Although Bill has finally begun to look his age—nascent crow's-feet now crease the corners of his eyes, and* *he's no longer the beanpole he was—the Buffetts and Graham still dote on him like a wunderkind. He, in turn, treats them with a warm hint of deference, quite a contrast to his usual debater's demeanor.*

*Finally the two made their way to the stage, pausing in the wings for University of Washington Business School dean Bill Bradford's introduction. Unfortunately, the dean's remarks, which mainly praised Microsoft for hiring University of Washington students, missed the point. The funny, philosophical, extraordinary conversation that followed would be much more than a pep talk from a local employer and his pal. See for yourself.* —Brent Schlender

What do you get when you put a billionaire buddy act in front of 350 students? $84 billion of inspiration. In a meeting of incomparable minds (and unspendable net worth), Buffett and Gates muse about taking risks, motivating employees, confronting mistakes, and giving back. The result: something pretty darn close to wisdom.

# 1. How We Got Here

### *Warren and Bill explain how they became richer than God*

**BUFFETT:** I thought I ought to start this off by announcing that Bill and I have a small bet as to who would get the most applause. I suggested that I bet my house against his. We settled on a small sum, but evidently it isn't such a small sum to Bill, because just before we came out he gave me this Nebraska Cornhusker shirt to wear, and then he puts on this purple University of Washington shirt himself.

They've asked us to start out talking, the two of us, about what got us here, but then it's on to your questions. How I got here is pretty simple in my case. It's not IQ, I'm sure you'll be glad to hear. The big thing is rationality. I always look at IQ and talent as representing the horsepower of the motor, but that the output—the efficiency with which that motor works—depends on rationality. A lot of people start out with 400-horsepower motors but only get a hundred horsepower of output. It's way better to have a 200-horsepower motor and get it all into output.

So why do smart people do things that interfere with getting the output they're entitled to? It gets into the habits and character and temperament, and behaving in a rational manner. Not getting in your own way. As I said, everybody here has the ability absolutely to do anything I do and much beyond. Some of you will, and some of you won't. For the ones who won't, it will be because you get in your own way, not because the world doesn't allow you.

So I have one little suggestion for you: Pick out the person you admire the most, and then write down why you admire them. You're not to name yourself in this. And then put down the person that, frankly, you can stand the least, and write down the qualities that turn you off in that person. The qualities of the one you admire are traits that you, with a little practice, can make your own, and that, if practiced, will become habit-forming.

The chains of habit are too light to be felt until they are too heavy to be broken. At my age, I can't change any of my habits. I'm stuck. But you will have the habits 20 years from now that you decide to put into practice today. So I suggest that you look at the behavior that you admire in others and make those your own habits, and look at what you really find reprehensible in others and decide that those are things you are not going to do. If you do that, you'll find that you convert all of your horsepower into output.

**GATES:** I think Warren's absolutely right about habit. I was lucky enough when I was quite young to have an exposure to computers, which were very expensive and kind of limited in what they could do, but still they were fascinating. Some friends of mine and I talked about that a lot and decided that, because of the miracle of chip technology, they would change into something that everybody could use. We didn't see any limit to the computer's potential, and we really thought writing software was a neat thing. So we hired our friends who wrote software to see what kind of a tool this could really be—a tool for the Information Age that could magnify your brainpower instead of just your muscle power.

By pursuing that with a pretty incredible focus and by being there at the very beginning of the industry, we were able to build a company that has played a very central role in what's been a pretty big revolution. Now, fortunately, the revolution is still at the beginning. It was 23 years ago when we started the company. But there's no doubt that if we take the habits we formed and stick with them, the next 23 years should give us a lot more potential and maybe even get us pretty close to our original vision—"a computer on every desk and in every home."

**I was wondering how you define success, personally?**

**BUFFETT:** I can certainly define happiness, because happy is what I am. I get to do what I like to do every single day of the year. I get to do it with people I like, and I don't have to associate with anybody who causes my stomach to churn. I tap dance to work, and when I get there I think I'm supposed to lie on my back and paint the ceiling. It's tremendous fun. The only thing in my job that I don't like—and this just happens every three or four years—is that occasionally I have to fire somebody.

They say success is getting what you want and happiness is wanting what you get. I don't know which one applies in this case, but I do know I wouldn't be doing anything else. I'd advise you that when you go out to work, work for an organization of people you admire, because it will turn you on. I always worry about people who say, "I'm going to do this for ten years; I really don't like it very well. And then I'll do this. . . ." That's a little like saving up sex for your old age. Not a very good idea.

I have turned down business deals that were otherwise decent deals because I didn't like the people I would have to work with. I didn't see any sense in pretending. To get involved with people who cause your stomach to churn—I say it's a lot like marrying for money. It's probably a bad idea under any circumstances, but it's absolutely crazy if you're already rich, right?

**GATES:** I agree that the key point is that you've got to enjoy what you do every day. For me, that's working with very smart people and it's working on new problems. Every time we think, "Hey, we've had a little bit of success," we're pretty careful not to dwell on it too much because the bar gets raised. We've always got customer feedback telling us that the machines are too complicated and they're not natural enough. The competition, the technological breakthroughs, and the research make the computer industry, and in particular software, the most exciting field there is, and I think I have the best job in that business.

**BUFFETT:** Don't you think Dairy Queen is more important than that? [Berkshire Hathaway bought International Dairy Queen last fall, for $585 million.]

**GATES:** You can manage Dairy Queen, Warren. I'll go and buy the Dilly Bars.

**BUFFETT:** We'll raise the price when you come.

**Starting a new company is very risky. How do you determine when is the best opportunity to start a new company?**

**GATES:** When I started Microsoft, I was so excited that I didn't think of it as being all that risky. It's true, I might have gone bankrupt, but I had a set of skills that were highly employable. And my parents were still willing to let me go back to Harvard and finish my education if I wanted to.

**BUFFETT:** You've always got a job with me, Bill.

**GATES:** The thing that was scary to me was when I started hiring my friends, and they expected to be paid. And then we had customers that went bankrupt—customers that I counted on to come through. And so I soon came up with this incredibly conservative approach that I wanted to have enough money in the bank to pay a year's worth of payroll, even if we didn't get any payments coming in. I've been almost true to that the whole time. We have about $10 billion now, which is pretty much enough for the next year.

Anyway, if you're going to start a company, it takes so much energy that you'd better overcome your feeling of risk. Also, I don't think that you should necessarily start a company at the beginning of your career. There's a lot to be said for working for a company and learning how they do things first. In our case, Paul Allen and I were afraid somebody else might get there before us. It turned out we probably could've waited another year, in fact, because things were a little slow to start out, but being on the ground floor seemed very important to us.

**How do you get people to support you?**

**GATES:** At first you'll run into some skepticism. If you're young, it's hard to go lease premises. You couldn't rent a car when you were under 25, so I was always taking taxis to go see customers. When people would ask me to go have discussions in the bar, well, I couldn't go to the bar.

That's fun, because when people are first skeptical, they say, "Oh, this kid doesn't know anything." But when you show them you've really got a good product and you know something, they actually tend to go overboard. So, at least in this country, our youth was a huge asset for us once we reached a certain threshold.

# 2. The World Is Our Oyster

*Why Warren is sure everyone in China will want to drink Coke*

**How do you as businessmen take your companies global?**

**BUFFETT:** [At Berkshire Hathaway] we don't take our businesses global directly. Our two largest commitments are Coke and Gillette. Coke has 80% of its earnings coming from abroad, and Gillette has two-thirds of its earnings coming from abroad. So they are participating in a worldwide improvement in living standards, and we go global by piggybacking on them. I can sit in Omaha and let Doug Ivester [CEO of Coca-Cola] fly all over the world.

**GATES:** Our business is truly global. The PC standard is a global standard. What you need in a spreadsheet in Korea or Egypt is about the same as what you need in the U.S. We have to do some adaptation for the local languages, and that's a fun part of our business—understanding bi-directional languages and the large alphabets that you have in Chinese, Japanese, and Korean.

In fact, our market share is much higher outside the U.S. than it is inside, because it's relatively hard to set up local subsidiaries and to understand local conditions, local distribution and relationships. Since most of our competitors are from the U.S. and aren't as good at doing international business, we thrive even better in these other countries.

Most of our growth will come from outside the U.S. Here it will get to the point where it is largely a replacement market. Now, that doesn't mean U.S. customers don't want better software that can see, listen, and learn. But outside the U.S. we still have that early-growth-slope phenomenon.

**What impelled you to make a trip together to China in 1995, and how has that trip affected your global business decisions since?**

**GATES:** We went to China for a lot of reasons. Partly to relax and have fun. We found a few McDonald's there, so we didn't feel too far away from home. It was also exciting to go and see all the changes taking place, to see different parts of the country, and to meet some of the leaders.

China is a market that Microsoft had already been investing in. We've upped that a lot since then. As a percentage of our sales, though, it's tiny—well under 1%—and so even though it will double every year for the next five years, it's really only by taking a ten-year view that we can say it's worth the emphasis we're putting on it.

Although about three million computers get sold every year in China, people don't pay for the software. Someday they will, though. And as long as they're going to steal it, we want them to steal ours. They'll get sort of addicted, and then we'll somehow figure out how to collect sometime in the next decade.

**BUFFETT:** My family was amazed that I went. I never traveled beyond the outer reaches of the county in Nebraska. I had a terrific time and also confirmed my feeling that there's going to be a lot of Coca-Cola sold there in the future. I told everyone over there that it acts as an aphrodisiac.

# 3. Innovations "R" Us

## *Warren ponders Internet chewing gum*

**Both of you are innovators in your given industries. I was wondering what your definition of innovation is?**

**BUFFETT:** I don't do a lot of innovating in my work. I really have just two functions: One is to allocate capital, which I enjoy doing. And the second one is to help 15 or 20 senior managers keep a group of people enthused about what they do when they have no financial need whatsoever to do it. At least three-quarters of the managers that we have are rich beyond any possible financial need, and therefore my job is to help my senior people keep them interested enough to want to jump out of bed at six o'clock in the morning and work with all of the enthusiasm they did when they were poor and starting. If I do those two things, they do the innovation.

**GATES:** The technology business has a lot of twists and turns. Probably the reason it's such a fun business is that no company gets to rest on its laurels. IBM was more dominant than any company will ever be in technology, and yet they missed a few turns in the road. That makes you wake up every day thinking, "Hmm, let's try to make sure today's not the day we miss the turn in the road. Let's find out what's going on in speech recognition, or in artificial intelligence. Let's make sure we're hiring the kinds of people who can pull those things together, and let's make sure we don't get surprised."

Sometimes we do get taken by surprise. For example, when the Internet came along, we had it as a fifth or sixth priority. It wasn't like somebody told me about it and I said, "I don't know how to spell that." I said, "Yeah, I've got that on my list, so I'm okay." But there came a point when we realized it was happening faster and was a much deeper phenomenon than had been recognized in our strategy. So as an act of leadership I had to create a sense of crisis, and we spent a couple of months throwing ideas and E-mail around, and we went on some retreats. Eventually a new strategy coalesced, and we said, "Okay, here's what we're going to do; here's how we're going to measure ourselves internally; and here's what the world should think about what we're going to do."

That kind of crisis is going to come up every three or four years. You have to listen carefully to all the smart people in the company. That's why a company like ours has to attract a lot of people who think in different ways, it has to allow a lot of dissent, and then it has to recognize the right ideas and put some real energy behind them.

**Which countries and companies are best prepared to take advantage of the information age that is revolutionizing society?**

**BUFFETT:** When you think about it, 15 years ago this country almost had an inferiority complex about its ability to compete in the world.

**GATES:** Everybody was talking about how the Japanese had taken over consumer electronics and that the computer industry was going to be next, and that their system of hard work somehow was superior, and that we had to completely rethink what we were doing. Now, if you look at what's happened in personal computers or in business in general, or at how we allocate capital, and how we let labor move around, the U.S. has emerged in a very strong position. And so the first beneficiary of all this information technology has been the U.S.

In places like Singapore, Hong Kong, and the Scandinavian countries, people are adopting the technology at basically the same rate that we are. And there are a few countries that, relative to their level of income, are going after the technology at an even higher rate than we are because they believe so much in education. In Korea and in many parts of China we see incredible penetration of personal computers even at very low income levels, because people there have decided it's a tool to help their kids get ahead.

The whole world is going to benefit in a big way. There will be this shift where, instead of your income level being determined by what country you are from, it will be determined by your education level. Today, a Ph.D. in India doesn't make nearly as much as a Ph.D. in the U.S. When we get the Internet allowing services and advice to be transported as efficiently as goods are transported via shipping, then you'll get essentially open-market bidding for that engineer in India vs. an engineer here in the U.S. And that benefits everyone, because you're taking better advantage of those resources. So the developed countries will get the early benefit of these things. But in the long run, the people in developing countries who are lucky enough to get a good education should get absolutely the biggest boost from all this.

**BUFFETT:** I didn't grasp it at first, but it's huge. The technological revolution will change the world in dramatic ways, and quickly. Ironically, however, our approach to dealing with that is just the opposite of Bill's. I look for businesses in which I think I can predict what they're going to look like in 10 or 15 or 20 years. That means businesses that will look more or less as they do today, except that they'll be larger and doing more business internationally.

So I focus on an absence of change. When I look at the Internet, for example, I try and figure out how an industry or a company can be hurt or changed by it, and then I avoid it. That doesn't mean I don't think there's a lot of money to be made from that change, I just don't think I'm the one to make a lot of money out of it.

Take Wrigley's chewing gum. I don't think the Internet is going to change how people are going to chew gum. Bill probably does. I don't think it's going to change the fact that Coke will be the drink of preference and will gain in per capita consumption around the world; I don't think it will change whether people shave or how they shave. So we are looking for the very predictable, and you won't find the very predictable in what Bill does. As a member of society, I applaud what he is doing, but as an investor, I keep a wary eye on it.

**GATES:** This is an area where I agree strongly with Warren. I think the multiples of technology stocks should be quite a bit lower than the multiples of stocks like Coke and Gillette, because we are subject to complete changes in the rules. I know very well that in the next 10 years, if Microsoft is still a leader, we will have had to weather at least three crises.

# 4. See You in Court!

*Bill and Warren talk about tangling with trustbusters*

**What is the appropriate role for antitrust law in American business?**

**BUFFETT:** We had one civil antitrust case at the *Buffalo Evening News* in 1977. And believe it or not, in the Salomon situation in 1991, in addition to having problems with the Federal Reserve in New York, and the SEC, and the U.S. Treasury, and the U.S. Attorney for the Southern District of New York, we also had the Department of Justice antitrust division after us. I don't know what happened to the Bureau of Indian Affairs. They missed us for some reason. Those are the only two experiences I had, and in neither case did I feel that we had done anything wrong. I might add that there was never any adjudication against us either time.

I am no antitrust scholar. I met Bill eight years ago, and he's a terrific teacher. He spent six or seven hours explaining Microsoft to me. Here I am the world's biggest dummy on technology, and he explained it to me pretty darn well. When he got through with it, I bought a hundred shares of stock so I could keep track of it. That shows two things: One is that I've got an IQ of about 50, and the second is that I didn't think he had any monopoly.

**GATES:** The key role of competition law is to protect consumers and to make sure that new products get created and that those products are very innovative. And you can look at different sectors of the economy and ask, "Where is that happening very well?" No matter how you score it, there's no doubt that one sector of economy would stand out as absolutely the best, and that's the personal computer industry. I don't say the computer industry at large, because you have to remember that before personal computers came along, the structure was very different. People were stuck. Once you bought a computer from Digital or IBM or Hewlett-Packard or anyone else, the software that you created only ran on that computer.

The vision of Microsoft was that all of these computers would work the same. The reason for that is that if you want to get a lot of great software, you have to have a lot of computers out there—millions and millions of them. So you've got to make them cheap, and make them so you don't have to test the software on all the different ones. The goal of the PC industry was to have every company competing to make the most portable one, or the fastest one, or the cheapest one. That would be great for consumers, and it would spark a big software market.

The price of computing before the PC came along was going down at a certain rate, and since the PC came along it's gone down at an incredible rate. The variety and quality of software has also increased at a phenomenal rate. We're absolutely at the peak of that today. The number of new software companies being started, the number of new jobs being created, the level of investment, the number of companies going public, you name it. It's way beyond even what it was three years ago. So consumers are doing very well.

Part of the PC dynamic is that instead of asking software developers to duplicate one another's work, we take anything that's typical in all those applications and put those features in Windows. So for things like connecting to the Internet, instead of everybody having to do that themselves, we put that in. That's been the evolution—graphical user interfaces came in, hard-disk support, networking support, now Internet support, including the browser.

I think antitrust laws as written are fine. There are people who will debate whether they should be weaker, but that's of academic interest. When I come in to do business, I'm very careful to check with our lawyers to be sure we're steering a hundred miles away from anything that would be questionable. So it is somewhat of a surprise to find ourselves in an antitrust controversy. Thank goodness for the judiciary, which is an environment in which facts are tested and people can see if competition worked in the way it should and has been beneficial to consumers. There's no doubt in our minds where that is going to come out.

In the meantime, we're going to be the focus of a lot of controversy because the filing of a lawsuit is a very big deal. You've got the government taking on that challenge and saying a lot of righteous things, and that's just something we'll have to be sure doesn't distract us from what we're really all about.

# 5. What's a Company Really Worth?

*Warren explains why Berkshire stock costs more than a Lexus*

**Mr. Buffett, I was told that you have a policy against splitting stock, and I wondered if you might comment on Microsoft's history of splitting stock?**

**BUFFETT:** I've never really felt that if I went into a restaurant and said, "I want two hatchecks instead of one for my hat," I'd really be a lot better off. But I also don't have any quarrel with companies that do split their stock, and I don't think Microsoft's been hurt by it.

I think that our policy fits us very well. There's nothing in my religious upbringing that causes me to recoil from stock splits. I'm on the boards of three companies, two of which have split their stock in the last couple of years. I happen to think that by not splitting Berkshire stock, we attract a slightly more long-term-oriented group of investors. What you want to do is attract shareholders that are very much like you, with the same time horizons and expectations. We don't talk about quarterly earnings, we don't have an investor relations department, and we don't have conference calls with Wall Street analysts, because we don't want people who are focusing on what's going to happen next quarter or even next year. We want people to join us because they want to be with us until they die.

If I were to split the stock dramatically, would I change that shareholder composition much? No, but I'd change it just a little. And remember, all the shareholder seats are filled, just like this auditorium. If I say something that offends all of you, and you all leave and another group comes in, am I better off or worse off? Well, that depends upon what they're like and what you're like. But I think I already have a very good group of shareholders who are attracted to these policies, and I think this policy reinforces it slightly.

**GATES:** Warren has done something admirable by signaling to people that it's a "different stock" and that they ought to think of Berkshire Hathaway as being a little different from your typical company. Having that unusual stock price is probably a good thing, as long as the newspaper doesn't screw it up. He's caused a lot of problems, you know, with the widths of those columns in the stock tables.

**Mr. Buffett, what's your response to those who say that traditional methods for valuing companies are obsolete in this market?**

**BUFFETT:** I think it's hard to find companies that meet our tests of being undervalued in this market, but I don't think that the methods of valuation have changed. It's just that in some markets, like in the mid-1970s, every security you looked at was really dramatically undervalued. I once ran an investment partnership for about 13 years, ending in 1969, and closed it up because I couldn't find anything. I hadn't lost the ability to value companies; there just weren't any left that were cheap enough, and I wasn't in the business of shorting stocks.

But I think that there's no magic to evaluating any financial asset. A financial asset means, by definition, that you lay out money now to get money back in the future. If every financial asset were valued properly, they would all sell at a price that reflected all of the cash that would be received from them forever until Judgment Day, discounted back to the present at the same interest rate. There wouldn't be any risk premium, because you'd know what coupons were printed on this "bond" between now and eternity. That method of valuation is exactly what should be used whether you're in 1974 or you're in 1998. If I can't do that, then I don't buy. So I'll wait.

**Would you look for a higher price-to-earnings ratio at this point than you did in 1969?**

**BUFFETT:** That ratio would be affected by interest rates. The difference between now and 1969 or any other time, in terms of calculating a valuation, wouldn't be affected by anything else. Now, if you looked at the overall market, returns on equity are much higher than they were in 1969 or 1974, or any other time in history. So if you're going to say you're going to value the overall market, the question becomes: "Do you crank in the present 20% returns on equity for American business in aggregate, and say that's a realistic figure to stick on for this future that runs out until eternity?" I'd say that's a fairly reckless assumption and doesn't leave much margin of safety. And I would say that present market levels discount a lot of that, and so that makes me quite cautious.

**Do you feel that technology has made businesses more efficient to the point that you can pay more for them?**

**GATES:** There's definitely a one-time lift when you start using technology, and particularly if U.S. companies are using it better than their competitors outside the U.S. You get the ability to communicate better, and you get global scale in a lot of businesses that wouldn't have had it before.

When you look at the really big earners, the ones generating this 20% return on equity and going to that worldwide marketplace—companies like Coca-Cola or Microsoft or Boeing or GE—I know that every one of those has been helped by technology. But that cannot explain why ten years from now they'd be getting that kind of return on equity. Almost certainly there's something ephemeral about current conditions.

**BUFFETT:** I'm sure technology has made companies more efficient, and if I thought otherwise, I'd be afraid to say so with Bill sitting right here beside me. But the question you might ponder is this: Let's just say that I found a way to clone Jack Welch, and ran off 499 clones of him. Jack continued to run General Electric, and these other 499 ran the rest of the *Fortune* 500. Is the *Fortune* 500 going to have a higher return on equity five years from now or not?

I don't think the answer to that is easy. Because if you get 500 Jack Welches out there, they are going to be doing things in a competitive way that may well produce lower returns for American business than if you've got a bunch of clods out there and a guy like Jack competing with them. If you've got great variation in the quality of management, it improves the chances enormously of a relatively significant number getting terrific returns.

So I would say that a lot of things in business, including technology, really have the same effect as if you went to a parade and the band started coming down the street and all of a sudden you stood up on tiptoe. In another 30 seconds everybody else is on tiptoe, and it would be hell on your legs and you still wouldn't be seeing any better.

Capitalism tends to be self-neutralizing like that in terms of improvements. That's marvelous because it means we have better everything than otherwise. But the real trick is to stand up on tiptoe and not have anyone notice you.

**The recent wave of mergers has been staggering. Could you comment on how any of these mergers will create value for shareholders?**

**BUFFETT:** Actually, the two of us have a small announcement we would like to make . . .

*[laughter]*

It won't stop. Mergers will be motivated by very good considerations. There truly are synergies in a great many mergers. But whether there are synergies or not, they are going to keep happening. You don't get to be the CEO of a big company by being a milquetoast. You are not devoid of animal spirits. And it gets contagious. I've been a director of 19 different public companies over the years, and I can tell you that the conversation turns to acquisitions and mergers much more when the competitors of the particular company are engaging in those. As long as our economy works the way it does—and I think it works very well—you're going to see a lot of it. A generally buoyant market tends to encourage mergers, because everybody's currency is more useful in those circumstances. [A few weeks later, Berkshire Hathaway agreed to pay $23.5 billion in stock to acquire General Re, the world's third-largest reinsurance company.]

**GATES:** I think it's good to have a healthy skepticism. But General Motors was created out of a restructuring of the automobile industry from a specialized orientation to companies that did the whole job. And anybody who missed that was basically wiped out.

We've bought a lot of small companies, and I'd say that's been vital to us. These are companies that on their own probably wouldn't have made it, but when their abilities are combined with ours, both of us were able to create a much better set of products than we could've otherwise.

I think in banking today, if you're a medium-sized bank, you're probably going to need to participate in all this stuff that's going on. It doesn't make that much sense to have so many banks in this country, and so there will be certain ones going after scale. But there are a lot of silly mergers too.

**At the end of the day, is the shareholder better off after a merger?**

**BUFFETT:** In most acquisitions, it's better to be the target than the acquirer. The acquirer pays for the fact that he gets to haul back to his cave the carcass of the conquered animal.

I am suspicious of people who just keep acquiring almost by the week, though. If you look at the outstanding companies—say, a Microsoft or an Intel or a Wal-Mart—their growth overwhelmingly has been internal. Frequently, if some company is on a real acquisition binge, they feel they're using funny money, and it has certain aspects of a chain-letter game.

Beyond that, I'd like to see a period where merged companies just run by themselves after a deal, rather than moving around the accounting and putting up big restructuring charges. I get suspicious when there's too much activity. I like to see organic growth.

# 6. Aw, Shucks!

*Warren and Bill muse on their mistakes, their business partners, and managerial succession*

### What was the best business decision you made?

**BUFFETT:** It was just jumping in the pool, basically. The nice thing about the investment business is that you don't need very many deals to succeed. In fact, if when you got out of business school here, you got a punch card with 20 punches on it, and every time you made an investment decision you used up one punch, and that's all you were going to get, you would make 20 very good investment decisions. And you could get very rich, incidentally. You don't need 50 good ideas at all.

I hope the one I made yesterday was a good one. But they've always been kind of simple and obvious to me. The truth is, you know them when you see them. They're so cheap. When I got out of Columbia University, I went through the Moody's manuals page by page—the industrial manual, the transportation manual, the banks and finance manual—just looking for things. And I found stocks at one times earnings. One was Genessee Valley Gas, a little tiny company up in upstate New York, a public utility selling at one times earnings. There were no brokerage reports on it, no nothing, but all you had to do was turn the page. It worked out so well I actually went through the book a second time. Bill was reading the World Book at that time. He's since put it out of business.

**GATES:** We were talking at breakfast this morning about which of all Warren's investment decisions was the worst one. They're tough to find because his track record is unbelievable. But we decided that, by some metric, buying the one that his company is named after—Berkshire Hathaway—was probably his worst investment decision.

**BUFFETT:** That's true. We went into a terrible business because it was cheap. It's what I refer to as the "used cigar butt" approach to investing. You see this cigar butt down there, it's soggy and terrible, but there's one puff left, and it's free. That's what Berkshire was when we bought it—it was selling below working capital—but it was a terrible, terrible mistake.

I've made all kinds of bad decisions that have cost us billions of dollars. They've been mistakes of omission rather than commission. I don't worry about not buying Microsoft, though, because I didn't understand that business. And I didn't understand Intel. But there are businesses that I did understand—Fannie Mae was one that was within my circle of competence. I made a decision to buy it, and I just didn't execute. We would've made many billions of dollars. But we didn't do it. Conventional accounting doesn't record that, but believe me, it happened.

**GATES:** In my case, I'd have to say my best business decisions have had to do with picking people. Deciding to go into business with Paul Allen is probably at the top of the list, and subsequently, hiring a friend—Steve Ballmer—who has been my primary business partner ever since. It's important to have someone who you totally trust, who is totally committed, who shares your vision, and yet who has a little bit different set of skills and who also acts as something of a check on you. Some of the ideas you run by him, you know he's going to say, "Hey, wait a minute, have you thought about this and that?" The benefit of sparking off somebody who's got that kind of brilliance is that it not only makes business more fun, but it really leads to a lot of success.

**BUFFETT:** I've had a partner like that—Charlie Munger—for a lot of years, and it does for me exactly what Bill is talking about. You have to calibrate with Charlie, though, because Charlie says everything I do is dumb. If he says it's really dumb, I know it is, but if he just says it's dumb, I take that as an affirmative vote.

**It seems that in both of your companies, your success is driven by yourselves and your leadership skills. What will happen when you're gone?**

**BUFFETT:** Your assumption is wrong. I will keep working until about five years after I die, and I've given the directors a Ouija board so they can keep in touch. But if the Ouija board doesn't work, we have outstanding people who can do what I do. People are not going to stop drinking Coca-Cola if I die tonight, they're not going to quit shaving tonight, they're not going to eat less See's candy, or fewer Dilly Bars, or anything of the sort. Those companies have terrific products, they've got outstanding managers, and all you'll need at the top of Berkshire is someone who can allocate capital and make sure you have the right managers down below. We've got the people identified to do that, and the board of directors of Berkshire knows who they are.

In fact, I've already sent out a letter that tells what should be done, and I've got another letter that's addressed that will go out at the time, and it starts out, "Yesterday I died," and then tells what the plans of the company are.

**GATES:** My attitude is a lot like Warren's. I want to keep doing what I'm doing for a long, long time. I think probably a decade from now or so, even though I'll still be totally involved with Microsoft because it's my career, I will pick somebody else to be CEO.

**BUFFETT:** I see some hands in the audience here.

**GATES:** That's a long time hence, and our top managers are always sitting down and talking about succession in general, because we want to make sure that we're giving people the opportunity to move up. We don't want to ever create a situation where they feel like it's clogged and they have to go off somewhere else to get big challenges. Our growth helps a lot. We're able to spawn off very, very big jobs for people. Picking that next person is something I give a lot of thought to, but it's probably five years before I have to do something very concrete about it. If there was a surprise, well, there's a contingency plan.

# 7. Charity Begins When I'm Ready

*Bill and Warren explain why they'll give away 99% of their wealth—someday*

**As two of the world's most successful business people, what role do you see for yourselves in giving back to your communities? And how do you use your influence to get others to give back as well?**

**BUFFETT:** We both have a similar philosophy on that. I know in my own case that 99%-plus will go back to society, just because we've been treated extraordinarily well by society.

I'm lucky. I don't run very fast, but I'm wired in a particular way that I thrive in a big capitalist economy with a lot of action. I'm not adapted for football, I'm not adapted for violin playing. I happen to be in something that pays off huge in this society. As Bill says, if I had been born some time ago I would've been some animal's lunch.

I do not believe in the divine right of the womb. Frankly, I don't think it's right that the quarterback of the Nebraska football team next year should be the eldest son of the quarterback of the Nebraska football team of 22 years ago. Nor do I think that our Olympic team in 2000 should be chosen from the same family that was on the Olympic team in the various respective sports in 1976.

We believe in a meritocracy when it comes to athletics and all sorts of things. Now, why not have a meritocracy in terms of what you go out into the world with in terms of the productive goods? Let the resources flow to those who use them best, and then I believe they should give them back to society when they get through.

**GATES:** That's a great philosophy, not to mention that passing along a lot of money can be bad for the people who receive it.

**BUFFETT:** You'd better not put it to a vote.

**How do you use your role as successful businessmen in influencing others, even those who are not as successful, to give back?**

**BUFFETT:** Let me suggest another way to think about this. Let's say that it was 24 hours before you were born, and a genie appeared and said, "You look like a winner. I have enormous confidence in you, and what I'm going to do is let you set the rules of the society into which you will be born. You can set the economic rules and the social rules, and whatever rules you set will apply during your lifetime and your children's lifetimes."

And you'll say, "Well, that's nice, but what's the catch?"

And the genie says, "Here's the catch. You don't know if you're going to be born rich or poor, white or black, male or female, able-bodied or infirm, intelligent or retarded." So all you know is that you're going to get one ball out of a barrel with, say, 5.8 billion balls in it. You're going to participate in what I call the ovarian lottery. It's the most important thing that will happen to you in your life, but you have no control over it. It's going to determine far more than your grades at school or anything else that happens to you.

Now, what rules do you want to have? I'm not going to tell you the rules, and nobody will tell you; you have to make them up for yourself. But they will affect how you think about what you do in your will and things of that sort. That's because you're going to want to have a system that turns out more and more goods and services. You've got a great quantity of people out there, and you want them to live pretty well, and you want your kids to live better than you did, and you want your grandchildren to live better than your kids. You're going to want a system that keeps Bill Gates and Andy Grove and Jack Welch working long, long after they don't need to work. You're going to want the most able people working more than 12 hours a day. So you've got to have a system that gives them an incentive to turn out the goods and services.

But you're also going to want a system that takes care of the bad balls, the ones that aren't lucky. If you have a system that is turning out enough goods and services, you can take care of them. You don't want people worrying about being sick in their old age, or fearful about going home at night. You want a system where people are free of fear to some extent.

So you'll try to design something, assuming you have the goods and services to solve that sort of thing. You'll want equality of opportunity—namely a good public school system—to make you feel that every piece of talent out there will get the same shot at contributing. And your tax system will follow from your reasoning on that. And what you do with the money you make is another thing to think about. As you work through that, everybody comes up with something a little different. I just suggest you play that little game.

**How do you see yourselves as leaders in facets of human experience other than business?**

**GATES:** You have to be careful, if you're good at something, to make sure you don't think you're good at other things that you aren't necessarily so good at. I come in every day and work with a great team of people who are trying to figure out how to make great software, listening to the feedback and doing the research. And it's very typical that because I've been very successful at that, people come in and expect that I have wisdom about topics that I don't.

I do think there are some ways that we've run the company—the way we've hired people, and created an environment and used stock options—that would be good lessons for other businesses as well. But I always want to be careful not to suggest that we've found the solutions to all problems.

**BUFFETT:** You can learn a lot by studying Microsoft and Bill. And you can learn the most by studying what it is he does year after year. But if he devoted 5% or 10% to what he's now doing, and then spread the remainder of his attention over a bunch of other things, well, society would be worse off, in my view.

Bill's right, occasionally there are things—like campaign finance reform—that he may want to take a position on. But you still don't want to say that the whole world ought to follow you on it. I'm very suspect of the person who is very good at one business—it also could be a good athlete or a good entertainer—who starts thinking they should tell the world how to behave on everything. For us to think that just because we made a lot of money, we're going to be better at giving advice on every subject—well, that's just crazy.

*Editor's Note: Having fielded their last question, the two billionaires briefly acknowledged the applause and bolted off the stage, leaving behind an audience that clearly would have relished another two hours of them. But no: they had a bridge game to play.*

# A House Built on Sand

October 26, 1998

### BY CAROL LOOMIS

*Of all the feats that Bill Gates has pulled off, one of the most remarkable is having persuaded Warren Buffett to go on vacations. Since Buffett regards his office in Omaha as the most pleasurable place to be in the world, being anywhere else does not intuitively appeal to him. Even so, Bill and Melinda Gates got him and his first wife, the late Susie Buffett, to come along for two weeks in China in 1996 and nearly two weeks in Alaska and U.S. western parks in 1998.*

*Unfortunately for Buffett, his August departure for Alaska that year coincided with his decision just hours before to try to buy the huge, trouble-fraught trading portfolio held by the collapsing hedge fund Long-Term Capital Management (LTCM). This story chronicles how that firm, under John Meriwether, floundered and how Buffett, operating at times from the fjords of Alaska, did not succeed in doing the deal.*

*Instead, a consortium of fourteen banks reluctantly put up $3.6 billion to keep LTCM afloat, because they feared that the firm's bankruptcy would lead to unbearable losses in their own trading positions. An oversight group established by the banks set about unwinding LTCM's huge 60,000 positions, working—ironically—with Meriwether and partners, who had insistently negotiated a place for themselves in the picture. By the end of 1999, the oversight group managed to return the $3.6 billion put up by the banks, and in 2000 LTCM was liquidated.*

*Just how the deal would have worked out for Buffett, had he instead bought that portfolio of 60,000 positions, is unknowable because there is no way of telling how his bidding group, which included Goldman Sachs, would have fared in dismantling the portfolio. Asked recently to reflect on his LTCM experience, Buffett says it still astounds him that the firm's managers, celebrated for their brilliance, let themselves get into a position in which they could lose all their money. Behavior of that kind is not socially acceptable at Berkshire, where there is a counter-reminder: "You only need to get rich once."*

*Apparently having never quite absorbed that message, Meriwether has since the LTCM debacle been working, none too successfully, on a second effort to get rich, in the same business yet. In 1999, he started hedge fund JWM Partners, which made money for years, grew to about $3 billion in size, and then suffered huge losses in the credit crisis. The fund liquidated in 2008. The following year, Meriwether opened JM Advisors Management, whose investment record has not been publicly disclosed. —CL*

It is a curiosity of the Long-Term Capital debacle that, although it has been endlessly and ably explained in the newspapers, it remains a mystery to many readers. Indeed, the affair has so many facets and is so complicated that it almost confounds complete understanding. For that reason, *Fortune* does not claim that this story will tell you all you need to know about Long-Term Capital or give more than a glimpse of all that is surely yet to unfold. But we do know we understand, to an extent that no other publication can, the role played in this affair by noted investor Warren Buffett, who is a longtime friend of this writer. Buffett's role in this saga was important, dramatic, and not without humor, coming to a climax in four particular September days. Moreover, his role is possibly not ended.

The outlines of what happened to Long-Term Capital in September are among the few clarities of this affair. For most of the month, the huge hedge fund hung on the edge of bankruptcy and was finally saved only by a $3.6 billion infusion from a consortium of 14 banks and brokerage firms—all creditors who feared what the bankruptcy of a fund that owed upwards of $100 billion would do to their own finances. Very much in the act also was the Federal Reserve Bank of New York, which wished to avert the domino effects that a fast liquidation of the fund's holdings might have exerted on an already reeling global securities market. So the New York Fed played godfather to the rescue deal, bringing the creditors together at its own offices and overseeing their negotiations.

In the center of this affair—always—was the hedge fund's founder and principal manager, former Salomon Brothers whiz John Meriwether. Meriwether had surrounded himself with brilliant colleagues, many of them Ph.D.s in mathematics and finance, and put them to work devising computer-driven trading strategies that were supposedly bulletproof. In the Greenwich, Conn., office of the hedge fund's management firm, Long-Term Capital Management, there may be more IQ points per square foot than in any other institution extant. There are certainly more Nobel Prize winners per square foot. LTCM has two: Myron Scholes and Robert Merton, who less than a year ago went jubilantly to Sweden to receive the world's highest accolade for achievement in economics.

The disaster that befell this brain trust recalls the first line of Allen Ginsberg's beatnik poem "Howl": "I saw the best minds of my generation destroyed by madness . . ." At LTCM the best minds were destroyed by the oldest and most famously addictive drug in finance, leverage. Had the fund not grievously overextended itself, it might still be trucking along, doing its thing, working those brain cells. But now its strategists have swapped their laurels for the booby prize of the financial markets, which is the ignominy of being largely wiped out and viewed as bumbling losers.

All of which raises the question of why Warren Buffett would want to pick up this particular piece of road kill—and yet he made a stab at doing exactly that. His move came on Wednesday, Sept. 23. It interrupted days of meetings that the New York Fed had been holding with the banks and brokerage firms that Long-Term Capital owed huge amounts of money to, which were being asked, in their own self-interest, to put up new money to stave off the fund's bankruptcy. The participants were an extraordinarily powerful group—every bank and firm that attended had sent its CEO or another top honcho—and the atmosphere was contentious. None of the members really wanted to ante up the money, and yet they dreaded a bankruptcy.

As the creditors' group was about to reconvene on this Wednesday morning, William McDonough, president of the New York Fed, learned from Goldman Sachs—itself one of Long-Term Capital's creditors—that it had an alternative financing proposition to present. McDonough recessed the meeting and listened to Goldman make the case for a bid, headed by Buffett's Berkshire Hathaway, to take over the fund. The terms were complicated—more on that later—but essentially the Buffett group proposed to put up $4 billion and make itself the manager of Long-Term Capital. Of the $4 billion, $3 billion was to come from Berkshire, $700 million from insurer American International Group, and $300 million from Goldman Sachs.

This bid then went to Meriwether, and that's when it began to die. There is disagreement as to why. Buffett believes that the deal did not happen because Meriwether and the other LTCM principals simply did not want to accept his terms, which would have left LTCM's principals with little money and no jobs. For their part, Meriwether and other LTCM partners told McDonough that the Buffett bid was structurally flawed and therefore not feasible.

Buying that argument, McDonough reconvened the meeting and told the creditors, in effect, that they were back to being the only game in town. One of the CEOs there told *Fortune* recently that McDonough explained that the other deal was not going to happen because it had "structural" problems. Grudgingly, the CEOs went back to negotiating their rescue plan, with each participant ultimately putting up very big money: $100 million to $350 million.

Suppose, *Fortune* asked that same CEO, that McDonough had said the deal would not happen because Long-Term Capital did not like its terms. "I think," answered the CEO, "that I would probably have told Meriwether to go screw himself." Of course, he adds, negotiations might then have turned into a game of chicken. Perhaps Meriwether would have countered that he preferred bankruptcy to Buffett. Then the creditors would be back to the question of whether they could stand bankruptcy. Squawk, squawk, which side flinches first?

To understand how both Long-Term Capital and the creditors—and the Fed, to boot—got themselves into this amazing bind and why Buffett volunteered to step into apparent chaos, it is necessary to look at the character of this hedge fund and its boss, John Meriwether. Until August 1991, Meriwether, now 51, was a vice chairman of Salomon, with responsibility for fixed-income trading and also "proprietary trading," which is a firm's investment of its own money. Meriwether was a huge money-maker for the firm, and was liked and admired to the point of reverence by the people who worked for him. "British Guiana actually comes to mind," said a former Salomon Brothers executive recently. "John had a kind of cultlike following."

Then came Salomon's Treasury bond scandal, precipitated by Paul Mozer, one of Meriwether's senior people. In the chain of disclosure, Mozer admitted to Meriwether in April 1991 that he had falsified bids for Treasury securities; Meriwether immediately went to his bosses, John Gutfreund and Thomas Strauss, with the news; everybody concluded that the Fed must be told; and then nobody did the telling. When the scandal finally erupted in August, Mozer was fired, and Gutfreund and Strauss resigned under pressure. To the rescue came Buffett, head of Salomon's biggest shareholder, Berkshire.

In the first two days of Buffett's regime as chairman of Salomon, Meriwether's fate was uncertain. Many of Salomon's managing partners had turned against him and wanted him out. But Buffett was not sure that it was fair to fire Meriwether, since he had acted responsibly in immediately disclosing Mozer's sins to the firm's bosses. In the end, Meriwether himself made the decision to resign, telling Buffett that he thought it was the best thing for the firm.

Gradually, a number of men who had worked for Meriwether left Salomon to join him in business. The specifics about what they were to do surfaced in 1993, when Meriwether announced plans to start a hedge fund called Long-Term Capital. Actually, Long-Term Capital is made up of a variety of investment vehicles, some partnerships, some corporations; some domiciled in the U.S., some in the Cayman Islands. Why the Caymans? So that offshore investors, as well as certain kinds of U.S. investors, can avoid U.S. income taxes—a point that grates, of course, when we recall that the Fed was scrambling around in September on the fund's behalf. However, all of these instruments feed their money into a master fund called Long-Term Capital Portfolio L.P., a Cayman partnership.

It is this fund that has taken the positions that its investment managers, Meriwether and crew, dictated. From its beginning, the fund was distinctive in that its managers proposed to carry out trading strategies that would take time—six months to two years or more—to deliver profits. For that reason, LTCM ruled that it would not allow investors in the fund to withdraw their money quarterly or annually, which are the common practices of hedge funds, but would instead lock up their money until the end of 1997.

As for the strategies, the fund's managers proposed to make relatively few trades that carried "directional" risk and instead to concentrate on capturing small profits from carefully hedged positions, particularly in the fixed-income markets. A couple of illustrations will illuminate some distinctions in risk, which are important in this tale. Imagine that an individual investor decided to buy the stock of Cendant, on the theory that it was headed up. That would be a directional trade, or a "position risk." Assuming the investor didn't buy on margin, the percentage gain or loss on each dollar at risk would be exactly equal to the percentage rise or fall in Cendant stock.

Long-Term Capital's main strategy, in contrast, was to make hedged trades that it thought could succeed regardless of the general trend of the markets. The fund put its financial technology and brains to work, for example, at identifying sectors of the bond market in which yields had gotten out of line with yields in related sectors. It would then buy one of the securities and short the other. A trade of this type can deliver a profit regardless of whether interest rates in general go up or down or stay flat. All that matters is that the two yields eventually converge.

In this kind of trading, the fund never expected to earn a large return on each dollar at risk. An investor in Long-Term Capital recalls talking by phone to some of its top managers in 1996 and asking them just how much they were annually realizing per dollar. The answer was 67 basis points, or 0.67 of a cent.

Returns like that were never going to make investors happy unless the invested capital could be greatly enlarged, and that's where the leverage came in. Confident that its position risk was very low, the fund took on a colossal amount of what's called "balance-sheet risk," piling a huge slab of debt on top of its relative sliver of capital. At the moment in 1996 when that investor was getting his answer of 67 basis points, the fund had a ratio of $30 in balance-sheet debt for every $1 in capital. Leveraged 30 to 1, a 0.67% return on each dollar at risk produces a healthy 20% return on capital.

Leverage that steep sounds terrifying—and eventually it was. But LTCM always maintained that its financial technologies and its meticulously constructed hedges gave the fund a conservative risk profile. In October 1994, LTCM spelled out this proposition in a paper sent to its investors. In the paper was a table that delineated a range of returns that the fund might aim for in a year and paired them with the probabilities of loss if things went bad. For example, the table said that if the fund were shooting for a 25% return—which was indeed a typical goal for the operation—the probability that it actually would end up losing 20% or more was an insignificant 1 in 100. The table never even contemplated a steeper loss.

That would all be funny if it weren't tragic. In the first eight months of 1998, the fund lost nearly 50% of its capital, and in September it hemorrhaged still more, with the loss going to around 90%. "What that tells you," says Warren Buffett, "is that underneath the mathematical elegance—underneath all those betas and sigmas—there was quicksand."

At least one of Long-Term Capital's investors was troubled by the same thought. The investor who was told about the fund's 67-basis-point return wrote himself two notes for the file after that conversation. He recently showed them to *Fortune*. One note said, "Are they no different from any Wall Street firm—Bear or Salomon or Goldman? It's the proprietary desks without the people, overhead, or agency business."

The second note leaned on a Yiddish word, *kishka*, which figuratively means "gut instincts." Said the note: "There is no *kishka* override over the portfolio. One gets a Nobel Prize-winning computer system. Will that collapse one day? Would one prefer a person, with *kishkas*, at the controls?"

From the looks of the fund's vitality in its first four years, from the late winter of 1994 until the spring of 1998, not many investors were worrying about *kishkas*. The structure of Long-Term Capital calls for its investors to pay the management company unusually steep fees: first, an annual 2% on the capital that an investor has in the fund, and second, 25% of profits earned. Even so, the fund's investors earned 20% in the ten months of 1994 that it was in operation, 43% in 1995, 41% in 1996, and 17% in 1997. Furthermore, monthly performance figures showed that the fund was having a smooth ride, experiencing very little volatility in its results.

Like a siren song, these facts brought in a flood of new money. That was true even though the fund's managers kept a tight veil of secrecy over their specific trading strategies, leaving their investors with little clue as to just how the fund was making its profits. By the fall of 1997, the combination of contributions and reinvested earnings had raised the capital of the fund to around $7 billion.

At that point, things took an unexpected turn: LTCM itself concluded that the fund had too much capital for the investment opportunities open to it and forced many of its investors, notably those who had come in late, to withdraw their money. Many of those expelled went kicking and screaming, and at least one protested so angrily that LTCM allowed him to stay onboard. The anger arose in part because LTCM's principals and other insiders were allowed to maintain their full stakes in the fund. In other words, maybe attractive investments weren't so scarce after all. When the smoke had cleared at year-end 1997, the fund had $4.7 billion in capital, of which about $1.5 billion belonged to insiders.

At that time, the fund also had about $125 billion in debt, which means that its balance-sheet leverage ratio was about 25 to one. But that far understates the true exposure, since the fund has always aggressively entered into off-balance-sheet derivatives contracts that by their nature create additional leverage. Only an insider would know, at any point, what the derivatives exposure amounted to—but be assured that if the balance-sheet leverage at year-end 1997 was 25 to one, the overall leverage was greater.

In a sense, all this debt owed its existence to another kind of near-cult following that Meriwether had acquired, this one made up of banks and brokerage firms enamored with the prospect of lending to him. Creditors love customers who are big, active, and solid, and that was precisely the image that Long-Term Capital projected. Most of the fund's creditors do not appear to have looked critically at its leverage. In fact, many were accommodating in granting favorable terms on loans—the waiving of collateral, for example. Many also happily entered into derivatives contracts with the fund, increasing their total exposure to what, unknown to them, was about to become a train wreck.

This year of the wreck, 1998, began calmly enough, but in May, volatile markets cost the fund a 6% loss, and in June, another 10%. Those lashes of the whip, unheard of in the fund's history, were enough to make Meriwether shoot off a special letter to his investors. It said that LTCM was "understandably disappointed" with the May and June results, but nevertheless believed that "the future expected returns [for the fund's investment strategies] are good." In July the fund was essentially flat.

And then came August—terrible, terrible August. Russia devalued its currency, and the world's investors fled to quality. That was not what LTCM had been banking on in several different trading strategies. For example, it had at some point done paired trades that in essence bet on a narrowing of the spread between the yields of AA-rated corporate bonds and comparable U.S. Treasuries. The bet looked good because the spread was relatively wide compared with its historical levels. But when the flight to quality began, Treasury yields plunged, and the gap between government and corporate yields dramatically and incredibly widened still more. The outcome was disastrous. The fund lost 40% of its capital in August alone, leaving it with just $2.5 billion. Astoundingly, it was still carrying about $100 billion in debt.

Around this time, the fund's principals and at least some creditors got really nervous. Stuffing their pride into the closet for the moment, the LTCM crew went on a search for investors who might buy out some of their trading positions or, alternatively, put fresh capital into the fund, thereby giving it a stronger base. The team solicited, among others, certain investors who'd been pushed out of the firm at the end of 1997, as well as the hedge fund moguls George Soros and Julian Robertson. All said no.

On the night of Sunday, Aug. 23, LTCM opened the Omaha front. The man assigned to call Buffett was Eric Rosenfeld, an LTCM principal and onetime Salomon trader who had earned Buffett's regard by loyally helping Salomon climb out of its hole after the 1991 crisis. Rosenfeld, 45, is normally laid back. But on this occasion, Buffett says there was a sense of urgency in Rosenfeld's offer to sell him some of the fund's large equity arbitrage positions. Buffett said no.

By Wednesday, Rosenfeld was back on the phone, joined this time by Meriwether. Could Buffett meet the following morning in Omaha with still another LTCM principal, Lawrence Hilibrand? At the meeting, Hilibrand, 39, also a former Salomon trader well regarded by Buffett, presented a rough, though still guarded, picture of Long-Term Capital's portfolio and urged Buffett to become a large investor in the fund. Hilibrand also pinpointed a reason for hurry: When August ended a few days later, the fund was going to have to tell its investors and lenders how much it had lost for the month and would be pleased to tell them also that it had secured financing arrangements that would ease the fund's leverage. Sorry, said Buffett politely, but he simply had no interest.

Later, Buffett talked to Berkshire's vice chairman, Charles Munger, and remembers telling him that though the fund's positions might have been logical, he had no desire to make Berkshire a hedge fund investor. He also pointed out the absurdity of "10 or 15 guys with an average IQ of maybe 170 getting themselves into a position where they can lose all their money."

After that, Buffett did not again think much about Long-Term Capital until late Friday afternoon, Sept. 18, when he returned a call from a Goldman Sachs partner he knew, Peter Kraus. Kraus said that Long-Term Capital's net assets—

■ FILLING TOMORROW'S JOBS ● TOKYO'S STOCK MARKET ● THE EASTERN AIR LINES MESS ■

APRIL 11, 1988                                                                    $3.50

# FORTUNE

## THE INSIDE STORY OF WARREN BUFFETT

The legendary investor is also an ace at running businesses. Here's how he does it.

*Fortune* has featured Warren Buffett on its cover thirteen times. Left: 1988, Berkshire Hathaway builder (and bridge player); below, left: 2006, megascale philanthropist; and 2008, true believer in America's ability to surmount tough economic times.

# FORTUNE

## WARREN BUFFETT GIVES IT AWAY

The bulk of his fortune, now worth $44 billion, will become the biggest charitable gift ever. His chief beneficiary? The Bill & Melinda Gates Foundation. Buffett reveals an extraordinary plan.

A FORTUNE EXCLUSIVE

GOING GREEN
SPECIAL REPORT

# FORTUNE

## What Warren Thinks...

ABOUT THE CREDIT CRISIS, THE ECONOMY, AND MORE

PLUS
Where to Invest Now!
THE BEST STOCKS AND BONDS TO BUY TODAY

Bob Iger on Where He's Taking Disney

FORTUNE.COM

Above: Buffett, in Omaha in late 1969, as he was closing down his hedge fund after thirteen years of shining results—and after a run of wild stock markets he despised. Below: In 1985, at his office (then and now), from a *Fortune* piece on his out-of-the-box buy of Whoops municipal bonds.

Guy Gillette

Mark Hanauer / Corbis Outline

Michael O'Neill / Corbis Outline

Clockwise from top: A 1998 photo staged by tour host Bill Gates as Buffett stalked Long-Term Capital by phone while ignoring Old Faithful; at Pebble Beach in 2002, during a sore-shoulder, nongolfing trip with pals; in Omaha, doing a Q&A with visiting Wharton students in chaotic 2008.

Ben Baker / Redux

Above: Berkshire Hathaway vice chairman and polymath Charlie Munger often weighs in on Buffett's big business decisions. Below: Gladys Kaiser (right) was Buffett's assistant for twenty-five years; successor Debbie Bosanek is nearing twenty. The three, says Buffett, have "made me look good."

Above: Friends and business stars Ajit Jain (left), Berkshire Hathaway's insurance whiz, and retired Capital Cities/ABC chairman Tom Murphy (right), whom Buffett thought "the top manager in the U.S." Below: Berkshire annual-meeting crowds at Nebraska Furniture Mart in Omaha.

Above: The family in Sun Valley before the death of Buffett's wife, Susie: in front row, Buffett, Susie, son Howard; in back row, son Peter and his wife, Jennifer; Howard's wife, Devon; and Buffett's daughter, Susie. Below, also in Sun Valley: Buffett in 2006 with his soon-to-be second wife Astrid Menks.

Photo by Albert Watson

Above: Bill and Melinda Gates posing with Buffett in 2006. Months before, he had announced he would begin giving away his fortune—the lion's share to go to the Gates Foundation. Below: Buffett and Gates meeting in 2010 at a Hollywood Diner near Omaha to discuss plans for creating the Giving Pledge.

Mark Peterson / Redux

Clockwise from top left: Buffett clowning in 1999 with Jimmy Buffett; at a 2000 Omaha Royals baseball game; holding, in 2006, a Berkshire stock certificate worth a colossal $11 billion; adding his wallet to Berkshire's $5 billion investment in Lloyd Blankfein's Goldman Sachs in 2008.

its capital—had sunk to $1.5 billion, and that Goldman was calling around looking for people who might want to become big investors in the fund. No interest, Buffett said once again. But the two men then bounced around other ideas relating to Long-Term Capital. Finally, Buffett got to focusing on the very-big-picture thought that Berkshire and Goldman might jointly bid for the entire fund, chuck the Meriwether management, and take on the fund's management themselves. The concept, says Buffett today, was to patiently stick with most of the fund's positions and gradually liquidate at what Buffett thought could be a decent profit.

It was a major idea, of a size suitable for Berkshire's billions in available cash, but it could not have come at a worse time. Buffett was trying to leave his office to get to a granddaughter's birthday party. That night he was scheduled to fly to Seattle to join a Bill Gates group that was going to spend nearly two weeks touring Alaska and a galaxy of Western parks. It was a highly uncharacteristic move; Buffett ordinarily has no interest in scenery of any kind. But his close friendship with Gates had lured him and his wife, Susan, into signing on for the trip.

If a bid was to be made, then Buffett would have to work it out with Kraus over the phone from the wild. And that's how it happened, although not without moments of exquisite frustration. Suffice it to say that not even a megabillionaire can establish and keep a phone connection from the canyonlike depths of an Alaskan fjord.

Nevertheless, the $4 billion bid took shape over four hectic days, with Goldman declining to be more than a $300 million partner and with AIG, at Buffett's suggestion, asked in. That invitation occurred because Buffett has had good relations with AIG's chairman, Maurice "Hank" Greenberg, and thought this gesture might further cement them. Another facet of the deal called for Goldman to be the fund's administrator, once the property was in the bidding group's hands.

It is essential to understand what the group proposed to buy and at what price. It wanted to own the fund's entire portfolio, and to accomplish that, it wished to purchase the master fund, Long-Term Capital Portfolio L.P. This is the fund that had $1.5 billion of capital on Friday, Sept. 18. By the following Wednesday, though, when the Buffett bid was made, the fund's net assets were maybe in the range of $600 million. Nobody knew for sure. In any case, Buffett, never a man to overpay, wanted to buy the fund at a discount, and his bid was $250 million. Had it been accepted, the sum would have gone to the fund's old investors—Meriwether's management team included—and would have tacitly said that a fund worth $4.7 billion at the start of 1998 had sunk in value to about a 20th of that. Once the $250 million was paid over, the Buffett group would have immediately put up an additional $3.75 billion, which would have restored capital adequacy to the fund.

Think a bit more about the $250 million. Once it went on the table, it would become the figure that Meriwether, given time, would quite understandably try to "shop," looking for more dollars. Also, when you are talking a $4 billion proposition and the markets are turbulent, it is not good to let a bid sit around and go stale. So Buffett put a tight time limit on his offer. The bid was faxed to Meriwether at 11:40 on Wednesday morning, and he was advised it would expire within an hour, at 12:30.

Meanwhile, McDonough and the creditors' group had already been trying for days to assemble its rescue plan and were meeting again that day. So even before the bid was faxed to Meriwether that morning, Goldman briefed McDonough on the deal, and McDonough called Buffett, now at a Montana ranch, to confirm the offer. Buffett says that McDonough seemed elated at the sudden appearance of an alternative plan to the one he'd been nursing with the creditors. Buffett then called Meriwether and told him a bid was on its way. Buffett made it clear that his group wanted to buy Long-Term Capital Portfolio in its entirety. Meriwether was noncommittal.

But when the call ended, Meriwether went into action, fast. After a quick conversation with LTCM's in-house lawyer, he got on the phone to McDonough and told him that Buffett's bid wouldn't work because Meriwether did not have the authority to sell. Meriwether is a general partner of the so-called portfolio company, but it also has other partners, and Meriwether contended he would have to seek the vote of each one before agreeing to sell. And obviously, he said, that could not be done before 12:30. Backing Meriwether up in the conversation was another LTCM principal and a former colleague of McDonough's, David Mullins, who was vice chairman of the Federal Reserve Board until he joined LTCM in 1994.

Buffett's group had not gone into its bid without its own legal opinion. Studying the Long-Term Capital documents available, incomplete though they were, the group's lawyers concluded that the bid was workable from Meriwether's side. Besides, everyone on the Buffett side believed that if Meriwether really had any interest in the bid, he could tentatively accept it and then tangle with the complications later.

But Meriwether displayed absolutely no interest when he spoke to McDonough. The Fed president concluded that he could not dismiss Meriwether's legal argument or, for that matter, stretch his authority as a central banker to force Meriwether to sell. Resignedly, McDonough returned to his surly band of creditors and flogged along their $3.6 billion rescue plan.

How do Meriwether and the fund's other investors fare under that scheme? Part of the answer is that they keep whatever shrunken capital they still have in the fund, which totaled something around $400 million in late September. That is the correct figure to compare with Buffett's $250 million, though it is worth mentioning that Buffett was to hand over cash, whereas the $400 million remains tied up in the fund.

As for Meriwether and the LTCM crew, they still run the fund, though the creditors have roughly halved their fees. The creditors have also put six of their people in LTCM's offices with instructions to liquidate the fund as fast as it can be sensibly done. Finishing within a year would be splendid, says one senior Wall Streeter.

There is, of course, another scenario: a prompt move by the creditors to find a bidder—a Buffett, say—who would step up and take this mess off their hands immediately. Would Buffett do that? Who knows, since he never telegraphs his moves. But he is aware that certain creditors have been thinking about him.

In any event, Buffett has returned from vacation, and he managed to catch C-Span's Oct. 1 coverage of the House hearings on Long-Term Capital. The vignette he liked best: Congressman James Leach's memory that his father had told him to avoid anyone doing business out of the Cayman Islands. That reminded Buffett of a favorite line that seems just about the perfect wrapup for Long-Term Capital: "You never know who's swimming naked until the tide goes out."

# Are Jimmy and Warren Buffett Related?

June 21, 1999

## BY TYLER MARONEY

We'll begin to answer this question of blood ties between the Oracle of Omaha and the Minstrel of Margaritaville by pointing out their similarities, which are haunting. Both play stringed instruments: Jimmy a tropical guitar, Warren a mean ukulele. ("I've probably had worse musicians in my band," jokes Jimmy.) They've both cashed in on unlikely investments: Warren bet on furniture, insurance, and vacuum cleaners and is now worth $35 billion; Jimmy bet on the illusion of a colada-drenched beach bum and forged a multi-million-dollar brand with over 30 albums, eight movies, a clothing line, nightclubs, a custom record label, three best-selling novels, and hundreds of gift-shop gimmicks. Jimmy's a Capricorn, adept at accumulating money; Warren's a Virgo, with a creative musical mind.

Both keep it real by sticking to what they know: Warren by avoiding tech stocks, Jimmy by milking a song he recorded more than a generation ago. Both attract cult followings: Parrotheads flock to Jimmy's summer concerts; investors flock to Warren's Berkshire Hathaway shareholder meetings—Warren himself calls it the capitalists' Woodstock. Both avoid changes in latitudes and changes in attitudes: Warren's a diehard Husker; Jimmy's still wasting away in mythical Margaritaville. ("Lethargy bordering on sloth" is how Buffett describes the cornerstone of his style. That's Warren on investing, not Jimmy on chilling.) And in his classic "Cheeseburger in Paradise," Jimmy croons, "Heaven on earth with an onion slice." Hamburgers are Warren's favorite food.

But really: Are they related? *Fortune* believes, but cannot prove beyond a doubt, that Warren and Jimmy are kin. It was Warren's sister Doris, the family genealogist, who first raised the subject. Two years after mailing out questionnaires to all 125 Buffetts in the U.S., she got a call from a curious Jimmy. "He said, 'I want to be related to your family because they're rich and famous,'" Doris recalls. "And I said, 'That's funny, we want to be related to you because you're rich and famous.'"

Doris' research has unearthed three possible ancestral links: John Buffett, a poor 17th-century pickle farmer from Long Island; a Newfoundland sailor whom Jimmy honors in "Son of a Son of a Sailor"; and Norfolk Island in the South Pacific, which is inhabited by hundreds of Buffetts (as well as a good many descendants of the mutineers of the Bounty). When Doris and Jimmy discovered that Norfolk Island used to be a penal colony, however, they lost hope: Centuries of inbreeding have blurred family lines.

Despite the lack of absolute proof that they're related (as of press time, no DNA testing had been conducted), Warren and Jimmy have become friends. While Jimmy insists "Uncle Warren" doesn't slip him any investing tips, the two have been known to break out in song. "I think he's angling to get into my will," the billionaire Buffett jokes. "But the way things are going, I'd rather be in his."

*And the final answer is . . .*

*Eight years and many scientific advances later, Jimmy and Warren did the requisite spitting into small receptacles and submitted to a DNA analysis, carried out by 23andMe (a company cofounded by Anne Wojcicki, who happens to be the wife of Google cofounder Sergey Brin). The results showed, alas, that Jimmy and Warren are not related. To find common ancestors for the two, you'd have to go back ten thousand years, which is before surnames—and that doesn't count. Case closed. —CL*

# Put Bite into Audit Committees

August 2, 1999

**BY CAROL LOOMIS**

*In the days before Sarbanes-Oxley became law, regulators struggled to end "cooking the books," and Buffett weighed in on the issue. —CL*

Eager for boards to have better audit committees than they do, Arthur Levitt got a special panel to make recommendations for improvement and now wants them adopted. But when the New York Stock Exchange asked its listed companies to comment on the recommendations, back came bullets.

The companies especially disliked a proposal that would have required audit committees to do their homework and then attest in annual reports that the financial statements therein conformed to GAAP. Some protesters thought such a rule would invite lawsuits against audit committee members. Others saw role confusion. Attesting, said one letter, "is what the external auditor is hired to do."

A related objection came from Warren Buffett . . . who, up to the minute he put up his hand on this one, had publicly and warmly applauded Levitt's campaign against earnings management. Here, though, Buffett disputed the thought that an audit committee, meeting for a few hours a year, could attest to anything meaningful about a company's financial statements. Instead, he said, the committee needs to learn what the outside auditors know—something that "frequently does not occur, even (perhaps especially) when major shortcomings exist."

Buffett said the committee should require the auditors to give detailed answers to three questions:

1. If the auditor were solely responsible for preparation of the company's financial statements, would they have been done differently, in either material or nonmaterial ways? If "differently," the auditor should explain both management's argument and his own.

2. If the auditor were an investor, would he have received the information essential to understanding the company's financial performance during the reporting period?

3. Is the company following the same internal audit procedure the auditor would if he himself were CEO? If not, what are the differences and why?

Buffett then said—in italics—that the auditors' answers should be spelled out in the minutes of the meeting. The point, he said, is to hang "monetary liability" on the auditors, that being the only thing that will drive them to truly do their job instead of becoming subservient to management.

*Fortune* asked Olivia Kirtley, chair of the American Institute of Certified Public Accountants and also chief financial officer of Vermont American Corp., for her opinion about Buffett's ideas. He'd "boiled down" his questions, she said, but they were "in the spirit" of what the AICPA's own audit committee asks of its outside auditors.

Whether her auditing-firm constituency would like a plan that seeks to get them either to do their job well or to accept monetary responsibility for failure is doubtful. Auditors have eased their legal troubles in the past decade, managing to establish that financial statements are the responsibility of management, and also getting help from new laws and a friendly Supreme Court decision. As a result, the number of suits auditors are having to defend is sharply down.

Of course, it is also during this decade that managements have learned all the subterranean routes for meeting "expectations." Is that simply coincidence or has the slimming of monetary consequences made auditors less diligent and more compliant than was once the case? That question is unanswerable. Buffett's three are not.

# Mr. Buffett on the Stock Market

November 22, 1999

### *A Buffett speech that Carol Loomis converted into an article*

*Warren Buffett almost never talks publicly about the general level of stock prices—neither in his famed annual report nor at Berkshire's thronged annual meetings nor in the rare speeches he gives. But in the last half of 1999, on four occasions, Buffett did step up to that subject, laying out his opinions, in ways both analytical and creative, about the long-term future for stocks. I heard the last of those talks, given in September to a group of Buffett's friends, and also watched a videotape of the first speech, given in July at Allen & Co.'s Sun Valley, Idaho, bash for business leaders. From those extemporaneous talks (the first made with the Dow Jones industrial average at 11,194), I distilled the following account of what Buffett said. Buffett reviewed it and weighed in with some clarifications.*

*Buffett's central message is contained in the first words of this article: "Investors in stocks these days are expecting far too much." As for the nascent Internet, whose promise swelled investors' hopes, he proceeded to emphasize how few people got rich from two other transforming industries, auto and aviation.*

*In his speeches, Buffett certainly did not anticipate the low interest rates—Treasury bills that pay pennies, for example—prevailing recently. Neither was he quite as grim about stock market returns as reality has proved them to be.*

*But he was absolutely right in his general bearishness about the market, so much so that he says today, "I wouldn't change a word of what I said." He was speaking at a time when investors had grown used to average annual total returns of 12 percent on their holdings. He expected instead that 7 percent was a reasonable estimate as to what investors—before inflation—could earn annually in total returns over the seventeen years from 1999 to 2016 (the article explains why he selected that oddball number of years). And that was a gross figure, before the heavy transactional costs that investors bear—commissions, sales loads, and management fees, for example. After these costs, Buffett thought that a reasonable expectation for the return would be about 6 percent annually.*

*In lamentable fact, the total return of the Dow Industrials, compounded annually, was was through mid-2013 (and the strong market of that first half) only 4.4 percent. The comparable figure for the S&P 500 (which is not as dividend-heavy as the Dow and suffered much more than the Dow when the Internet bubble burst) was absolutely abysmal: 2.6 percent.*

*As this book is published, there are still three years to go, of course, before the seventeen years end. But they will have to deliver superb results if investors are to speed across the ground they've lost and end up with even a 6 percent annual total return. —CL* nvestors in stocks these days are expecting far too much, and I'm going to explain why. That will inevitably set me to talking about the general stock market, a subject I'm usually unwilling to discuss. But I want to make one thing clear going in: Though I will be talking about the level of the market, I will *not* be predicting its next moves. At Berkshire we focus almost exclusively on the valuations of individual companies, looking only to a very limited extent at the valuation of the overall market. Even then, valuing the market has nothing to do with where it's going to go next week or next month or next year, a line of thought we never get into. The fact is that markets behave in ways, sometimes for a very long stretch, that are not linked to value. Sooner or later, though, value counts. So what I am going to be saying—assuming it's correct—*will* have implications for the long-term results to be realized by American stockholders.

Let's start by defining "investing." The definition is simple but often forgotten: Investing is laying out money now to get more money back in the future—more money in *real* terms, after taking inflation into account.

Now, to get some historical perspective, let's look back at the 34 years before this one—and here we are going to see an almost Biblical kind of symmetry, in the sense of lean years and fat years—to observe what happened in the stock market. Take, to begin with, the first 17 years of the period, from the end of 1964 through 1981. Here's what took place in that interval:

---

### DOW JONES INDUSTRIAL AVERAGE

Dec. 31, 1964: *874.12*

Dec. 31, 1981: *875.00*

---

Now I'm known as a long-term investor and a patient guy, but that is not my idea of a big move.

And here's a major and very opposite fact: During that same 17 years, the GDP of the U.S.—that is, the business being done in this country—almost quintupled, rising by 370%. Or, if we look at another measure, the sales of the *Fortune* 500 (a changing mix of companies, of course) more than sextupled. And yet the Dow went exactly nowhere.

To understand why that happened, we need first to look at one of the two important variables that affect investment results: interest rates. These act on financial valuations the way gravity acts on matter: The higher the rate, the greater the downward pull. That's because the rates of return that investors need from any kind of investment are directly tied to the risk-free rate that they can earn from government securities. So if the government rate rises, the prices of all other investments must adjust downward, to a level that brings their expected rates of return into line. Conversely, if government interest rates fall, the move pushes the prices of all other investments upward. The basic proposition is this: What an investor should pay today for a dollar to be received tomorrow can only be determined by first looking at the risk-free interest rate.

Consequently, every time the risk-free rate moves by one basis point—by 0.01%—the value of every investment in the country changes. People can see this easily in the case of bonds, whose value is normally affected only by interest rates. In the case of equities or real estate or farms or whatever, other very important variables are almost always at work, and that means the effect of interest rate changes is usually obscured. Nonetheless, the effect—like the invisible pull of gravity—is constantly there.

In the 1964-81 period, there was a tremendous increase in the rates on long-term government bonds, which moved from just over 4% at year-end 1964 to more than 15% by late 1981. That rise in rates had a huge depressing effect on the value of all investments, but the one we noticed, of course, was the price of equities. So *there*—in that tripling of the gravitational pull of interest rates—lies the major explanation of why tremendous growth in the economy was accompanied by a stock market going nowhere.

Then, in the early 1980s, the situation reversed itself. You will remember Paul Volcker coming in as chairman of the Fed and remember also how unpopular he was. But the heroic things he did—his taking a two-by-four to the economy and breaking the back of inflation—caused the interest rate trend to reverse, with some rather spectacular results. Let's say you put $1 million into the 14% 30-year U.S. bond issued Nov. 16, 1981, and reinvested the coupons. That is, every time you got an interest payment, you used it to buy more of that same bond. At the end of 1998, with long-term governments by then selling at 5%, you would have had $8,181,219 and would have earned an annual return of more than 13%.

That 13% annual return is better than stocks have done in a great many 17-year periods in history—in most 17-year periods, in fact. It was a helluva result, and from none other than a stodgy bond.

The power of interest rates had the effect of pushing up equities as well, though other things that we will get to pushed additionally. And so here's what equities did in that same 17 years: If you'd invested $1 million in the Dow on Nov. 16, 1981, and reinvested all dividends, you'd have had $19,720,112 on Dec. 31, 1998. And your annual return would have been 19%.

The increase in equity values since 1981 beats anything you can find in history. This increase even surpasses what you would have realized if you'd bought stocks in 1932, at their Depression bottom—on its lowest day, July 8, 1932, the Dow closed at 41.22—and held them for 17 years.

The second thing bearing on stock prices during this 17 years was after-tax corporate profits, which the chart on the facing page displays as a percentage of GDP. In effect, what this chart tells you is what portion of the GDP ended up every year with the shareholders of American business.

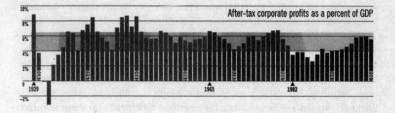

After-tax corporate profits as a percent of GDP

The chart, as you will see, starts in 1929. I'm quite fond of 1929, since that's when it all began for me. My dad was a stock salesman at the time, and after the Crash came, in the fall, he was afraid to call anyone—all those people who'd been burned. So he just stayed home in the afternoons. And there wasn't television then. Soooo . . . I was conceived on or about Nov. 30, 1929 (and born nine months later, on Aug. 30, 1930), and I've forever had a kind of warm feeling about the Crash.

As you can see, corporate profits as a percentage of GDP peaked in 1929, and then they tanked. The left-hand side of the chart, in fact, is filled with aberrations: not only the Depression but also a wartime profits boom—sedated by the excess-profits tax—and another boom after the war. But from 1951 on, the percentage settled down pretty much to a 4% to 6.5% range.

By 1981, though, the trend was headed toward the bottom of that band, and in 1982 profits tumbled to 3.5%. So at that point investors were looking at two strong negatives: Profits were sub-par and interest rates were sky-high.

And as is so typical, investors projected out into the future what they were seeing. That's their unshakable habit: looking into the rear-view mirror instead of through the windshield. What they were observing, looking backward, made them very discouraged about the country. They were projecting high interest rates, they were projecting low profits, and they were therefore valuing the Dow at a level that was the same as 17 years earlier, even though GDP had nearly quintupled.

Now, what happened in the 17 years beginning with 1982? One thing that didn't happen was comparable growth in GDP: In this second 17-year period, GDP less than tripled. But interest rates began their descent, and after the Volcker effect wore off, profits began to climb—not steadily, but nonetheless with real power. You can see the profit trend in the chart, which shows that by the late 1990s, after-tax profits as a percent of GDP were running close to 6%, which is on the upper part of the "normalcy" band. And at the end of 1998, long-term government interest rates had made their way down to that 5%.

These dramatic changes in the two fundamentals that matter most to investors explain much, though not all, of the more than tenfold rise in equity prices—the Dow went from 875 to 9,181—during this 17-year period. What was at work also, of course, was market psychology. Once a bull market gets under way, and once you reach the point where everybody has made money no matter what system he or she followed, a crowd is attracted into the game that is responding not to interest rates and profits but simply to the fact that it seems a mistake to be out of stocks. In effect, these people superimpose an I-can't-miss-the-party factor on top of the fundamental factors that drive the market. Like Pavlov's dog, these "investors" learn that when the bell rings—in this case, the one that opens the New York Stock Exchange at 9:30 A.M.—they get fed. Through this daily reinforcement, they become convinced that there is a God and that He wants them to get rich.

Today, staring fixedly back at the road they just traveled, most investors have rosy expectations. A Paine Webber and Gallup Organization survey released in July shows that the least experienced investors—those who have invested for less than five years—expect annual returns over the next ten years of 22.6%. Even those who have invested for more than 20 years are expecting 12.9%.

Now, I'd like to argue that we can't come even remotely close to that 12.9%, and make my case by examining the key value-determining factors. Today, if an investor is to achieve juicy profits in the market over 10 years or 17 or 20, one or more of three things must happen. I'll delay talking about the last of them for a bit, but here are the first two:

1. **Interest rates must fall further**. If government interest rates, now at a level of about 6%, were to fall to 3%, that factor alone would come close to doubling the value of common stocks. Incidentally, if you think interest rates are going to do that—or fall to the 1% that Japan has experienced—you should head for where you can really make a bundle: bond options.

2. **Corporate profitability in relation to GDP must rise**. You know, someone once told me that New York has more lawyers than people. I think that's the same fellow who thinks profits will become larger than GDP. When you begin to expect the growth of a component factor to forever outpace that of the aggregate, you get into certain mathematical problems. In my opinion, you have to be wildly optimistic to believe that corporate profits as a percent of GDP can, for any sustained period, hold much above 6%. One thing keeping the percentage down will be competition, which is alive and well. In addition, there's a public-policy point: If corporate investors, in aggregate, are going to eat an ever-growing portion of the American economic pie, some other group will have to settle for a smaller portion. That would justifiably raise political problems—and in my view a major reslicing of the pie just isn't going to happen.

So where do some reasonable assumptions lead us? Let's say that GDP grows at an average 5% a year—3% real growth, which is pretty darn good, plus 2%

inflation. If GDP grows at 5%, and you don't have some help from interest rates, the aggregate value of equities is not going to grow a whole lot more. Yes, you can add on a bit of return from dividends. But with stocks selling where they are today, the importance of dividends to total return is way down from what it used to be. Nor can investors expect to score because companies are busy boosting their per-share earnings by buying in their stock. The offset here is that the companies are just about as busy issuing new stock, both through primary offerings and those ever present stock options.

So I come back to my postulation of 5% growth in GDP and remind you that it is a limiting factor in the returns you're going to get: You cannot expect to forever realize a 12% annual increase—much less 22%—in the valuation of American business if its profitability is growing only at 5%. The inescapable fact is that the value of an asset, whatever its character, cannot over the long term grow faster than its earnings do.

Now, maybe you'd like to argue a different case. Fair enough. But give me your assumptions. If you think the American public is going to make 12% a year in stocks, I think you have to say, for example, "Well, that's because I expect GDP to grow at 10% a year, dividends to add two percentage points to returns, and interest rates to stay at a constant level." Or you've got to rearrange these key variables in some other manner. The Tinker Bell approach—clap if you believe—just won't cut it.

Beyond that, you need to remember that future returns are always affected by current valuations and give some thought to what you're getting for your money in the stock market right now. Here are two 1998 figures for the *Fortune* 500. The companies in this universe account for about 75% of the value of all publicly owned American businesses, so when you look at the 500, you're really talking about America Inc.

---

### *FORTUNE* 500

1998 profits: $334,335,000,000

Market value on March 15, 1999: $9,907,233,000,000

---

As we focus on those two numbers, we need to be aware that the profits figure has its quirks. Profits in 1998 included one very unusual item—a $16 billion bookkeeping gain that Ford reported from its spinoff of Associates—and profits also included, as they always do in the 500, the earnings of a few mutual companies, such as State Farm, that do not have a market value. Additionally, one major corporate expense, stock-option compensation costs, is not deducted from profits. On the other hand, the profits figure has been reduced in some cases by write-offs that probably didn't reflect economic reality and could just as well be added back in. But leaving aside these qualifications, investors were saying on March 15 this year that they would pay a hefty $10 trillion for the $334 billion in profits.

Bear in mind—this is a critical fact often ignored—that investors as a whole cannot get anything out of their businesses except what the businesses earn. Sure, you and I can sell each other stocks at higher and higher prices. Let's say the *Fortune* 500 was just one business and that the people in this room each owned a piece of it. In that case, we could sit here and sell each other pieces at ever-ascending prices. You personally might outsmart the next fellow by buying low and selling high. But no money would leave the game when that happened: You'd simply take out what he put in. Meanwhile, the experience of the *group* wouldn't have been affected a whit, because its fate would still be tied to profits. The absolute most that the owners of a business, in aggregate, can get out of it in the end—between now and Judgment Day—is what that business earns over time.

And there's still another major qualification to be considered. If you and I were trading pieces of our business in this room, we could escape transactional costs because there would be no brokers around to take a bite out of every trade we made. But in the real world investors have a habit of wanting to change chairs, or of at least getting advice as to whether they should, and that costs money—big money. The expenses they bear—I call them frictional costs—are for a wide range of items. There's the market maker's spread, and commissions, and sales loads, and 12b-1 fees, and management fees, and custodial fees, and wrap fees, and even subscriptions to financial publications. And don't brush these expenses off as irrelevancies. If you were evaluating a piece of investment real estate, would you not deduct management costs in figuring your return? Yes, of course—and in exactly the same way, stock market investors who are figuring their returns must face up to the frictional costs they bear.

And what do they come to? My estimate is that investors in American stocks pay out well over $100 billion a year—say, $130 billion—to move around on those chairs or to buy advice as to whether they should! Perhaps $100 billion of that relates to the *Fortune* 500. In other words, investors are dissipating almost a third of everything that the *Fortune* 500 is earning for them—that $334 billion in 1998—by handing it over to various types of chair-changing and chair-advisory "helpers." And when that handoff is completed, the investors who own the 500 are reaping less than a $250 billion return on their $10 trillion investment. In my view, that's slim pickings.

Perhaps by now you're mentally quarreling with my estimate that $100 billion flows to those "helpers." How do they charge thee? Let me count the ways. Start with transaction costs, including commissions, the market maker's take, and the spread on underwritten offerings: With double counting stripped out, there will this year be at least 350 billion shares of stock traded in the U.S., and I would estimate that the transaction cost per share for each side—that is, for both the buyer and the seller—will average 6 cents. That adds up to $42 billion.

Move on to the additional costs: hefty charges for little guys who have wrap accounts; management fees for big guys; and, looming very large, a raft of expenses for the holders of domestic equity mutual funds. These funds now have assets of about $3.5 trillion, and you have to conclude that the annual cost of these to their investors—counting management fees, sales loads, 12b-1 fees, general operating costs—runs to at least 1%, or $35 billion.

And none of the damage I've so far described counts the commissions and spreads on options and futures, or the costs borne by holders of variable annuities, or the myriad other charges that the "helpers" manage to think up. In short, $100 billion of frictional costs for the owners of the *Fortune* 500—which is 1% of the 500's market value—looks to me not only highly defensible as an estimate, but quite possibly on the low side.

It also looks like a horrendous cost. I heard once about a cartoon in which a news commentator says, "There was no trading on the New York Stock Exchange today. Everyone was happy with what they owned." Well, if that were really the case, investors would every year keep around $130 billion in their pockets.

Let me summarize what I've been saying about the stock market: I think it's very hard to come up with a persuasive case that equities will over the next 17 years perform anything like—*anything* like—they've performed in the past 17. If I had to pick the most probable return, from appreciation and dividends combined, that investors in aggregate—repeat, aggregate—would earn in a world of constant interest rates, 2% inflation, and those ever hurtful frictional costs, it would be 6%. If you strip out the inflation component from this nominal return (which you would need to do however inflation fluctuates), that's 4% in real terms. And if 4% is wrong, I believe that the percentage is just as likely to be less as more.

Let me come back to what I said earlier: that there are three things that might allow investors to realize significant profits in the market going forward. The first was that interest rates might fall, and the second was that corporate profits as a percent of GDP might rise dramatically. I get to the third point now: Perhaps you are an optimist who believes that though investors as a whole may slog along, you yourself will be a winner. That thought might be particularly seductive in these early days of the information revolution (which I wholeheartedly believe in). Just pick the obvious winners, your broker will tell you, and ride the wave.

Well, I thought it would be instructive to go back and look at a couple of industries that transformed this country much earlier in this century: automobiles and aviation. Take automobiles first: I have here one page, out of 70 in total, of car and truck manufacturers that have operated in this country. At one time, there was a Berkshire car and an Omaha car. Naturally I noticed those. But there was also a telephone book of others.

All told, there appear to have been at least 2,000 car makes, in an industry that had an incredible impact on people's lives. If you had foreseen in the early days of cars how this industry would develop, you would have said, "Here is the road to riches." So what did we progress to by the 1990s? After corporate carnage that never let up, we came down to three U.S. car companies—themselves no lollapaloozas for investors. So here is an industry that had an enormous impact on America—and also an enormous impact, though not the anticipated one, on investors.

Sometimes, incidentally, it's much easier in these transforming events to figure out the losers. You could have grasped the importance of the auto when it came along but still found it hard to pick companies that would make you money. But there was one obvious decision you could have made back then— it's better sometimes to turn these things upside down—and that was to short horses. Frankly, I'm disappointed that the Buffett family was not short horses through this entire period. And we really had no excuse: Living in Nebraska, we would have found it super-easy to borrow horses and avoid a short squeeze.

---

## U.S. HORSE POPULATION

1900: 21 million

1998: 5 million

---

The other truly transforming business invention of the first quarter of the century, besides the car, was the airplane—another industry whose plainly brilliant future would have caused investors to salivate. So I went back to check out aircraft manufacturers and found that in the 1919-39 period, there were about 300 companies, only a handful still breathing today. Among the planes made then—we must have been the Silicon Valley of that age—were both the Nebraska and the Omaha, two aircraft that even the most loyal Nebraskan no longer relies upon.

Move on to failures of airlines. Here [says Buffett in his speech, waving a piece of paper] is a list of 129 airlines that in the past 20 years filed for bankruptcy. Continental was smart enough to make that list twice. As of 1992, in fact—though the picture would have improved since then—the money that had been made since the dawn of aviation by all of this country's airline companies was zero. Absolutely zero.

Sizing all this up, I like to think that if I'd been at Kitty Hawk in 1903 when Orville Wright took off, I would have been farsighted enough, and public-spirited enough—I owed this to future capitalists—to shoot him down. I mean, Karl Marx couldn't have done as much damage to capitalists as Orville did.

I won't dwell on other glamorous businesses that dramatically changed our lives but concurrently failed to deliver rewards to U.S. investors: the manufacture of radios and televisions, for example. But I will draw a lesson from these businesses: The key to investing is not assessing how much an industry is going to affect society, or how much it will grow, but rather determining the competitive advantage of any given company and, above all, the durability of that advantage. The products or services that have wide, sustainable moats around them are the ones that deliver rewards to investors.

This talk of 17-year periods makes me think—incongruously, I admit—of 17-year locusts. What could a current brood of these critters, scheduled to take flight in 2016, expect to encounter? I see them entering a world in which the public is less euphoric about stocks than it is now. Naturally, investors will be feeling disappointment—but only because they started out expecting too much.

Grumpy or not, they will have by then grown considerably wealthier, simply because the American business establishment that they own will have been chugging along, increasing its profits by 3% annually in real terms. Best of all, the rewards from this creation of wealth will have flowed through to Americans in general, who will be enjoying a far higher standard of living than they do today. That wouldn't be a bad world at all—even if it doesn't measure up to what investors got used to in the 17 years just passed.

# Warren Buffett: Revivalist

May 19, 2000

**BY AMY KOVER**

**B**erkshire Hathaway Chairman Warren Buffett calls his annual shareholders' meeting the "Woodstock weekend for capitalists," but investor Michael Cleveland has a better analogy: "It's a religious revival, and Buffett is our evangelist!" For years shareholders have flocked to Omaha each spring to hear Buffett preach the virtues of investing in—and holding on to—strong, proven businesses. As the incredible returns piled up, so have conversions to Buffettism.

But last year Buffett seemed to have lost his heavenly touch. This year Berkshire's per share book value underperformed the S&P 500 index, by 20.5 percentage points—the first time in 20 years it lagged the index. The problem: Most of Buffett's blessed stocks—including Coca-Cola and Gillette—tumbled. Meanwhile, infant Net stocks soared, making many instant millionaires. Buffett still refused to jump in (he doesn't feel comfortable betting on companies and industries subject to great uncertainties). Berkshire Hathaway fell 50%, to a 52-week low of $40,800 a share, by early March. Enough to rattle the faith of even the most devout.

Like any good revivalist, Buffett had a higher power on his side: Wall Street. Miraculously, his stock staged a 47% recovery, to around $60,000, just in time for the meeting in late April. What's more, technology stocks tanked. "We're in this stock for the long haul anyway," notes Brian Goebel of Huntington Beach, Calif. "We're not day traders."

Certainly not. Unlike the nouveaux riches dot-com clique, Buffett-heads aren't glam. Rather than Prada slip dresses and Manolo Blahnik pumps, the weekend uniform was a forest-green Berkshire T-shirt (emblazoned with a fistful of cash) and matching baseball cap. Few of the folks who lined up for free Danish and coffee looked as if they could afford a $60,000 share of Class A stock. This crowd was particularly pumped when Buffett announced that See's Candies, a company that Berkshire owns outright, was working in collaboration with Mattel to make a Barbie doll dressed in See's classic 1950s salesgirl outfit. Everyone clamored for order sheets.

Of course, the weekend wasn't all about Barbies. The meat of the conference was the seven-hour meeting on Saturday in the cavernous Omaha Civic Auditorium. Buffett kicked off the event with a goofy one-hour movie in which he strummed on a ukulele and played *Who Wants to Be a Jillionaire?* with Regis Philbin. (Sample question: What is the sure-fire investment for the new millennium? Buffett opted for a lifeline call to Bill Gates, after noting, "Value investing hasn't been working so hot lately.") Then the gang settled down to business. For almost five hours shareholders posed questions to Buffett and his vice chairman, Charlie Munger. Some shed their worshipful attitude, pressing Buffett on the company's underwhelming performance last year. One 15-year-old said, "I bought Class B shares two years ago for college. When they dipped below $1,500, I decided to investigate correspondence courses." Buffett laughed, as if to say, "You got me."

Throughout the weekend, Omaha became a trade-show floor showcasing Berkshire's wide-ranging businesses: International Dairy Queen, See's Candies, Dexter Shoe, and World Book. Shareholders scooped up discounted knives, mattresses, and diamonds with a hungry vengeance. On Saturday night Buffett lured the faithful to a minor-league baseball game (though many missed half the game waiting in line for Buffett's autograph). And others took part in their favorite pastime: trading Buffett tales. "Have you driven by his house?" one woman asked. "It's so modest!" Another woman says she went to high school with the chairman. She had her photo taken with him at the last reunion. "I had a lot of boasting to do the next day," she laughed.

Some had more pressing reasons to make the pilgrimage this year. Bong Jung, who has owned Berkshire stock for a decade, needed to get back in touch with his Buffett values. "It's been hard not to be tempted by Internet stocks," explains Jung. "When you play golf, you chat about investing. My friend is telling me that he's making 80% in tech, while my stock is down 30%! It's hard not to be jealous. So I came here to renew my faith." "Exactly," chimes in his wife. "Renew." Once again, Sage Buffett gave his minions something to believe in.

# Warren Buffett Invests in the First Lady

October 20, 2000

## BY JEFFREY BIRNBAUM

*Warren Buffett, a Democrat through most of his adult life, has over the years supported many a party candidate. But he gained particular attention—as witness the article that follows—when he backed Hillary Clinton's successful bid in 2000 to be elected senator from New York. The plot then thickened in 2008, as Senator Clinton sought to become the Democrats' candidate for president. That gave Buffett a certain problem, in that he had also developed a cordial relationship with another contender, Barack Obama.*

*Through a friend, Buffett had met Obama earlier when the Chicagoan was preparing to run for senator from Illinois. Obama came to Omaha then for lunch and conversation. Buffett liked the young man and his views, and the two men parted friends.*

*What to do in 2008, then, when Clinton and Obama were both seeking the Democratic nomination? Buffett resolved that question by making himself, in his jest, a "political bigamist." That is, he told the candidates that he would back both of them, which indeed he did.*

*And we know who won. —CL*

Warren Buffett started life as a Republican. He all but inherited the preference from his father, a four-term Republican Congressman from Nebraska. Buffett was so zealous that he was president of the Young Republicans Club at the University of Pennsylvania and in 1948 planned to ride an elephant down a Philadelphia thoroughfare to celebrate the election of Thomas Dewey—until Harry Truman defeated Dewey.

How times have changed! Buffett these days is decidedly Democratic. He has even raised and given money to, of all people, Hillary Clinton. That's right, the Sage of Omaha is putting his money on Clinton's bid to become a Senator from New York. Buffett went to Columbia University to appear on the First Lady's behalf alongside former Treasury Secretary Robert Rubin. He also co-hosted fundraisers for her at the Russian Tea Room in Manhattan and at the Omaha home of Vin Gupta, CEO of Info USA.

Has he lost his mind? Not at all. "I support politicians, irrespective of party, when I think their ideas on important issues are largely in sync with my own," says Buffett, a registered Democrat. In this case he likes Clinton's pro-choice position on abortion and her backing of campaign-finance reform, a pet project of his (unlike some of Clinton's donors, Buffett has not slept over at the White House or Camp David—not even on a couch, he notes). "I support her ideas—it's that simple," Buffett says. "It's the same reason I voted for her husband." He also has a special affinity for New York. His company, Berkshire Hathaway, owns the *Buffalo News*, and he says that what happens in the state has an effect well beyond its borders.

The surprise is that Buffett gives money to politicians at all. He has pushed hard and publicly in recent years to reform campaign financing. He has focused his ire on the system's most flagrant abuse, so-called soft money—the unlimited contributions to political parties. To avoid being labeled a hypocrite, Buffett donates only "hard" money to federal candidates, which is limited to $1,000 per election per candidate. In other words, he has given Clinton $2,000 ($1,000 for the primary and $1,000 for the general election). Buffett also doesn't ask others to contribute to his chosen candidates. He says he wants people to donate because they believe in the aspirant, not because he asks them to.

Still, the name Warren Buffett on a fundraising invitation is sure to draw a crowd. And he has been careful about which candidates to back. They've mostly been Democrats, including his friend Senator Bob Kerrey of Nebraska and, for President, former New Jersey Senator Bill Bradley. He also supported such champions of campaign-finance reform as Democratic Senator Russ Feingold of Wisconsin and Connecticut's Representative Chris Shays, a Republican. In years past he backed such well-regarded lawmakers as GOP Senator Nancy Kassebaum of Kansas and Democratic Senator Daniel Patrick Moynihan, whose seat Clinton is fighting to win. "I think she's quite effective and articulate," Buffett says of Clinton. "If she's elected, she'll be more than one in 100." Does that mean the First Lady is an undervalued asset?

# ADMIRED—AGAIN AND AGAIN

FORTUNE *PUBLISHES ITS LIST of the Most Admired Companies every year, and this year—2001—our editors plucked Berkshire (and Buffett) from its No. 7 spot on the list to write about and feature on the cover. History, and maybe foresight, justified that. Berkshire had then been in the top ten of the Most Admired for five years and has stayed ever since, even after* Fortune *merged its U.S. and "global" lists into one "world" list beginning in 2008. For the last sixteen years, 1997 through 2013, Berkshire is the only company that has always made the top ten.*

*Buffett loves it all. Having Berkshire finish high in a list ranked by revenues, as is the* Fortune 500 *(where Berkshire has risen to the top ten) matters little to him. But he values a good reputation immensely. Talking to* Fortune *in 2010 about how a business earns trust, he said, "You can't do it in a day or week or month. You do it one grain of sand at a time. And you can destroy it fast, but you build it slowly."*

*Being a perennial object of admiration does not rule out a company having operating problems, or perhaps flunking the best use of its assets, and this story, "The Value Machine," talks about Berkshire's intractable difficulties with its Maine subsidiary Dexter Shoe. Naturally Buffett did not anticipate problems— he was, in fact, an enthusiastic acquirer—when Berkshire bought the company in 1993, paying stock worth $419 million. But Buffett severely underestimated the low-cost overseas competition that Dexter was facing and by the 1999 annual report was forced to acknowledge that things at the company were not good. In 2000, Berkshire wrote off $219 million of Dexter accounting goodwill. And the next year Buffett threw in the towel, conceding that he a) shouldn't have bought Dexter in the first place; b) particularly shouldn't have bought it with stock; and c) had procrastinated in attacking its problems.*

*The management of Dexter was turned over in 2001 to another Berkshire shoe company, whose managers, Frank Rooney and Jim Issler, reduced its business— amid plant shutdowns and layoffs—to a few operations. By 2005, the Dexter name had disappeared entirely from Berkshire's annual report.*

*Today, Buffett says of Dexter, "This is definitely the worst acquisition I have ever made—so far."*

*Harold Alfond, chairman and majority owner of Dexter when Berkshire bought it and a well-known philanthropist before and after, died in 2007 and left most of his fortune to the Harold Alfond Foundation. When his will was settled, the foundation's assets jumped fivefold, to $500 million (about 80 percent of that in Berkshire stock). The foundation principally gives to Maine education, medical, and youth development causes. So that is another example—a paradoxical one—of Berkshire wealth going to philanthropy. —CL*

# The Value Machine

February 19, 2001

## BY CAROL LOOMIS

A small quiz, if you don't mind: Kindly describe what each of the companies in the top ten of the Most Admired does.

Most readers could breeze through eight of these paragons. They're into megastores (Wal-Mart) and securities brokerages (Schwab) and computer chips (Intel) and so on. General Electric is tougher to parse: It's financial services, but also a TV network and an electrical equipment and aerospace empire, soon to include Honeywell. But the real puzzler is No. 7, Berkshire Hathaway of Omaha. Using a sharp No. 2 pencil, could you please write 500 words on that company's business?

If you're like many people, you couldn't get past four of them: "That's Warren Buffett's company." It would take a Berkshire groupie, of whom there are carloads, to elucidate the fine points: What we've got here is a highly unusual combination of a very profitable operating company—insurance in a big way, plus a crazy quilt of other businesses—and a CEO, now 70, who invests its money and who, in that department, has a strong, long-standing claim to being the best in the world.

In the 36 years that Buffett has run the company, Berkshire's per-share book value—the performance statistic that best describes the success of an insurance company—has grown, on average, by more than 23% a year. There have been a couple of ugly lurches, notably a terrible year in 1999, but in 32 of the 36 years Berkshire's per-share results have beaten the total return of the S&P 500, often by miles. Berkshire's stock, which Buffett wouldn't dream of splitting—he sends birthday greetings to friends that say, "May you live until Berkshire splits"—has tracked the company's success and then some. In those same 36 years, it has gone from about $12 a share to a year-end price of $71,000, which is an annual growth rate of 27%.

Famous though this record may be, even many of the business people who vote for the Most Admired don't understand the machinery behind Berkshire's value proposition. A few may not even connect with the fact that they're voting—lawdy!—for an insurance company. But clearly they like something: This is the fifth straight year that Berkshire has made the top ten.

We now interrupt this account for some disclosure: I'm an admirer too, and a longtime friend of Buffett's, and perennial editor of his annual report (though he's most certainly the writer), and a Berkshire shareholder for decades. Buffett and I have talked forever about collaborating on a book about his business career—in terms of words actually written, this has been all hat and no cattle—and as a result I have had unusual access to his thinking.

What I know at this moment is that Berkshire had a remarkable year in 2000, in ways largely unrecognized. I'm not talking about the stock, although that's what most Berkshire followers were looking at. While tech stocks were skyrocketing early in the year, Berkshire was tanking. It got all the way down to $40,800 in March, when, says Buffett, "we were on that other list—the Most Admired by Short-Sellers." The stock then came back to that $71,000, which from the bottom was a gain of 74%. (In late January the stock was $68,000.) The rebound left Berkshire climbing 26.6% for the calendar year—in a down year for most companies, including seven of the ten at the top of the Most Admired list.

So what! The real story is what was going on in the company, not the stock. In a grand sweep of allocating capital—which has been his greatest talent—Buffett completed or initiated the purchase of no fewer than eight companies. We're not talking stocks here (though some of the lot were publicly owned) but rather entire companies.

One of the acquisitions, U.S. Liability of Wayne, Pa., adds to Berkshire's insurance empire. The others contribute new swatches to the Berkshire crazy quilt, being in businesses as ludicrously diverse, and as old economy, as bricks and boots (Justin Industries of Fort Worth) and fine jewelry (the Ben Bridge chain, headquartered in Seattle) and carpets (Shaw Industries of Dalton, Ga.). The purchase price, in total, was $8 billion. That's an amount dwarfed by the $22 billion in stock that Berkshire paid for reinsurer General Re in 1998. But the $8 billion paid for the pieces of eight was almost all cash. That's a lot of cash—more than five times as much, for example, as the $1.5 billion that Berkshire put some years ago into its biggest stock investment ever, American Express. None of the $8 billion, furthermore, was borrowed. Buffett just reached into the big bucket of cash equivalents he's been patiently sitting with, and handed over the money.

When all the acquisitions are complete, Berkshire will have more than doubled the number of its employees and added about $13 billion in revenues—although $5 billion of that, from MidAmerican Energy, will not be consolidated because of regulatory restrictions. Even so, when Berkshire's 2000 revenues are reported, they ought to be close to $30 billion. This year, for the first time, Berkshire will be among the top 50 companies on the *Fortune* 500 list. The company's profits should be in the range of $3 billion, including significant capital gains that Berkshire realized during the year, from the sale of certain stocks whose identity Buffett hasn't yet disclosed.

Buffett never set out to climb into the upper reaches of the *Fortune* 500 list. Neither did he have some grand plan for acquisitions—"other than answering the phone," he says—as he entered 2000. The truth is, when it comes to creating value for investors, he doesn't see the world the way many chief executives do. He doesn't focus on his company's stock price; on a given day, he may not know where it stands. He is not searching for synergy; he likes to buy businesses that generate healthy earnings and leave them alone. And he is a switch hitter: He has always shown a willingness to buy whole businesses or, alternatively, to buy portions of businesses in the stock market. It's just that in 2000 he went on a kind of buying binge in the whole-company camp.

And was he concurrently putting new capital into the stock market? No. He's been buying some junk bonds, among them Finova's (but not Conseco's, even though some publications recently reported he was). He was, however, a net seller of stocks in 2000, and in each of the four years before as well. This retreat fits his well-known opinion that future returns from stocks can't begin to match those that investors earned in the 1980s and '90s. Among the stocks he's known to have chopped in the past few years are McDonald's and Disney.

In fact, for all his renown as a stock picker, Buffett has long preferred to have Berkshire grow not by buying stocks that go up, which is what most people would assume, but by adding businesses. Yes, that can add problems too—he's had some—but he'd still rather head in that direction.

The preference is emotional, in that he likes dealing with the managers of Berkshire's subsidiaries and building a real, working business. And the preference is often economic as well, because of taxes. Imagine that (1) a subsidiary of Berkshire, such as See's Candies, makes $10 million after-tax, and that (2) Coca-Cola simultaneously makes $125 million after-tax, which would mean Berkshire's share of that—given that it owns 8% of Coke—would be $10 million. The $10 million earned by See's is totally Berkshire's. The Coke $10 million, however, is ensnared: To capture that money Berkshire must pay additional taxes, either on Coke dividends it receives or on capital gains it realizes upon selling Coke shares (it has never sold any). If the opportunities for reinvesting capital within Coke are sufficiently good, which means that the profits "belonging" to Berkshire will grow, Buffett happily accepts the tax toll. But otherwise he has no problem identifying the $10 million earned inside as what he'd like to have.

He likes cash of all kinds, of course, and in Berkshire he has built a machine that produces prodigious amounts of it. The engine in the machine is the company's insurance business, which yields that wonderful thing called "float"—money an insurer can invest while it's holding premiums that will eventually go to pay claims. The businesses Buffett buys with his available funds become parts of the machinery too, generating cash for further investment.

As for what he buys: Buffett likes companies at sensible prices—which leaves him avoiding the auctions investment bankers run—that throw off cash and have capable, honest, and trustworthy people running them. He wants substantial earnings, for sure, but cares not at all whether they are consistent: "I'd rather have a lumpy 15% return on capital," he has often said, "than a smooth 12%." And he wants businesses that he can understand and that are not subject to major change. It is the rapid change in technology that has kept him away from tech investments. He feels that he cannot be sure how much cash flow a tech company will be producing ten years from now, so he stays away.

To get good companies at good prices, it helps to be perceived as a great owner, and Buffett has that reputation. He has piled up furniture retailers more or less by word of mouth—the first one in Omaha, the next in Utah, then Texas, then Massachusetts, then Iowa. For some sellers Berkshire is a refuge, a place to land when, say, some members of a family that controls a private company want cash and others wish to keep running the business. To the latter Buffett promises independence and respect and then—barring some irreconcilable problem that just has to be dealt with—delivers on the commitment. "We don't have any MBAs running around telling these people what to do," Buffett says. "And God knows I wouldn't know what to tell them." To public companies that may also have a family reason for selling, or that just want to escape the cold world of regrettable stock prices, unrealistic quarterly demands, and unfriendly suitors, he is equally a haven.

These are acquisition parameters that have logic in any year. But 2000 had a tightening financial character that gave Berkshire an edge in buying companies. The money available for purchases of companies got short as the year went on, with junk bonds tough to sell and big equity investors skittish. In fact, a New York investment banker visiting Buffett told him that he thought of Berkshire as the only investor in the country that could lay out $5 billion for an equity position.

There is no better example of Berkshire's edge—and of Buffett's agility in exploiting it—than the Johns Manville purchase, the eighth acquisition of the year. Manville's profile in 2000 included $2 billion in revenues from insulation and roofing products, more than $200 million in profits, and a controlling stockholder—a trust that had been set up in Manville's bankruptcy days to assume its asbestos liabilities. In mid-2000 a buyout group made a deal to acquire the company for $2.8 billion. But Manville's business later went into a cyclical slide, and the buyers ran into financing problems. They bowed out Dec. 8, a Friday. Among those left stranded was Manville's CEO, Charles "Jerry" Henry, who had been set to participate in the buyout and was looking forward to getting divorced from the trust.

Buffett and the man he's long called his partner, Berkshire's vice chairman, Charles Munger (who lives in Los Angeles), had been wishfully watching the Manville action from the wings. And three days later, on Monday, they called the trust and offered $2.2 billion for Manville, cash on the barrel. They had a deal, negotiated by phone, in 24 hours and an announcement Dec. 20. That afternoon, Jerry Henry went before Manville's Denver employees and announced, to cheers, "There is a Santa Claus. But he's not located at the North Pole, my friends. He's in Omaha."

Henry, 59, has since met with Buffett in Omaha, for about six hours. He went into the meeting, Henry says, thinking about plans he had to retire and ready to say "I'm gone" if he got any clue that he couldn't work with Buffett. Instead, he says, he emerged from the meeting charged up: "I came out totally committed to making this thing work. It's easy to see what happens with Buffett's companies. You end up saying you don't want to let this guy down."

For this article, I talked to the heads of all eight of the companies Berkshire bought. I heard no complaints about their new owner, just compliments. True, there's no reason these people should publicly grouse about their boss, especially to one of his friends. But it's also true that I heard stories from the sellers about money renounced, just so a Berkshire deal could be made.

Ed Bridge, 44, the fourth-generation co-head of Ben Bridge Jeweler, got to thinking a couple of years ago, in a period when he was ill, that he should sell his family's much treasured, privately owned company. He considered an IPO, or an LBO, or selling to a "strategic" buyer, meaning someone in a related business. But he also got a push toward Berkshire from Barnett Helzberg of Kansas City, who'd sold his own jewelry store business to Buffett in 1995. Bridge couldn't quite see why Buffett would be interested in his relatively small company, described by Bridge as "65 doors in 11 Western states." Bridge nonetheless talked by phone to Buffett early last year and then sent him some financial data. Back came Buffett's enthusiastic reply, recalled by Bridge as "You guys are great, great, great."

Things then moved toward a deal. But a strategic buyer heard that Bridge might be selling and began edging up to an offer. "I think," says Bridge, "that we probably could have received 20% more from this buyer than we got from Berkshire. But I also think we would have destroyed the business if we had gone that way." So in early May he and Buffett agreed on the details of a deal (including a price not being made public). They didn't shake hands, because they hadn't ever met at that point. That suited Buffett just fine—"I buy companies all the time over the phone," he told Bridge—but Bridge really wanted to see this fellow personally. He got the chance later in May, when Buffett, on his way to a Microsoft conference, stopped to do a Bridge visit.

The managers and employees that he talked to that day got hours of his attention: He has great stamina when doing something he likes. They also got a dose of the usual Buffett: bespectacled, Midwestern looks; carelessly combed gray hair; unbuttoned suit coat, suspenders, and probably the same tie he'd worn for a month straight; plain talk dressed in metaphors. One directive Buffett gave that day is familiar to many of his companies: "Just keep on doing what you're doing. We're never going to tell a .400 hitter how to change his batting stance."

Bridge also recalls that, as he and Buffett drove past a See's Candies store, Buffett reeled off its dollar sales. To Bridge's marveling at this feat of memory,

Buffett replied, "Well, I love numbers." That made Bridge think back to what the head of a Berkshire subsidiary had warned when Bridge inquired about Buffett: "Don't show him any number you don't want him to see, because he'll remember it."

Buffett's buying binge naturally raises a question: How have his past acquisitions performed? Generally they have been very successful, but not all have been unequivocal winners. General Re, his $22 billion purchase of 1998, has slogged through a tough reinsurance market and been hurt by its own pricing mistakes. It's working its way out of those and had improved results in 2000, but some insurance analysts have argued that Buffett goofed in making this purchase. He himself mourns any deal that must be made in stock, as this one was, because he so dislikes relinquishing pieces of ownership in Berkshire. But he says he is confident Gen Re will turn into a valuable Berkshire asset.

In Buffett's noninsurance companies—the manufacturers, retailers, and service companies, in other words—the profit margins generally look good, especially considering that these businesses are largely mundane. In 1999 the companies made $700 million pretax on $5.7 billion in revenues. After-tax, their margin was around 7.7%, which was well above the *Fortune* 500's median of 5%.

Furthermore, the managers of many Berkshire subsidiaries work under compensation agreements that encourage them to hold their use of capital to a minimum—and to zip any spare dollars off to Omaha headquarters. ("That's why," says Buffett, "I always come down to the office on Saturday to personally open the mail.") Once the dollars get to headquarters, by the way, they don't go to paying Buffett: His Berkshire salary is $100,000 a year and not set to rise. On the other hand, he owns 31% of Berkshire's stock, recently worth about $32 billion, so we won't feel sorry for him.

In his manufacturing lineup, Buffett's biggest disappointment has been Dexter Shoe, a Maine company he bought in the early 1990s for some $440 million in stock. Encountering severe foreign competition, Dexter tried hard to stick with U.S. plants, and all it got for its pains was drastically reduced profits, and then losses. Making the kind of statement he has had very little experience with, Buffett will say in his annual report that he clearly overpaid for Dexter and that he compounded the mistake by paying in stock. He will add that he does not consider Dexter's management to have been at fault.

But he has had to deal occasionally with other situations in which management was patently the problem and in which he has had to resort to firing people. Some of the problems have arisen in companies he's bought from families, in which the older, highly competent managers initially in charge do not have children with comparable abilities (which may be, he recognizes, the reason the elders decided to sell). He hit that kind of trouble at Fechheimer, a Cincinnati manufacturer of uniforms that Berkshire bought in 1986, when it was run by two brothers in their mid-60s. One brother then retired, and the other, the CEO, became ill. The CEO's son took over but couldn't cut the mustard and was ousted. Years went by with no CEO settled upon. Finally, in 1999, Buffett made a rare attempt to cross-pollinate, making a manager from one of his insurance companies, Brad Kinstler, the head of Fechheimer. "And he's just terrific," says Buffett, relievedly. "We may have to try this kind of thing more often."

The vigor with which Buffett goes at fixing up his machine, or doing anything that involves Berkshire, belies his 70 years. Nonetheless, his age is a subject that often preys on the minds of the company's shareholders. Their concern is rational, given what Berkshire is. First, it is a fine collection of assets, whose value would survive Buffett's not being around. Second, it is his skill at investing the cash flow from these assets—and this talent is probably irreplaceable.

The age topic got special attention last summer when Buffett underwent an operation to remove several polyps (all benign) in his colon. He recovered quickly, resumed his morning run on a treadmill, and returned to eating hamburgers, French fries snowed under by salt, and the occasional Dairy Queen sundae, all washed down by Cherry Cokes.

Nonetheless, the operation drove the press to review what he had said in his annual report about management succession. If he were to die today, his 46-year-old son, Howard, chairman of an agricultural equipment firm in Assumption, Ill., and also a working farmer, would become nonexecutive chairman of Berkshire. The sweeping job that the boss does now would be split between two people. Louis Simpson, 64, who manages the investments of Berkshire's GEICO subsidiary, would probably take over Berkshire's portfolio. The job of overseeing Berkshire's operating subsidiaries would go to some insider whom Buffett has selected but not identified publicly. In an October article, the Wall Street Journal speculated that three executives in Berkshire's subsidiaries had the lead: Ajit Jain, 49, who works with Buffett in constructing big, arcane insurance deals; Tony Nicely, 57, head of GEICO; and Richard Santulli, 56, CEO of Executive Jet.

Buffett says any one of them could do his job better than he can—"but don't let that get around." He has a solution anyway: "Forget about splitting the stock; we're just going to split my age."

The fact is that it's hard to take any discussion of successors seriously because Buffett (and his doctor) consider his health good, and he simply plans to keep doing his job indefinitely. He loves his work—loves it! So does Jack Welch, of course, but GE has retirement rules and Berkshire doesn't. Buffett sent Welch a kidding reminder of that recently, after Welch, 65, made a comment to the Financial Times about age: "There is nothing worse than seeing the old, drooling chairman sitting in the seat." Buffett faxed that sentence to Welch with a scrawled message: "Jack, we don't tolerate this sort of talk at Berkshire. I keep Charlie on-stage"—that would be vice chairman Munger, 77, on the stage at Berkshire's annual meeting—"so the stockholders know it could be worse."

It may seem odd to ask a 77-year-old whether he thinks his 70-year-old friend is still sharp, but that's what we did recently with the aforesaid Charlie, who is recognized as astute by all who know him. Does he see, we asked Munger, any diminution of Buffett's mental powers or ability to think outside the box? Munger first came through with a totally typical monosyllabic answer: "No." Prodded to elaborate, he said the Buffett of today might just be "a little better" than the Buffett of all the yesterdays. "Because he knows more," Munger says. "Now, I've watched enough people age to know that things can happen pretty fast. Some people go along at 90 miles an hour, and then—like an orange tree does—they go into a quick decline. So you can't make extrapolations. But I don't see the slightest diminution in Warren's mental powers." Munger adds that Berkshire has built up a reputational advantage. "That gives you shortcuts," he says. "We basically made a deal to buy Johns Manville without meeting any of the people."

To those who know him, it also seems that Buffett keeps coming up with fresh ideas. They don't have much to do with product innovation, unless you count his dedication to helping See's pick new lollipop flavors. But Berkshire has repeatedly dealt with its shareholders in an innovative way: giving them an "owner's manual" that states Berkshire's operating principles; permitting them to personally determine (based on how many shares each has) where Berkshire's charitable contributions should go; even structuring an annual meeting that permits shareholders five hours of opportunity to ask the bosses, Buffett and Munger, any business-related question they want.

And, of course, the annual meeting in Omaha is itself unique. Around 10,000 shareholders turn up, many from abroad, for an entire weekend of festivities: a baseball game at which Buffett throws the first pitch, usually poorly; out-of-control shopping ("I *hope*," says Buffett) at Borsheim's, Berkshire's Omaha jewelry store; and those hours of Buffett and Munger teaching, because that's what it is, at the meeting itself.

In sum, this is a company that thinks first and foremost about its shareholders—though there may be one point on which Buffett and some of his flock disagree. Other than Buffett, I have never met a CEO who didn't think his stock was undervalued. Buffett, however, has gone through periods—one was in 1998, when Berkshire rose above $80,000—in which he felt the stock was overpriced. And he agonized about it, because he does not like to think of Berkshire shareholders as either buying or selling at prices that are significantly out of line with what he views as a zone of fairness. "I'll say this," he said recently. "I'm bothered more by Berkshire getting too high than too low." Will this heresy get him ejected from the top ten of the Most Admired?

For Berkshire shareholders the fresh ideas that probably matter most are those that come out of the company's core insurance company, National Indemnity. Over the years the insurer has built a worldwide reputation for its willingness to write a policy covering just about any risk, of almost any size (though the company always caps its exposure), if the premium is satisfactory. Figuring the odds on these policies is a joint project of Buffett and Ajit Jain—both eminently suited to the game—and the two sometimes take Berkshire into weird territory. It would require pages to discuss that terrain fully, but here's an example: Last year they wrote a policy protecting Grab.com against having to pay a $1 billion prize (with a present value of $170 million), a lure that Grab.com used to attract millions of people to its Internet site, so as to gather information about them that would be useful to marketers. The game for visitors to the site was to pick seven numbers between one and 77; bulletins warned that the odds against anybody's picking the right seven were formidable. Nobody knew that better than Buffett and Jain, and in fact no one did win. But obviously somebody could have, which would have put a huge hole in Berkshire's earnings. "I wouldn't have thrown a party if we had had to pay off," says Buffett, "but we take well-judged chances like that all the time. That's what we do that almost no one else is willing to do."

Jain, whose office is in Connecticut, is someone who has actually seen a change in Buffett. In the early '90s the two used to talk almost every night around nine, Omaha time, about the day's insurance happenings. Then Buffett started playing bridge on the Internet, and that's where he normally is now at nine. Jain says the change is okay: "We just talk now before or after the bridge game."

Having frequently played bridge with Buffett, both as partner and opponent, I have come to think that his bridge style, in some ways, resembles his business and investing style (though he is far harder on some of his bridge partners than on his managers). In bridge he does not employ some of the modern bidding conventions that most players accept as standard. He knows all the odds in the game, and both bids and plays his hands with them in mind. He is analytical and focused when playing, and he keeps getting better—though he's not what bridge folk call expert. When he makes a stupid mistake, he tends to be hard on himself. "I can't believe I did that," he said recently after one hand. "That was incredible." The self-accusatory remark reminded me of something he once said about his mistakes in business: "It wouldn't matter to me that nobody else knew. I'd know."

The record shows there can't have been too many of those mistakes. And given continued good health, Buffett is likely to keep on burnishing the record as well. An interesting fact about Berkshire at the moment is that its three largest stock holdings—Coke, American Express, and Gillette—all have new CEOs (Douglas Daft at Coke; Kenneth Chenault at American Express; and James Kilts, a Nabisco executive who was just hired at Gillette). That will give Buffett something to watch. And as he says, with relish, "I've got all these wonderful companies that we own to look at."

He also still has cash. "This place reminds me of Mickey Mouse as the Sorcerer's Apprentice in *Fantasia*," he says. "His problem was floods of water. Ours is cash." The stuff never burns a hole in Buffett's pocket—patience is one of his strengths. Now that he's into serial buying, though, you wouldn't want to lay odds—unless you covered yourself with a Berkshire insurance policy—that he won't strike again.

# A Letter from *Fortune*'s Letters Column

March 26, 2001

"The Value Machine" is a great article, but I'd like to quibble with one point you make: "Buffett isn't searching for synergy." Whether he's searching for it or not, he has an uncanny record for delivering it. Time after time a good return on equity has become a great one under the Berkshire umbrella. Consider See's Candy, Buffalo News, Scott Fetzer, and so on. Double the return on equity of a company, and you get much more than a doubling of the company's intrinsic value.

While the record for synergy is interesting, the source of that record is important. Buffett is the only conglomerateur I can think of who doesn't hew to the command and control model. To that extent, he has created a new management model.

Buffett is one of the greatest managers in history. He created the most successful of all the '60s conglomerates, the most successful of all the '70s inflation hedges, and he's on the verge of creating the biggest category killer of all time (a collection of category killers). He should get his due as a manager.

CHARLES WALLMAN
Washington Island, Wisconsin

# Warren Buffett on the Stock Market

### December 10, 2001

#### *A Buffett speech that Carol Loomis converted into an article*

*Buffett's speech at Allen & Co.'s 1999 Sun Valley, Idaho, conclave of business leaders (see page 166) was so widely admired that Herbert Allen, head of the company, asked Buffett two years later for a reprise. Once again I worked with Buffett to convert his speech (given in July 2001) into a* Fortune *article. On the opening page, we set up the piece with a question: "So where do we stand now— with the stock market seeming to reflect a dismal profit outlook, an unfamiliar war, and rattled consumer confidence?"*

*Buffett's discussion, an exemplar of his out-of-the-box thinking, turns to several themes he feels deeply about: the resilience of the U.S. economy; the inability of investors, very much including pension funds, to ignore the rearview mirror; the importance of price in gauging when it's time to buy.*

*In the two years between his first speech and the second, indeed, the Dow Industrials had dropped from 11,194 to 9,500 as the Internet bubble deflated. Just on the basis of price, Buffett's expectations for long-term stock returns had therefore improved.*

*But not by a lot. A chart in the article, based on a Buffett metric, showed that prices were still historically high in relation to GNP. The chart became famous: Over the years that followed I would frequently get calls and e-mails asking* Fortune *to update it. And in fact we ultimately did, running a new version of the chart in early 2009 (see page 286) when for a time it appeared that stocks would never hit bottom. —CL*

The last time I tackled this subject, in 1999, I broke down the previous 34 years into two 17-year periods, which in the sense of lean years and fat were astonishingly symmetrical. Here's the first period. As you can see, over 17 years the Dow gained exactly one-tenth of one percent.

---

### DOW JONES INDUSTRIAL AVERAGE

Dec. 31, 1964: 874.12

Dec. 31, 1981: 875.00

---

And here's the second, marked by an incredible bull market that, as I laid out my thoughts, was about to end (though I didn't know that).

---

### DOW INDUSTRIALS

Dec. 31, 1981: 875.00

Dec. 31, 1998: 9181.43

---

Now, you couldn't explain this remarkable divergence in markets by, say, differences in the growth of gross national product. In the first period—that dismal time for the market—GNP actually grew more than twice as fast as it did in the second period.

---

### GAIN IN GROSS NATIONAL PRODUCT

1964-1981: 373%

1981-1998: 177%

---

So what was the explanation? I concluded that the market's contrasting moves were caused by extraordinary changes in two critical economic variables—and by a related psychological force that eventually came into play.

Here I need to remind you about the definition of "investing," which though simple is often forgotten. Investing is laying out money today to receive more money tomorrow.

That gets to the first of the economic variables that affected stock prices in the two periods—interest rates. In economics, interest rates act as gravity behaves in the physical world. At all times, in all markets, in all parts of the world, the tiniest change in rates changes the value of every financial asset. You see that clearly with the fluctuating prices of bonds. But the rule applies as well to farmland, oil reserves, stocks, and every other financial asset. And the effects can be huge on values. If interest rates are, say, 13%, the present value of a dollar that you're going to receive in the future from an investment is not nearly as high as the present value of a dollar if rates are 4%.

So here's the record on interest rates at key dates in our 34-year span. They moved dramatically up—that was bad for investors—in the first half of that period and dramatically down—a boon for investors—in the second half.

## INTEREST RATES, LONG-TERM GOVERNMENT BONDS

Dec. 31, 1964: 4.20%

Dec. 31, 1981: 13.65%

Dec. 31, 1998: 5.09%

The other critical variable here is how many dollars investors expected to get from the companies in which they invested. During the first period expectations fell significantly because corporate profits weren't looking good. By the early 1980s Fed Chairman Paul Volcker's economic sledgehammer had, in fact, driven corporate profitability to a level that people hadn't seen since the 1930s.

The upshot is that investors lost their confidence in the American economy: They were looking at a future they believed would be plagued by two negatives. First, they didn't see much good coming in the way of corporate profits. Second, the sky-high interest rates prevailing caused them to discount those meager profits further. These two factors, working together, caused stagnation in the stock market from 1964 to 1981, even though those years featured huge improvements in GNP. The business of the country grew while investors' valuation of that business shrank!

And then the reversal of those factors created a period during which much lower GNP gains were accompanied by a bonanza for the market. First, you got a major increase in the rate of profitability. Second, you got an enormous drop in interest rates, which made a dollar of future profit that much more valuable. Both phenomena were real and powerful fuels for a major bull market. And in time the psychological factor I mentioned was added to the equation: Speculative trading exploded, simply because of the market action that people had seen. Later, we'll look at the pathology of this dangerous and oft-recurring malady.

Two years ago I believed the favorable fundamental trends had largely run their course. For the market to go dramatically up from where it was then would have required long-term interest rates to drop much further (which is always possible) or for there to be a major improvement in corporate profitability (which seemed, at the time, considerably less possible). If you take a look at a 50-year chart of after-tax profits as a percent of gross domestic product, you find that the rate normally falls between 4%—that was its neighborhood in the bad year of 1981, for example—and 6.5. For the rate to go above 6.5% is rare. In the very good profit years of 1999 and 2000, the rate was under 6% and this year it may well fall below 5%.

So there you have my explanation of those two wildly different 17-year periods. The question is, How much do those periods of the past for the market say about its future?

To suggest an answer, I'd like to look back over the 20th century. As you know, this was really the American century. We had the advent of autos, we had aircraft, we had radio, TV, and computers. It was an incredible period. Indeed, the per capita growth in U.S. output, measured in real dollars (that is, with no impact from inflation), was a breathtaking 702%.

The century included some very tough years, of course—like the Depression years of 1929 to 1933. But a decade-by-decade look at per capita GNP [which is presented in the chart on the facing page] shows something remarkable: As a nation, we made relatively consistent progress throughout the century. So you might think that the economic value of the U.S.—at least as measured by its securities markets—would have grown at a reasonably consistent pace as well.

That's not what happened. We know from our earlier examination of the 1964-98 period that parallelism broke down completely in that era. But the whole century makes this point as well. At its beginning, for example, between 1900 and 1920, the country was chugging ahead, explosively expanding its use of electricity, autos, and the telephone. Yet the market barely moved, recording a 0.4% annual increase that was roughly analogous to the slim pickings between 1964 and 1981.

---

### DOW INDUSTRIALS

Dec. 31, 1899: 66.08

Dec. 31, 1920: 71.95

---

In the next period, we had the market boom of the '20s, when the Dow jumped 430% to 381 in September 1929. Then we go 19 years—*19 years*—and there is the Dow at 177, half the level where it began. That's true even though the 1940s displayed by far the largest gain in per capita GDP (50%) of any 20th-century decade. Following that came a 17-year period when stocks finally took off—making a great five-to-one gain. And then the two periods discussed at the start: stagnation until 1981, and the roaring boom that wrapped up this amazing century.

To break things down another way, we had three huge, secular bull markets that covered about 44 years, during which the Dow gained more than 11,000 points. And we had three periods of stagnation, covering some 56 years. During those 56 years the country made major economic progress and yet the Dow actually *lost* 292 points.

How could this have happened? In a flourishing country in which people are focused on making money, how could you have had three extended and anguishing periods of stagnation that in aggregate—leaving aside dividends—

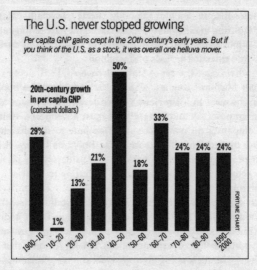

### The U.S. never stopped growing

Per capita GNP gains crept in the 20th century's early years. But if you think of the U.S. as a stock, it was overall one helluva mover.

20th-century growth in per capita GNP (constant dollars)

50%
33%
29%
24% 24% 24%
21%
18%
13%
1%

1900–10  '10–20  '20–30  '30–40  '40–50  '50–60  '60–70  '70–80  '80–90  1990–2000

FORTUNE CHART

would have lost you money? The answer lies in the mistake that investors repeatedly make—that psychological force I mentioned above: People are habitually guided by the rear-view mirror and, for the most part, by the vistas immediately behind them.

The first part of the century offers a vivid illustration of that myopia. In the century's first 20 years, stocks normally yielded more than high-grade bonds. That relationship now seems quaint, but it was then almost axiomatic. Stocks were known to be riskier, so why buy them unless you were paid a premium?

And then came along a 1924 book—slim and initially unheralded, but destined to move markets as never before—written by a man named Edgar Lawrence Smith. The book, called *Common Stocks as Long Term Investments*, chronicled a study Smith had done of security price movements in the 56 years ended in 1922. Smith had started off his study with a hypothesis: Stocks would do better in times of inflation, and bonds would do better in times of deflation. It was a perfectly reasonable hypothesis.

But consider the first words in the book: "These studies are the record of a failure—the failure of facts to sustain a preconceived theory." Smith went on: "The facts assembled, however, seemed worthy of further examination. If they would not prove what we had hoped to have them prove, it seemed desirable to turn them loose and to follow them to whatever end they might lead."

Now, there was a smart man, who did just about the hardest thing in the world to do. Charles Darwin used to say that whenever he ran into something that contradicted a conclusion he cherished, he was obliged to write the new finding down within 30 minutes. Otherwise his mind would work to reject the discordant information, much as the body rejects transplants. Man's natural inclination is to cling to his beliefs, particularly if they are reinforced by recent experience—a flaw in our makeup that bears on what happens during secular bull markets and extended periods of stagnation.

To report what Edgar Lawrence Smith discovered, I will quote a legendary thinker—John Maynard Keynes, who in 1925 reviewed the book, thereby putting it on the map. In his review, Keynes described "perhaps Mr. Smith's most important point . . . and certainly his most novel point. Well-managed industrial companies do not, as a rule, distribute to the shareholders the whole of their earned profits. In good years, if not in all years, they retain a part of their profits and put them back in the business. Thus *there is an element of compound interest* (Keynes' italics) operating in favor of a sound industrial investment."

It was that simple. It wasn't even news. People certainly knew that companies were not paying out 100% of their earnings. But investors hadn't thought through the implications of the point. Here, though, was this guy Smith saying, "Why do stocks typically outperform bonds? A major reason is that businesses retain earnings, with these going on to generate still more earnings—and dividends, too."

That finding ignited an unprecedented bull market. Galvanized by Smith's insight, investors piled into stocks, anticipating a double dip: their higher initial yield over bonds, and growth to boot. For the American public, this new understanding was like the discovery of fire.

But before long that same public was burned. Stocks were driven to prices that first pushed down their yield to that on bonds and ultimately drove their yield far lower. What happened then should strike readers as eerily familiar: The mere fact that share prices were rising so quickly became the main impetus for people to rush into stocks. What the few bought for the *right* reason in 1925, the many bought for the *wrong* reason in 1929.

Astutely, Keynes anticipated a perversity of this kind in his 1925 review. He wrote: "It is dangerous . . . to apply to the future inductive arguments based on past experience, unless one can distinguish the broad reasons why past experience was what it was." If you can't do that, he said, you may fall into the trap of expecting results in the future that will materialize only if conditions are exactly the same as they were in the past. The special conditions he had in mind, of course, stemmed from the fact that Smith's study covered a half century during which stocks generally yielded more than high-grade bonds.

The colossal miscalculation that investors made in the 1920s has recurred in one form or another several times since. The public's monumental hangover from its stock binge of the 1920s lasted, as we have seen, through 1948. The country was then intrinsically far more valuable than it had been 20 years before; dividend yields were more than double the yield on bonds; and yet stock prices were at less than half their 1929 peak. The conditions that had produced Smith's wondrous results had reappeared—in spades. But rather than seeing what was in plain sight in the late 1940s, investors were transfixed by the frightening market of the early 1930s and were avoiding re-exposure to pain.

Don't think for a moment that small investors are the only ones guilty of too much attention to the rear-view mirror. Let's look at the behavior of professionally managed pension funds in recent decades. In 1971—this was Nifty Fifty time—pension managers, feeling great about the market, put more than 90% of their net cash flow into stocks, a record commitment at the time. And then, in a couple of years, the roof fell in and stocks got way cheaper. So what did the pension fund managers do? They quit buying because stocks got cheaper!

---

## PRIVATE PENSION FUNDS

**% of cash flow put into equities**

1971: 91% (record high)

1974: 13%

---

This is the one thing I can never understand. To refer to a personal taste of mine, I'm going to buy hamburgers the rest of my life. When hamburgers go down in price, we sing the "Hallelujah Chorus" in the Buffett household. When hamburgers go up, we weep. For most people, it's the same way with everything in life they will be buying—*except* stocks. When stocks go down and you can get more for your money, people don't like them anymore.

That sort of behavior is especially puzzling when engaged in by pension fund managers, who by all rights should have the longest time horizon of any investors. These managers are not going to need the money in their funds tomorrow, not next year, nor even next decade. So they have total freedom to sit back and relax. Since they are not operating with their own funds, moreover, raw greed should not distort their decisions. They should simply think about what makes the most sense. Yet they behave just like rank amateurs (getting paid, though, as if they had special expertise).

In 1979, when I felt stocks were a screaming buy, I wrote in an article, "Pension fund managers continue to make investment decisions with their eyes firmly fixed on the rear-view mirror. This generals-fighting-the-last-war approach has proved costly in the past and will likely prove equally costly this time around." That's true, I said, because "stocks now sell at levels that should produce long-term returns far superior to bonds."

Consider the circumstances in 1972, when pension fund managers were still loading up on stocks: The Dow ended the year at 1020, had an average book value of 625, and earned 11% on book. Six years later, the Dow was 20% cheaper, its book value had gained nearly 40%, and it had earned 13% on book. Or as I wrote then,

"Stocks were demonstrably cheaper in 1978 when pension fund managers wouldn't buy them than they were in 1972, when they bought them at record rates."

At the time of the article, long-term corporate bonds were yielding about 9.5%. So I asked this seemingly obvious question: "Can better results be obtained, over 20 years, from a group of 9.5% bonds of leading American companies maturing in 1999 than from a group of Dow-type equities purchased, in aggregate, around book value and likely to earn, in aggregate, about 13% on that book value?" The question answered itself.

Now, if you had read that article in 1979, you would have suffered—oh, how you would have suffered!—for about three years. I was no good then at forecasting the near-term movements of stock prices, and I'm no good now. I never have the faintest idea what the stock market is going to do in the next six months, or the next year, or the next two.

But I think it is very easy to see what is likely to happen over the long term. Ben Graham told us why: "Though the stock market functions as a voting machine in the short run, it acts as a weighing machine in the long run." Fear and greed play important roles when votes are being cast, but they don't register on the scale.

By my thinking, it was not hard to say that, over a 20-year period, a 9.5% bond wasn't going to do as well as this disguised bond called the Dow that you could buy below par—that's book value—and that was earning 13% on par.

Let me explain what I mean by that term I slipped in there, "disguised bond." A bond, as most of you know, comes with a certain maturity and with a string of little coupons. A 6% bond, for example, pays a 3% coupon every six months.

A stock, in contrast, is a financial instrument that has a claim on future distributions made by a given business, whether they are paid out as dividends or to repurchase stock or to settle up after sale or liquidation. These payments are in effect "coupons." The set of owners getting them will change as shareholders come and go. But the financial outcome for the business' owners as a whole will be determined by the size and timing of these coupons. Estimating those particulars is what investment analysis is all about.

Now, gauging the size of those "coupons" gets very difficult for individual stocks. It's easier, though, for groups of stocks. Back in 1978, as I mentioned, we had the Dow earning 13% on its average book value of $850. The 13% could only be a benchmark, not a guarantee. Still, if you'd been willing then to invest for a period of time in stocks, you were in effect buying a bond—at prices that in 1979 seldom inched above par—with a principal value of $891 and a quite possible 13% coupon on the principal.

How could that not be better than a 9.5% bond? From that starting point, stocks had to outperform bonds over the long term. That, incidentally, has been true during most of my business lifetime. But as Keynes would remind us, the superiority of stocks isn't inevitable. They own the advantage only when certain conditions prevail.

Let me show you another point about the herd mentality among pension funds—a point perhaps accentuated by a little self-interest on the part of those who oversee the funds. In the table below are four well-known companies— typical of many others I could have selected—and the expected returns on their pension fund assets that they used in calculating what charge (or credit) they should make annually for pensions.

## EXPECTED PENSION FUND RETURNS

|                                      | 1975 | 1978  | 2000  |
|--------------------------------------|------|-------|-------|
| Exxon                                | 7.0% | 7.8%  | 9.5%  |
| General Electric                     | 6.0% | 7.5%  | 9.5%  |
| General Motors                       | 6.0% | 7.0%  | 10.0% |
| IBM                                  | 4.8% | 5.5%  | 10.0% |
| Yield on long-term government bonds  | 8.0% | 10.4% | 5.5%  |

Now, the higher the expectation rate that a company uses for pensions, the higher its reported earnings will be. That's just the way that pension accounting works—and I hope, for the sake of relative brevity, that you'll just take my word for it.

As the table shows, expectations in 1975 were modest: 7% for Exxon, 6% for GE and GM, and under 5% for IBM. The oddity of these assumptions is that investors could then buy long-term government noncallable bonds that paid 8%. In other words, these companies could have loaded up their entire portfolio with 8% no-risk bonds, but they nevertheless used lower assumptions. By 1982, as you can see, they had moved up their assumptions a little bit, most to around 7%. But now you could buy long-term governments at 10.4%. You could in fact have locked in that yield for decades by buying so-called strips that guaranteed you a 10.4% reinvestment rate. In effect, your idiot nephew could have managed the fund and achieved returns far higher than the investment assumptions corporations were using.

Why in the world would a company be assuming 7.5% when it could get nearly 10.5% on government bonds? The answer is that rear-view mirror again: Investors who'd been through the collapse of the Nifty Fifty in the early 1970s were still feeling the pain of the period and were out of date in their thinking about returns. They couldn't make the necessary mental adjustment.

Now fast-forward to 2000, when we had long-term governments at 5.4%. And what were the four companies saying in their 2000 annual reports about expectations for their pension funds? They were using assumptions of 9.5% and even 10%.

I'm a sporting type, and I would love to make a large bet with the chief financial officer of any one of those four companies, or with their actuaries or auditors, that over the next 15 years they will not average the rates they've postulated. Just look at the math, for one thing. A fund's portfolio is very likely to be one-third bonds, on which—assuming a conservative mix of issues with an appropriate range of maturities—the fund cannot today expect to earn much more than 5%. It's simple to see then that the fund will need to average more than 11% on the two-thirds that's in stocks to earn about 9.5% overall. That's a pretty heroic assumption, particularly given the substantial investment expenses that a typical fund incurs.

Heroic assumptions do wonders, however, for the bottom line. By embracing those expectation rates shown in the far right column, these companies report much higher earnings—much higher—than if they were using lower rates. And that's certainly not lost on the people who set the rates. The actuaries who have roles in this game know nothing special about future investment returns. What they do know, however, is that their clients desire rates that are high. And a happy client is a continuing client.

Are we talking big numbers here? Let's take a look at General Electric, the country's most valuable and most admired company. I'm a huge admirer myself. GE has run its pension fund extraordinarily well for decades, and its assumptions about returns are typical of the crowd. I use the company as an example simply because of its prominence.

If we may retreat to 1982 again, GE recorded a pension *charge* of $570 million. That amount cost the company 20% of its pretax earnings. Last year GE recorded a $1.74 billion pension *credit*. That was 9% of the company's pretax earnings. And it was 2 1/2 times the appliance division's profit of $684 million. A $1.74 billion credit is simply a lot of money. Reduce that pension assumption enough and you wipe out most of the credit.

GE's pension credit, and that of many another corporation, owes its existence to a rule of the Financial Accounting Standards Board that went into effect in 1987. From that point on, companies equipped with the right assumptions and getting the fund performance they needed could start crediting pension income to their income statements. Last year, according to Goldman Sachs, 35 companies in the S&P 500 got more than 10% of their earnings from pension credits, even as, in many cases, the value of their pension investments shrank.

Unfortunately, the subject of pension assumptions, critically important though it is, almost never comes up in corporate board meetings. (I myself have been on 19 boards, and I've never heard a serious discussion of this subject.) And now, of course, the need for discussion is paramount because these assumptions that are being made, with all eyes looking backward at the glories of the 1990s, are so extreme. I invite you to ask the CFO of a company having a large defined-benefit pension fund what adjustment would need to be made to the company's earnings if its pension assumption was lowered to 6.5%. And then, if you want to be mean, ask what the company's assumptions were back in 1975 when both stocks and bonds had far higher prospective returns than they do now.

With 2001 annual reports soon to arrive, it will be interesting to see whether companies have reduced their assumptions about future pension returns. Considering how poor returns have been recently and the reprises that probably lie ahead, I think that anyone choosing not to lower assumptions—CEOs, auditors, and actuaries all—is risking litigation for misleading investors. And directors who don't question the optimism thus displayed simply won't be doing their job.

The tour we've taken through the last century proves that market irrationality of an extreme kind periodically erupts—and compellingly suggests that investors wanting to do well had better learn how to deal with the next outbreak. What's needed is an antidote, and in my opinion that's quantification. If you quantify, you won't necessarily rise to brilliance, but neither will you sink into craziness.

On a macro basis, quantification doesn't have to be complicated at all. Below is a chart, starting almost 80 years ago and really quite fundamental in what it says. The chart shows the market value of all publicly traded securities as a percentage of the country's business—that is, as a percentage of GNP. The ratio has

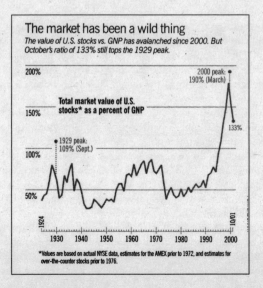

The market has been a wild thing

The value of U.S. stocks vs. GNP has avalanched since 2000. But October's ratio of 133% still tops the 1929 peak.

*Values are based on actual NYSE data, estimates for the AMEX prior to 1972, and estimates for over-the-counter stocks prior to 1976.

certain limitations in telling you what you need to know. Still, it is probably the best single measure of where valuations stand at any given moment. And as you can see, nearly two years ago the ratio rose to an unprecedented level. That should have been a clear warning signal.

For me, the message of that chart is this: If the percentage relationship falls to the 70% or 80% area, buying stocks is likely to work very well for you. If the ratio approaches 200%—as it did in 1999 and a part of 2000—you are playing with fire. As you can see, the ratio was recently 133%.

Even so, that is a good-sized drop from when I was talking about the market in 1999. I ventured then that the American public should expect equity returns over the next decade or two (with dividends included and 2% inflation assumed) of perhaps 7%. That was a gross figure, not counting frictional costs, such as commissions and fees. Net, I thought returns might be 6%.

Today stock market "hamburgers," so to speak, are cheaper. The country's economy has grown and stocks are lower, which means that investors are getting more for their money. I would expect now to see long-term returns run somewhat higher, in the neighborhood of 7% after costs. Not bad at all—that is, unless you're still deriving your expectations from the 1990s.

# The Mash Note Everybody Wants

September 16, 2002

### *A Sidebar by Jerry Useem*

*The following sidebar ran in a post-Enron article describing the rush of corporations to make themselves into model institutions.*

What are the most coveted words in corporate America today?
That's simple: "Sincerely, Warren."

With companies competing to clean up their act, a letter of praise from super-investor Warren Buffett has become the ultimate Good Housekeeping Seal of Approval. General Electric got one for announcing it would expense stock options. "For long, GE has brought good things to life," Buffett wrote. "Now GE has brought good things to accounting."

Standard & Poor's got one, too, for its new "core earnings" measure. "Your move is both courageous and correct," Buffett wrote in his letter, which S&P liked enough to post on its website. "In the future, investors will look back at your action as a milestone event." Other lucky recipients have included Bank One and Amazon.

"He's the only person or entity out there that still has an unblemished reputation," says S&P analyst Robert Friedman. Well, a few other voices still command credulity, such as John Bogle, the outspoken founder of Vanguard Group. But how did Bogle know that a speech about corporate accountability went over well? "[Buffett] gave me a very nice note after reading that speech," he says.

# The Oracle of Everything

November 11, 2002

**BY ANDY SERWER**

*In the forty-eight years that Warren Buffett has run Berkshire Hathaway, the company's stock has fallen roughly 40 percent to 50 percent at four different times. We will identify three of those episodes—1973–1974, 1987–1988, and 2007–2008—and move on to the other perpetrator, the Internet bubble. This cover story picks up Buffett in late 2002, when the bubble had clearly burst and Berkshire's A stock had climbed back from just over $40,000 in early 2000 to more than $70,000. Meantime, the word abroad about Buffett was that maybe he wasn't a relic after all, as so many market pundits had adamantly asserted him to be in the days when their heads were in the bubble.*

*Andy Serwer, who was then writing copious amounts of copy for* Fortune *under the name* Street Life *and who in 2006 became managing editor of the magazine, happened to get assigned to this "Buffett's back" story at a time when Buffett was headed to California with a group of men on a golfing trip. Not that Buffett was himself playing golf; he couldn't because of a torn rotator cuff. But this particular group of men had been playing Pebble Beach, Spyglass, and Cypress Point every other year for two decades, and Buffett wasn't inclined to give up the sociability of it all.*

*So Andy went to Pebble Beach, too. He hung around with Buffett throughout the day: in a scenic spot when the rooms of neither were available; in Buffett's room; and at night when Buffett and the golfers congregated. Among the others were Charlie Munger, Tom Murphy of Cap Cities/ABC, George Gillespie of Cravath Swaine & Moore, Don Graham of Washington Post, and Sandy Gottesman and my husband, John Loomis, of First Manhattan Co.*

*Andy quickly decided it would not be all bad to do the entirety of his future reporting at Pebble Beach. Unsurprisingly, no other reporting assignment has since taken him there. —CL*

F or decades the name Warren Buffett has conjured up the image of a golden-touch investor—a solid, straight-shooting, deep value-minded soul who (as dozens of biographies and investing primers will tell you) believes in buying "companies," not stocks. His effect on the stock market rivals that of Federal Reserve chairmen and U.S. Presidents; his investing style is studied and copied by legions of acolytes from Wall Street to small-town America; his missives in Berkshire Hathaway's annual reports are read (and cited) as if they were the Gospel itself.

So it is a little strange, to say the least, to see the *man* Warren Buffett up close in his PJs. It is a sumptuous California morning, and I am sitting with the 72-year-old Buffett in his spacious ground-floor suite at the Lodge at Pebble Beach. Outside, the October sun is brilliant. The view of Carmel Bay is glorious.

The 18th green frames the scene to the right; a large cypress tree stands to the left. As for the Oracle of Omaha, well, he is kicked back, picking at a room-service omelet, lounging around in a white terry-cloth bathrobe and pastel-blue pajamas.

Fittingly, for such Left Coast perfection, we are talking about the tech bubble of the century just ended. "It was a mass hallucination," Buffett says, "by far the biggest in my lifetime." Scary stuff, yet Buffett looks hardly perturbed. There is no self-regret on his face. Maybe that's because he wasn't a party to any of that malarkey—the bubble or its popping.

Which brings us to another facet of Buffett. And that's the fact that he not only has been dead-on with the vast majority of his investments over time but has also—in his own calm, self-effacing, almost goofy way—been right about much else: right on his views about corporate governance, right about stock options and accounting reform, right about the demise of corporate ethics, uncannily right about the stock market.

Indeed, he has been right on those fronts for years. What has changed during the recent months of corporate scandal, a soggy economy, and a vicious bear market is that the rest of the world seems to be coming back around to the Buffett worldview. Take that a step further: More and more people seem to be expecting (or at least hoping) that he will step in and save them from their own past mistakes. Because he controls, through his company Berkshire Hathaway, one of the most liquid sources of capital on earth, Buffett has recently been able to step up and buy huge chunks of American businesses, especially in hard-hit sectors like telecom, utilities, and energy. He is doing what he has always done these many years: buying at the bottom of the market, not the top.

As simple as that feat may sound, no one has been able to match it. For us mere mortals, that is reason enough to watch his every move. And that is also why *Fortune* has returned to this subject. When we asked for a little bit of Buffett's precious time, we got instead an extraordinary 48-hour peek into the Oracle's mind and a marathon conversation that spanned everything from nuclear bombs to junk bonds to Barry Bonds to Barry Switzer to Eliot Spitzer.

Right now, though, we are talking about a time many believed he was wrong. Hard to imagine, but it wasn't long ago that a good number of people on Wall Street and in Silicon Valley thought this fabled investor was irrelevant, washed up. Buffett's take on things seemed out of tune. The rules of the game had changed, and he just didn't get it. "Warren Buffett should say, 'I'm sorry,'" fumed Harry Newton, publisher of *Technology Investor Magazine*, in early 2000. "How did he miss the silicon, wireless, DSL, cable, and biotech revolutions?"

It is hardly necessary to point out that this was during the age of irrational exuberance, when the Nasdaq was flying and Berkshire's stock was flopping. Buffett's fixation on value (and values too), his focus on the long term, not the short term—that was old hat. What was wrong with the stock option culture, financial engineering, and "situational ethics" (to use one of Buffett's own phrases)? The stuff worked, didn't it?

"Did it ever bother you," I ask him, "that people said you were a has-been, that you were through?"

"Never," he says in his folksy, gravelly voice. "Nothing bothers me like that. You can't do well in investments unless you think independently. And the truth is, you're neither right nor wrong because people agree with you. You're right because your facts and your reasoning are right. In the end that's all that counts. And there wasn't any question about the facts or reasoning being correct."

My time with Buffett begins back in Omaha on a Sunday and continues on a NetJets Gulfstream out to Monterey, where his sister Bertie picks us up and drives us over to Pebble Beach. At Pebble he spends most of his time holed up in his room instead of out on the links with his usual biennial eightsome, due to a torn left rotator cuff. The injury is not a huge problem for Buffett. For one thing, it isn't that painful, and for another, he's not that crazy about golf. ("I've got the highest handicap of any member of Augusta," he brags.) The shoulder injury affords him more time to work—reading, writing, and phoning—which is what he loves anyway.

There is only one logical thing to do when you have the world's greatest financial mind cornered in his room with an injured wing. And that is to ask him about the stock market. The problem is, Buffett doesn't like to talk about stock prices per se—though he did so in a November 1999 *Fortune* article, in which he strongly implied that the market was too high. (Historians might do well to observe the parallels between that article and the warning Bernard Baruch famously gave in the 1920s.) *Fortune* ran a follow-up piece about his views last year, in which Buffett said that many corporations would be forced to lower their inflated expectations for the returns on their pension funds. (He is proving to be right.) And he pointed out that the value of all U.S. stocks was then a full third higher than the U.S. gross national product, well above that ratio's peak in 1929. The message was clear: Stocks could continue falling. (Right again.)

So what does Buffett think about the market now? Not much more than: "The bubble has popped, but stocks are still not cheap." There is no question, however, that now is a better time to buy stocks than it was in 1999, he confirms. Buffett's investing precepts remain unflinching as well: "Investors need to avoid the negatives of buying fads, crummy companies, and timing the market," he says. "Buying an index fund over a long period of time makes the most sense." What about buying Berkshire Hathaway stock? "I don't know about that; it's kind of high right now," he says, "though I'd rather own it than the S&P 500. When we were talking about buying back our stock [in early 2000 when it dipped into the low 40,000s], now that was a *real* sign!" He lets out one of his patented guffawing chuckles, kicking his feet up on the glass coffee table. His stock has risen to more than $70,000 since then. Investors take note: Next time Buffett talks about a buyback, *buy*!

The center of Buffett's life isn't the broader stock market but his company, Berkshire Hathaway—and understanding how it works is key to understanding

Buffett's thinking. For that I first check in with Buffett's partner, Charlie Munger, who is a member of the golfing party, along with Tom Murphy, former head of CapCities, and Don Graham, CEO of the Washington Post Co. "It's so extreme the way Berkshire is operated that I think a lot of people don't fully understand it," Munger tells me. "We have less overhead and faster decision-making than any other place of our size in the world."

It is truly difficult to overstate just how different Berkshire Hathaway is from other companies. For the record, it is a conglomerate with sizable operations in insurance. It holds large stakes in giant American companies such as Coke, Gillette, and American Express. Berkshire also controls a significant utility and gas pipeline business, and it owns an amazing cornucopia of mundane operations—things like furniture retailers, jewelry shops, and shoe factories.

The company has grown with no master plan or strategic road map, and yet the physical makeup of Berkshire provides investors with a pretty good window into the mind of Buffett. For instance: For years Berkshire was best known as an insurance company with those big stockholdings. But a couple of things have happened. First, Buffett has largely stopped buying huge blocks of stock of companies. His purchases of the Washington Post, for instance, date back to the 1970s. Why has he stopped? Simple: Stock prices have been too high to his taste for years. "I bought my first stock 60 years ago," Buffett says. "Of those 60 years, probably 50 have been attractive to buy common stocks. In probably ten years I've not been able to find anything." Many of those ten, notably, have been recent ones.

Instead Buffett has shifted to buying entire companies (often of the old-economy and private variety), many of which were selling cheap during the tech boom. Some of the acquisitions have also been insurance operations, but others have been part of the aforementioned cornucopia—Benjamin Moore paint, Shaw carpets, a utility called MidAmerican Energy, and most recently the Pampered Chef, a privately held direct-marketer of kitchenware. The result is that Berkshire's famous stockholdings have become somewhat deaccentuated (recently that portfolio was worth some $26 billion). And while the insurance segment has grown, the part of the conglomerate made up of manufacturing and service companies is now much larger than before. Insurance still accounts for about half of Berkshire's revenues; on a relative basis, though, it's falling.

Through the acquisition of these various businesses—some 20 over the past five years—the number of employees working at Berkshire Hathaway companies has grown at a healthy clip. Today more than 145,000 folks around the country can stand up and say, "I work for Warren Buffett." That would make Berkshire about the 25th-largest private employer in the U.S. (That's more than the head count at PepsiCo or Marriott.)

How does Warren Buffett find new companies to add to the fold? Typically they come to him. These days, Buffett says, sellers appear in a couple of varieties: "We're now getting two kinds of calls. We get contacted where people only want us [meaning they want their businesses to become Berkshire companies], and now we get calls where people only want cash—and fast. We're the buyer who can come up with cash over a weekend."

Fitting into the former category—sellers who approach him because they want to be Berkshire companies—is Buffett's latest acquisition, the Pampered Chef. If you are male or hate to cook, you may not have heard of this company. But if you don't fit that description, it's very likely you have. Pampered Chef "consultants" sell cookware and utensils at parties in their homes. It's a sort of upscale Tupperware model.

Twenty-two years ago founder Doris Christopher borrowed $3,000 from a life insurance policy to start the business so that she could work flexible hours and spend time with her young daughters. Today her company has more than $700 million in sales, which come from some 70,000 direct-marketers, who host more than 19,000 in-house demonstrations a week. (As for profits, we can say only that Pampered is plenty profitable, with mouthwatering margins.)

Even though her business was flourishing, Christopher knew she needed a plan in the event she (a) dropped dead or (b) decided, upon aging, to step back from the business. She had heard about Warren Buffett years ago, "and in the back of my mind I thought, 'Wouldn't it be great to be part of his company?' but we dismissed it at the time." The name Berkshire came up again, though, and in mid-September, Christopher's bankers at Goldman Sachs contacted Buffett, who immediately liked what he saw.

Within a matter of days Christopher and her president, Sheila O'Connell Cooper, were winging from Chicago to Omaha for a sitdown with the Oracle. "I could tell that in a few minutes—and Doris could tell in a few minutes—that we were made for each other," says Buffett, who made her an offer on the spot. He positively gushes when he talks about the Pampered Chef: "I didn't know the name two months ago, but I could tell that Doris and Sheila love running the business. All I have to do is not get in their way. It's a better story than I am." Well, not quite.

For Buffett, though, this story has all the right plot lines: Pampered is a proprietary, high-margin, growing franchise—and one that's already big to start with. The fact is, size matters to Buffett. That's because Berkshire is actually growing pretty fast and is a heckuva lot bigger than it was ten years ago. Annual revenues have grown from $3 billion to nearly $38 billion over that time—with most of that growth having come from acquisitions like Gen Re and Shaw. "They said that Berkshire wasn't *scalable*," scoffs the 79-year-old Munger. "Well, they were wrong."

While Berkshire clearly has grown and will grow still, Buffett's acquisition diet is limited mostly to big fish. With a few exceptions, a company must now have some $50 million in pretax profits for Buffett even to consider buying it. That is why he tells me that he may broaden his search for great companies to other countries.

The reason is simple: An acquisition needs to be plenty large to have any impact on Berkshire's bottom line—a line, we should point out, that tends to be somewhat erratic. That's partly because in any given year Berkshire may be taking huge capital gains, a factor that makes following the company's net earnings on a short-term basis a rather fruitless exercise. Example: Because of insurance losses from Sept. 11, last year's earnings plunged 76%, to $795 million, matching the company's profit tally in 1995. But in 2000 earnings more than doubled, to $3.3 billion.

If those kinds of gyrations bother you, look elsewhere. Buffett is interested only in investors who have a long-term horizon.

One evening in Pebble Beach, Buffett invites me to join him and his crew over at his sister Bertie's cozy house in nearby Carmel to have dinner. It's a casual get-together: a few drinks and a buffet supper, with Bertie's beloved San Francisco Giants playing on a big-screen TV. The talk here is much the same as it is with any group of guys. A lot of sports, which Buffett can do with the best of them—though a pained look flashes across his face when I remind him that his Nebraska Cornhuskers are out of the top 25 for the first time in decades. At one point during the evening Buffett, his ever-present Cherry Coke in hand, leans over and says to me, "For me, MidAmerican started here, you know. In this house." He is referring to what is likely to be the next cornerstone of Berkshire—MidAmerican Energy Holdings Co., an electric power and gas pipeline utility, based in Des Moines. No, I didn't know, I say to him. Could he explain? Almost exactly three years ago, it seems, Bertie was having another party for her brother and a different group of pals. One of the guests was Walter Scott, chairman of the telco Level 3 and also former CEO of Peter Kiewit Sons', the large Omaha construction firm.

"Walter pulled me aside and asked if he could speak with me for a minute in another room," Buffett says. "He talked about this public-utility company called MidAmerican that he was into, which wasn't going anywhere. They had tried to explain the business to Wall Street, but the analysts didn't like it because they were looking for companies like AES or Calpine that had what was called 'deal velocity' [meaning they were doing a lot of deals]. Walter said they were thinking of taking MidAmerican private and asked if I would be interested. I said yes."

You have to remember that at that point many utility stocks were just as hot and overhyped as Internet incubators or B2B stocks. Calpine and AES, for instance, traded at $56 and $70, respectively, at their peaks. Today each sells for around $2. The origin of the utility bubble goes back to the Energy Policy Act of 1992, which lured companies into the seemingly sexy, unregulated end of the business. (Unregulated utilities produce power on a speculative basis, without guaranteed customers, but can sell that power at market rates. A regulated utility has guaranteed customers and regulated rates.) As more and more money streamed into unregulated businesses, Dave Sokol, CEO of MidAmerican, saw what he thought was a tremendous opportunity: Regulated assets were being overlooked.

By the mid-1990s, MidAmerican owned regulated utilities in California, Iowa, and Britain. But while Enron and its ilk sported P/Es of 30 to 50, MidAmerican was selling for six to eight times earnings. "We couldn't figure out what the other companies were doing," says Sokol. "They kept on building power plants and adding capacity, I guess because they thought demand would go up forever. And their trading businesses were also a mystery. The profits seemed impossible to us." Meanwhile MidAmerican's stock was languishing. So Sokol decided in October 1999 to abandon the public markets and sell out to Buffett. Berkshire effectively ended up buying 80% of the company for $35.05 a share, a cost of $3.3 billion.

Buffett's timing wasn't impeccable, but it was close. By the summer of 2001 the unregulated energy business—headlined by Enron—began its spectacular collapse. By early this year the situation had become dire for many of these players, including Williams Cos., which suddenly found itself in need of a large amount of cash. What Williams had to offer was the Kern River Pipeline, which transports 850 million cubic feet of gas (cfg) per day over 935 miles from the Rocky Mountains to Las Vegas and California. The price tag: $950 million— which was hundreds of millions less than the market would have valued it two years earlier.

Even sweeter for Buffett was MidAmerican's purchase this past July of the 4.3 billion-cfg-per-day, 16,600-mile Northern Natural Gas pipeline. With obvious pleasure Buffett leans back on the couch and tells the story, as though relating the hooking of a giant tuna: "Northern Natural used to be a prominent Omaha company. In 1986 a guy came up from Houston with a smaller company and said, 'Let's merge, and I'll come to Omaha.' Most people in Omaha feel they got double-crossed, because within six or eight months the company had gone back to Houston. Of course, the guy from Houston was Ken Lay, and the company became Enron. When Enron got in trouble a year ago, they made this deal with Dynegy where Dynegy puts in $1.5 billion and they more or less get Northern Natural as collateral. So Dynegy takes over the pipeline for its one and a half billion, and then Dynegy gets in trouble. So they call us on a Friday and say we need a deal by next week that we're sure will close for cash. So we sent a team down, and we sign a contract by the following Monday morning."

Here's how the math works: Enron effectively sells the pipeline to Dynegy in January for $1.5 billion. Dynegy sells it to Buffett's MidAmerican six months later for . . . get this . . . $928 million. Nice!

MidAmerican now transports about 10% of the nation's gas. "It may be that we'll never make another deal, but it could be a very big company," Buffett says. "MidAmerican is useful because it is big scale." As in potentially very big scale. Berkshire could ultimately end up investing some $10 billion to $15 billion or more in this company. If that sounds like a mammoth sum, consider that Berkshire now generates some $5 billion in cash flow annually from its investments, insurance, and operating companies. "We've got $100 million a week that I have to figure out what to do with," he says. "It's a happy problem, but it's a problem, especially if I do something dumb with it—and that's easy to do."

After dinner at Bertie's house, Don Graham, Buffett, and I pile into Graham's rented Ford Taurus, and we begin to try to find our way back to Pebble Beach. Easier said than done. It's pitch-black, and I'm in the back seat with a map trying to navigate. "I'm glad Don's driving," says Buffett, as we wend our way through Pebble Beach's myriad dark ocean roads. "I don't like driving at night. Don't see that well at night."

Yes, the man is mortal—even getting on in years. He has $100 million a week to figure out how to invest, but he has trouble driving at night. Earlier in our visit Buffett had me in stitches with off-color palindromes. (Sorry, but this is a family magazine.) Can this be the same Public Citizen who pens op-ed pieces in the *New York Times* on the slipperiness of stock option accounting?

Another seeming contradiction: The man whom shareholders count on to defy gravity, time and again, is telling those same shareholders that gravity always wins.

Partly because of Berkshire's ever-increasing size, Buffett had been warning his Berkshire flock for years that the future performance of their company's stock couldn't match the spectacular returns of the past. The future became now in 1999 when Berkshire posted its worst relative return ever. The metric Buffett likes to use to gauge his performance is comparing the annual change in the per-share book value of Berkshire with the total return of the S&P 500. In 1999, Berkshire's book value nudged up 0.5%, while the S&P soared 21% (ergo, relative underperformance of 20.5 percentage points). Since then the company has reverted to its outperforming ways, although 2001 produced another Berkshire anomaly. It was the first year ever that Berkshire's book value declined. The 6.2% drop was due in large part to the fact that Berkshire's insurance operations lost more than $2 billion in the Sept. 11 terror attack on the World Trade Center.

That's the bad news. The good news is that because of Sept. 11, pricing in the insurance business has firmed up (meaning the cost of coverage has risen), which is potentially good for the bottom line of Berkshire's insurance operations. (Recently there have been rumors in the market that Berkshire will buy Employers Re, GE's reinsurance business.) With the S&P down some 20% year to date and Berkshire's operations mostly purring along—as of June 30, Berkshire's book value was up 7.6%—another year of relative outperformance seems likely. As for Berkshire's stock—well, it has certainly held its own recently. On March 10, 2000, the Nasdaq peaked (interday) at 5,132. That same day Berkshire hit a multiyear low of $40,800. Recently the Nasdaq traded for 1,270, down 75%, while Berkshire traded for $74,000, up 81%. And, of course, BRK has beaten up on the S&P 500 over the past one, two, five, ten, 15 years—you name the period.

The week after my visit with Buffett, I spent time speaking with some of the CEOs of Berkshire's companies. They number close to 40 now, and Buffett happily points out that in Berkshire's 38 years, not a single one has elected to leave the fold to go work someplace else. This, in part, has to reflect an underrated aspect of Buffett's managerial prowess: his people skills. "He is the best judge of human talent there is," says Rich Santulli, who heads up NetJets, a company that leases fractional shares of aircraft. "And people want to work for him."

Judging by the success of Buffett's companies, Santulli has a point. It is a remarkable group of CEOs, impressive not only in their ability but also in their love of work. There are several octogenarians in the group, including Al Ueltschi, 85, CEO of Flight Safety, and Frank Rooney, 80, at shoe company H.H. Brown.

Joe Brandon, on the other hand, at 43 is one of the youngest Berkshire CEOs. Named head of General Re a year ago, Brandon is also sitting in Berkshire's hottest of hot seats. Even before Sept. 11, Gen Re—which Berkshire bought for $22 billion of stock in 1998—has had troubles. Its underwriting had been undisciplined, its returns subpar. Buffett has gone so far as to apologize to shareholders for the company's performance.

So, Joe, how's the old man been treating you? "He has been supportive in every way," insists Brandon. "Yes, you are working for one of the smartest guys in the world, so you'd better be prepared. But people just don't understand what a great manager he is." Brandon's point is dead-on and again unrecognized. In part this is because of Buffett himself. "I just buy the businesses and get out of the way," Buffett says over and over. Well, not exactly.

Dig deeper and you discover that Buffett is engaged with each of his companies to a varying degree, depending on his interest and whether the particular business warrants his attention. For instance, Brandon says that he speaks to Buffett up to a couple of times a week. But Buffett talks with Ajit Jain, head of Berkshire's other reinsurance operations, every day. That is not because Jain is doing a bad job. On the contrary, Buffett will tell you that Jain is one of his ablest executives; it's just that insuring jumbo risks—the Olympic Games, for instance—has major financial implications for Berkshire. It's also true that pricing insurance for huge pieces of business like this happens to be a discipline that Buffett loves dearly. As for some of his other companies, here's what Buffett says: "GEICO sends me figures every Tuesday—Internet hits, business closed on the Internet, telephone inquiries closed. I love all that. Shaw sends me the daily sales figures by fax. And around Christmas—the month before, I like to get daily sales figures from our jewelry stores and from our candy business."

Even with the staggering pile of numbers that Buffett sifts through, and even though he works like the dickens, Buffett is no type-A boss. "Yes, I need roller skates to keep up with him," says Debbie Bosanek, his secretary of nine years, "but I've never seen him get mad. I don't think he'd like to be lied to, though. If you make a mistake and tell him about it, that's okay, but you wouldn't want to cover it up." Adds Tom Murphy, the founder of CapCities: "He wakes up every morning and goes to work to have fun. It's not work. He's only with people he likes, so he isn't stressed out." Buffett is probably one of the few CEOs in America who spends much of the day reading. Buffett doesn't e-mail, and there are no time-squandering meetings at Berkshire's headquarters. "Warren gets blinding headaches if he sits in a room full of people around a table, and a lot of people are saying dumb things on and on," says his partner, Charlie Munger. Buffett and Munger, who have been together 40-plus years, used to talk all the time, but less so now: "By now Warren knows pretty much everything I think. Once in a while I'll know something that's useful to him."

The bottom line is that Buffett's ability to allocate his time and brainpower among all these various businesses is as impressive as his vaunted ability to allocate capital. "Most supersmart people tend to make things more complicated," says Don Graham of the Washington Post Co., where Buffett sits on the board. "He has an extraordinary ability to state things clearly and make them simpler."

But wait a minute—stop the music. There must be *some* people out there who don't like the guy, right? Well, sure. A long list actually. Buffett has lobbied hard for expensing stock options, so the Silicon Valley crowd aren't big fans. Some also point out that for all of Buffett's grousing about corporate governance, Berkshire has a paucity of outside directors. Buffett gives money to Planned Parenthood, so he's not a favorite of the right-to-lifers. Many investment bankers don't like him—they can't snow him—and he's no friend to the Wall Street analysts—he won't give them any guidance. And as someone (the only one!) who routinely and consistently beats the market, he must drive disciples of the efficient-market theory crazy. Harvey Pitt may be a bit peeved at him, since Buffett has been less than supportive of his tenure. And then there's the matter of the 16,712 votes cast earlier this year *against* Buffett for director of Berkshire. (For the record, he received 1,140,816 votes in his favor.)

Overall, though, Buffett's stature has never been loftier—and he is using that prominence to weigh in on significant economic and political issues. In addition to the stock option fight, for instance, he has been vocal in his support for a federal terrorism insurance fund similar to the FDIC. "Nuclear attack would bankrupt the insurance industry," he says. "The federal government would have to bail out the country anyway. Why not create this fund before something happens rather than after the fact?"

If talking about nuclear destruction on the sixth green at Pebble Beach is incongruous, it doesn't seem to bother Buffett. A nuclear bomb, he says, "is the ultimate depressing thing. It will happen. It's inevitable. I don't see any way that it won't happen. But we can reduce the probabilities. If there's a 10% probability of something happening in a given year—and I don't know if that's the right probability; nobody knows—then the chances that it will happen in 50 years are 99.5%. If you get it down to 3%, there is about a 78% chance. If you get it down to 1% per year, there's like a 40% chance, so reducing the probabilities per annum of anything happening obviously increases the chance significantly that your kids will get through their lifetimes without this happening. You can't get rid of the knowledge. You can try to control the materials. You'll never get rid of the intent. It is the ultimate problem of mankind."

Late in the afternoon, as the setting sun gilds the back nine outside Buffett's window, I ask him the inevitable question of succession. Or put less delicately, what happens when he dies? Buffett has been through this a million times, and he has a million lines—"I hope the stock doesn't go up too much" being one of his favorites. But this time he turns serious. "Look, this company is going to outlast me for years to come," he says. "These businesses are going to run for 50 years. We have a great team of managers. They know how this company works. It's pretty simple really."

Really? Well, this is one time I beg to differ. It's not so much the operational businesses that are a problem. Presumably those managements would stay and continue their money-coining ways. And never mind that the insurance businesses are pretty darn complicated. It's the capital allocation skills of Buffett's that would be so hard to replicate. Even Buffett's friends privately wonder about filling those shoes.

As for Buffett's family, they are connected to Berkshire today and Berkshire tomorrow in various ways. Buffett's wife, Susie, is a board member of Berkshire and lives in San Francisco—but frequently travels with Buffett. (For more than 20 years Buffett has lived in Omaha with a woman named Astrid Menks. It's a unique arrangement, but one that seems to suit all parties.) Susie Buffett is also CEO of the Buffett Foundation. Buffett's Berkshire stock, now valued at $34 billion, will go to Susie when he dies (assuming he dies first)—and then, when she dies, virtually all of her assets will go to the Buffett Foundation, which will then distribute the assets. Buffett's elder son, Howard, until recently an executive at an agricultural equipment company, is also a director of Berkshire, and upon his father's death would become nonexecutive chairman of the company. Buffett's two other children, Susie, a homemaker, and Peter, a musician, are trustees of the foundation.

After Buffett is gone, the foundation will become one of the largest philanthropic organizations in the world—though one intriguing point is that Buffett hasn't designated where the money goes. The trustees of the foundation will have full discretion over that disbursement. For now that may be the only part of Buffett's glorious legacy that isn't yet crystal clear.

# A Letter from *Fortune*'s Letters Column

February 17, 2003

The bold type in "Playing the Dividend Market" (Investor's Guide 2003, Dec. 9) saying "Not just any dividend payer is a good investment. Many of the most tempting are quite risky" rang a very loud bell. In January 1956, I bought some shares in a textile company because it appeared to be paying an 8.5% dividend. But it turned out that dividends hadn't yet caught up with a decrease in net income. I sold the stock a year later for a 64% loss. That was the biggest mistake of my life. The company was Berkshire Hathaway, which Warren Buffett [took over] a few years after that. Please don't tell me what the stock I sold is now worth.

ROBERT H. PASCHALL
Bishop, California

# Avoiding a "Mega-Catastrophe"

March 17, 2003

*An excerpt from Buffett's letter to shareholders in the 2002 Berkshire Hathaway annual report*

*"Financial weapons of mass destruction." That Buffett blast at derivatives—a phrase soon to become famous around the world—made its inaugural public appearance in* Fortune, *as we published this excerpt from Berkshire's 2002 annual report a short time before the report itself came out.*

*But then . . . In the mid-2000s, just in time for the financial crisis, Buffett bought a range of derivatives contracts for Berkshire, many of them appearing to take large amounts of risk with its money. The situation is further complicated by the fact that Charlie Munger, were he boss of the financial world, would banish all derivatives, whose social value he thinks to be far less than zero.*

*Shall we say that all of this left many Berkshire shareholders deeply confused? And some angry, as proved by a few rancorous questions at annual meetings?*

*A beginning explanation for this puzzle is that Buffett believes derivatives, just like other securities, can be safely bought if the buyer truly understands both risk and pricing. Buffett, displaying a confidence built on experience, feels himself able to handle both challenges. He has in fact gone gleefully through life trying to spot mispricing wherever it occurs—in stocks and businesses, of course, but also in bonds, commodities, currencies, and even television stations (see "A Small College Scores Big in the Investment Game," page 23). No one can say that his detective work has been unsuccessful. Its controversial extension in recent years to derivatives may therefore be easy to explain as just one more expedition into a land of mispricing—one more lovely garden to tend. And then, of course, if you're Buffett and you see something terrific, you have to act. I do not believe that Buffett is capable of ignoring mispriced securities.*

*To date, the derivatives contracts that Buffett controversially entered into during the mid-2000s have increased the volatility of Berkshire's earnings (a fact to which Buffett assigns zero importance) but have otherwise had only beneficial effects. Buffett, in fact, has referred again and again in his annual letter to a) the billions of dollars of float that have been generated by Berkshire's derivatives and b) his expectation, as well, that satisfying amounts of underwriting profit will be earned on them. Since some of the contracts on the books extend to 2028, two years before the centennial of his birth, he wishes also to be around at the end to see how it all worked out. —CL*

Charlie [Munger] and I are of one mind in how we feel about derivatives and the trading activities that go with them: We view them as time bombs, both for the parties that deal in them and the economic system.

Having delivered that thought, which I'll get back to, let me retreat to explaining derivatives, though the explanation must be general because the word covers an extraordinarily wide range of financial contracts. Essentially, these instruments call for money to change hands at some future date, with the amount to be determined by one or more reference items, such as interest rates, stock prices, or currency values. If, for example, you are either long or short an S&P 500 futures contract, you are a party to a very simple derivatives transaction—with your gain or loss *derived* from movements in the index. Derivatives contracts are of varying duration (running sometimes to 20 or more years), and their value is often tied to several variables.

Unless derivatives contracts are collateralized or guaranteed, their ultimate value also depends on the creditworthiness of the counterparties to them. In the meantime, though, before a contract is settled, the counterparties record profits and losses—often huge in amount—in their current earnings statements without so much as a penny changing hands.

The range of derivatives contracts is limited only by the imagination of man (or sometimes, so it seems, madmen). At Enron, for example, newsprint and broadband derivatives, due to be settled many years in the future, were put on the books. Or say you want to write a contract speculating on the number of twins to be born in Nebraska in 2020. No problem—at a price, you will easily find an obliging counterparty.

When we purchased Gen Re, it came with General Re Securities, a derivatives dealer that Charlie and I didn't want, judging it to be dangerous. We failed in our attempts to sell the operation, however, and are now terminating it.

But closing down a derivatives business is easier said than done. It will be a great many years before we are totally out of this operation (though we reduce our exposure daily). In fact, the reinsurance and derivatives businesses are similar: Like Hell, both are easy to enter and almost impossible to exit. In either industry, once you write a contract—which may require a large payment decades later—you are usually stuck with it. True, there are methods by which the risk can be laid off with others. But most strategies of that kind leave you with residual liability.

Another commonality of reinsurance and derivatives is that both generate reported earnings that are often wildly overstated. That's true because today's earnings are in a significant way based on estimates whose inaccuracy may not be exposed for many years.

Errors will usually be honest, reflecting only the human tendency to take an optimistic view of one's commitments. But the parties to derivatives also have enormous incentives to cheat in accounting for them. Those who trade derivatives are usually paid (in whole or part) on "earnings" calculated by mark-to-market accounting. But often there is no real market (think about our contract involving twins) and "mark-to-model" is utilized. This substitution can bring on large-scale mischief. As a general rule, contracts involving multiple reference items and distant settlement dates increase the opportunities for counterparties to use fanciful assumptions. In the twins scenario, for example, the two parties to the contract might well use differing models allowing *both* to show substantial profits for many years. In extreme cases, mark-to-model degenerates into what I would call mark-to-myth.

Of course, both internal and outside auditors review the numbers, but that's no easy job. For example, General Re Securities at year-end (after ten months of winding down its operation) had 14,384 contracts outstanding, involving 672 counterparties around the world. Each contract had a plus or minus value derived from one or more reference items, including some of mind-boggling complexity. Valuing a portfolio like that, expert auditors could easily and honestly have widely varying opinions.

The valuation problem is far from academic: In recent years some huge-scale frauds and near-frauds have been facilitated by derivatives trades. In the energy and electric utility sectors, for example, companies used derivatives and trading activities to report great "earnings"—until the roof fell in when they actually tried to convert the derivatives-related receivables on their balance sheets into cash. "Mark-to-market" then turned out to be truly "mark-to-myth."

I can assure you that the marking errors in the derivatives business have not been symmetrical. Almost invariably, they have favored either the trader who was eyeing a multimillion-dollar bonus or the CEO who wanted to report impressive "earnings" (or both). The bonuses were paid, and the CEO profited from his options. Only much later did shareholders learn that the reported earnings were a sham.

Another problem about derivatives is that they can exacerbate trouble that a corporation has run into for completely unrelated reasons. This pile-on effect occurs because many derivatives contracts require that a company suffering a credit downgrade immediately supply collateral to counterparties. Imagine, then, that a company is downgraded because of general adversity and that its derivatives instantly kick in with *their* requirement, imposing an unexpected and enormous demand for cash collateral on the company. The need to meet this demand can then throw the company into a liquidity crisis that may, in some cases, trigger still more downgrades. It all becomes a spiral that can lead to a corporate meltdown.

Derivatives also create a daisy-chain risk that is akin to the risk run by insurers or reinsurers that lay off much of their business with others. In both cases, huge receivables from many counterparties tend to build up over time. (At Gen Re Securities, we still have $6.5 billion of receivables, though we've been in a liquidation mode for nearly a year.) A participant may see himself as prudent, believing his large credit exposures to be diversified and therefore not dangerous. Under certain circumstances, though, an exogenous event that causes the receivable from Company A to go bad will also affect those from Companies B through Z. History teaches us that a crisis often causes problems to correlate in a manner undreamed of in more tranquil times.

In banking, the recognition of a "linkage" problem was one of the reasons for the formation of the Federal Reserve System. Before the Fed was established, the failure of weak banks would sometimes put sudden and unanticipated liquidity demands on previously strong banks, causing them to fail in turn. The Fed now insulates the strong from the troubles of the weak. But there is no central bank assigned to the job of preventing the dominoes toppling in insurance or derivatives. In these industries, firms that are fundamentally solid can become troubled simply because of the travails of other firms further down the chain. When a "chain reaction" threat exists within an industry, it pays to minimize links of any kind. That's how we conduct our reinsurance business, and it's one reason we are exiting derivatives.

Many people argue that derivatives reduce systemic problems, in that participants who can't bear certain risks are able to transfer them to stronger hands. These people believe that derivatives act to stabilize the economy, facilitate trade, and eliminate bumps for individual participants. And, on a micro level, what they say is often true. Indeed, at Berkshire, I sometimes engage in large-scale derivatives transactions in order to facilitate certain investment strategies.

Charlie and I believe, however, that the macro picture is dangerous and getting more so. Large amounts of risk, particularly credit risk, have become concentrated in the hands of relatively few derivatives dealers, who in addition trade extensively with one another. The troubles of one could quickly infect the others. On top of that, these dealers are owed huge amounts by nondealer counterparties. Some of these counterparties, as I've mentioned, are linked in ways that could cause them to contemporaneously run into a problem because of a single event (such as the implosion of the telecom industry or the precipitous decline in the value of merchant power projects). Linkage, when it suddenly surfaces, can trigger serious systemic problems.

Indeed, in 1998, the leveraged and derivatives-heavy activities of a single hedge fund, Long-Term Capital Management, caused the Federal Reserve anxieties so severe that it hastily orchestrated a rescue effort. In later congressional testimony, Fed officials acknowledged that, had they not intervened, the outstanding trades of LTCM—a firm unknown to the general public and employing only a few hundred people—could well have posed a serious threat to the stability of American markets. In other words, the Fed acted because its leaders were fearful of what might have happened to other financial institutions had the LTCM domino toppled. And this affair, though it paralyzed many parts of the fixed-income market for weeks, was far from a worst-case scenario.

One of the derivatives instruments that LTCM used was total-return swaps, contracts that facilitate 100% leverage in various markets, including stocks. For example, Party A to a contract, usually a bank, puts up all of the money for the purchase of a stock, while Party B, without putting up any capital, agrees that at a future date it will receive any gain or pay any loss that the bank realizes.

Total-return swaps of this type make a joke of margin requirements. Beyond that, other types of derivatives severely curtail the ability of regulators to curb leverage and generally get their arms around the risk profiles of banks, insurers, and other financial institutions. Similarly, even experienced investors and analysts encounter major problems in analyzing the financial condition of firms that are heavily involved with derivatives contracts. When Charlie and I finish reading the long footnotes detailing the derivatives activities of major banks, the only thing we understand is that *we don't* understand how much risk the institution is running.

The derivatives genie is now well out of the bottle, and these instruments will almost certainly multiply in variety and number until some event makes their toxicity clear. Knowledge of how dangerous they are has already permeated the electricity and gas businesses, in which the eruption of major troubles caused the use of derivatives to diminish dramatically. Elsewhere, however, the derivatives business continues to expand unchecked. Central banks and governments have so far found no effective way to control, or even monitor, the risks posed by these contracts.

Charlie and I believe Berkshire should be a fortress of financial strength—for the sake of our owners, creditors, policyholders, and employees. We try to be alert to any sort of mega-catastrophe risk, and that posture may make us unduly apprehensive about the burgeoning quantities of long-term derivatives contracts and the massive amount of uncollateralized receivables that are growing alongside. In our view, however, derivatives are financial weapons of mass destruction, carrying dangers that, while now latent, are potentially lethal.

# Where We're Putting Our Money Now

March 17, 2003

*A second excerpt from Buffett's letter to shareholders
in the 2002 annual report*

We continue to do little in equities. Charlie and I are increasingly comfortable with our holdings in Berkshire's major investees because most of them have increased their earnings while their valuations have decreased. But we are not inclined to add to them. Though these enterprises have good prospects, we don't yet believe their shares are undervalued.

In our view, the same conclusion fits stocks generally. Despite three years of falling prices, which have significantly improved the attractiveness of common stocks, we still find very few that even mildly interest us. That dismal fact is testimony to the insanity of valuations reached during The Great Bubble. Unfortunately, the hangover may prove to be proportional to the binge.

The aversion to equities that Charlie and I exhibit today is far from congenital. We love owning common stocks—if they can be purchased at attractive prices. In my 61 years of investing, 50 or so years have offered that kind of opportunity. There will be years like that again. Unless, however, we see a very high probability of at least 10% pretax returns (which translate to 6% to 7% after corporate tax), we will sit on the sidelines. With short-term money returning less than 1% after-tax, sitting it out is no fun. But occasionally successful investing requires inactivity.

Last year we were, however, able to make sensible investments in a few "junk" bonds and loans. Overall, our commitments in this sector sextupled, reaching $8.3 billion by year-end.

Investing in junk bonds and investing in stocks are alike in certain ways: Both activities require us to make a price-value calculation and also to scan hundreds of securities to find the very few that have attractive reward/risk ratios. But there are important differences between the two disciplines as well. In stocks, we expect every commitment to work out well because we concentrate on conservatively financed businesses with strong competitive strengths, run by able and honest people. If we buy into these companies at sensible prices, losses should be rare. Indeed, during the 38 years we have run the company's affairs, gains from the equities we manage at Berkshire (that is, excluding those managed at General Re/Cologne and GEICO) have exceeded losses by a ratio of about 100 to one.

Purchasing junk bonds, we are dealing with enterprises that are far more marginal. These businesses are usually overloaded with debt and often operate in industries characterized by low returns on capital. Additionally, the quality of management is sometimes questionable. Management may even have interests that are directly counter to those of debtholders. Therefore, we expect that we will have occasional large losses in junk issues. So far, however, we have done reasonably well in this field.

# The Sage Goes to Asia

May 26, 2003

## BY CLAY CHANDLER

Remember that Warren Buffett line about how, if he taught business school, he'd ask every student to compute the value of an Internet company, and then flunk anyone who answered? He could say the same about Chinese stocks. The People's Republic may boast the world's fastest-growing economy, but the finances of its publicly traded companies are as murky as the Yangtze.

So why is the Sage of Omaha boosting his stake in Beijing's biggest state oil firm, PetroChina? In April, Buffett's Berkshire Hathaway socked $50 million into PetroChina, increasing its stake to more than 13% of the company's publicly traded equities. Citigroup's Thomas Hilboldt says the Buffett Effect drove the stock up 12% in a week. The purchase raises Buffett's total investment in the company to nearly $500 million, making him the second-largest outside investor after Britain's BP.

It's tough to square PetroChina with the "buy what you know" mantra that has helped make Buffett the world's second-richest man. This is a guy who for decades has mainly stuck to businesses in his own backyard. Investors hoping for an explanation at Berkshire Hathaway's annual meeting in May didn't find one. "We think we understand the oil business in China reasonably well," Buffett said. "We don't make any great judgments about China."

Countless investors have been burned over the years betting against Buffett. Still, some China analysts question the move. "There must be some other reason for it," speculates CSFB's Peter Best.

Viewed from a computer screen on the other side of the earth, PetroChina, which produces two-thirds of China's oil and natural gas, may look like a winner. China guzzles more than five million barrels of oil a day, and that thirst will surely grow. Car sales surged nearly 60% last year. And PetroChina, which trades at about seven times earnings, looks like a steal compared with Exxon Mobil's P/E of 15.

But there are reasons to worry that Buffett's PetroChina claim will come up dry. The company's three main oilfields have been thoroughly plumbed. Management has kept production stable, but observers say that has come with unsustainable outlays on exploration. Others question PetroChina's bloated payroll of 400,000 workers.

Cost concerns are a key reason some investors favor CNOOC, the China National Offshore Oil Corp., as the smarter China oil play. Investors give CNOOC higher marks for corporate governance, and its annual revenue has grown by 13% over the past three years vs. 4% for PetroChina. Then again, PTR has Buffett.

*Editor's note: Berkshire sold its PetroChina stock in 2007, and here is what Buffett said in that year's annual report about the holding: "In 2002 and 2003 Berkshire* bought 1.3% of PetroChina for $488 million, a price that valued the entire business at about $37 billion. Charlie and I felt that the company was worth about $100 billion. By 2007, two factors had materially increased its value: The price of oil had climbed significantly, and PetroChina's management had done a great job in building oil and gas reserves. In the second half of last year, the market value of the company rose to $275 billion, about what we thought it was worth compared to other giant oil companies. So we sold our holdings for $4 billion."

The price of PetroChina stock fell off a cliff at the very end of 2007 and has never returned to its bull-market levels—so Buffett made a good sale. On the other hand, he piled money into another oil company, ConocoPhillips, in 2007 and 2008—with "terrible timing," he said soon after, because oil prices promptly fell. In 2009 and 2010 Berkshire sold about two-thirds of its ConocoPhillips position. The losses Berkshire took on that oil investment roughly balanced what it had made on PetroChina.

# THE POWER ISSUE

## From "The 25 Most Powerful People in Business"

### August 11, 2003

*Excerpts from an article by Jerry Useem*

*Editor's Note: This article began with a description of a Sun Valley golf game in July 2003 that the writer thought might have established "a new record for aggregate economic might." The players: "They included the CEO of the world's largest company, the world's most successful investor, and the world's richest man. Picture all that clout piled into one battery-powered cart and you have the right visual for opening this Power Issue."*

*Move past a dozen or so paragraphs about the meaning of power to the editors' discussion of who should be first on the list. Said the article, and we quote several paragraphs:*

After several months of internal debate about our power list, two things became clear: first, that power is a *really* deep topic; second, that any list we published would provoke the same howls of protest and counterprotest that filled our offices. . . . And yet in one area a strange civility broke out. When it came to deciding the list's highest slots, there was something close to unanimity. In fact, we'd narrowed the top three contenders to the trio who, coincidentally (hand on the Bible here), were set to play golf in Sun Valley.

We had our three biggest fish. That left the question: Who's the kingfish?

There's no debating who runs the most powerful company. Lee Scott's Wal-Mart is reshaping about 20 industries at once and would probably qualify for a seat on the UN Security Council if that body's membership weren't limited to "countries." Yet Scott may be the most replaceable of the three. Bill Gates, as lead brain in a company powered by brainpower, is still Mr. Microsoft—and as

Huck Finn might have said, he's got a powerful amount of green stuff to go with his gray. Yet the company's $46 billion war chest is only potential, unrealized power unless it finds new behavior-changing ways to use it. Lately Microsoft has been parceling it out to investors as dividends.

Which brings us to our third golfer. Besides overseeing an empire known as Berkshire Hathaway, Warren Buffett has his hand in a lot of important pies (Coca-Cola, Gillette, the Washington Post Co.) and a personal fortune second only to Gates'. But the most arresting fact about Buffett may come from a recent Duke University survey of graduating MBAs. After their own father, the person the graduates admire most—more than the President, more than the Pope, more than Gandhi—is Warren Buffett. That remarkable stature gives him a power of moral suasion that's been made all the stronger by his sparing use of it. It's the ability to shape the behavior of people far beyond his direct reach merely through his words, and it's added to Buffett's image as American capitalism's unofficial Lord Protector.

He's got the rock, the scissors, and the paper, And now he's got something else: the top spot on our list.

## The Most Powerful Businessperson: Warren Buffett

August 11, 2003

**BY ANDY SERWER**

The most powerful businessperson in America is famously understated about his station in life. Sure, Warren Buffett enjoys some of the trappings that come from being the second-richest man in the world, such as winging around in one of his Netjets and playing bridge with pal (and No. 2 on our list) Bill Gates. Mostly, though, the 72-year-old brushes aside the notion that he is the Atlas of American business. "It really just means that if I do something dumb, I can do it on a very big scale," he says with his trademark chuckle. "It means you could add a lot of zeros to the losses."

There haven't been many of the latter. Buffett's company, Berkshire Hathaway, has become an all-American juggernaut, with multibillion-dollar interests in everything from insurance—where Buffett is one of the world's leading players—to newspapers, carpets, and cowboy boots. In racking up compound annual returns of 21% over the past 15 years (vs. the market's 11%), Buffett has proved himself the world's greatest investor. As such, his influence on stocks and the market is unparalleled. Word that Buffett is buying or selling certain shares (be it fact or fiction) will move a stock like a pinball, which is why he is extra-guarded when it comes to discussing investments.

One of the few places where he does talk about investments—his annual letter to shareholders—is far and away the most widely read communication from a CEO in the world. When former Chinese President Jiang Zemin discussed the mystifying nature of the U.S. stock market with a visiting Bill Gates, Gates told him that there was really only one guy who understood it: Warren Buffett. Gates added that when he got back to the U.S., he would send Buffett's most recent annual report to him. Which he did. (No word on whether Jiang is now long BRK.)

What's more, Buffett is without question the world's most sought-after businessman by other CEOs who want guidance. "CEOs are surrounded by people who are getting paid," says Buffett. "I'm getting nothing, so I can give them unbiased advice." Over the past five years dozens of CEOs have come to Omaha to visit the sage, including General Electric's Jeff Immelt (No. 7 on our list). "I've been there two or three times to speak with him and have a steak," says Immelt. "He's the world's most astute investor, and I'm trying to pick his brain."

The U.S. Congress hangs on Buffett's words too. On May 20, just days before lawmakers voted on the Bush tax bill, Buffett wrote an op-ed piece in the *Washington Post* that pointed out what he perceived as the folly of eliminating taxes on dividends. The tax cut, Buffett argued, would mostly benefit the wealthy. Powerful stuff coming from Buffett—powerful enough to persuade certain members of Congress to water down the final version of the tax cut.

Quite simply, Buffett is respected and admired more than any other businessperson alive, not only by others in business but by the general public as well. Now *that's* power. —AS

*The complete Power article, including all 25 of the people listed, is available at fortune.com/buffettbook.*

# America's Growing Trade Deficit Is Selling the Nation Out from Under Us. Here's a Way to Fix the Problem— And We Need to Do It Now.

<hr>

November 10, 2003

<hr>

## BY WARREN BUFFETT, WORKING WITH CAROL LOOMIS

*This article by Buffett, running under a title that surely set new* Fortune *records for length, deplored the U.S. trade deficit and proposed a Buffett idea, "import certificates," as a way to bring imports and exports into balance. Being both creative and well thought out, the idea sparked some interest in Washington, catching the fleeting attention, for example, of both Senators Ted Kennedy and Joe Biden. Even today, with Buffett in no way stumping for his idea, he will occasionally get an e-mail from someone admiring his concept and wondering how to advance it.*

*But overall Buffett's idea did not gain traction. Certainly no acclaim came from economists: They are almost universally free traders who despise quotas and all else that would interfere with the market's working its Adam Smith magic. Charlie Munger himself is enough of a traditionalist to have disliked Buffett's plan, which he happened to learn about in a brand-new copy of* Fortune *that I, while visiting him and his now-late wife in California, hand-delivered to him. He immediately read the article from start to finish, then said, "Warren is right, of course, in abhorring our trade deficits. I wish, though, that he would not push gimmicks like this."*

*Just as Buffett was sure would happen, nonetheless, the problems that he spotlighted in 2003 have worsened. The U.S. trade deficit that year was about $500 billion. It ran $100 billion to $250 billion higher in each of the next five years, abating to under $500 billion only in 2009, when the credit crisis so terrified U.S. citizens that they at least temporarily cut their consumption of goods in favor of higher rates of saving. After 2009, the trade deficit began working its way up. Its level in 2012 was $535 billion.*

*Today, though Buffett talks about the import certificate idea only when asked, he still thinks it has merit. Other ideas for achieving a balance between exports and imports might work as well, he adds. "But," he says with conviction, "somehow we have to get to balance. The current situation of huge deficits is simply untenable."*

*The article's opening revelation that Buffett had put Berkshire into foreign currencies—trading against the dollar for the first time in his life—led him in the next few years to report periodically on where this bet stood. He wound up this narrative in early 2006 by stating that Berkshire had made about $2.2 billion on currencies and had closed out almost all of its positions. That was not because he expected the dollar to strengthen—he in fact said it would probably weaken,* *which indeed it has, by a significant amount—but because interest-rate differentials between countries had changed and lessened the attractiveness of direct investments in currencies. Putting Berkshire's money into companies making a large proportion of their earnings overseas would be a better strategy for the future, Buffett said.*

*One follow-on, just a few months later, to that declaration: Berkshire's first-ever acquisition of a foreign company, namely Iscar, an Israeli manufacturer of cutting tools that makes almost all of its profits outside the U.S. Berkshire's original stake in Iscar, acquired in 2004, was 80 percent, bought for $4 billion. Nine years later, in 2013, Berkshire bought the residual 20 percent of the company for $2.05 billion. The two purchase prices imply that the total value of Iscar had risen in nine years from $5 billion to just over $10 billion.*

*The article that immediately follows this one on the trade deficit appeared as a sidebar. —CL*

I'm about to deliver a warning regarding the U.S. trade deficit and also suggest a remedy for the problem. But first I need to mention two reasons you might want to be skeptical about what I say. To begin, my forecasting record with respect to macroeconomics is far from inspiring. For example, over the past two decades I was excessively fearful of inflation. More to the point at hand, I started way back in 1987 to publicly worry about our mounting trade deficits—and, as you know, we've not only survived but also thrived. So on the trade front, score at least one "wolf" for me. Nevertheless, I am crying wolf again and this time backing it with Berkshire Hathaway's money. Through the spring of 2002, I had lived nearly 72 years without purchasing a foreign currency. Since then Berkshire has made significant investments in—and today holds—several currencies. I won't give you particulars; in fact, it is largely irrelevant which currencies they are. What does matter is the underlying point: To hold other currencies is to believe that the dollar will decline.

Both as an American and as an investor, I actually hope these commitments prove to be a mistake. Any profits Berkshire might make from currency trading would pale against the losses the company and our shareholders, in other aspects of their lives, would incur from a plunging dollar.

But as head of Berkshire Hathaway, I am in charge of investing its money in ways that make sense. And my reason for finally putting my money where my mouth has been so long is that our trade deficit has greatly worsened, to the point that our country's "net worth," so to speak, is now being transferred abroad at an alarming rate.

A perpetuation of this transfer will lead to major trouble. To understand why, take a wildly fanciful trip with me to two isolated, side-by-side islands of equal size, Squanderville and Thriftville. Land is the only capital asset on these islands, and their communities are primitive, needing only food and producing only food. Working eight hours a day, in fact, each inhabitant can produce enough food to sustain himself or herself. And for a long time that's how things go along. On each island everybody works the prescribed eight hours a day, which means that each society is self-sufficient.

Eventually, though, the industrious citizens of Thriftville decide to do some serious saving and investing, and they start to work 16 hours a day. In this mode they continue to live off the food they produce in eight hours of work but begin exporting an equal amount to their one and only trading outlet, Squanderville.

The citizens of Squanderville are ecstatic about this turn of events, since they can now live their lives free from toil but eat as well as ever. Oh, yes, there's a quid pro quo—but to the Squanders, it seems harmless: All that the Thrifts want in exchange for their food is Squanderbonds (which are denominated, naturally, in Squanderbucks).

Over time Thriftville accumulates an enormous amount of these bonds, which at their core represent claim checks on the future output of Squanderville. A few pundits in Squanderville smell trouble coming. They foresee that for the Squanders both to eat and to pay off—or simply service—the debt they're piling up will eventually require them to work more than eight hours a day. But the residents of Squanderville are in no mood to listen to such doomsaying.

Meanwhile, the citizens of Thriftville begin to get nervous. Just how good, they ask, are the IOUs of a shiftless island? So the Thrifts change strategy: Though they continue to hold some bonds, they sell most of them to Squanderville residents for Squanderbucks and use the proceeds to buy Squanderville land. And eventually the Thrifts own all of Squanderville.

At that point, the Squanders are forced to deal with an ugly equation: They must now not only return to working eight hours a day in order to eat—they have nothing left to trade—but must also work additional hours to service their debt and pay Thriftville rent on the land so imprudently sold. In effect, Squanderville has been colonized by purchase rather than conquest.

It can be argued, of course, that the present value of the future production that Squanderville must forever ship to Thriftville only equates to the production Thriftville initially gave up and that therefore both have received a fair deal. But since one generation of Squanders gets the free ride and future generations pay in perpetuity for it, there are—in economist talk—some pretty dramatic "intergenerational inequities."

Let's think of it in terms of a family: Imagine that I, Warren Buffett, can get the suppliers of all that I consume in my lifetime to take Buffett family IOUs that are payable, in goods and services and with interest added, by my descendants. This scenario may be viewed as effecting an even trade between the Buffett family unit and its creditors. But the generations of Buffetts following me are not likely to applaud the deal (and, heaven forbid, may even attempt to welsh on it).

Think again about those islands: Sooner or later the Squanderville government, facing ever greater payments to service debt, would decide to embrace highly inflationary policies—that is, issue more Squanderbucks to dilute the value of each. After all, the government would reason, those irritating Squanderbonds are simply claims on specific *numbers* of Squanderbucks, not on bucks of specific *value*. In short, making Squanderbucks less valuable would ease the island's fiscal pain.

That prospect is why I, were I a resident of Thriftville, would opt for direct ownership of Squanderville land rather than bonds of the island's government. Most governments find it much harder morally to seize foreign-owned property than they do to dilute the purchasing power of claim checks foreigners hold. Theft by stealth is preferred to theft by force.

So what does all this island hopping have to do with the U.S.? Simply put, after World War II and up until the early 1970s we operated in the industrious Thriftville style, regularly selling more abroad than we purchased. We concurrently invested our surplus abroad, with the result that our net investment—that is, our holdings of foreign assets less foreign holdings of U.S. assets—increased (under methodology, since revised, that the government was then using) from $37 billion in 1950 to $68 billion in 1970. In those days, to sum up, our country's "net worth," viewed in totality, consisted of all the wealth within our borders plus a modest portion of the wealth in the rest of the world.

Additionally, because the U.S. was in a net ownership position with respect to the rest of the world, we realized net investment income that, piled on top of our trade surplus, became a second source of investable funds. Our fiscal situation was thus similar to that of an individual who was both saving some of his salary and reinvesting the dividends from his existing nest egg.

In the late 1970s the trade situation reversed, producing deficits that initially ran about 1% of GDP. That was hardly serious, particularly because net investment income remained positive. Indeed, with the power of compound interest working for us, our net ownership balance hit its high in 1980 at $360 billion.

Since then, however, it's been all downhill, with the pace of decline rapidly accelerating in the past five years. Our annual trade deficit now exceeds 4% of GDP. Equally ominous, the rest of the world owns a staggering $2.5 trillion more of the U.S. than we own of other countries. Some of this $2.5 trillion is invested in claim checks—U.S. bonds, both governmental and private—and some in such assets as property and equity securities.

In effect, our country has been behaving like an extraordinarily rich family that possesses an immense farm. In order to consume 4% more than we produce—that's the trade deficit—we have, day by day, been both selling pieces of the farm and increasing the mortgage on what we still own.

To put the $2.5 trillion of net foreign ownership in perspective, contrast it with the $12 trillion value of publicly owned U.S. stocks or the equal amount of U.S. residential real estate or what I would estimate as a grand total of $50 trillion in national wealth. Those comparisons show that what's already been transferred abroad is meaningful—in the area, for example, of 5% of our national wealth.

More important, however, is that foreign ownership of our assets will grow at about $500 billion per year at the present trade-deficit level, which means that the deficit will be adding about one percentage point annually to foreigners' net ownership of our national wealth. As that ownership grows, so will the annual net investment income flowing out of this country. That will leave us paying ever-increasing dividends and interest to the world rather than being a net receiver of them, as in the past. We have entered the world of negative compounding—goodbye pleasure, hello pain.

We were taught in Economics 101 that countries could not for long sustain large, ever-growing trade deficits. At a point, so it was claimed, the spree of the consumption-happy nation would be braked by currency-rate adjustments and by the unwillingness of creditor countries to accept an endless flow of IOUs from the big spenders. And that's the way it has indeed worked for the rest of the world, as we can see by the abrupt shutoffs of credit that many profligate nations have suffered in recent decades.

The U.S., however, enjoys special status. In effect, we can behave today as we wish because our past financial behavior was so exemplary—and because we are so rich. Neither our capacity nor our intention to pay is questioned, and we continue to have a mountain of desirable assets to trade for consumables. In other words, our national credit card allows us to charge truly breathtaking amounts. But that card's credit line is not limitless.

The time to halt this trading of assets for consumables is now, and I have a plan to suggest for getting it done. My remedy may sound gimmicky, and in truth it is a tariff called by another name. But this is a tariff that retains most free-market virtues, neither protecting specific industries nor punishing specific countries nor encouraging trade wars. This plan would increase our exports and might well lead to increased overall world trade. And it would balance our books without there being a significant decline in the value of the dollar, which I believe is otherwise almost certain to occur.

We would achieve this balance by issuing what I will call Import Certificates (ICs) to all U.S. exporters in an amount equal to the dollar value of their exports. Each exporter would, in turn, sell the ICs to parties—either exporters abroad or importers here—wanting to get goods into the U.S. To import $1 million of goods, for example, an importer would need ICs that were the by-product of $1 million of exports. The inevitable result: trade balance.

Because our exports total about $80 billion a month, ICs would be issued in huge, equivalent quantities—that is, 80 billion certificates a month—and would surely trade in an exceptionally liquid market. Competition would then determine who among those parties wanting to sell to us would buy the certificates and how much they would pay. (I visualize that the certificates would be issued with a short life, possibly of six months, so that speculators would be discouraged from accumulating them.)

For illustrative purposes, let's postulate that each IC would sell for 10 cents— that is, 10 cents per dollar of exports behind them. Other things being equal, this amount would mean a U.S. producer could realize 10% more by selling his goods in the export market than by selling them domestically, with the extra 10% coming from his sales of ICs.

In my opinion, many exporters would view this as a reduction in cost, one that would let them cut the prices of their products in international markets. Commodity-type products would particularly encourage this kind of behavior. If aluminum, for example, was selling for 66 cents per pound domestically and ICs were worth 10%, domestic aluminum producers could sell for about 60 cents per pound (plus transportation costs) in foreign markets and still earn normal margins. In this scenario, the output of the U.S. would become significantly more competitive and exports would expand. Along the way, the number of jobs would grow.

Foreigners selling to us, of course, would face tougher economics. But that's a problem they're up against no matter what trade "solution" is adopted—and make no mistake, a solution must come. (As Herb Stein said, "If something cannot go on forever, it will stop.") In one way the IC approach would give countries selling to us great flexibility, since the plan does not penalize any specific industry or product. In the end, the free market would determine what would be sold in the U.S. and who would sell it. The ICs would determine only the aggregate dollar volume of what was sold.

To see what would happen to imports, let's look at a car now entering the U.S. at a cost to the importer of $20,000. Under the new plan and the assumption that ICs sell for 10%, the importer's cost would rise to $22,000. If demand for the car was exceptionally strong, the importer might manage to pass all of this on to the American consumer. In the usual case, however, competitive forces would take hold, requiring the foreign manufacturer to absorb some, if not all, of the $2,000 IC cost.

There is no free lunch in the IC plan: It would have certain serious negative consequences for U.S. citizens. Prices of most imported products would increase, and so would the prices of certain competitive products manufactured domestically. The cost of the ICs, either in whole or in part, would therefore typically act as a tax on consumers.

That is a serious drawback. But there would be drawbacks also to the dollar continuing to lose value or to our increasing tariffs on specific products or instituting quotas on them—courses of action that in my opinion offer a smaller chance of success. Above all, the pain of higher prices on goods imported today dims beside the pain we will eventually suffer if we drift along and trade away ever larger portions of our country's net worth.

I believe that ICs would produce, rather promptly, a U.S. trade equilibrium well above present export levels but below present import levels. The certificates would moderately aid all our industries in world competition, even as the free market determined which of them ultimately met the test of "comparative advantage."

This plan would not be copied by nations that are net exporters, because their ICs would be valueless. Would major exporting countries retaliate in other ways? Would this start another Smoot-Hawley tariff war? Hardly. At the time of Smoot-Hawley we ran an unreasonable trade surplus that we wished to maintain. We now run a damaging deficit that the whole world knows we must correct.

For decades the world has struggled with a shifting maze of punitive tariffs, export subsidies, quotas, dollar-locked currencies, and the like. Many of these import-inhibiting and export-encouraging devices have long been employed by major exporting countries trying to amass ever larger surpluses—yet significant trade wars have not erupted. Surely one will not be precipitated by a proposal that simply aims at balancing the books of the world's largest trade debtor. Major exporting countries have behaved quite rationally in the past and they will continue to do so—though, as always, it may be in their interest to attempt to convince us that they will behave otherwise.

The likely outcome of an IC plan is that the exporting nations—after some initial posturing—will turn their ingenuity to encouraging imports from us. Take the position of China, which today sells us about $140 billion of goods and services annually while purchasing only $25 billion. Were ICs to exist, one course for China would be simply to fill the gap by buying 115 billion certificates annually. But it could alternatively reduce its need for ICs by cutting its exports to the U.S. or by increasing its purchases from us. This last choice would probably be the most palatable for China, and we should wish it to be so.

If our exports were to increase and the supply of ICs were therefore to be enlarged, their market price would be driven down. Indeed, if our exports expanded sufficiently, ICs would be rendered valueless and the entire plan made moot. Presented with the power to make this happen, important exporting countries might quickly eliminate the mechanisms they now use to inhibit exports from us.

Were we to install an IC plan, we might opt for some transition years in which we deliberately ran a relatively small deficit, a step that would enable the world to adjust as we gradually got where we need to be. Carrying this plan out, our government could either auction "bonus" ICs every month or simply give them, say, to less-developed countries needing to increase their exports. The latter course would deliver a form of foreign aid likely to be particularly effective and appreciated.

I will close by reminding you again that I cried wolf once before. In general, the batting average of doomsayers in the U.S. is terrible. Our country has consistently made fools of those who were skeptical about either our economic potential or our resiliency. Many pessimistic seers simply underestimated the dynamism that has allowed us to overcome problems that once seemed ominous. We still have a truly remarkable country and economy.

But I believe that in the trade deficit we also have a problem that is going to test all of our abilities to find a solution. A gently declining dollar will not provide the answer. True, it would reduce our trade deficit to a degree, but not by enough to halt the outflow of our country's net worth and the resulting growth in our investment-income deficit.

Perhaps there are other solutions that make more sense than mine. However, wishful thinking—and its usual companion, thumb sucking—is not among them. From what I now see, action to halt the rapid outflow of our national wealth is called for, and ICs seem the least painful and most certain way to get the job done. Just keep remembering that this is not a small problem: For example, at the rate at which the rest of the world is now making net investments in the U.S., it could annually buy and sock away nearly 4% of our publicly traded stocks.

In evaluating business options at Berkshire, my partner, Charles Munger, suggests that we pay close attention to his jocular wish: "All I want to know is where I'm going to die, so I'll never go there." Framers of our trade policy should heed this caution—and steer clear of Squanderville.

# WHY FOREIGNERS CAN'T DITCH THEIR DOLLARS
## NOVEMBER 10, 2003

### *A Sidebar by Warren Buffett with Carol Loomis*

How often have you seen a comment like this in articles about the U.S. dollar? "Analysts say that what really worries them is that foreigners will start moving out of the dollar."

Next time you see something like that, dismiss it. The fact is that foreigners—as a whole—cannot ditch their dollars. Indeed, because our trade deficit is constantly putting new dollars into the hands of foreigners, they have to just as constantly increase their U.S. investments.

It's true, of course, that the rest of the world can choose which U.S. assets to hold. They can decide, for example, to sell U.S. bonds to buy U.S. stocks. Or they can make a move into real estate, as the Japanese did in the 1980s. Moreover, any of those moves, particularly if they are carried out by anxious sellers or buyers, can influence the price of the dollar.

But imagine that the Japanese both want to get out of their U.S. real estate and entirely away from dollar assets. They can't accomplish that by selling their real estate to Americans, because they will get paid in dollars. And if they sell their real estate to non-Americans—say, the French, for euros—the property will remain in the hands of foreigners. With either kind of sale, the dollar assets held by the rest of the world will not (except for any concurrent shift in the price of the dollar) have changed.

The bottom line is that other nations simply can't disinvest in the U.S. unless they, as a universe, buy more goods and services from us than we buy from them. That state of affairs would be called an American trade surplus, and we don't have one.

You can dream up some radical plots for changing the situation. For example, the rest of the world could send the U.S. massive foreign aid that would serve to offset our trade deficit. But under any realistic view of things, our huge trade deficit guarantees that the rest of the world must not only hold the American assets it owns but consistently add to them. And that's why, of course, our national net worth is gradually shifting away from our shores.

# The Market According to Buffett

May 17, 2004

**BY DAVID STIRES**

How much would you pay to get close to Warren Buffett? In what must set a new record for business fandom, some admirers were bidding as much as $117 on eBay for a ticket to Berkshire Hathaway's May 1 annual meeting. Determined to secure access for all, Buffett posted 10,000 tickets on the site, at $2.50 apiece (a bargain, given that one share of Class A stock goes for $93,500).But it's hardly the only time Buffett-mania has reared its head. Below, a sampling of the robust Buffett aftermarket:

**$16.95**
The best-selling Buffett tome

**$210,000**
Buffett's 20-year-old wallet, sold at a charity auction in 1999

**$5**
Two tickets to Berkshire Hathaway's annual meeting

**$250,100**
Lunch with Buffett, sold on eBay in 2003

**$100**
Dollar bill signed by Buffett, sold at a church auction in Nebraska in 2004

**$20**
Bobble-head doll, sold on the Omaha Royals' website

*Editor's note: The eBay auction for a Buffett lunch to benefit San Francisco's Glide Foundation continues— and also jumps in price every year. In 2012, the winning bid, once again a record, was $3,456,789.*

# The Best Advice I Ever Got

March 11, 2005

### *A Warren Buffett recollection, edited by Carol Loomis*

*Three times in the 2000s decade,* Fortune *lined up twenty or so well-known people and asked each to relate the best advice he or she had ever been given. Buffett agreed to be in the first of these packages, and within about one second of his acceptance, managing editor Rik Kirkland scheduled him for the cover.*

*I had the Buffett interview assignment, and as I opened my notebook to record whatever he had to say, I was genuinely curious as to what it would be. I simply didn't think I'd ever heard him on this subject. So I said, "Okay, what is the best advice you ever got?"*

*Back came an out-of-the-box answer that was a real doozy. He didn't have any best advice to talk about. Instead, he went on at length about the "worst advice" he had ever received, with it coming to boot from the two men he admired most.*

*I can't remember how I presented Rik with this surprise twist on what he had in mind. Perhaps I have suppressed the whole scene from my brain. But you know what? We put Buffett on the cover anyway.* —CL

"I had two mentors: my dad, Howard Buffett, and Ben Graham. Here were these two guys who I revered and who over the years gave me tons of good advice. But when I think about what they said to me, the truth is, the first thing that comes to mind is bad advice.

"I was not quite 21 when this happened, in 1951, and just getting out of business school at Columbia. I had just taken Ben's class there—and I was the most interested student you ever saw. I wanted to work for Ben at Graham-Newman Corp., and I had famously gone to him and offered to work for nothing. He said no.

"But I still was determined to go into the securities business, and that's where Ben and my dad gave me the bad advice. They both thought it was a bad time to start. One thing on their minds was that the Dow Jones industrials had been above 200 all year, and yet there had never been a year when it didn't sell below 200. So they both said, 'You'll do fine, but this is not a good time to start.'

"Now there's one thing that may have influenced my dad, and maybe Ben too. I was so immature. I was not only young-looking, I was young-acting. I was skinny. My hair looked awful. Maybe their advice was their polite way of saying that before I started selling stocks, I needed to mature a little, or I wasn't going to be successful. But they didn't say that to me; they said the other. Anyway, I didn't pay any attention. I went back to Omaha and started selling securities at my dad's firm, Buffett Falk.

"My dad was a totally independent thinker. I suppose the fact that he was has influenced my own thinking some when it comes to buying stocks. Ben instructed me some there too. He said, 'You're neither right nor wrong because others agree with you. You're right because your facts and reasoning are right.'

"Now, Ben—I started learning from him when I read his books on investing at the University of Nebraska. I had tried all kinds of investing up to then, but what he said, particularly in *The Intelligent Investor,* just lifted the scales from my eyes—things like 'margin of safety' and how to use 'Mr. Market' rather than letting him use you. I then went to Columbia just to take his class and later got that turndown when I asked him for a job. But I kept thinking about that idea when I went back to Omaha. I kept trying to sell Ben stocks and pestering him, sort of. And finally one day in 1954 I got a letter from him saying something to the effect of the next time you're in New York, I'd like to talk to you about something. I was elated! And I made a point of getting to New York immediately.

"I went to work for Ben in August 1954, without ever having asked what my salary would be. It turned out to be $12,000, plus the next year I got a $2,000 bonus. I worked for both parts of the business: Graham-Newman was a regulated investment company, and Newman & Graham Ltd. was what we'd today call a hedge fund. But together they ran only $12 million!

"Walter Schloss and I—though he left before long to start a hedge fund— worked together in a little room. We had a lot of fun with each other, plus we kept poring through the manuals, looking for cheap stocks. We never went out to visit any companies. Ben thought that would be cheating. And when we found something terrific, Ben would put 50,000 bucks into it.

"By early 1956, Ben was planning to leave the firm to go to California. And I had already decided by then to go back to Omaha. I had a terrible time telling Ben about that: I'd go into his office and come back, and then go in and not do it, for a really long time. But his reaction was kind of the same as my dad would have had: whatever's best for you.

"I had $9,800 at the end of 1950, and by 1956 I had $150,000. I figured with that I could live like a king. And I didn't know what I was going to do in Omaha. Maybe go to law school. I did not have a plan. I certainly didn't know I was going to start an investing partnership. But then a couple of months later, seven people wanted me to invest their money for them, and a partnership was the way to do it. And that began it all."

# The $91 Billion Conversation

October 31, 2005

**BY DANIEL ROTH**

*Fair's fair—that is, if it's Warren Buffett and Bill Gates, and it's time for the University of Nebraska to finally match the event held by the University of Washington eight years earlier (see page 133).*

*News jumped out of this conversation, which signaled that Buffett had gone a long way toward deciding that he would give his money away while he was still alive. That was a sharp swerve in his philanthropic intentions, but there had also been a swerve—a very sad one—in Buffett's life: the death in the summer of 2004 of his wife, Susie, who died from a sudden stroke. As noted earlier in this book, Buffett had always expected that Susie, two years younger than he, would outlive him and quickly apply her superabundant wisdom and compassion to giving his billions away. With Susie gone, the job of determining how his philanthropy should proceed had become a weight on Buffett's mind. By early 2006, though, he had settled on his stunning plan to gradually give away his Berkshire stock to five foundations, chief among them the one run by the Bill of this conversation and his wife, Melinda. (See "Warren Buffett Gives It Away," page 256.)*

*The "Buffett Speaks Out" sidebar that follows the Q&A attests to how strongly Buffett felt even in 2005 about the unfairness of the ultra-rich (including himself and Gates, of course) paying very low tax rates on their income. He made that argument often in the next few years and by 2011 his views—or at least something loosely resembling them—were shaped by the Obama camp into the so-called Buffett Rule. In 2013 taxes were raised for upper-income filers, with the increases beginning at levels lower than the $1 million Buffett had proposed. —CL*

It's the Friday before the University of Nebraska's Big 12 Conference opener in football-mad Lincoln, but the Cornhuskers game isn't the only hot ticket in town. On a beautiful late September afternoon, some 2,000 students are lined up outside the school's Lied Center auditorium, an hour before the doors open. Andrew Schoemacher, a lanky 19-year-old chemical-engineering sophomore, doesn't even have a ticket but hopes he can scrounge one to get inside. How could he miss seeing this show? After all, he says, "It's Bill Gates and Warren Buffett."

Gates and Buffett—friends who just happen to be the two richest men in the world, worth $51 billion and $40 billion, respectively—are coming together for a free-ranging question-and-answer session. They have done this kind of talk before—once. The two met up in Gates' hometown of Seattle in 1998 with students at the University of Washington. Back then both men were on the verge of turbulent times: Microsoft about to face off against the government in its epic antitrust trial, and Buffett weeks away from buying reinsurer General Re, now the thorn in his company Berkshire Hathaway's side, thanks to its involvement with the troubled AIG. *Fortune*, the only magazine invited to attend their first chat, found the interaction "something pretty darn close to wisdom" and put the talk on the cover. So when the billionaires decided to meet again, we went along for an inside peek at the event—and more important, some private time with the two men to pose our own questions.

Over lunch with *Fortune*'s Daniel Roth—Cherry Coke and sliced turkey on white bread for Buffett; roast beef with mustard on white for Gates—the two moguls loosened up, talking about their close relationship, their plans for poker that night, and Wall Street's willingness to lead investors down the wrong path. Both men are shaping up: Gates, 50 in October, has dropped 20 pounds by running regularly; Buffett, 75, has shed 12 pounds thanks to three-times-a-week personal-training sessions. And they're reshaping their plans as well: Buffett reverses himself and says for the first time that he may begin giving away his fortune before he dies. What follows are excerpts of that conversation.

**FORTUNE:** A few quick hits. First: best book you've read lately.

**BUFFETT:** Katharine Graham's *Personal History* is sensational. I think everybody ought to read that.

**GATES:** There's one called *The Bottomless Well*, about energy, that I love. There's one about computer science, Ray Kurzweil's book—I have a pre-print, so I'm not sure when it's coming out—called *Singularity Is Near*, about artificial intelligence. The Tom Friedman book [*The World Is Flat*] is supergood. Jeffrey Sachs wrote a book called *The End of Poverty*, the Jack Welch book *Winning* came out this year, and don't forget [Jared Diamond's] *Collapse*, which is the follow-on to one of the best books of all time [*Guns, Germs, and Steel*].

**FORTUNE:** Your last big splurge?

**BUFFETT:** You mean personal expenditure?

**FORTUNE:** Right.

**BUFFETT:** Plane. That's the only way in which having a lot of money has changed my life—a NetJets G4. [Note: Berkshire owns NetJets.] I spend a couple hundred thousand dollars a year, or maybe a little more.

**GATES:** Splurge . . . I guess if I lose at poker tonight, it's a $500 splurge.

**BUFFETT:** That is a splurge.

**GATES:** Warren's and my betting has always been confined to $1 bets.

**BUFFETT:** This fellow in Omaha called me about a poker game, and it sounded like fun. But with Texas Hold 'Em you've got to play for money. That's the nature of the game. I think bridge is a better game, but poker is a lot of fun.

**GATES:** If we'd had an ideal fourth here, we might have opted for bridge.

*FORTUNE:* What does your friend think when you say, "Oh yeah, I'll come over for poker. I'm going to bring my buddy Bill Gates"?

**BUFFETT:** We kept it quiet. The guy that's setting up the game knows, but the other participants don't.

*FORTUNE:* Back to the lightning round: Make a call on the market. Seven years from now, will the S&P 500 have returned over or under 10% annually?

**BUFFETT:** More likely to be under than over. You're not going to have the GDP in nominal terms grow 5% a year and everybody make 10% a year.

**GATES:** I'd say under, most likely. The notion that returns will continue to be superhigh—there are some clouds out there.

*FORTUNE:* The last time you did a talk like this, Warren, you said that people were making "fairly reckless assumptions" about big stock market returns. Is the same thing happening today with hedge funds and private equity?

**BUFFETT:** In the late 1990s people were looking in their rearview mirror, and they thought that God had granted Americans the right to 15% a year. They built that into pension assumptions. They built it to some extent into what endowment funds spent. Now, six or seven years later, people look in the rearview mirror, and they see that conventional investments haven't produced remotely anything like that. And so they say to themselves, "Well, how do I get it? I'll turn to alternative investments." You can be sure that vacuum will be filled by Wall Street people who say, "You're right looking in that rearview mirror and seeing conventional investments don't work. Come with us, because we have the Holy Grail." And the thing about the Holy Grail is that you have to pay a lot more.

**GATES:** In venture capital there were very high returns with small amounts of money, and then very poor returns with large amounts of money. This desire to have high absolute returns—and seeing that places like Harvard University were cleverly in alternative assets—has led to this thought that "Okay, there must be something out there returning 10%. I just haven't found it yet." So the fact that expectations of returns exceed reality, that's still true today.

**BUFFETT:** And Wall Street feeds that.

**GATES:** It's Wall Street's job. [Both laugh.]

**FORTUNE:** Warren gave a speech to Allen & Co. this summer about his worries surrounding the ballooning U.S. trade deficit. I'm curious, Bill, whether you have the same sort of fears that Warren does.

**GATES:** Warren has got me thinking hard about it. I watched that speech twice, and after each time I'm more concerned. I believe in the basic principle that trade is a supergood thing. I'm very worried that the reaction to this imbalance is to put on trade restrictions to bring imports down, which would lead other nations to do similar things. I think the greatest danger is something that would slow down the benefits that the free trade system has brought.

**FORTUNE:** Don't companies like yours, as they move production overseas, add to the trade deficit problem?

**GATES:** Microsoft is a net exporter—more than any other business. We do way more of our R&D here than we get in sales here. If the U.S. had about 100 more Microsofts, the trade deficit would be gone.

**BUFFETT:** High tech has been one of our huge advantages. You're looking for the things in the world that you're good at, and let the other guy turn out bananas. We're never going to be good at growing bananas in this country. But I don't think the trade deficit is a stable thing. If you had a major economic disruption, and people just had a general feeling that "look at what this situation has done"—you get some very bad political consequences. It's almost inevitable.

**FORTUNE:** Is that your biggest fear about what happens to the U.S.?

**BUFFETT:** The biggest problem we have is in terms of rogue states, terrorists, and nuclear, chemical, or biological weapons. Economically, I think the U.S. is going to be fine. If the rest of the world's GDP per capita grows faster than ours, that's the way it should be.

**GATES:** It's too bad that economics isn't taught or a hobby for lots of people, because you do run into those who seem to say, "There's only a certain number of jobs." That's not the case. Let's say tomorrow we could decide that everyone in India is as rich as we are. Would the world be a better place? Certainly. Would the U.S. thrive more because of the great products and work that would be done over there? Absolutely. The world getting richer is a great thing. It has been a great thing. It will continue to be.

**BUFFETT:** It's not a zero-sum game.

**GATES:** Right, that's the key.

*FORTUNE:* You have different philosophies about philanthropy, with Bill giving a lot of his money away today and Warren waiting until he dies to give it away. What arguments would you make to the other that your way is the right way?

**BUFFETT:** Well, I think his way is better. He and Melinda, they're devoting a huge amount of money, terrific brains, and heart to it. That's a great combination. I couldn't have done that when I was in my 40s and added anything meaningful.

At my age now, you can argue that a very significant percentage of the money has been made. And I don't need the stock to control Berkshire, so it may make sense to do something very significant before I die.

*FORTUNE:* Is this a change for you?

**BUFFETT:** It's an evolution.

**GATES:** In 1998 I was just getting started [in philanthropy], and back then I would have said, "Look, it's too confusing and distracting to be making money and giving money away at the same time." I didn't think I could spare the time. As my dad encouraged me to jump in, as Melinda weighed in on that side, and both of them were willing to put time into it, we got a great person in Steve Ballmer, who actually I'd known at Microsoft a long time—the pieces really fell together. I'd always thought that I would wait until I was done working full-time before I'd do a lot of philanthropy. But it's worked amazingly well to be able to do some of both.

**BUFFETT:** Bill's got a better mind for it. I couldn't do what he does. I wouldn't get any enjoyment, because I would know I wasn't that good at it. I want to see the money used intelligently. I don't regard my death as being the perfect timing, necessarily.

*FORTUNE:* Do you two talk about this?

**BUFFETT**: Oh, sure.

**GATES**: Absolutely.

**FORTUNE**: Are you trying to persuade Warren to be as hands-on in philanthropy as you are?

**GATES**: No, but I share the enjoyment I get out of it and some of the fun dynamics, the dynamics of what works and doesn't work. It's a lot like the world of business—not enough that you can just walk into it, but you learn some of the specifics and then the experience of business applies.

**BUFFETT**: Berkshire is so much a part of me that I never could walk away from it. But I don't think that I'm going to quintuple [my personal fortune] in six or eight years. The amount is big enough now to do very significant things, and way different than when I was in my 40s. I mean, if I had done this in my 40s, it might have been $20 million. Now we've got a sum that can do something significant. And I don't need it to control Berkshire. Nobody's going to take over Berkshire at its present size, which was not the case 20 years ago.

**GATES**: I'd never thought that giving wealth to my own kids could be disadvantageous until I read a *Fortune* article—

**BUFFETT**: "Should You Leave It All to the Children?"

**GATES**: Right. Warren was a strong voice in that article. And after I read it, I thought, Wow, it would be a mistake as you get past a certain amount [to hand it all down]. So this idea that it should all go back to society, Warren influenced me dramatically on that.

**BUFFETT**: And he's doing a better job. [Laughter.] It's interesting that the same people who talk about the terrible cycle of dependency that welfare brings will then hand their kids when they emerge from the womb a lifetime supply of food stamps. But some poor woman who's had two pregnancies by the time she's 17, they say, Oh, this is terrible to give her anything.

**FORTUNE**: Warren, I know that you don't typically invest in tech companies, but I'm curious if Microsoft is looking tempting.

**BUFFETT**: With Bill on my board, people would assume that I had inside information if I made money. And if I didn't make money, it wouldn't be a good idea. [Both start laughing.]

**GATES:** Yeah, they'd assume I misled you.

*FORTUNE:* But, Bill, you've been buying more Berkshire Hathaway.

**GATES:** Well, out of all the board members, I have the smallest percentage of my net worth in Berkshire stock.

*FORTUNE:* So this isn't a takeover attempt of Berkshire . . .

**GATES:** [Laughing.] No, no, no.

**BUFFETT:** If anybody takes over, I hope it's Bill.

**GATES:** When I get up to 1%, I'll let you know.

*FORTUNE:* Speaking of Berkshire, you both like its subsidiary, Dairy Queen. So, last question: Dilly Bar or Blizzard?

**BUFFETT:** Well, I actually prefer something I call a Dusty Sundae. But given the choice I would have to say a Blizzard.

**GATES:** I would pick a Dilly Bar.

Later, Dan Roth talked to the men separately. Here is his Buffett report:

## Buffett speaks out . . .

### On the idea of a flat tax

I wouldn't support it. We have, in my view, a taxation system that's much too flat already. If you look at the payroll tax—which is over 12% now, and that applies on the first $80,000 or $90,000 of income—Bill and I pay practically none of that in relation to our income. For the people that work for us, their tax rate in many cases is the same or even higher than my own, since the rate on capital gains and dividends was cut to 15%. What has gone on in this country in recent years is a huge benefit to the very rich and not that much relief to people down below.

Frankly, I think that Bill and I should have a higher tax rate on the income we get. We pay less than half the rate that I was paying 25 years ago when I was making a lot less money. They have really taken care of the rich.

### On his worst investment decisions

The biggest mistakes are mistakes of omission rather than commission. We've never lost that much money on any one investment, but it's the things that I knew enough to do but didn't do. We have missed profits of as much as $10 billion. The fact that I didn't buy Microsoft way back is not a foregone opportunity because I didn't know enough to make that decision, but there have been other investments where I did know enough and for one reason or other I either didn't invest at all or I did it on a small scale. I was sucking my thumb when I should have been writing checks, basically.

But, you know, if you were a golfer and you had a hole in one on every hole, the game wouldn't be any fun. At least that's my explanation of why I keep hitting them in the rough.

### On giving money to his children

Our kids are going to be rich, in the top half-a-percent of the world, but 99% of what I have will go to philanthropy, and Bill has the same attitude, basically. We are not going to turn out super-superwealthy kids. They'll be wealthy, there's no question about that, but the idea of dynastic fortune turns me off. If you talk about equality of opportunity in this country and really having everybody with talent having a fair shot at getting the brass ring, the idea that you hand over huge positions in society simply because someone came from the right womb, I just think it's almost un-American.

# Cut Your Gains!

March 20, 2006

*An excerpt from Buffett's letter to shareholders in the*
*2005 Berkshire Hathaway annual report*

*"He is such a reductionist," said a business associate of Warren Buffett's not long ago, using that uncommon word to refer to Buffett's uncommon ability to reduce a problem or issue to its essence. Buffett displays that talent in this excerpt from his 2005 shareholder letter, averring "the most that owners in aggregate can earn between now and Judgment Day is what their businesses in aggregate earn." He then goes on, under the "Cut Your Gains!" headline that* Fortune *supplied for the excerpt, to lament "frictional costs" and their expensive effect on a family named Gotrocks.*

*"Frictional costs" have been on Buffett's mind since he started his Buffett Partnership Ltd. in 1956. By today's definition, it was a hedge fund. But in a practice emulated by few other funds, Buffett assigned the first 6 percent of the fund's annual gains to his limited partners, before beginning to collect any part of the gains for himself. Later, as his shareholder letters became famous, he advised most individual investors to head for low-cost index funds rather than to try to deal with the stock market themselves.*

*Still later, he made the now famous bet against Protégé Partners, in which he wagered that an unmanaged and low-cost S&P index fund could over ten years beat the performance of five hedge fund of funds carefully selected for this bet. The burden that limited partners in those funds bear, of course, is two sets of frictional costs, the first at the hedge fund level, the second at the fund of funds level. As this book is published in 2013, five years of the bet have passed and Buffett has for the first time moved into the lead. More about the bet can be found in "Buffett's Big Bet," page 279. —CL*

It's been an easy matter for Berkshire and other owners of American equities to prosper over the years. Between Dec. 31, 1899, and Dec. 31, 1999, to give a really long-term example, the Dow rose from 66 to 11,497. (Guess what annual growth rate is required to produce this result; the surprising answer is at the end of this piece.) This huge rise came about for a simple reason: Over the century, American businesses did extraordinarily well and investors rode the wave of their prosperity. Businesses continue to do well. But now shareholders, through a series of self-inflicted wounds, are in a major way cutting the returns they will realize from their investments.

The explanation of how this is happening begins with a fundamental truth: With unimportant exceptions, such as bankruptcies in which some of a company's losses are borne by creditors, *the most that owners in aggregate can earn between now and Judgment Day is what their businesses in aggregate earn.* True, by buying and selling that is clever or lucky, investor A may take more than his share of the pie at the expense of investor B. And, yes, all investors *feel* richer when stocks soar. But an owner can exit only by having someone take his place. If one investor sells high, another must buy high. For owners as a whole, there is simply no magic—no shower of money from outer space—that will enable them to extract wealth from their companies beyond that created by the companies themselves.

Indeed, owners must earn less than their businesses earn because of "frictional" costs. And that's my point: These costs are now being incurred in amounts that will cause shareholders to earn *far* less than they historically have.

To understand how this toll has ballooned, imagine for a moment that all American corporations are, and always will be, owned by a single family. We'll call them the Gotrocks. After paying taxes on dividends, this family—generation after generation—becomes richer by the aggregate amount earned by its companies. Today that amount is about $700 billion annually. Naturally, the family spends some of these dollars. But the portion it saves steadily compounds for its benefit. In the Gotrocks household everyone grows wealthier at the same pace, and all is harmonious.

But let's now assume that a few fast-talking Helpers approach the family and persuade each of its members to try to outsmart his relatives by buying certain of their holdings and selling them certain others. The Helpers—for a fee, of course—obligingly agree to handle these transactions. The Gotrocks still own all of corporate America; the trades just rearrange who owns what. So the family's annual gain in wealth diminishes, equaling the earnings of American business minus commissions paid. The more that family members trade, the smaller their share of the pie and the larger the slice received by the Helpers. This fact is not lost upon these broker-Helpers: Activity is their friend, and in a wide variety of ways, they urge it on.

After a while, most of the family members realize that they are not doing so well at this new "beat my brother" game. Enter another set of Helpers. These newcomers explain to each member of the Gotrocks clan that by himself he'll never outsmart the rest of the family. The suggested cure: "Hire a manager—yes, us—and get the job done professionally." These manager-Helpers continue to use the broker-Helpers to execute trades; the managers may even increase their activity so as to permit the brokers to prosper still more. Overall, a bigger slice of the pie now goes to the two classes of Helpers.

The family's disappointment grows. Each of its members is now employing professionals. Yet overall, the group's finances have taken a turn for the worse. The solution? More help, of course.

It arrives in the form of financial planners and institutional consultants, who weigh in to advise the Gotrocks on selecting manager-Helpers. The befuddled family welcomes this assistance. By now its members know they can pick neither the right stocks nor the right stock pickers. Why, one might ask, should they expect success in picking the right consultant? But this question does not occur to the Gotrocks, and the consultant-Helpers certainly don't suggest it to them.

The Gotrocks, now supporting three classes of expensive Helpers, find that their results get worse, and they sink into despair. But just as hope seems lost, a fourth group—we'll call them the hyper-Helpers—appears. These friendly folk explain to the Gotrocks that their unsatisfactory results are occurring because the existing Helpers—brokers, managers, consultants—are not sufficiently motivated and are simply going through the motions. "What," the new Helpers ask, "can you expect from such a bunch of zombies?"

The new arrivals offer a breathtakingly simple solution: *Pay more money.* Brimming with self-confidence, the hyper-Helpers assert that huge contingent payments—in addition to stiff fixed fees—are what each family member must fork over in order to *really* outmaneuver his relatives.

The more observant members of the family see that some of the hyper-Helpers are really just manager-Helpers wearing new uniforms, bearing sewn-on sexy names like HEDGE FUND or PRIVATE EQUITY. The new Helpers, however, assure the Gotrocks that this change of clothing is all-important, bestowing on its wearers magical powers similar to those acquired by mild-mannered Clark Kent when he changed into his Superman costume. Calmed by this explanation, the family decides to pay up.

And that's where we are today: A record portion of the earnings that would go in their entirety to owners—if they all just stayed in their rocking chairs—is now going to a swelling army of Helpers. Particularly expensive is the recent pandemic of profit arrangements under which Helpers receive large portions of the winnings when they are smart or lucky, and leave family members with all the losses—and large fixed fees to boot—when the Helpers are dumb or unlucky (or occasionally crooked).

A sufficient number of arrangements like this—heads, the Helper takes much of the winnings; tails, the Gotrocks lose and pay dearly for the privilege of doing so—may make it more accurate to call the family the Hadrocks. Today, in fact, the family's frictional costs of all sorts may well amount to 20% of the earnings of American business. In other words, the burden of paying Helpers may cause American equity investors, overall, to earn only 80% or so of what they would earn if they just sat still and listened to no one.

Long ago, Sir Isaac Newton gave us three laws of motion, which were the work of genius. But Sir Isaac's talents didn't extend to investing: He lost a bundle in the South Sea Bubble, explaining later, "I can calculate the movement of the stars, but not the madness of men." If he had not been traumatized by this loss, Sir Isaac might well have gone on to discover the fourth law of motion: *For investors as a whole, returns decrease as motion increases.*

Here's the answer to the question posed at the beginning of this piece: To get very specific, the Dow increased from 65.73 to 11,497.12 in the 20th century, and that amounts to a gain of 5.3% compounded annually. (Investors would also have received dividends, of course.) To achieve an equal rate of gain in the 21st century, the Dow will have to rise by Dec. 31, 2099, to—brace yourself—precisely 2,011,011.23. But I'm willing to settle for 2,000,000; six years into this century, the Dow has gained not at all.

# Buffett's Alter Ego

May 29, 2006

## BY ANDY SERWER

*The matchup of Warren Buffett and Charles Munger is regarded as so perfect—so impossible to imagine not happening—that two different Omahans claim they made the introduction. This argument will not be settled here. But it is worth recalling what one of the contenders, Richard Holland, has written in his book* Truth and Other Tall Tales, *about the evening in which he claims to have brought the pair together: "Our living room was arranged with two chairs in one corner for conversations, and that's where Warren and Charlie parked for the evening. To my memory, they never got out of their chairs nor stopped talking until it was time to leave. . . . Charlie talked so much he hyperventilated occasionally."*

*In the article that follows, Andy Serwer describes the unique talents that Munger brings to the Berkshire party, among them making the annual meeting the best two-man show that never made it to Broadway. For this introduction, I thought it might be interesting as well to ask Charlie himself to look back on his Buffett/Berkshire years and articulate, in his distinctive way, what he thinks have been the most important contributions he has made to the extraordinary success that Berkshire has become.*

*He didn't quite rise to that bait. Instead, he employed a pronoun, "we," that is an integral part of Berkshire's culture. Said Charlie: "We chose our style of operation to fit our natures, which demanded that plenty of time be spent thinking and learning, while engaging in lifelong self-criticism, light contrition for every error, and much humor. Naturally this caused extreme delegation, which is what we would have wanted as recipients of trust. We knew our methods would create good financial results for us and those who relied on us. But we did not anticipate that we would draw so much more admiration than we deserved and that this would help us to be happy as we in effect became teachers who to some extent copied Warren's mentor, Ben Graham." —CL*

Ask folks about Berkshire Hathaway, and most will tell you that it's Warren Buffett's company, which is true as far as it goes. But those in the know recognize that Berkshire's success is actually the product of a tag-team effort by Buffett and his long-standing partner, Charlie Munger. Sure, Buffett is the top banana—he's the chairman and CEO as well as the very public face of the company, while Munger is merely vice chairman and more of a behind-the-scenes type—but Munger has long been the co-thinker at Berkshire, which is no small thing.

In early May I made the pilgrimage to Omaha to attend Berkshire's now world-famous annual meeting and to get a taste of what Munger calls "festival capitalism." I had another agenda, however, which was to do some close-up Munger-watching and also to sit down with him and pick his brain. You've probably read plenty about Berkshire's annual meetings, and I have too. But it was still a surreal experience to stroll into the filled-to-capacity Qwest Center in Omaha and find 17,000 shareholders, plus another 7,000 spread throughout the facility in overflow rooms. And almost every single one of them (many of whom are multimillionaires) was sitting in rapt attention as a couple of gee-zers—Buffett is 75 and Munger is 82—waxed on for some five hours. It's the kind of scene where you'd expect to see a couple of high-powered motivational speakers—which, in a sense, is what Buffett and Munger are.

Over the years the Buffett-and-Munger show has taken on a somewhat for-mulaic choreography. The two men sit center stage, facing a dark sea of share-holders. Questions are usually fielded first by Buffett, who will answer and then ramble a bit in his inimitable way—often with a one-liner or two mixed in—for five minutes or so. At that point he will look over to his partner and inquire, "Charlie?" Then one of two things occurs: Munger will either lean in and make a pointed, pithy, often scathing comment (which sometimes elicits gasps or loud guffaws from the crowd). Or Munger will simply remark, "I have nothing to say." (Which, after a particularly long-winded Buffett digression, can be amusing as well.) After that Buffett likes to come back for a two-minute coda. This goes on for 2½ hours in the morning. Then there's a break for lunch. And then another couple of hours in the afternoon. "We stumbled into this two-person format," Munger told me the day after this year's marathon. "It would not work if it was just one person. You could have the wittiest, wisest person on earth up there, and people would find it very tiresome. It takes a little interplay of personalities to handle the extreme length of the festival."

Berkshire watchers say that Munger, who can be prickly and does not suf-fer fools particularly well, has been coming into his own lately. Unlike Buf-fett, who intends to engage in postmortem philanthropy, Munger has been actively doling out big bucks, mostly to educational and health-care causes in his adopted state of California. And then there's the lavish coffee-table book, *Poor Charlie's Almanack: The Wit and Wisdom of Charles T. Munger*, the sec-ond edition of which came out just in time for this year's annual meeting. The book's title and conceit is, of course, a nod to Benjamin Franklin, a man whom Munger greatly admires. "There is the sheer amount of Franklin's wis-dom," says Munger who just for a second flashes a cherubic grin. "And the talent. Franklin played four instruments. He was the nation's leading scientist and inventor, plus a leading author, statesman, and philanthropist. There has never been anyone like him."

To Berkshire shareholders, Munger's pretty singular himself. "Warren is ob-viously so brilliant," one stockholder told me, "but I just love what Charlie says." In a way, Buffett and Munger remind me of the Rolling Stones. Buffett, like Mick Jagger, is certainly the main dude. But many believe that Munger, like Keith Richards, is just as cool, if not more so. (Let's just hope that Munger stays out of coconut trees.)

So what were some of Charlie's zingers this year? Well, at one point Buffett was talking about his shareholders investing on their own, which, he said, would work out just fine for many of them. To which Charlie followed up, "Many of you won't do fine." Munger blasted auditors, saying they are "contemptible. They've totally sold out." Corrupt foreign governments are "kleptocracies." A well-regarded author of business books is "demented." As for executive comp, America is "exporting poison to Europe," he says. The hedge fund and private equity businesses are due for a comeuppance at some point, and Wall Street is filled with "racetrack touts." And so on. But Munger isn't just about calling out charlatans. Many Mungerisms are exercises in humility and simple wisdom. "Warren and I avoid doing anything that someone else at Berkshire can do better," he tells me. "You don't really have a competency if you don't know the edge of it."

On the eve of the meeting, Berkshire announced that, for $4 billion, it had purchased an 80% stake in Iscar, an Israeli metal-cutting tool manufacturer (and Berkshire's first acquisition overseas). In Iscar, Munger says he and his partner have found management with "super talent and super integrity." I hear that Munger, who's usually more skeptical of deals than Buffett, was highly enthusiastic about Iscar from the get-go and even more eager to do the deal than Buffett. "Who the hell wouldn't be excited by this deal?" Munger says.

What's always been maddening to me about Berkshire and Buffett and Munger is how they make both their business and the art of investing, which I find to be so complicated and bewildering, seem so simple. "Berkshire is in the business of making easy predictions," Munger explains. If a deal looks too hard, the partners simply shelve it. But the line of Munger's that I really remember best from this year's meeting is this: "We have a high moral responsibility to be rational," he says. Think about that for a minute. Have you ever heard any business leader describe their charge thusly? There's a reason that there's just one Berkshire Hathaway and one Warren Buffett. And one Charlie Munger too.

# Buffett Backs GM—And Buys a Caddy

May 29, 2006

**BY ALEX TAYLOR III**

Warren Buffett isn't one of those guys who always has to have the fanciest bling on the block. This is, after all, the billionaire who loves to dine at Dairy Queen. And his daily commute takes only five minutes. But after he saw Rick Wagoner, the chairman and CEO of General Motors, on CBS's *Face the Nation* in early April, Buffett decided it was time to splurge for a new ride. He faxed Wagoner a note that praised him for being "candid, composed, and rational" in discussing problems that GM faced that weren't of his making, and added a P.S.: "I don't buy cars very often, but the next one will be a Cadillac." Wagoner wrote back offering to help Buffett with the purchase, but it wasn't necessary. Buffett dispatched his daughter to a nearby dealer so that he could, as he put it, cast "one vote for the guy." She picked out a DTS—a sedan that is the model of choice for senior-citizen drivers and starts at $41,900. "I think I'll become a car salesman, because I would have no trouble selling this car to anyone," Buffett says. "I'm behind GM 100%." In case you were wondering, he paid cash.

# THE PHILANTHROPIST EMERGES

IN EARLY MAY OF 2006, *I went into the office of my managing editor, Eric Pooley, shut his door, and told him we had a chance to break a big story. "As you know," I said in these general words, "Warren Buffett has always said that most of his fortune would go to charity, but has never spelled out any plan for making that happen. Now he's set to announce in June that he will start the giving right away. His money will gradually go to five foundations, and the biggest recipient by far will be the Gates Foundation. Fortune can do a story—a Q&A with him maybe—in which we can disclose all this, if we want it."*

*Eric looked stunned, but in a microsecond said, "We want it." No doubt thinking immediately of a cover story, he said we needed to call in Greg Pond, the head of our photo department. When Greg arrived, Eric asked me to repeat my news. I began the recital, and when I got to the part about where the money would go, Eric interrupted and said, in a voice that surely penetrated the closed door, "And he's giving it to Bill Gates!"*

*Buffett wanted to make his announcement in late June, and we scheduled our article for an issue closing June 23. But the story did not go on the tentative list made up for each issue, which is routinely circulated to the staff. Instead, a small team of us huddled over the secret, while quietly carrying out the normal workings of a magazine: Reporting, writing, and editing took place; a photographer who didn't exactly know what the story was set up a cover shoot; our art director, pulled into the secret, designed pages and a cover.*

*In what amounted to a small miracle, we managed to keep this story absolutely secret from even the staff for more than a month. It was not until a few days before publication that some bright soul asked, in our morning meeting, "Is there maybe some story that we don't know about that's in this issue?" Eric Pooley said there was indeed, and that the absence of further questions would be appreciated. When Fortune's public relations crew put out a long press release on Sunday, June 25, that disclosed the news, it was a complete surprise to the world (and most of the magazine's staff).*

*Buffett made his first gifts to the five foundations in August 2006, and they have continued each summer. Counting all the donations made through 2013, he has given almost $16 billion to the five donees. Of that, about $13 billion went to*

*the Bill and Melinda Gates Foundation; $1.3 billion to the Susan Thompson Buf-*
*fett Foundation; and $1.6 billion—that is, more than $500 million apiece—to the*
*foundations run by his three children.*

*Because the contributions to all the foundations are a set, though annually*
*declining, number of Berkshire Hathaway shares, the value of what Buffett gives*
*swings yearly with the price of Berkshire stock. As one example, the gifts to the*
*Gates foundation have ranged from a high of $2 billion in the good stock-market*
*days of 2013 to a low of $1.25 billion in battered 2009.*

*One note: The data given for the Berkshire B shares in this article and the one*
*that follows are not adjusted for the 50-to-1 split of the shares that took place in*
*2010. —CL*

# Warren Buffett Gives It Away

July 10, 2006

## BY CAROL LOOMIS

We were sitting in a Manhattan living room on a spring afternoon, and Warren Buffett had a Cherry Coke in his hand as usual. But this unremarkable
scene was about to take a surprising turn. "Brace yourself," Buffett warned with
a grin. He then described a momentous change in his thinking. Within months,
he said, he would begin to give away his Berkshire Hathaway fortune, then and
now worth well over $40 billion. This news was indeed stunning. Buffett, 75,
has for decades said his wealth would go to philanthropy but has just as steadily
indicated the handoff would be made at his death. Now he was revising the
timetable. "I know what I want to do," he said, "and it makes sense to get going."
On that spring day his plan was uncertain in some of its details; today it is essentially complete. And it is typical Buffett: rational, original, breaking the
mold of how extremely rich people donate money.

Buffett has pledged to gradually give 85% of his Berkshire stock to five foundations. A dominant five-sixths of the shares will go to the world's largest philanthropic organization, the $30 billion Bill & Melinda Gates Foundation,
whose principals are close friends of Buffett's (a connection that began in 1991,
when a mutual friend introduced Buffett and Bill Gates). The Gateses credit
Buffett, says Bill, with having "inspired" their thinking about giving money
back to society. Their foundation's activities, internationally famous, are focused on world health—fighting such diseases as malaria, HIV/AIDS, and tu-
berculosis—and on improving U.S. libraries and high schools. Up to now, the
two Gateses have been the only trustees of their foundation. But as his plan gets
underway, Buffett will be joining them. Bill Gates says he and his wife are

"thrilled" by that and by knowing that Buffett's money will allow the foundation to "both deepen and accelerate" its work. "The generosity and trust Warren has shown," Gates adds, "is incredible."

Beginning in July and continuing every year, Buffett will give a set, annually declining number of Berkshire B shares—starting with 602,500 in 2006 and then decreasing by 5% per year—to the five foundations. The gifts to the Gates foundation will be made either by Buffett or through his estate as long as at least one of the pair—Bill, now 50, or Melinda, 41—is active in it. Berkshire's price on the date of each gift will determine its dollar value. Were B shares, for example, to be $3,071 in July—that was their close on June 23—Buffett's 2006 gift to the foundation, 500,000 shares, would be worth about $1.5 billion.

With so much new money to handle, the foundation will be given two years to resize its operations. But it will then be required by the terms of Buffett's gift to annually spend the dollar amount of his contributions as well as those it is already making from its existing assets. At the moment, $1.5 billion would roughly double the foundation's yearly benefactions.

But the $1.5 billion has little relevance to the value of Buffett's future gifts, since their amount will depend on the price of Berkshire's stock when they are made. If the stock rises yearly, on average, by even a modest amount—say, 6%— the gain will more than offset the annual 5% decline in the number of shares given. Under those circumstances, the value of Buffett's contributions will rise. Buffett himself thinks that will happen. Or to state that proposition more directly: He believes the price of Berkshire, and with it the dollar size of the contributions, will trend upward—perhaps over time increasing substantially.

The other foundation gifts that Buffett is making will also occur annually and start in July. At Berkshire's current price, the combined 2006 total of these gifts will be $315 million. The contributions will go to foundations headed by Buffett's three children, Susan, Howard, and Peter, and to the Susan Thompson Buffett Foundation. This last foundation was for 40 years known simply as the Buffett Foundation and was recently renamed in honor of Buffett's late wife, Susie, who died in 2004, at 72, after a stroke. Her will bestows about $2.5 billion on the foundation, to which her husband's gifts will be added. The foundation has mainly focused on reproductive health, family planning, and pro-choice causes, and on preventing the spread of nuclear weapons.

Counting the gifts to all five foundations, Buffett will gradually but sharply reduce his holdings of Berkshire stock. He now owns close to 31% of the company—worth nearly $44 billion in late June—and that proportion will ultimately be cut to around 5%. Sticking to his long-term intentions, Buffett says the residual 5%, worth about $6.8 billion today, will in time go for philanthropy also, perhaps in his lifetime and, if not, at his death.

Because the value of Buffett's gifts are tied to a future, unknowable price of Berkshire, there is no way to put a total dollar value on them. But the number of shares earmarked to be given have a huge value today: $37 billion. That alone would be the largest philanthropic gift in history. And if Buffett is right in thinking that Berkshire's price will trend upward, the eventual amount given could far exceed that figure.

So that's the plan. What follows is a conversation in which Buffett explains how he moved away from his original thinking and decided to begin giving now. The questioner is yours truly, *Fortune* editor-at-large Carol Loomis. I am a longtime friend of Buffett's, a Berkshire Hathaway shareholder, and a director of the Susan Thompson Buffett Foundation.

**Coming from you, this plan is pretty startling. Up to now you haven't been famous for giving away money. In fact, you've been roundly criticized now and then for not giving it away. So let's cut to the obvious question: Are you ill?**

No, absolutely not. I feel terrific, and when I had my last physical, in October, my doctor gave me a clean bill of health.

**Then what's going on here? Does your change in plans have something to do with Susie's death?**

Yes, it does. Susie was two years younger than I, and women usually live longer than men. She and I always assumed that she would inherit my Berkshire stock and be the one who oversaw the distribution of our wealth to society, where both of us had always said it would go. And Susie would have enjoyed overseeing the process. She was a little afraid of it, in terms of scaling up. But she would have liked doing it, and would have been very good at it. And she would really have stepped on the gas.

**By that you mean that she always wanted to give away more money, faster, than you did?**

Yes, she said that many times. As for me, I always had the idea that philanthropy was important today, but would be equally important in one year, ten years, 20 years, and the future generally. And someone who was compounding money at a high rate, I thought, was the better party to be taking care of the philanthropy that was to be done 20 years out, while the people compounding at a lower rate should logically take care of the current philanthropy.

**But that theory also happened to fit what you wanted to do, right?**

(*He laughs, hard.*) And how! No question about that. I was having fun— and still am having fun—doing what I do. And for a while I also thought in terms of control of Berkshire. I had bought effective control of Berkshire in the early 1970s, using $15 million I got when I disbanded Buffett Partnership. And I had very little money—considerably less than $1 million—outside of Berkshire. My salary was $50,000 a year. So if I had engaged in significant philanthropy back then, I would have had to give away shares of Berkshire. I hadn't bought those to immediately give them away.

**Even so, you and Susie set up the Buffett Foundation way back in the 1960s, which means you obviously expected to be giving away money sometime. What was your thinking back then?**

Well, when we got married in 1952, I told Susie I was going to be rich. That wasn't going to be because of any special virtues of mine or even because of hard work, but simply because I was born with the right skills in the right place at the right time. I was wired at birth to allocate capital and was lucky enough to have people around me early on—my parents and teachers and Susie—who helped me to make the most of that.

In any case, Susie didn't get very excited when I told her we were going to get rich. She either didn't care or didn't believe me—probably both, in fact. But to the extent we did amass wealth, we were totally in sync about what to do with it—and that was to give it back to society. In that, we agreed with Andrew Carnegie, who said that huge fortunes that flow in large part from society should in large part be returned to society. In my case, the ability to allocate capital would have had little utility unless I lived in a rich, populous country in which enormous quantities of marketable securities were traded and were sometimes ridiculously mispriced. And fortunately for me, that describes the U.S. in the second half of the last century.

Certainly neither Susie nor I ever thought we should pass huge amounts of money along to our children. Our kids are great. But I would argue that when your kids have all the advantages anyway, in terms of how they grow up and the opportunities they have for education, including what they learn at home—I would say it's neither right nor rational to be flooding them with money. In effect, they've had a gigantic headstart in a society that aspires to be a meritocracy. Dynastic mega-wealth would further tilt the playing field that we ought to be trying instead to level.

**From the fact that you've given your kids money before to set up foundations and are planning to give them more now, I gather you don't think that kind of flooding them with money is wrong.**

No, I don't. What they're doing with their foundations is giving money back to society—just where Susie and I thought it should go. And they aren't just writing checks: They've put enormous thought and effort into the process. I'm very proud of them for the way they've handled it all, and I have no doubt they're going to keep on the right track.

**So what about the Susan Thompson Buffett Foundation and what all this means for it?**

As you know, because as a director you've seen it close up, Allen Green-berg, the foundation's president, has done an excellent and thoughtful job of running it. His results-to-cost ratio is as good as I've ever seen. And he'll keep on that same path now, not just with Susie's money, but with mine too. Actually, if I had died before Susie and she had begun to dis-tribute our wealth, this is the foundation that would have scaled up to a much bigger size—right now it has only five employees—and become her main vehicle for giving. And the foundation anchored my plans too. Un-til I changed my thoughts about when to give, this was to be where my fortune would go also.

**And what changed your mind?**

The short answer is that I came to realize that there was a terrific founda-tion that was already scaled-up—that wouldn't have to go through the real grind of getting to a megasize like the Buffett Foundation would—and that could productively use my money now. The longer answer is that over the years I had gotten to know Bill and Melinda Gates well, spent a lot of time with them having fun and, way beyond that, had grown to admire what they were doing with their foundation. I've seen them give presenta-tions about its programs, and I'm always amazed at the enthusiasm and passion and energy they're pouring into their work. They've gone at it, you might say, with both head and heart. Bill reads many thousands of pages annually keeping up with medical advances and means of delivering help. Melinda, often with Bill along, travels the world looking at how well good intentions are being converted into good results. Life has dealt a terrible hand to literally billions of people around the world, and Bill and Melinda are bent on reducing that inequity to the extent they possibly can.

If you think about it—if your goal is to return the money to society by attacking truly major problems that don't have a commensurate funding base—what could you find that's better than turning to a couple of people who are young, who are ungodly bright, whose ideas have been proven, who already have shown an ability to scale it up and do it right? You don't get an opportunity like that ordinarily. I'm getting two people enor-mously successful at something, where I've had a chance to see what they've done, where I know they will keep doing it—where they've done it with their own money, so they're not living in some fantasy world—and where in general I agree with their reasoning. If I've found the right ve-hicle for my goal, there's no reason to wait.

Compare what I'm doing with them to my situation at Berkshire, where I have talented and proven people in charge of our businesses. They do a much better job than I could in running their operations. What can be more logical, in whatever you want done, than finding someone better equipped than you are to do it? Who wouldn't select Tiger Woods to take his place in a high-stakes golf game? That's how I feel about this decision about my money.

**People will be very curious, I think, as to how much your decision—and its announcement at this particular time—is connected to Bill Gates's announcement in mid-June that he would phase out of his operating responsibilities at Microsoft and begin to devote most of his time to the foundation. What's the story here?**

I realize that the close timing of the two announcements will suggest they're related. But they aren't in the least. The timing is just happenstance. I would be disclosing my plans right now whether or not he had announced his move—and even, in fact, if he were indefinitely keeping on with all of his work at Microsoft. On the other hand, I'm pleased that he's going to be devoting more time to the foundation. And I think he and Melinda are pleased to know they're going to be working with more resources.

**Does it occur to you that it's somewhat ironic for the second-richest man in the world to be giving untold billions to the first-richest man?**

When you put it that way, it sounds pretty funny. But in truth, I'm giving it *through* him—and, importantly, Melinda as well—not *to* him.

**Some people say the Gates foundation is bureaucratic, and bureaucracy is just about your No. 1 dislike. So how do you react to that charge?**

I would say that most large organizations—though Berkshire is a shining exception—are bureaucratic to some degree. Anyway, what some people really mean when they claim that the Gates foundation is bureaucratic is that big decisions don't get made by anybody except Bill and Melinda. That suits me fine. I want the two of them to make the big calls.

**What is the significance of your going on the board of the Gates foundation?**

Not much. The biggest reason for my doing that is if they were ever to go down on an airplane together. Beyond that, I hope to have a constructive thought now and then. But I don't think I'm as well cut out to be a philanthropist as Bill and Melinda are. The feedback on philanthropy is very slow, and that would bother me. I'd have to be too involved with a lot of people I wouldn't want to be involved with and have to listen to more opinions than I would enjoy. In philanthropy also, you have to make some big mistakes. I know that. But it would bother me more to make the mistakes myself, rather than having someone else make them whom I trust overall to do a good job. In general, Bill and Melinda will have a better batting average than I would.

**Did you talk this huge decision over with other people before deciding to go ahead with the plan?**

Yes, I talked to my children and Allen Greenberg, and to four Berkshire directors, including my son Howard and Charlie Munger. I got lots of questions, and some people had qualms about the plan initially because it was such an abrupt change from what they had been anticipating. But I'd say everybody, and that certainly includes Allen—who knows what a bear it would have been to scale up the Buffett Foundation—came around to seeing the logic of what I was proposing to do. Now all concerned can't wait to get started—particularly me.

And frankly, I have some small hopes that what I'm doing might encourage other very rich people thinking about philanthropy to decide they didn't necessarily have to set up their own foundations but could look around for the best of those that were up and running and available to handle their money. People do that all the time with their investments. They put their money with people they think are going to do a better job than they could. There's some real merit to extending that thought to your wealth, rather than setting up something to be run after your death by a bunch of old business cronies or a staff that eventually comes to dictate the agenda. Some version of this plan I've got is not a crazy thing for some of the next 20 people who are going to die with $1 billion or more to adopt themselves. One problem most rich people have is that they're old, with contemporaries who are not at their peak years and who don't have much time ahead of them. I'm lucky in that respect in that I can turn to younger people.

**Okay, now what does that mean for Berkshire?**

I'd say virtually nothing. Anybody who knows me also knows how I feel about making Berkshire as good as it can be, and that goal is still going to be there. I won't do anything differently, because I'm not capable of doing things differently. The name on the stock certificates will change, but nothing else will.

I've always made it clear to Berkshire's shareholders that my wealth from the company would go to philanthropy, so the fact that I'm starting the process is basically a nonevent for them. And, you know, though this may surprise some people, it's a nonevent for me too in some ways. Ted Turner, whose philanthropic activities I admire enormously, once told me that his hands shook when he signed a $1 billion pledge. Well, I have zero of that. To me, there's just no emotional downside to this at all.

**Won't the foundations that are getting your stock need to sell it?**

Yes, in some cases. The Buffett Foundation and the kids' foundations will have to sell their stock relatively soon after they get it, because it will be their only asset—and they'll need to raise cash to give away. The Gates foundation will have more options because it has lots of other assets, so it will have some flexibility to choose which it should turn into cash. Bill and Melinda will make the decisions about that. I'm going to totally insulate myself from any investment decisions their foundation makes, which leaves them free to do whatever they think makes sense. Perhaps they will decide to sell bigger portions of other assets and hang on to some Berkshire. It's a great mix of businesses and wouldn't be an inappropriate asset for a foundation to own. But I won't tie the foundation up in any shape or form.

**So it could be that all the shares you give annually will be sold in the market?**

Yes, that may well happen. And naturally people are going to be interested in whether that selling could weigh down Berkshire's price. I don't think so in the least—and that's true even though the annual turnover ratio for Berkshire has been running only about 15% a year, which is extremely low for large-cap stocks. Let's say the five foundations sell all the stock they get this year. If trading volume continues as it has, their selling will raise turnover to less than 17%. It would be ridiculous to think that much new selling could affect the price of the stock. In fact, the added supply could even be beneficial in increasing the stock's liquidity and should make it more likely that Berkshire would eventually be included in the S&P 500.

I'd say this: I would not be making the gifts if they would in any way harm Berkshire's shareholders. And they won't.

**This plan seems to settle the fate, over the long term, of all your Berkshire shares. Does that mean you're giving *nothing* to your family in straight-out gifts?**

No, what I've always said is that my family won't receive *huge* amounts of my net worth. That doesn't mean they'll get nothing. My children have already received some money from me and Susie and will receive more. I still believe in the philosophy—*Fortune* quoted me saying this 20 years ago—that a very rich person should leave his kids enough to do anything but not enough to do nothing. (The *Fortune* article was "Should You Leave It All to the Children?", page 54).

Remember I said that way back when I was buying Berkshire, I had less than $1 million in outside cash? Well, I've made a few decent investments with that money in the years since—taking positions that were too small for Berkshire, doing some fixed-income arbitrage, and selling my interest in a bank that was split off from Berkshire. So I'm glad to say I've got quite a bit of cash now. Overall I can—and will—use my Berkshire shares for philanthropic purposes and will have plenty left over to provide well for all those close to me.

## What the Legends Gave

Their philanthropies were immense, given the small economic worlds of their time. But Buffett's contribution is miles bigger.

| PHILANTHROPIST | SPAN OF GIVING | AMOUNT | IN CURRENT DOLLARS |
|---|---|---|---|
| ANDREW CARNEGIE | 1902-1919 | $350 million | $7.2 billion |
| JOHN D. ROCKEFELLER | 1889-1937 | $530 million | $7.1 billion |
| JOHN D. ROCKEFELLER JR. | 1927-1960 | $475 million | $5.5 billion |

*Fortune* table/Sources: American Philanthropy by Robert H. Bremner, *Fortune* research

# How Buffett's Giveaway Will Work

July 10, 2006

## BY CAROL LOOMIS

*The mind that built the fortune also came up with a complex plan to hand it off.*

**W**arren Buffett holds only Berkshire Hathaway A stock (474,998 shares), but his gifts are to be made in Berkshire B stock, into which each A share is convertible at a ratio of 30 to 1. He will convert A shares to obtain the B shares he needs for his gifts.

Buffett is earmarking a set number of B shares for each of the five foundations he has chosen to receive his gifts. In 2006 he will give 5% of the designated shares to each recipient. Next year the gifts will be 5% of the residual shares, and so on for every year until either Buffett's death or until certain conditions are no longer met at the foundations. At Buffett's death, his estate will distribute, in a way not yet definite, the remaining earmarked shares.

Here are the recipients and the number of B shares to be allocated to them.

## Bill and Melinda Gates Foundation

### 10 Million Shares

This foundation, the largest in the world, has around $30 billion of assets right now and has given away $8 billion in its 12 years of existence. Most of its money (typically funneled through partners) has gone to world health programs and to U.S. education. Buffett's gifts to this foundation will continue only as long as either Bill or Melinda Gates is alive and active in its work.

## Susan Thompson Buffett Foundation

### 1 Million Shares

Once called simply the Buffett Foundation and renamed in 2004 for Buffett's wife, who died that year, this foundation has $270 million in assets. Most of its funds came from the estate of Susan T. Buffett, and $2.1 billion more is expected from that source. This foundation has focused on reproductive health, family planning, and pro-choice causes, and on preventing the spread of nuclear weapons.

## Susan A. Buffett Foundation

### 350,000 Shares

This philanthropy is named for and chaired by Buffett's daughter, 52, who lives in Omaha (and who has also chaired the Susan Thompson Buffett Foundation since her mother's death). The daughter's foundation, which today has $118 million in assets, has funded early education for children of low-income families. With her father's new gifts, Susan Buffett expects to continue that work and expand into public-education and foster-care grants.

## Howard G. Buffett Foundation

### 350,000 Shares

Now holding $129 million in assets, this foundation was set up by Buffett's older son, 51, who farms 840 acres outside Decatur, Ill., and is on several corporate boards, including Berkshire's. (His middle name, by the way, is Graham—for famed investor Ben Graham.) This foundation's giving has been very international, taking in 42 countries and often aimed at conservation goals such as the protection of African wildlife habitats. But with its new money, the foundation plans to move much more heavily into clean-water projects, food relief, the plight of children entangled in illegal immigration, and other humanitarian areas.

## NoVo Foundation

### *350,000 Shares*

Named for the Latin word novo (meaning "I alter"), this foundation is run by Peter Buffett, 48, a musician and composer, and his wife, Jennifer, who live in New York City. Currently holding $120 million in assets, it has focused on funding individuals and organizations working to open up education opportunities, reverse environmental degradation, uphold human rights, and improve understanding and respect among various cultures and ethnicities.

# Would You Like That $11 Billion in Twenties?

July 24, 2006

## BY CAROL LOOMIS

On July 3, Warren Buffett drove himself downtown, walked into the cavernous and nearly deserted central branch of U.S. Bank in Omaha, descended a flight of steps, and opened his large safe-deposit box. He took out a 1979-dated certificate for 121,737 shares of Berkshire Hathaway A stock, on that day worth about $11 billion—roughly one-quarter of his Berkshire fortune. Driving back to his office, he pondered the next step: getting that certificate and a few others (worth only tens of millions) to Wells Fargo in Minneapolis for conversion at a 30-to-1 ratio into around 3.75 million shares of Berkshire B stock. He considered FedEx and elected instead to turn one of the 16 people working at Berkshire headquarters into a courier.

As *Fortune* first reported last month, Buffett has begun to give his money to charity. Converting the astoundingly valuable 1979 certificate is an initial step in that process. When it is switched over, Buffett will have the B stock he needs for handing out the 602,500 shares he has committed this year—the first of his huge philanthropic program—to the Bill & Melinda Gates Foundation and four smaller foundations. Because of the size of that one certificate, he will also be up to his eyeballs in B shares, having manufactured enough to fill his giving needs for most of the next decade. (He'll keep the excess shares in a brokerage account to be used as needed.)

Buffett says the whole exercise on July 3 made him think of the time almost 70 years ago, when he was 6 years old and his father, Howard Buffett, took him to the same bank to open a $20 savings account. The money was a gift, the bank was then called Omaha National, and the small passbook he got was maroon. After that, he says, it took him five years of gifts, chores, and money-earning schemes to build the account to $120. Having accrued this fortune, he bought, at age 11, his first stock: three shares of Cities Service preferred for $114.

Well, if you are going to amass $44 billion, you have to start someplace.

# Buffett to Gates: Spend It!

March 19, 2007

**BY JIA LYNN YANG**

Last summer Warren Buffett stunned the business world when he told *Fortune* that he would give away the bulk of his $44 billion Berkshire Hathaway fortune to charity.

Now comes the news . . . that in the latest Berkshire annual report Buffett states strict rules about what should happen to any Berkshire shares he retains when he dies—rules that challenge the way most charitable foundations are run. As he previously said, these shares will go to charity, but the new stipulations are all about speed. Once his estate is closed, which he estimates will take three years, every dollar of his gifts must be used within ten years.

By establishing this timetable, Buffett has thrust himself into a long-running debate: Should foundations focus on spending their resources or perpetuating them? And because of his reputation and the scale of his wealth, Buffett's endorsement of the latter is a landmark moment in philanthropy.

The vast majority of large foundations operate with the intent of lasting forever and therefore rarely exceed the minimum spending ratio of 5% (calculated on an organization's asset value of the previous year) which they need to retain tax-exempt status. According to data compiled by Buffett's staff, 28 of the 30 largest foundations paid out less than 5% of assets in grants in 2005. (They reached the 5% threshold by counting operating costs).

But a small number of foundations both past and current have decided to follow a spend-down model. Why? Many want greater control over how their money is used. As Buffett writes in the Berkshire annual report, "I've set this schedule because I want the money to be spent more promptly by people I know to be capable, vigorous, and motivated." Buffett's gifts are going to the Bill & Melinda Gates Foundation, three foundations run by his children, and the Susan Thompson Buffett Foundation, named after his late first wife. (The Gateses, too, have put a time limit on the spending of their donation, stipulating that their foundation must disburse all the money within 50 years of their death).

"As foundations grow over time the risk of bureaucracy and mission drift grows," says Harvey Dale, director of New York University's National Center on Philanthropy and the Law. Dale is also the former president, CEO, and now director of Atlantic Philanthropies, an oft-cited modern example of a spend-down foundation. Adds Dale: "[Spending down] focuses the mind."

But don't expect the Ford Foundation to go on a wild spending spree or to go out of business anytime soon. "Foundations set up in perpetuity aren't looking at this," says Gene Tempel, executive director of the Center on Philanthropy at

Indiana University. "It's a lot more common with younger donors who are setting up new foundations."

Or donors who are young at heart. Buffett is 76. And he's also overseeing a charitable obligation that's increasing in size. Last June, when Buffett unveiled his plan to give away 85% of his Berkshire shares, the gift was worth $37 billion. Since then the stock has risen about 15%.

# Marking to Myth

September 3, 2007

## BY WARREN BUFFETT

*Fortune asked a baker's dozen of financial thinkers to share both their reactions to the tightening credit crisis and their insights about the road ahead. Here are Buffett's comments:*

Many institutions that publicly report precise market values for their holdings of CDOs and CMOs are in truth reporting fiction. They are marking to model rather than marking to market. The recent meltdown in much of the debt market, moreover, has transformed this process into marking to myth.

Because many of these institutions are highly leveraged, the difference between "model" and "market" could deliver a huge whack to shareholders' equity. Indeed, for a few institutions, the difference in valuations is the difference between what purports to be robust health and insolvency. For these institutions, pinning down market values would not be difficult: They should simply sell 5% of all the large positions they hold. That kind of sale would establish a true value, though one still higher, no doubt, than would be realized for 100% of an oversized and illiquid holding.

In one way, I'm sympathetic to the institutional reluctance to face the music. I'd give a lot to mark my weight to "model" rather than "market."

# The Oracle's Credit Crisis

March 31, 2008

## BY TELIS DEMOS

**W**arren Buffett may be the world's richest man, but you might have a better credit score. When the Berkshire Hathaway CEO recently checked his credit history, his FICO score in one report was 718, slightly below the U.S. median. "I've been telling my family for years that my credit was sort of shaky," Buffett insists. He's kidding, of course, referring to his self-proclaimed stinginess with his kids. In truth, the score may have been due to an imposter; the report cites 23 missed payments on a $294 loan at an HSBC branch in Nevada, where Buffett says he has never had an account. A 2004 study found that 25% of reports contain serious errors, which is why watchdogs say low scores shouldn't be cause to deny a loan. Fortunately for Buffett, he was able to pay for his last car, a Cadillac DTS, in cash.

# What Warren Thinks . . .

April 28, 2008

## BY NICHOLAS VARCHAVER

*The tagline on this story read, "With Wall Street in chaos, Fortune naturally went to Omaha looking for wisdom," and, with some twists, that describes the article's origins. Bear Stearns had just collapsed into the arms of JPMorgan Chase and the U.S. government, and the economy was shuddering. Fortune's managing editor, Andy Serwer, proposed to me that we seek out Buffett's views about the markets and the economic outlook. Knowing, as Andy himself did, that Buffett resists predicting the direction of stock prices and normally ducks macro questions about the economy, I was dubious about our ability to land that article.*

*I instead suggested a different angle: Buffett's practice of holding Q&A sessions and then lunching with business school students who had trekked to Omaha for the occasion. One of those events was coming up. Why not, I said, have a Fortune writer observe, and then write about, what Buffett told the students? We would be getting, I also argued, a picture of Buffett the teacher—the role for which he has said he would most like to be remembered.*

*The resulting piece turned out to be a mix of Andy's idea and mine. Assigned at the eleventh hour to the story, Fortune writer Nick Varchaver raced to Omaha and listened in as Buffett spent four hours with 150 Wharton School students. Then Buffett—never quite totally keeping his eyes on the road—drove Nick and a Fortune photographer back to Berkshire's headquarters for a straight-on interview. Recalling his impressions that day, Nick says he was struck by how freely and informatively Buffett talked to the students and was amazed by his ability to crystallize issues.*

*Nick also added a reporter's insight: "I once spent days interviewing a businessman almost as smart as Buffett, and this guy never exhibited the slightest curiosity about my background or how I got to Fortune. But before that car ride with Buffett was over, he had asked me one question after another about myself. You don't see that often among the people we interview."*

*The 150 students that Buffett talked to on that April day were among 2,400, from 31 different schools, who visited Berkshire in the 2007–2008 school year. By the 2011–2012 school year Buffett had faced up to the demands on his time and begun to reduce the number of these student events. In the 2013–2014 year he will probably hold only five, with each including 160 students from eight different schools given twenty slots apiece. Having noted a few years ago that his guests were overwhelmingly male and having suspected some gender bias, Buffett has since required that each contingent be at least one-third female.*

*One of his assistants meanwhile keeps track of a wait list of more than 200 schools hoping to be chosen for the visits. —CL*

**W**ith Wall Street in chaos, *Fortune* naturally went to Omaha looking for wisdom.

If Berkshire Hathaway's annual meeting, scheduled for May 3 this year, is known as the Woodstock of Capitalism, then perhaps this is the equivalent of Bob Dylan playing a private show in his own house: Some 15 times a year Berkshire CEO Warren Buffett invites a group of business students for an intensive day of learning. The students tour one or two of the company's businesses and then proceed to Berkshire headquarters in downtown Omaha, where Buffett opens the floor to two hours of questions and answers. Later everyone repairs to one of his favorite restaurants, where he treats them to lunch and root beer floats. Finally, each student gets the chance to pose for a photo with Buffett.

In early April the megabillionaire hosted 150 students from the University of Pennsylvania's Wharton School (which Buffett attended) and offered *Fortune* the rare opportunity to sit in as he expounded on everything from the Bear Stearns bailout to the prognosis for the economy to whether he'd rather be CEO of GE—or a paperboy. What follows are edited excerpts from his question-and-answer session with the students, his lunchtime chat with the Whartonites over chicken parmigiana at Piccolo Pete's, and an interview with *Fortune* in his office.

Buffett began by welcoming the students with an array of Coca-Cola products. ("Berkshire owns a little over 8% of Coke, so we get the profit on one out of 12 cans. I don't care whether you drink it, but just open the cans, if you will.") He then plunged into weightier matters:

> Before we start in on questions, I would like to tell you about one thing going on recently. It may have some meaning to you if you're still being taught efficient-market theory, which was standard procedure 25 years ago. But we've had a recent illustration of why the theory is misguided. In the past seven or eight or nine weeks, Berkshire has built up a position in auction-rate securities [bonds whose interest rates are periodically reset at auction] of about $4 billion. And what we have seen there is really quite phenomenal. Every day we get bid lists. The fascinating thing is that on these bid lists, frequently the same credit will appear more than once.
>
> Here's one from yesterday. We bid on this particular issue—this happens to be Citizens Insurance, which is a creature of the state of Florida. It was set up to take care of hurricane insurance, and it's backed by premium taxes, and if they have a big hurricane and the fund becomes inadequate, they raise the premium taxes. There's nothing wrong with the credit. So we bid on three different Citizens securities that day. We got one bid at an 11.33% interest rate. One that we didn't buy went for 9.87%, and one went for 6.0%. It's the same bond, the same time, the same dealer. And a big issue. This is not some little anomaly, as they like to say in academic circles every time they find something that disagrees with their theory.

So wild things happen in the markets. And the markets have not gotten more rational over the years. They've become more *followed*. But when people panic, when fear takes over, or when greed takes over, people react just as irrationally as they have in the past.

**Do you think the U.S. financial markets are losing their competitive edge? And what's the right balance between confidence-inspiring standards and . . .**

Between regulations and the Wild West? Well, I don't think we're losing our edge. I mean, there are costs to Sarbanes-Oxley, some of which are wasted. But they're not huge relative to the $20 trillion in total market value. I think we've got fabulous capital markets in this country, and they get screwed up often enough to make them even more fabulous. I mean, you don't want a capital market that functions perfectly if you're in my business. People continue to do foolish things no matter what the regulation is, and they always will. There are significant limits to what regulation can accomplish. As a dramatic illustration, take two of the biggest accounting disasters in the past ten years: Freddie Mac and Fannie Mae. We're talking billions and billions of dollars of misstatements at both places.

Now, these are two incredibly important institutions. I mean, they accounted for over 40% of the mortgage flow a few years back. Right now I think they're up to 70%. They're quasi-governmental in nature. So the government set up an organization called OFHEO. I'm not sure what all the letters stand for. [Note to Warren: They stand for Office of Federal Housing Enterprise Oversight.] But if you go to OFHEO's website, you'll find that its purpose was to just watch over these two companies. OF-HEO had 200 employees. Their job was simply to look at two companies and say, "Are these guys behaving like they're supposed to?" And of course what happened were two of the greatest accounting misstatements in history while these 200 people had their jobs. It's incredible. I mean, two for two!

It's very, very, very hard to regulate people. If I were appointed a new regulator—if you gave me 100 of the smartest people you can imagine to work for me, and every day I got the positions from the biggest institutions, all their derivative positions, all their stock positions and currency positions, I wouldn't be able to tell you how they were doing. It's very, very hard to regulate when you get into very complex instruments where you've got hundreds of counterparties. The counterparty behavior and risk was a big part of why the Treasury and the Fed felt that they had to move in over a weekend at Bear Stearns. And I think they were right to do it, incidentally. Nobody knew what would be unleashed when you had thousands of counterparties with, I read someplace, contracts with a $14 trillion notional value. Those people would have tried to unwind all those contracts if there had been a bankruptcy. What that would have done to the markets, what that would have done to other counterparties in turn—it gets very, very complicated. So regulating is an important part of the system. The efficacy of it is really tough.

*At Piccolo Pete's, where he has dined with everyone from Microsoft's Bill Gates to the New York Yankees' Alex Rodriguez, Buffett sat at a table with 12 Whartonites and bantered over many topics.*

**How do you feel about the election?**

Way before they both filed, I told Hillary that I would support her if she ran, and I told Barack I would support him if he ran. So I am now a political bigamist. But I feel either would be great. And actually, I feel that if a Republican wins, John McCain would be the one I would prefer. I think we've got three unusually good candidates this time.

**They're all moderate in their approach.**

Well, the one we don't know for sure about is Barack. On the other hand, he has the chance to be the most transformational too.

**I know you had a paper route. Was that your first job?**

Well, I worked for my grandfather, which was really tough, in the [family] grocery store. But if you gave me the choice of being CEO of General Electric or IBM or General Motors, you name it, or delivering papers, I would deliver papers. I would. I enjoyed doing that. I can think about what I want to think. I don't have to do anything I don't want to do. It might be wonderful to be head of GE, and Jeff Immelt is a friend of mine. And he's a great guy. But think of all the things he has to do whether he wants to do them or not.

**How do you get your ideas?**

I just read. I read all day. I mean, we put $500 million in PetroChina. All I did was read the annual report. [Editor's note: Berkshire purchased the shares five years ago and sold them in 2007 for $4 billion.]

**What advice would you give to someone who is not a professional investor? Where should they put their money?**

Well, if they're not going to be an active investor—and very few should try to do that—then they should just stay with index funds. Any low-cost index fund. And they should buy it over time. They're not going to be able to pick the right price and the right time. What they want to do is avoid the wrong price and wrong stock. You just make sure you own a piece of American business, and you don't buy all at one time.

*When Buffett said he was ready to pose for photographs, all 150 students stampeded out of the room within seconds and formed a massive line. For the next half hour, each one took his or her turn with Buffett, often in hammy poses (wrestling for his wallet was a favorite). Then, as he started to leave, a 77-year-old's version of* A Hard Day's Night *ensued, with a pack of 30 students trailing him to his gold Cadillac. Once free, he drove this* Fortune *writer back to his office and continued fielding questions.*

### How does the current turmoil stack up against past crises?

Well, that's hard to say. Every one has so many variables in it. But there's no question that this time there's extreme leveraging and in some cases the extreme prices of residential housing or buyouts. You've got $20 trillion of residential real estate and you've got $11 trillion of mortgages, and a lot of that does not have a problem, but a lot of it does. In 2006 you had $330 billion of cash taken out in mortgage refinancings in the United States. That's a hell of a lot—I mean, we talk about having $150 billion of stimulus now, but that was $330 billion of stimulus. And that's just from prime mortgages. That's not from subprime mortgages. So leveraging up was one hell of a stimulus for the economy.

### If that was one hell of a stimulus, do you think the $150 billion government stimulus plan will make an impact?

Well, it's $150 billion more than we'd have otherwise. But it's not like we haven't had stimulus. And then the simultaneous, more or less, LBO boom, which was called private equity this time. The abuses keep coming back—and the terms got terrible and all that. You've got a banking system that's hung up with lots of that. You've got a mortgage industry that's deleveraging, and it's going to be painful.

### The scenario you're describing suggests we're a long way from turning a corner.

I think so. I mean, it seems everybody says it'll be short and shallow, but it looks like it's just the opposite. You know, deleveraging by its nature takes a lot of time, a lot of pain. And the consequences kind of roll through in different ways. Now, I don't invest a dime based on macro forecasts, so I don't think people should sell stocks because of that. I also don't think they should *buy* stocks because of that.

**Your OFHEO example implies you're not too optimistic about regulation.**

Finance has gotten so complex, with so much interdependency. I argued with Alan Greenspan some about this at [*Washington Post* chairman] Don Graham's dinner. He would say that you've spread risk throughout the world by all these instruments, and now you didn't have it all concentrated in your banks. But what you've done is you've interconnected the solvency of institutions to a degree that probably nobody anticipated. And it's very hard to evaluate. If Bear Stearns had not had a derivatives book, my guess is the Fed wouldn't have had to do what it did.

**Do you find it striking that banks keep looking into their investments and not knowing what they have?**

I read a few prospectuses for residential-mortgage-backed securities— mortgages, thousands of mortgages backing them, and then those all tranched into maybe 30 slices. You create a CDO by taking one of the lower tranches of that one and 50 others like it. Now if you're going to understand that CDO, you've got 50-times-300 pages to read, it's 15,000. If you take one of the lower tranches of the CDO and take 50 of those and create a CDO squared, you're now up to 750,000 pages to read to understand one security. I mean, it can't be done. When you start buying tranches of other instruments, nobody knows what the hell they're doing. It's ridiculous. And of course, you took a lower tranche of a mortgage-backed security and did 100 of those and thought you were diversifying risk. Hell, they're all subject to the same thing. I mean, it may be a little different whether they're in California or Nebraska, but the idea that this is uncorrelated risk and therefore you can take the CDO and call the top 50% of it super-senior—it isn't super-senior or anything. It's a bunch of juniors all put together. And the juniors all correlate.

**If big financial institutions don't seem to know what's in their portfolios, how will investors ever know when it's safe?**

They can't, they can't. They've got to, in effect, try to read the DNA of the people running the companies. But I say that in any large financial organization, the CEO has to be the chief risk officer. I'm the chief risk officer at Berkshire. I think I know my limits in terms of how much I can sort of process. And the worst thing you can have is models and spreadsheets. I mean, at Salomon, they had all these models, and you know, they fell apart.

**What should we say to investors now?**

The answer is you don't want investors to think that what they read today is important in terms of their investment strategy. Their investment strategy should factor in that (a) if you knew what was going to happen in the economy, you still wouldn't necessarily know what was going to happen in the stock market. And (b) they can't pick stocks that are better than average. Stocks are a good thing to own over time. There's only two things you can do wrong: You can buy the wrong ones, and you can buy or sell them at the wrong time. And the truth is you never need to sell them, basically. But they could buy a cross section of American industry, and if a cross section of American industry doesn't work, certainly trying to pick the little beauties here and there isn't going to work either. Then they just have to worry about getting greedy. You know, I always say you should get greedy when others are fearful and fearful when others are greedy. But that's too much to expect. Of course, you shouldn't get greedy when others get greedy and fearful when others get fearful. At a minimum, try to stay away from that.

**By your rule, now seems like a good time to be greedy. People are pretty fearful.**

You're right. They are going in that direction. That's why stocks are cheaper. Stocks are a better buy today than they were a year ago. Or three years ago.

**But you're still bullish about the U.S. for the long term?**

The American economy is going to do fine. But it won't do fine every year and every week and every month. I mean, if you don't believe that, forget about buying stocks anyway. But it stands to reason. I mean, we get more productive every year, you know. It's a positive-sum game, long term. And the only way an investor can get killed is by high fees or by trying to outsmart the market.

# Buffett's Big Bet

June 23, 2008

### BY CAROL LOOMIS

*This ten-year investment-performance wager runs through 2017, and at yearend 2012—the halfway point and the last marker before this book went to press— there was double-barreled news.*

Item one: For the first time since the bet started five years earlier, Buffett had moved ahead. That meant his horse—a low-cost Vanguard S&P 500 index fund—was besting five funds of hedge funds carefully picked by Buffett's opponent, Protégé Partners, a New York asset management firm. (By the terms of the bet, the names of those funds have never been disclosed.) The averaged return to investors in those five funds of funds, after all costs, fees, and expenses, is what counts in the bet.

Item two: For the first time ever as well, both sides had crawled out of the ditch (though the hedge funds barely made it) into slightly positive territory.

So, yes, there's been a history of terrible results, created most of all by the bet having started in the gut-wrenching year of 2008. Both contestants fell deep into the red then—with Buffett slammed the hardest. His index fund contender, Vanguard's Admiral shares, lost 37 percent in 2008 versus a 24 percent drop, on the average, for investors in Protégé's five funds of funds.

Reporting then on the bet, Fortune quoted Buffett as just hoping he could be like the fabled tortoise that ultimately passes the hare. And that's how it has gradually played out: The tortoise—aka the Admiral shares—got to the halfway point up 8.69 percent. Protégé's funds of funds were up, on the average, only— "gulp," said Protégé partner Ted Seides—0.13 percent.

Seides nonetheless is talking a turnaround: "Day ain't over yet," he says, quoting a famous line from the movie City Slickers.

As the contest entered its second half, the stakes were changed by mutual agreement of the participants. In this bet, there has always been $1 million at stake. That is, each side put up enough to buy a ten-year zero-coupon bond that at its maturity would be worth $500,000, with the total of $1 million to go to the charity chosen by the winner. But, as interest rates dove, the bonds performed so well, so fast, that they neared their ultimate value in late 2012.

With so little upside left in the bonds, Seides and Buffett agreed they should be sold and the proceeds put into Berkshire Hathaway stock. That gives the winning charity a prospect of getting far more than $1 million. At mid-2013, indeed, the value of the Berkshire stock bought when the bonds were sold was $1,255,000.

Covering the risk that Berkshire might fall by the bet's end—which its chairman naturally believes will not happen—Buffett has personally guaranteed that at least $1 million will be paid to the winner's charity.

There is still another relevant point about Buffett's role in this bet, tied to his argument that the high costs imposed by hedge funds and funds of funds on their *investors will cause them, on the average, to lose out to an index fund holder. The paradox there, of course, is that in his early days, Buffett was himself part of the hedge fund world, as managing partner of Omaha's Buffett Partnership.*

*But he did not adopt that world's typical "2-and-20" compensation arrangement, meaning an annual 2 percent-of-assets management fee and a 20 percent share of profits. Instead, Buffett charged no management fee at all and stipulated that the first 6 percent earned on capital each year would go entirely to his limited partners. After that, he received 25 percent of profits.*

*And, as noted earlier, his hedge fund put together thirteen straight years of profits before he decided to shut it down. The average annual return he delivered his limited partners—after they paid Buffett his 25 percent take—was 23.8 percent. —CL*

**W**ill a collection of hedge funds, carefully selected by experts, return more to investors over the next ten years than the S&P 500? That question is now the subject of a bet between Warren Buffett, the CEO of Berkshire Hathaway, and Protégé Partners LLC, a New York City money-management firm that runs funds of hedge funds—in other words, a firm whose existence rests on its ability to put its clients' money into the best hedge funds and keep it out of the underperformers. You can guess which party is taking which side. Protégé has placed its bet on five funds of hedge funds—specifically, the averaged returns that those vehicles deliver net of all fees, costs, and expenses. On the other side, Buffett, who has long argued that the fees that such "helpers" as hedge funds and funds of funds command are onerous and to be avoided, has bet that the returns from a low-cost S&P 500 index fund sold by Vanguard will beat the results delivered by the five funds that Protégé has selected.

We're way past theory here. This bet, being reported for the first time in this article (whose author is both a longtime friend of Buffett's and editor of his chairman's letter in the Berkshire annual report), has been in existence since Jan. 1 of this year. It's between Buffett (not Berkshire) and Protégé (the firm, not its funds). And there's serious money at stake. Each side put up roughly $320,000. The total funds of about $640,000 were used to buy a zero-coupon Treasury bond that will be worth $1 million at the bet's conclusion. That $1 million will then go to charity. If Protégé wins, it has asked that the money be given to Absolute Return for Kids (ARK), an international philanthropy based in London. If Buffett wins, the intended recipient is Girls Inc. of Omaha, whose board includes his daughter, Susan Buffett.

And who's holding the money, by way of owning the zero-coupon bond? That's an esoteric institution most readers of this article will never have heard of, the Long Now Foundation, of San Francisco, which exists to encourage long-term thinking and combat what one of its founders, Stewart Brand (of the *Whole Earth Catalog*) calls the "pathologically short attention span" that seems to afflict the world. Six years ago the foundation set up a mechanism for—what else?—Long Bets. The foundation receives wagers as donations, oversees the bets until they are decided, and then pays off the winner's designated charity. For this work, the foundation normally gets a $50 fee from each side and then shares fifty-fifty with the charitable winner-to-be in the returns earned on the funds being held. In the Buffett-Protégé bet, however, there will be no such sharing; each side simply made a $20,000 charitable gift to the Long Now Foundation.

To see today's Long Bets listings (to which, following publication of this article, the Buffett-Protégé bet will be added), go to www.longbets.org. Some bets catalogued there sound as though they were made in sports bars: Actor Ted Danson garnered $2,000 for a charity when the Red Sox won the World Series before a U.S. men's soccer team won the World Cup. On a more cosmic front, Lotus founder Mitchell Kapor and inventor and futurist Ray Kurzweil have a $20,000 bet on the proposition that "by 2029 no computer—or 'machine intelligence'—will have passed the Turing Test," meaning that a computer won't have successfully impersonated a human. Kapor made that prediction; Kurzweil disagrees with it. Each man, following the rules of Long Bets, has supported his point of view with a brief statement that is posted on the website. Buffett's and Protégé's arguments will appear there as well (and follow in the sidebars below).

Through 2007 the Kapor-Kurzweil bet of $20,000 was the largest on Long Bets. The Buffett-Protégé bet obviously vaults the stakes to the stratosphere. And to that there is a certain history, which began at Berkshire's May 2006 annual meeting. Expounding that weekend on the transaction and management costs borne by investors, Buffett offered to bet any taker $1 million that over ten years and after fees, the performance of an S&P index fund would beat ten hedge funds that any opponent might choose. Some time later he repeated the offer, adding that since he hadn't been taken up on the bet, he must be right in his thinking.

But in July 2007, Ted Seides, a principal of Protégé but speaking for himself at that point, wrote Buffett to say he'd like to make the bet—or at least some version of it. Months of sporadic negotiation ensued. The two sides eventually agreed that Seides would bet on five funds of funds rather than ten hedge funds. Seides, stepping way beyond his usual stakes—say, the cost of a meal—suggested that he and Buffett make the bet for $100,000 (which, he noted, was Buffett's annual salary). Buffett, not knowing then that Long Bets even existed, said that considering his age—he's now 77—and the complications that a ten-year bet might add to his estate's being settled, he'd only be interested in wagering at least $500,000. Even then, he wrote Seides, "my estate attorney is going to think I'm out of my mind for complicating things."

If $500,000 seemed too steep to Seides, Buffett (for whom it's obviously more of a trifle) had no problem with Seides recruiting partners to help out. And that's what in effect happened, by way of Protégé Partners LLC making the bet rather than Seides. Protégé, which manages around $3.5 billion, is principally owned by Seides, 37, and two other men, CEO Jeffrey Tarrant, 52, and Scott Bessent, 45. Each has a strong investment background, and two of the three have worked with well-known market practitioners: Seides learned the world of alternative investments under Yale's David Swensen; Bessent worked with both George Soros and short-seller Jim Chanos.

Upon its founding in 2002 by Tarrant and Seides, Protégé set up a fund of funds and began recruiting the kind of sophisticated investors—both institutions and wealthy individuals—who put their money in such funds. Very aware that the Securities and Exchange Commission prohibits broad-scale marketing by hedge funds and funds of funds, neither Seides nor Tarrant will disclose the precise names of the funds they now run, much less their performance records. But a London publication, *InvestHedge*, whose parent runs a hedge fund database, provided *Fortune* with several years of returns for the firm's flagship U.S. fund, Protégé Partners LP. From its inception in July 2002 through the end of 2007, the Protégé fund gained 95% (after all fees), soundly beating the Vanguard S&P 500 index fund's 64%. Protégé's performance was hugely helped by the fact that by mid-2006 the firm was extremely bearish on subprime mortgage securities, including CDOs, and had dispersed its investments in hedge funds to capitalize on that opinion. Most significant, it made an investment in Paulson & Co.'s hedge funds, which under John Paulson made a highly publicized killing in 2007 by short-selling securities linked to subprimes.

All that's history, of course, so let's get back to the bet: Buffett and Seides agreed that they'd periodically disclose where the wager stood. Seides wanted this disclosure to take place whenever the market fell by 10%, because he believes that one of the virtues of hedge funds is their ability to weather tough times. Indeed, in the first quarter of this year, during a down market, Protégé Partners LP fell by only 1.9%, while the Vanguard fund dropped 9.5%. Buffett insisted, though, that the logical time for disclosure was at Berkshire's annual meeting every spring—and that was the final agreement.

Just how much Buffett will have to say about the bet every year may be limited by one fact: The names of the five funds of funds that Protégé has selected are to be kept confidential. Of course, Buffett knows what the names are, because Protégé must supply him with the audited results of these funds every year. But other than that, the designated funds of funds saw no advantage (at least for now) to declaring their participation in the bet and agreed to go along only if confidentiality was promised. The first fund that Protégé tried to recruit, in fact, wouldn't sign up even then.

Seides and Tarrant do have a few general things to say about the five funds picked. They are equity-oriented (favoring stocks over bonds), tend to invest in hedge funds that avoid in-and-out trading, and are run mostly run by seasoned investment folk rather than tenderfoots. And we can probably assume that Protégé Partners LP is one of the five, if only because its exclusion would leave the firm with the difficult job of explaining to its investors why the firm didn't care to bet on the success of its own hedge fund choices.

As for the fees that investors pay in the hedge fund world—and that, of course, is the crux of Buffett's argument—they are both complicated and costly.

A fund of funds normally charges a 1% annual management fee. The hedge funds it puts that money into charge an annual management fee of their own, which for funds of funds is typically 1.5%. (The fees are paid quarterly by an investor and are figured on the value of his account at the time.) So that's 2.5% of an investor's capital that continually goes for these fees, regardless of the returns earned during a year. In contrast, Vanguard's S&P 500 index fund had an expense ratio last year of 15 basis points (0.15%) for ordinary shares and only seven basis points for Admiral shares, which are available to large investors. Admiral shares are the ones "bought" by Buffett in the bet.

On top of the management fee, the hedge funds typically collect 20% of any gains they make. That leaves 80% for the investors. The fund of funds takes 5% (or more) of that 80% as its share of the gains. The upshot is that only 76% (at most) of the annual return made on an investor's money accrues to him, with the rest going to the "helpers" that Buffett has written about. Meanwhile, the investor is paying his inexorable management fee of 2.5% on capital. The summation is pretty obvious. For Protégé to win this bet, the five funds of funds it has picked must do much, much better than the S&P.

And maybe they will. Buffett himself assesses his chances of winning at only 60%, which he grants is less of an edge than he usually likes to have. Protégé figures its own probabilities of winning at a heady 85%. Some people will say, of course, that just by making this bet, Protégé has acquired some priceless publicity. But then, Protégé clearly wants to win, and it's up against a man who hasn't made a lot of losing bets in his life. Seides himself sees one strong ray of light: "Fortunately for us, we're betting against the S&P's performance, not Buffett's."

## The Prediction and the Arguments

Prediction: Over a ten-year period commencing Jan. 1, 2008, and ending Dec. 31, 2017, the S&P 500 will outperform a portfolio of funds of hedge funds, when performance is measured on a basis net of fees, costs, and expenses.

### Warren Buffett: Agree

A lot of very smart people set out to do better than average in securities markets. Call them active investors.

Their opposites, passive investors, will by definition do about average. In aggregate their positions will more or less approximate those of an index fund. Therefore the balance of the universe—the active investors—must do about average as well. However, these investors will incur far greater costs. So, on balance, their aggregate results after these costs will be worse than those of the passive investors.

Costs skyrocket when large annual fees, large performance fees, and active trading costs are all added to the active investor's equation. Funds of hedge funds accentuate this cost problem because their fees are superimposed on the large fees charged by the hedge funds in which the funds of funds are invested.

A number of smart people are involved in running hedge funds. But to a great extent their efforts are self-neutralizing, and their IQ will not overcome the costs they impose on investors. Investors, on average and over time, will do better with a low-cost index fund than with a group of funds of funds.

### Protégé Partners LLC: Disagree

Mr. Buffett is correct in his assertion that, on average, active management in a narrowly defined universe like the S&P 500 is destined to underperform market indexes. But applying that argument to hedge funds is a bit of an apples-to-oranges comparison.

Having the flexibility to invest both long and short, hedge funds do not set out to beat the market. Rather, they seek to generate positive returns over time regardless of the market environment. For hedge funds, success can mean outperforming the market in lean times, while underperforming in the best of times. Through a cycle, nevertheless, top hedge fund managers have surpassed market returns net of all fees, while assuming less risk as well. We believe such results will continue.

There is a wide gap between the returns of the best hedge funds and the average ones. This differential affords sophisticated institutional investors, among them funds of funds, an opportunity to pick strategies and managers that these investors think will outperform the averages. Funds of funds with the ability to sort the wheat from the chaff will earn returns that amply compensate for the extra layer of fees their clients pay.

# From "What Obama Means for Business"

July 2, 2008

*An excerpt from an article by Nina Easton*

Already [Obama's] circle of advisors has expanded beyond a small core of academics to include veteran capitalists inside the Democratic Party. . . . He is frequently on the phone with billionaire CEO Warren Buffett ("one of my favorite people," says Obama, "he's just completely down-to-earth and as smart as they come"), a critic of the financial industry and of tax breaks for the rich who also happens to understand capital markets better than just about anyone.

# Buffett's Market Metric Says Buy

### February 16, 2009

## BY CAROL LOOMIS AND DORIS BURKE

*The stock market kept going down and down in the first days of 2009, and we decided at Fortune that it just might be time to update Buffett's market metric— the relationship of the total value of U.S. stocks to GNP. We had run a chart of that metric in late 2001, in "Warren Buffett on the Stock Market" (see page 191). The message then was a clarion "Don't buy!"*

*But, this time, when my coauthor on this piece, Doris Burke, ran the numbers, they showed that the market was definitely in Buffett's buying range. So we published this article and chart in an issue that reached subscribers around February 1.*

*Okay, this buy signal wasn't perfect: From February 1, the S&P 500 viciously went down another 18 percent before bottoming on March 9. Even so, if you'd bought an S&P 500 total return ETF on that February 1 and held until midyear 2012, you would have earned a 78 percent total return—and been very happy that Buffett shared this metric. —CL*

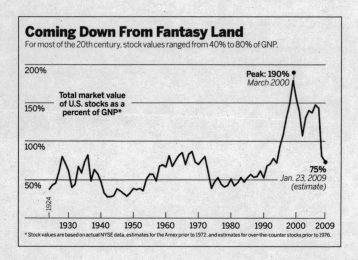

**Coming Down From Fantasy Land**

For most of the 20th century, stock values ranged from 40% to 80% of GNP.

Total market value of U.S. stocks as a percent of GNP*

Peak: 190%
March 2000

75%
Jan. 23, 2009
(estimate)

\* Stock values are based on actual NYSE data, estimates for the Amex prior to 1972, and estimates for over-the-counter stocks prior to 1976.

I s it time to buy stocks? According to both this 85-year chart and famed investor Warren Buffett, it just might be. The point of the chart is that there should be a rational relationship between the total market value of U.S. stocks and the output of the U.S. economy—its GNP.

*Fortune* first ran a version of this chart in late 2001. Stocks had by that time retreated sharply from the manic levels of the Internet bubble. But they were still very high, with stock values at 133% of GNP. That level certainly did not suggest to Buffett that it was time to buy stocks.

But he visualized a moment when purchases might make sense, saying, "If the percentage relationship falls to the 70% to 80% area, buying stocks is likely to work very well for you."

Well, that's where stocks were in late January, when the ratio was 75%. Nothing about that reversion to sanity surprises Buffett, who told *Fortune* that the shift in the ratio reminds him of investor Ben Graham's statement about the stock market: "In the short run it's a voting machine, but in the long run it's a weighing machine."

Not just liking the chart's message in theory, Buffett also put himself on record in an Oct. 17 *New York Times* op-ed piece, saying that he was personally buying U.S. stocks after a long period of owning nothing (outside of Berkshire Hathaway stock) but U.S. government bonds. He said that if prices kept falling, he expected to soon have 100% of his net worth in U.S. equities. Prices did keep falling—the Dow Jones industrials have dropped by about 10% since Oct. 17— so presumably Buffett kept buying. Alas for all curious investors, he isn't saying what he bought.

# Buffett Takes Charge

April 27, 2009

## BY MARC GUNTHER

*The headline on this story works as a pun, but does not exactly portray Buffett's behavior when a shareholder at the Berkshire annual meeting asks about the company's 10% ownership of the Chinese car and battery company, BYD. At such moments, Buffett invariably hands off the question to Charles Munger, Berkshire's vice-chairman. "Charlie is our expert on BYD," Buffett will say. In turn, Munger owes much of his expertise to Pasadena investment manager Li Lu, who was born in China and was a pro-democracy protester at Tiananmen Square in 1989.*

*Berkshire made its investment of $230 million in BYD in late 2008, amid the financial crisis, at a price of about $1 per share—which is, to use the Hong Kong currency in which BYD share prices are commonly quoted, HK$8. After Berkshire's entry into the picture, BYD's stock went into roller-coaster mode, rising to HK$77 by March 2010 and then falling to HK$11 in May 2012, as prospects for electric cars worsened and BYD's profits fell. By mid-2013 the stock had climbed to HK$29. That price leaves Berkshire having more than tripled its money. Still, BYD has not so far prospered as Munger thought it would.*

*Today, Munger says that he "retains both great admiration for BYD's founder and CEO, Wang Chuan-Fu, and high hopes for the company," yet is pessimistic about the speed of gain in sales for electric cars as a class. BYD's long-term prospects are good, Munger thinks, because "the company has large and extremely modern facilities, talented employees, including many thousands of engineers, and low-cost operations that deliver products with few defects."*

*The "few defects" would get an argument from some people who believe that BYD's cars are not made well. Munger, however, says that complaints about the company's products are themselves few and only a minor problem in BYD's picture. —CL*

**W**arren Buffett is famous for his rules of investing: When a management with a reputation for brilliance tackles a business with a reputation for bad economics, it is usually the reputation of the business that remains intact. You should invest in a business that even a fool can run, because someday a fool will. And perhaps most famously, Never invest in a business you cannot understand.

So when Buffett's friend and longtime partner in Berkshire Hathaway, Charlie Munger, suggested early last year that they invest in BYD, an obscure Chinese battery, mobile phone, and electric car company, one might have predicted Buffett would cite rule No. 3 above. He is, after all, a man who shunned the booming U.S. tech industry during the 1990s.

But Buffett, who is 78, was intrigued by Munger's description of the entrepreneur behind BYD, a man named Wang Chuan-Fu, whom he had met through a mutual friend. "This guy," Munger tells *Fortune*, "is a combination of Thomas Edison and Jack Welch—something like Edison in solving technical problems, and something like Welch in getting done what he needs to do. I have never seen anything like it."

Coming from Munger, that meant a lot. Munger, the 85-year-old vice chairman of Berkshire Hathaway, is a curmudgeon who frowns on most investment ideas. "When I call Charlie with an idea," Buffett tells me, "and he says, 'That is really a dumb idea,' that means we should put 100% of our net worth into it. If he says, 'That is the dumbest thing I've ever heard,' then you should put 50% of your net worth into it. Only if he says, 'I'm going to have you committed,' does it mean he really doesn't like the idea." This time Buffett asked another trusted partner, David Sokol, chairman of a Berkshire-owned utility company called MidAmerican Energy, to travel to China and take a closer look at BYD.

Last fall Berkshire Hathaway bought 10% of BYD for $230 million. The deal, which is awaiting final approval from the Chinese government, didn't get much notice at the time. It was announced in late September, as the global financial markets teetered on the abyss. But Buffett and Munger and Sokol think it is a very big deal indeed. They think BYD has a shot at becoming the world's largest automaker, primarily by selling electric cars, as well as a leader in the fast-growing solar power industry.

Wang Chuan-Fu started BYD (the letters are the initials of the company's Chinese name) in 1995 in Shenzhen, China. A chemist and government researcher, Wang raised some $300,000 from relatives, rented about 2,000 square meters of space, and set out to manufacture rechargeable batteries to compete with imports from Sony and Sanyo. By about 2000, BYD had become one of the world's largest manufacturers of cellphone batteries. The company went on to design and manufacture mobile-phone handsets and parts for Motorola, Nokia, Sony Ericsson, and Samsung.

Wang entered the automobile business in 2003 by buying a Chinese state-owned car company that was all but defunct. He knew very little about making cars but proved to be a quick study. In October a BYD sedan called the F3 became the bestselling sedan in China, topping well-known brands like the Volkswagon Jetta and Toyota Corolla. BYD has also begun selling a plug-in electric car with a backup gasoline engine, a move putting it ahead of GM, Nissan, and Toyota. BYD's plug-in, called the F3DM (for "dual mode"), goes farther on a single charge—62 miles—than other electric vehicles and sells for about $22,000, less than the plug-in Prius and much-hyped Chevy Volt are expected to cost when they hit the market in late 2010. Put simply, this little-known upstart has accelerated ahead of its much bigger rivals in the race to build an affordable electric car.

Today BYD employs 130,000 people in 11 factories, eight in China and one each in India, Hungary, and Romania. Its U.S. operations are small—about 20 people work in a sales and marketing outpost in Elk Grove Village, Ill., near Motorola, and another 20 or so work in San Francisco, not far from Apple. BYD makes about 80% of Motorola's RAZR handsets, as well as batteries for iPods and iPhones and low-cost computers, including the model distributed by Nicholas Negroponte's One Laptop per Child nonprofit based in Cambridge, Mass. Revenues, which have grown by about 45% annually during the past five years, reached $4 billion in 2008.

In acquiring a stake in BYD, Buffett broke a couple of his own rules. "I don't know a thing about cellphones or batteries," he admits. "And I don't know how cars work." But, he adds, "Charlie Munger and Dave Sokol are smart guys, and they do understand it. And there's no question that what's been accomplished since 1995 at BYD is extraordinary."

One more thing reassured him. Berkshire Hathaway first tried to buy 25% of BYD, but Wang turned down the offer. He wanted to be in business with Buffett—to enhance his brand and open doors in the U.S., he says—but he would not let go of more than 10% of BYD's stock. "This was a man who didn't want to sell his company," Buffett says. "That was a good sign."

We're lost in Shenzhen. I've flown 8,000 miles to meet Wang, and on the way to the interview, my driver pulls to the side of a dusty highway. He's yelling in Cantonese into his phone and frenetically sketching Chinese characters on the touchscreen of a GPS navigator. The PR woman beside me looks worried. "The GPS isn't working," she says. "Too many new roads."

I can't blame the driver or the GPS—which, it occurs to me, was probably made nearby, since Shenzhen is the manufacturing hub of the global electronics industry, the place your cellphone, digital camera, and laptop probably came from. Just across a river from Hong Kong, Shenzhen is the biggest and fastest-growing city in the world that most Americans cannot find on a map. It's also the Chinese city most like America, because people who live here have come from elsewhere in search of a better life.

When Deng Xiaoping designated Shenzhen as China's first "special economic zone" in 1980, inviting capitalism to take root, it was a fishing village; today it's a sprawling megacity of 12 million to 14 million people, most of them migrant workers who toil in vast factories like those run by BYD and earn about 1,300 renminbi, or $190, per month.

When we find BYD's new headquarters—a silvery office building that would not look out of place in Silicon Valley—I'm given a tour of the company "museum," which celebrates products and milestones from the firm's brief history, and then escorted into a conference room where plates of apples, bananas, and cherry tomatoes are spread on a table. Wang takes a seat across from me—he is 43, a smallish man, with black hair and glasses—and begins, through an interpreter, to tell me his story.

He started BYD with a modest goal: to edge in on the Japanese-dominated battery business. "Importing batteries from Japan was very expensive," Wang says. "There were import duties, and delivery times were long." He studied Sony and Sanyo patents and took apart batteries to understand how they were made, a "process that involved much trial and error," he says. (Sony and Sanyo later sued BYD, unsuccessfully, for infringing on their patents.)

BYD's breakthrough came when Wang decided to substitute migrant workers for machines. In place of the robotic arms used on Japanese assembly lines, which cost $100,000 or more apiece, BYD actually cut costs by hiring hundreds, then thousands, of people.

"When I first visited the BYD factory, I was shocked," says Daniel Kim, a Merrill Lynch technology analyst based in Hong Kong, who has been to the fully automated production lines in Japan and Korea. "It's a completely different business model." To control quality, BYD broke every job down into basic tasks and applied strict testing protocols. By 2002, BYD had become one of the top four manufacturers worldwide—and the largest Chinese manufacturer—in each of the three rechargeable battery technologies (Li-Ion, NiCad, and NiMH), according to a Harvard Business School case study of the company. And Wang stresses that BYD, unlike Sony and Sanyo, has never faced a recall of its batteries.

Deploying the armies of laborers at BYD is an officer corps of managers and engineers who invent and design the products. Today the company employs about 10,000 engineers who have graduated from the company's training programs—some 40% of those who enter either drop out or are dismissed—and another 7,000 new college graduates are being trained. Wang says the engineers come from China's best schools. "They are the top of the top," he says. "They are very hard-working, and they can compete with anyone." BYD can afford to hire lots of them because their salaries are only about $600 to $700 a month; they also get subsidized housing in company-owned apartment complexes and low-cost meals in BYD canteens. "They're basically breathing, eating, thinking, and working at the company 24/7," says a U.S. executive who has studied BYD.

Wang typically works until 11 P.M. or midnight, five or six days a week. "In China, people of my generation put work first and life second," says the CEO, whose wife takes responsibility for raising their two children.

This "human resource advantage" is "the most important part" of BYD's strategy, Wang says. His engineers investigate a wide array of technologies, from automobile air-conditioning systems that can run on batteries to the design of solar-powered streetlights. Unlike most automakers, BYD manufactures nearly all its cars by itself—not just the engines and body but air conditioning, lamps, seatbelts, airbags, and electronics. "It is difficult for others to compete," Wang says. "If we put our staff in Japan or the U.S., we could not afford to do anything like this."

Wang himself grew up in extreme poverty. His parents, both farmers, died before he entered high school, and he was raised by an older brother and sister. The train ride from the village where he grew up to Central South Industrial University of Technology, where he earned his chemistry degree, took him by Yellow Mountain, a popular destination for hikers and tourists, but he has never visited there. "I didn't go then because we had no money," he says. "I don't go now because we have no time."

As for accumulating wealth? "I'm not interested in it," he claims. He certainly doesn't live a very lavish lifestyle. He was paid about $265,000 in 2008, and he lives in a BYD-owned apartment complex with other engineers. His only indulgences are a Mercedes and a Lexus, and they have a practical purpose: He takes their engines apart to see how they work. On a trip to the U.S., he once tried to disassemble the seat of a Toyota owned by Fred Ni, an executive who was driving him around. Shortly after BYD went public, Wang did something extraordinary: He took approximately 15% of his holdings in BYD and distributed the shares to about 20 other executives and engineers at the company. He still owns roughly 28% of the shares, worth about $1 billion.

The company itself is frugal. Until recently, executives always flew coach. One told me he was appalled when he learned that Ford, which lost billions last year, had staged a gala at the Hotel George V during the Paris auto show. By contrast, the last time BYD executives traveled to the Detroit auto show they rented a suburban house to save the cost of hotel rooms.

This attention to costs is one reason that BYD has made money consistently even as it has expanded into new businesses. Each of BYD's business units— batteries, mobile-phone components, and autos—was profitable in 2008, albeit on a small scale. Overall, net profits were around $187 million. BYD, which is traded on the Hong Kong exchange, has a market value of about $3.8 billion. That's less than Ford ($7 billion at the beginning of April), but more than General Motors ($1.3 billion).

Near the end of our conversation, I ask Wang about the company name. It's been reported that BYD stands for "Build your dreams," but he says he added that as the company motto only later. Others say that as Motorola, Apple, and Berkshire Hathaway have made their way to Shenzhen, the name has taken on yet another meaning: Bring your dollars.

When David Sokol toured BYD's operations last summer, Wang took him to a battery factory and explained that BYD wants to make its batteries 100% recyclable. To that end, the company has developed a nontoxic electrolyte fluid. To underscore the point, Wang poured battery fluid into a glass and drank it. "Doesn't taste good," he said, making a face and offering a sip to Sokol.

Sokol declined politely. But he got the message. "His focus there was that if we're going to help solve environmental problems, we can't create new environmental problems with our technology," Sokol says.

Sokol, author of a slim volume on management principles called *Pleased but Not Satisfied*, sized up Wang during that visit and decided he was an unusually purposeful executive. Sokol says, "Many good entrepreneurs can go from zero to a couple of million in revenues and a couple of hundred people. He's got over 100,000 people. Few can do that." When he got back to the U.S., Sokol told Buffett, "This guy's amazing. You want to meet him."

Even before visiting BYD, Sokol believed in electric cars. His people at MidAmerican have studied clean technologies like batteries and wind power for years because of the threat of climate change. One way or another, Sokol says, energy companies will need to produce more energy while emitting less carbon dioxide.

Electric cars will be one answer. They generate fewer greenhouse gas emissions than cars that burn gasoline, and they have lower fuel costs, even when oil is cheap. That's because electric engines are more efficient than internal-combustion engines, and because generating energy on a large scale (in coal or nuclear plants) is less wasteful than doing it on a small scale (by burning gasoline in an internal-combustion engine).

The numbers look something like this: Assume you drive 12,000 miles a year, gas costs $2 a gallon, and electricity is priced at 12¢ per kilowatt, about what most Americans pay. A gasoline-powered car that gets 20 miles to the gallon—say, a Chevy Impala or a BMW X3—will have annual fuel costs of $1,200 and generate about 6.6 tons of carbon dioxide. Equip those cars with electric motors, and fuel costs drop to $400 a year and emissions are reduced to about 1.5 tons.

The big problem is that they are expensive to make, and the single largest cost is the battery. Manufacturing a safe, reliable, long-lasting, and fast-charging battery for a car is a complex and costly undertaking. BYD claims to have achieved a breakthrough with its lithium ion ferrous phosphate technology, but no one can be sure whether it will work as promised.

Skeptics say that BYD's battery cannot be both more powerful and cheaper than those made by competitors, and the U.S. Department of Energy has purchased an F3DM to take the battery apart. Chitra Gopal, an analyst with Nomura Securities in Singapore who follows the company closely, says BYD is betting on "entirely new technology, and the ability to produce it at scale and at a low cost remains unproven." William Moore, publisher and editor-in-chief of EV World, an electric car website, says, "They need to persuade people that they are selling a reliable, durable, quality automobile."

Even BYD's admirers say the fit and finish of the company's cars leave much to be desired. "Their cars are way behind Toyota, for sure," Sokol admits. BYD currently exports gasoline-powered cars to Africa, South America, and the Middle East, but they compete on price, not quality.

BYD's first plug-in hybrid, called a dual-mode car, is designed to run primarily on electricity, with an internal-combustion engine for backup. Two all-electric cars—the E3 and the E6—will follow later this year. Both will be sold first in China, primarily to fleet users: the government, post office, utilities, and taxi companies, all of which will build central fast-charging facilities. Europe, with its high gas prices, is the most promising export market for BYD's electric cars. Wang signed an agreement last year with Autobinck, a Dutch dealer group, to distribute its cars in the Netherlands and five Eastern European countries.

The company hasn't yet decided whether it will enter the U.S. market, where the economics of electric cars are not as compelling. Sokol, who now sits on BYD's board, says BYD could instead become a battery supplier to global automakers. Some Americans, though, are eager to do business with BYD. The day after *Fortune*'s visit to BYD, Oregon Gov. Ted Kulongoski arrived to test-drive an electric car and urge the company to import through the port of Portland.

Meanwhile, BYD researchers are on to their next big idea, a product they call a Home Clean Power Solution. It's essentially a set of rooftop solar photovoltaic panels with batteries built in to store power for use when the sun's not out, all to be designed and manufactured by BYD. "Solar is an endless source of energy," Wang says. "With better technology, we can reduce the costs."

Wang is also focused on building a stronger executive team to drive the company forward. "The good news is, he's 42 years old," Sokol says. "The bad news is that he's clearly the brains behind the organization, and the drive. He has to develop a team faster, but I think he knows that." Last winter it was Sokol's turn to lead Wang on a tour of his home country. They started in Detroit, where BYD's cars generated buzz at the North American Auto Show, and wound up on the West Coast, where Wang met for the first time with Charlie Munger. In between, they stopped in Omaha.

"How did BYD get so far ahead?" Warren Buffett asked Wang, speaking through a translator. "Our company is built on technological know-how," Wang answered. Wary as always of a technology play, Buffett asked how BYD would sustain its lead. "We'll never, never rest," Wang replied.

Buffett may not understand batteries or cars, or Mandarin for that matter. Drive, however, is something that needs no translation.

# From "Riders on the Storm"

---

May 4, 2009

*An excerpt from an article by Adam Lashinsky*

Warren Buffett delights in telling an anecdote about Wells [Fargo]'s banking relationship with his own company, Berkshire Hathaway. In 2001, when Berkshire and a partner bought Finova, a bankrupt lender, it solicited banks to become part of a loan syndicate. "Wells wasn't interested," says Buffett, who is Wells' largest shareholder, with 315 million shares, or a 7.4% stake. The others offered to lend Berkshire money at the ultralow rate of 0.2 percentage points above its cost, a loss leader intended to win follow-on investment-banking business from Berkshire. Not Wells. "I got a big kick out of that because that's exactly how they should think," says Buffett, with a hearty guffaw. . . . "The real insight you get about a banker is how they bank. Their speeches don't make any difference. It's what they do and what they don't do. And what Wells doesn't do is what defines its greatness."

# From "Who the Admired Admire"

March 22, 2010

*An excerpt from an article by Anna Bernasek*

*In its annual Most Admired issue, Fortune asked six CEOS heading admired companies to say what CEO each most admired. Ken Chenault, of American Express, picked Buffett, saying:*

> He embodies this incredible blend of high intellect and business judgment with the ability to emotionally engage with people.

# THE GIVING PLEDGE

IN JUNE 2010, ALMOST *exactly four years after Warren Buffett announced his huge gift to the Bill and Melinda Gates Foundation and four other foundations (see page 256), he and the Gateses returned momentously to the philanthropic scene with their announcement of the Giving Pledge—their drive to expand the thinking of billionaires about how much of their fortunes to give away to charity.* Fortune *did this cover article breaking the news. Attached to it was Buffett's personal pledge (reprinted here, on page 314), which was simultaneously posted on the Giving Pledge's brand-new website.*

*Three months before this pledge news was announced, and even before there was certainty as to how and when it would be, Bill Gates and Warren Buffett met for lunch near the Omaha airport to discuss the venture (which at that point lacked even a name). I knew a little about their plan to meet and thought it presented a photo op apt to be important. My managing editor, Andy Serwer, agreed when I told him about the philanthropic milestone in the making. And so it was that when we published the cover story in June, we had a lead-off shot of Warren and Bill eating lunch at a Hollywood Diner outside Omaha that March—with Bill on a recess from a cross-country flight and Warren having driven himself from his office in the city.*

*As of September 2013, there were 114 signers of the Giving Pledge (not including their co-signing spouses). Considering that a much larger collection of the very rich—namely, the* Forbes 400*—were the targets Buffett and the Gateses had in mind, there are still plenty of prospects. But Buffett, for one, believes that the crowd already signed up makes the Giving Pledge a real success. "I would have defined success as a whole lot less than 114," he says. "And I know that we have changed the minds of some people about how much to give—in a couple of cases by a lot."*

*Furthermore, Buffett and Gates have organized and attended dinners in India and China that have spread the idea of the Giving Pledge to lands where philanthropy usually finishes a poor second to dynastic inheritances. The India dinner, in March 2011, attracted scores of businesspeople and government officials. So there is no telling at this point how far the Giving Pledge philosophy can be extended. —CL*

# The $600 Billion Challenge

July 5, 2010

## BY CAROL LOOMIS

Just over a year ago, in May 2009, word leaked to the press that the two richest men in America, Bill Gates and Warren Buffett, had organized and presided over a confidential dinner meeting of billionaires in New York City. David Rockefeller was said to have been a host, Mayor Michael Bloomberg and Oprah Winfrey to have been among those attending, and philanthropy to have been the main subject.

Pushed by the press to explain, Buffett and Gates declined. But that certainly didn't dim the media's interest in reaching for descriptions of the meeting: *The Chronicle of Philanthropy* called it "unprecedented"; both *ABC News* and the *Houston Chronicle* went for "clandestine"; a *New York* magazine parody gleefully imagined George Soros to have been starstruck in the presence of Oprah. One radio broadcaster painted a dark picture: "Ladies and gentlemen, there's mischief afoot and it does not bode well for the rest of us." No, no, rebutted the former CEO of the Bill & Melinda Gates Foundation, Patty Stonesifer, who had been at the meeting and had reluctantly emerged to combat the rumors. The event, she told the *Seattle Times*, was simply a group of friends and colleagues "discussing ideas" about philanthropy.

And so it was. But that discussion—to be fully described for the first time in this article—has the potential to dramatically change the philanthropic behavior of Americans, inducing them to step up the amounts they give. With that dinner meeting, Gates and Buffett started what can be called the biggest fundraising drive in history. They'd welcome donors of any kind. But their direct target is billionaires, whom the two men wish to see greatly raise the amounts they give to charities, of any and all kinds. That wish was not mathematically framed at the time of the New York meeting. But as two other U.S. dinners were held (though not leaked), Buffett and Gates and his wife, Melinda, set the goal: They are driving to get the super-rich, starting with the *Forbes* list of the 400 wealthiest Americans, to pledge—literally *pledge*—at least 50% of their net worth to charity during their lifetimes or at death.

Without a doubt, that plan could create a colossal jump in the dollars going to philanthropy, though of what size is a puzzle we'll get to. To begin with, a word about this article you are reading. It is the first public disclosure of what Buffett and Melinda and Bill Gates are trying to do. Over the past couple of months *Fortune* has interviewed the three principals as the project has unfolded, as well as a group of billionaires who have signed up to add their names to the Gates/Buffett campaign.

In a sense this article is also an echo of two other *Fortune* stories, both featuring Buffett on the cover. The first, published in 1986, was "Should You

Leave It All to the Children?" To that query, Buffett emphatically said no. The second article, which appeared in 2006, disclosed Buffett's intention to gradually give away his Berkshire Hathaway fortune to five foundations, chief among them the world's largest, the Bill & Melinda Gates Foundation. (For Buffett's thinking on the disposition of his wealth, see his pledge that follows this article).

Since then, in four years of contributions, Buffett has given the foundation $6.4 billion, not counting the 2010 gift, to be made this summer. The foundation in turn has in that same period combined Buffett's money and its immense gifts from the Gateses to raise its level of giving to about $3 billion a year, much of it for world health. One small example: the Medicines for Malaria Venture, heavily funded by the Gates Foundation, has worked with pharmaceutical company Novartis to develop good-tasting malaria pills and distribute them to millions of children—the principal victims of the disease—in 24 countries.

Another fact about the 2006 Buffett article is that it was written by yours truly, Carol Loomis, a senior editor-at-large of *Fortune*. Besides that, I am a longtime friend of Buffett's and editor of his annual letter to Berkshire's shareholders. Through him, my husband, John Loomis, and I have also come to know Melinda and Bill Gates socially. The Loomis team has even occasionally played bridge against Warren and Bill.

All that said, the question of what philanthropy might gain from the Gates/Buffett drive rests, at its outset, on a mystery: what the wealthiest Americans are giving now. Most of them aren't telling, and outsiders can't pierce the veil. For that matter, the *Forbes* 400 list, while a valiant try, is a best-guess estimate both as to the cast of characters and as to their net worth. (Buffett says he knows of two Berkshire shareholders who should be on the list but have been missed.) As Bill Gates sums it up, "The list is imprecise."

Those qualifiers noted, the magazine stated the 2009 net worth of the *Forbes* 400 to be around $1.2 trillion. So if those 400 were to give 50% of that net worth away during their lifetimes or at death, that would be $600 billion. You can think of that colossal amount as what the Buffett and Gates team is stalking—at a minimum.

Leaving aside the *Forbes* 400 and looking simply at Internal Revenue Service data for both annual giving and estate taxes, we can piece together a picture of how far the very rich might be from a figure like that $600 billion. Start with an admirable fact about Americans as a whole: The U.S. outdoes all other countries in philanthropic generosity, annually giving in the neighborhood of $300 billion.

Some of that gets reported as charitable deductions on the tax filings made by individuals. But taxpayers at low income levels don't tend to itemize, taking the standard deduction instead. At higher income levels, charitable gift data begin to mean something. To take one example for 2007 (the latest data available), the 18,394 individual taxpayers having adjusted gross income of $10 million or more reported charitable gifts equal to about $32.8 billion, or 5.84% of their $562 billion in income.

And billionaires? Here, the best picture—though it's flawed—emerges from statistics that the IRS has for almost two decades been releasing on each year's 400 largest individual taxpayers, a changing universe obviously. The decision of the government to track this particular number of citizens may or may not have been spurred by the annual publication of the *Forbes* list. In any case, the two 400 batches, though surely overlapping, cannot be identical—for one reason because the IRS data deal with income, not net worth.

The IRS facts for 2007 show that the 400 biggest taxpayers had a total adjusted income of $138 billion, and just over $11 billion was taken as a charitable deduction, a proportion of about 8%. The amount deducted, we need quickly to add, must be adjusted upward because it would have been limited for certain gifts, among them very large ones such as Buffett's $1.8 billion donation that year to the Gates Foundation. Even so, it is hard to imagine the $11 billion rising, by any means, to more than $15 billion. If we accept $15 billion as a reasonable estimate, that would mean that the 400 biggest taxpayers gave 11% of their income to charity—just a bit more than tithing.

Is it possible that annual giving misses the bigger picture? One could imagine that the very rich build their net worth during their lifetimes and then put large charitable bequests into their wills. Estate tax data, unfortunately, make hash of that scenario, as 2008 statistics show. The number of taxpayers making estate tax filings that year was 38,000, and these filers had gross estates totaling $229 billion. Four-fifths of those taxpayers made no charitable bequests at death. The 7,214 who did make bequests gave $28 billion. And that's only 12% of the $229 billion gross estate value posted by the entire 38,000.

All told, the data suggest that there is a huge gap between what the very rich are giving now and what the Gateses and Buffett would like to suggest is appropriate—that 50%, or better, of net worth. The question is how many people of wealth will buy their argument.

The seminal event in this campaign was that billionaires' gathering in May 2009—the First Supper, if you will. The Gateses credit Buffett with the basic idea: that a small group of dedicated philanthropists be somehow assembled to discuss strategies for spreading the gospel to others. The Gateses proceeded to arrange the event. Bill Gates says, with a grin, "If you had to depend on Warren to organize this dinner, it might never have happened." In his office, meanwhile, Buffett scrawled out a name for a new file, "Great Givers."

The first item filed was a copy of a March 4 letter that Buffett and Gates sent to the patriarch of philanthropy, David Rockefeller, to ask that he host the meeting. Rockefeller, now 95, told *Fortune* that the request was "a surprise but a pleasure." As a site for the event, he picked the elegant and very private President's House at Rockefeller University in New York City, whose board he has been on for 70 years. He also tapped his son David Jr., 68, to go with him to the meeting.

The event was scheduled for 3 P.M. on Tuesday, May 5—a day urgently desired by Bill Gates, who wanted to fit the meeting into a short U.S. break he'd be taking from a three-month European stay with his family. Because Melinda elected to remain in Europe with their three children, she did not attend the first dinner, but lined herself up for any that followed. (The Gateses have considered this campaign to be a personal matter for them, not in any way a project of the Gates Foundation.)

Melinda also insisted from the start that both husbands and wives be invited to the dinners, sure that both would be important to any discussion. Her reasoning: "Even if he's the one that made the money, she's going to be a real gatekeeper. And she's got to go along with any philanthropic plan, because it affects her and it affects their kids."

The letter of invitation, dated March 24, went to more people than could come. But the hosts and guests who arrived on May 5 certainly had enough economic tickets to be there: a combined net worth of maybe $130 billion and a serious history of having depleted that amount by giving money to charity. Leaving aside the semi-observers, Patty Stonesifer and David Rockefeller Jr., there were 14 people present, starting with the senior Rockefeller, Buffett, and Gates. The local guests included Mayor Bloomberg; three Wall Streeters, "Pete" Peterson, Julian Robertson, and George Soros; and Charles "Chuck" Feeney, who made his money as a major owner of Duty Free Shoppers and has so far given away $5 billion through his foundations, called Atlantic Philanthropies. When Feeney was dropped from the *Forbes* 400 in 1997, the magazine explained his departure in words not often hauled out for use: "Gave bulk of holdings to charity."

The out-of-towners included Oprah, Ted Turner, and two California couples, Los Angeles philanthropists Eli and Edythe Broad, and Silicon Valley's John and Tashia Morgridge, whose fortune came from Cisco Systems. Both the Broads and the Morgridges had equivocated over whether to accept the invitation, regarding the trip as an inconvenience. But there were the signatures at the bottom of the letter—from left to right, Rockefeller, Gates, Buffett. "Impressive," Eli Broad thought.

So on the appointed day the Broads found themselves seated with everyone else around a big conference table, wondering what came next. They mainly got that message from Buffett, whose quick sense of humor left him playing, says David Rockefeller Jr., "the enlivener role." He remembers Buffett as keeping the event from being "too somber" and "too self-congratulatory." Buffett set the ball rolling by talking about philanthropy, describing the meeting as "exploratory," and then asking each person, going around the table, to describe his or her philosophy of giving and how it had evolved.

The result was 12 stories, each taking around 15 minutes, for a total of nearly three hours. But most participants whom *Fortune* has talked to found the stories riveting, even when they were familiar. David Rockefeller Sr. described learning philanthropy at the knees of his father and grandfather. Ted

Turner repeated the oft-told tale of how he had made a spur-of-the-moment decision to give $1 billion to the United Nations. Some people talked about the emotional difficulty of making the leap from small giving to large. Others worried that their robust philanthropy might alienate their children. (Later, recalling the meeting, Buffett laughed that it had made him feel like a psychiatrist.)

The charitable causes discussed in those stories covered the spectrum: education, again and again; culture; hospitals and health; the environment; public policy; the poor generally. Bill Gates, who found the whole event "amazing," regarded the range of causes as admirable: "The diversity of American giving," he says, "is part of its beauty."

At the dinner that followed, the conversation turned specifically to how giving by the rich could be increased. The ideas advanced included national recognition of great philanthropists (presidential medals, for example), or a film, or a philanthropy guidebook, or a conference of the rich. There was no talk of a pledge. Of the dinner, the junior Rockefeller says, "The most important thing my dad and I came away with was that increasing giving would take work by many in that room—delicate, and probably prolonged, one-on-one work."

The dinner, of course, had its unexpected coda: the leak. The leaker, with little doubt, was Chuck Feeney, and the leakee was his longtime friend Niall O'Dowd, the New York publisher behind the grandly unknown IrishCentral .com. (*Fortune* did not succeed in reaching Feeney; of our account, O'Dowd said, "I can't confirm that.") On May 18, two weeks after the meeting, IrishCentral.com posted an article of 14 short paragraphs headlined SECRET MEETING OF WORLD'S RICHEST PEOPLE HELD IN NEW YORK. With that, the fame of the website spiked, as the rest of the press picked up the news and ran with it.

The IrishCentral article exhibited some confusion about which Rockefeller starred at the dinner, or was even there, but otherwise provided the names of all the participants—with the notable exception of Feeney, who apparently didn't realize he looked more conspicuous to the others by being left out. Feeney, however, appears to have been quoted anonymously in the piece, once as an "attendee" who thought Gates the most impressive speaker of the day, Turner the most outspoken (surprise!), and Buffett the most insistent on his agenda for change. In a second instance, Feeney was a good bet to have been the awed "participant" who extolled his fellow guests: "They were all there, the great and the good."

The main effect of the leak was to place a "cone of silence"—that's a description from the Gates camp—over everything that transpired in the giving campaign over the next year. But there was certainly action, including a few small dinners abroad. Bill and Melinda Gates hosted a dinner in London, and Bill held a few others in India and China. Raising the philanthropic bar in foreign countries is a special challenge: Dynastic wealth is widely taken for granted; tax laws do not commonly allow deductions for gifts to charity; a paucity of institutions and organizations ready for gifts makes knowing whom to give to just not that obvious. Nonetheless, were the Gateses and Buffett to succeed in their campaign in the U.S., they would probably take it overseas.

But as last summer and fall progressed, Buffett and the Gateses did not even have a plan for how the campaign was to be structured. In this vacuum the idea of a pledge took hold and gained strength. It helped that more dinners were to be held. At them, says Melinda, the three principals would "float the pledge idea to see if it would fly."

There then occurred the second and third U.S. dinners, most of whose guests have not been publicly outed because of the cone of silence. Secrecy, a Gates spokesman says, is partly a bow to moguls who have been exposed to the philanthropic sales pitch but would be embarrassed to have been identified in case they chose not to step up to the challenge.

In any event, the names of some of the participants are known. The noted philanthropists at the second dinner, held at the New York Public Library in November last year, included New York investment banker Kenneth Langone and his wife, Elaine, and H.F. "Gerry" Lenfest and his wife, Marguerite, from Philadelphia. Lenfest got rich when he sold his Pennsylvania cable television company to Comcast in 2000, netting $1.2 billion for himself and his family. He promptly vowed that he would give most of it to charity in his lifetime. Now 80, he has so far meted out $800 million, a good part of it to schools he attended (Columbia Law School, Washington and Lee, Mercersburg Academy).

Lenfest's favorite moment at the November dinner was Buffett's declaration that Marguerite Lenfest had put forward the best idea of the evening when she said that the rich should sit down, decide how much money they and their progeny need, and figure out what to do with the rest of it. Says Lenfest: "The value of Buffett and Gates is that they're going to make people sit down and think these things through."

The Third Supper, held in December in Menlo Park, Calif., at the Rosewood Sand Hill hotel, is known as the Bay Area dinner but drew from all over the state, including its entertainment precincts. In attendance were some veteran philanthropists, including venture capitalist John Doerr of Kleiner Perkins and his wife, Ann, and the Morgridges, who had selected the meeting site. This dinner was somewhat different from the other two, says Melinda Gates, because a few people there were relatively new to huge wealth and were still forming their opinions about giving. Talk went on for hours, so long that the beef being prepared for dinner became somewhat overcooked. This is reported to have dismayed Rosewood's management, which may have noticed that the crowd in the Dogwood room was worth having back.

The dinner also brought out some of the fears that people have about philanthropy. What does going public with big gifts do to the peace in your life?

Won't pleas from charities be unending? How do you deal with giving internationally, which too often seems like throwing money down a hole? These are valid concerns, say the Gateses, the kind raised by people who want to feel as smart about giving as they were about making their money. But the questions didn't stop the two from plugging the satisfactions of philanthropy. At those dinners, says Bill, "no one ever said to me, 'We gave more than we should have.'"

Nor did the idea of a pledge get shot down at those dinners. It "floated" nicely, in other words. So as 2010 arrived, a pledge became the strategy. The idea of aiming for a 50% slice of net worth was pragmatically pulled from the sky, being less than the principals would have liked to ask for but perhaps as much, at least initially, as they can get. The pledges, meanwhile, were never envisioned as legal contracts but rather moral obligations to be both memorialized in writing and taken very seriously. They are in fact to be posted on a new website, Givingpledge.org, whose construction Melinda Gates oversaw. The 99% pledge that Buffett is making is likely to be the No. 1 document on the website, if he is not beaten out by his Seattle friends.

Enthusiastic about leading the search for Great Givers, the Gateses and Buffett nonetheless have wanted a phalanx of strong supporters. Already committed to at least a 50% pledge are the Broads, the Doerrs, the Lenfests, and the Morgridges. With the online publication of this article, moreover, the three principals will send e-mails and make calls to other billionaires judged likely prospects. A bit later, all of the pledgers may join in sending a letter to a large number of other billionaires, asking them to join the growing crowd. In the fall there may even be a Great Givers conference.

The definition of success in this venture may take years to figure out, but each of the principals has reflections about the matter. Buffett knows that everyone rich has thought about what to do with his or her money: "They may not have reached a decision about that, but they have for sure thought about it. The pledge that we're asking them to make will put them to thinking about the whole issue again." He warns, most of all, against the rich delaying the decision of what to do with their money: "If they wait until they're making a final will in their nineties, the chance of their brainpower and willpower being better than they are today is nil."

Bill Gates regards the 50% as a "low bar" encouraging high participation. People, he thinks, may be drawn in by that proportion and then surprise themselves and find they are giving at higher levels. "This is about moving to a different realm," he thinks, and it will take time for everything to sort out.

Melinda Gates separates the near-term from the far. There are so many reasons that rich people don't give, she says: They don't want to plan for their death; they worry that they'll need to hire someone to help with the work; they just don't want to take the time to think about it all. So the initial goal of the pledge campaign, she thinks, must be simply to cut through that and get them moving in the direction of giving. And eventually? "Three to five years down the road, we need to have a significant number of billionaires signed up. That would be success."

Society cannot help but be a beneficiary here, by virtue of at least some dollars and perhaps many. Nor will it be just the very rich who will perhaps bend their minds to what a pledge of this kind means. It could also be others with less to give but suddenly more reason to think about the rightness of what they do.

# My Philanthropic Pledge

July 5, 2010

## BY WARREN BUFFETT

In 2006, I made a commitment to gradually give all of my Berkshire Hathaway stock to philanthropic foundations. I couldn't be happier with that decision.

Now, Bill and Melinda Gates and I are asking hundreds of rich Americans to pledge at least 50% of their wealth to charity. So I think it is fitting that I reiterate my intentions and explain the thinking that lies behind them.

First, my pledge: More than 99% of my wealth will go to philanthropy during my lifetime or at death. Measured by dollars, this commitment is large. In a comparative sense, though, many individuals give more to others every day.

Millions of people who regularly contribute to churches, schools, and other organizations thereby relinquish the use of funds that would otherwise benefit their own families. The dollars these people drop into a collection plate or give to United Way mean forgone movies, dinners out, or other personal pleasures. In contrast, my family and I will give up nothing we need or want by fulfilling this 99% pledge.

Moreover, this pledge does not leave me contributing the most precious asset, which is time. Many people, including—I'm proud to say—my three children, give extensively of their own time and talents to help others. Gifts of this kind often prove far more valuable than money. A struggling child, befriended and nurtured by a caring mentor, receives a gift whose value far exceeds what can be bestowed by a check. My sister, Doris, extends significant person-to-person help daily. I've done little of this.

What I can do, however, is to take a pile of Berkshire Hathaway stock certificates—"claim checks" that when converted to cash can command far-ranging resources—and commit them to benefit others who, through the luck of the draw, have received the short straws in life. To date about 20% of my shares have been distributed (including shares given by my late wife, Susan Buffett). I will continue to annually distribute about 4% of the shares I retain. At the latest, the proceeds from all of my Berkshire shares will be expended for philanthropic purposes by 10 years after my estate is settled. Nothing will go to endowments; I want the money spent on current needs.

This pledge will leave my lifestyle untouched and that of my children as well. They have already received significant sums for their personal use and will receive more in the future. They live comfortable and productive lives. And I will continue to live in a manner that gives me everything that I could possibly want in life.

Some material things make my life more enjoyable; many, however, would not. I like having an expensive private plane, but owning a half-dozen homes would be a burden. Too often, a vast collection of possessions ends up possessing its owner. The asset I most value, aside from health, is interesting, diverse, and long-standing friends.

My wealth has come from a combination of living in America, some lucky genes, and compound interest. Both my children and I won what I call the ovarian lottery. (For starters, the odds against my 1930 birth taking place in the U.S. were at least 30 to 1. My being male and white also removed huge obstacles that a majority of Americans then faced.)

My luck was accentuated by my living in a market system that sometimes produces distorted results, though overall it serves our country well. I've worked in an economy that rewards someone who saves the lives of others on a battlefield with a medal, rewards a great teacher with thank-you notes from parents, but rewards those who can detect the mispricing of securities with sums reaching into the billions. In short, fate's distribution of long straws is wildly capricious.

The reaction of my family and me to our extraordinary good fortune is not guilt, but rather gratitude. Were we to use more than 1% of my claim checks on ourselves, neither our happiness nor our well-being would be enhanced. In contrast, that remaining 99% can have a huge effect on the health and welfare of others. That reality sets an obvious course for me and my family: Keep all we can conceivably need and distribute the rest to society, for its needs. My pledge starts us down that course.

# Buffett's Mr. Fix-It

## August 16, 2010

### BY BRIAN DUMAINE

*No one could have imagined when we published this laudatory 2010 article about David Sokol that less than a year later he would have resigned from Berkshire and come to be seen by many in the press as a bad actor. In fact, the article—in a picture display—described him as the man "mentioned most often as Buffett's successor." The other five Berkshire executives pictured were Greg Abel of MidAmerican Energy, Ajit Jain of Berkshire Reinsurance, Tad Montross of General Re, Tony Nicely of GEICO, and Matt Rose of railroad company BNSF.*

*Sokol abruptly removed himself as a contender in March 2011, resigning by his own choice from Berkshire and telling Buffett he'd been planning to leave for some time because he wanted to do something on his own. But the same Buffett press release that disclosed the resignation, and Sokol's explanation of it, also revealed that Sokol had bought stock in Lubrizol just weeks before proposing to Buffett that it would be a good company for Berkshire to buy. Buffett took care in the release to point out that Sokol had bought the stock before presenting his idea to Buffett and with no knowledge of how Buffett would react. Even so, the facts about Sokol's buying—combined with the lift in Lubrizol's stock that accompanied Buffett's decision to indeed buy—put Sokol into disrepute for what some onlookers thought might be insider trading.*

*The Securities and Exchange Commission did investigate Sokol's trading. But almost two years later, in January 2013, Sokol's lawyer told the press that he had learned from the SEC that it would not bring charges.*

*The Berkshire press release that went out about the whole affair caused its writer, Buffett, reputational troubles of his own. (The release, issued March 30, 2011, is on Berkshire Hathaway's website.) Much of the world thought the release was too soft on Sokol and weirdly devoid of the outrage that Buffett had long said he would display if anyone at Berkshire lost the company a shred of reputation. Critics of Buffett also questioned why he did not bore in for information when Sokol told him at one point that he owned Lubrizol stock.*

*The Sokol issue became not only a magnet for the press but also Topic A at Berkshire's 2011 annual meeting, held April 30. As one of the three journalists recruited to receive e-mailed questions from shareholders, and as the first scheduled to be at the mic, I read a question that wondered accusingly why Buffett had not reacted more harshly to what Sokol had done. Some applause followed my merely posing the question. Buffett then delivered a long answer that both called Sokol's behavior "inexplicable" and conceded that he himself might have handled some things better. He could have, he said specifically, asked more questions when Sokol said he owned Lubrizol stock.*

*After the meeting, the Sokol affair largely dropped out of the news. Sokol*

*himself moved from Omaha to the Jackson Hole, Wyoming area, where he set up*
*an investment management business, Teton Capital.*

*Because the Sokol news hit very soon after* Fortune *had closed an issue, we did*
*not publish a story about it in the magazine. But Brian Dumaine, who wrote the*
*Sokol article that follows, put up a Fortune.com story about Sokol the day after*
*Buffett's press release was issued. In that piece, Brian did not use the word "inex-*
*plicable," but that is what he regards Sokol's actions to have been. You can find a*
*copy of that online article at fortune.com.* —CL

The day after Lehman collapsed in September 2008, David Sokol noticed
that the stock of Constellation Energy, a Baltimore utility, was plummet-
ing. He called his boss, Warren Buffett, and said, "I see an opportunity here."
Buffett, who had noticed the same thing, replied after a brief discussion:
"Let's go after it."

Constellation held vast amounts of energy futures contracts that had gone
sour, and the company appeared to be on the verge of bankruptcy. Sokol, as
chairman of the Berkshire subsidiary MidAmerican Energy Holdings, knew
the utility industry and saw a chance to buy solid assets at a bargain price. The
deal, however, had to be done within 48 hours or the company would have to
file for bankruptcy.

Sokol phoned the office of Constellation CEO Mayo Shattuck III, who was in
an emergency board meeting. When his assistant answered, Sokol told her he'd
like to speak to him. The secretary replied that if she interrupted the meeting,
she might lose her job. Sokol replied, "If you *don't* interrupt the meeting, you
might lose your job."

Sokol boarded a Falcon 50EX and sped to Baltimore. He met with Shattuck
and struck a deal that evening to buy the company for $4.7 billion, staving off
bankruptcy.

Within weeks, before the acquisition was completed, Constellation's board
received a competing bid from Électricité de France for about a 30% premium.
The board liked the offer, and so did Sokol—who walked away with a $1.2 bil-
lion breakup fee for Berkshire.

When investors think of Berkshire Hathaway, they of course think of Warren Buffett and his record as a hands-off, if highly attentive, CEO. He gives free
rein to the heads of his large collection of companies, ranging from GEICO to
Dairy Queen to Benjamin Moore to the Buffalo News to NetJets. Yet even in
Buffett's empire, sometimes a CEO blows it, and his business needs to be fixed
or a deal needs to get done—fast. When that happens, Buffett's go-to guy is
David Sokol.

Of all Berkshire's lieutenants, Sokol, 53, is mentioned most often as Buffett's
heir, although Sokol shrugs off such speculation. Buffett likes Sokol just where
he is, getting deals done, boosting profits, and turning around ailing businesses. In the foreword to Sokol's book, *Pleased but Not Satisfied*, Buffett writes,

"He brings the business equivalent of Ted Williams' .406 batting average to the field of business management."

Buffett first met Sokol in 1999 when Berkshire was buying MidAmerican, the Iowa utility. With longtime Buffett friend Walter Scott, Sokol had bought a small, $28-million-a-year geothermal business in 1991 and built it into that utility powerhouse. MidAmerican, headquartered in Des Moines, now represents an $11.4 billion slice of Berkshire's revenue (about 10%), and Sokol is its chairman. In 2007, Buffett asked Sokol to get Johns Manville, an underperforming roofing and insulation company, on track, and he did; he is now its chairman. In 2008, Charlie Munger, Buffett's vice chairman, asked Sokol to fly to China to conduct due diligence on BYD, a battery and electric car maker. Sokol liked what he saw, and Berkshire invested $230 million for 10% of the company. That stake is now worth around $1.8 billion. In April, when Buffett had concerns about a provision in the Senate financial regulation bill that would have required Berkshire and other companies to post billions of collateral on their existing derivatives, it was Sokol he sent to argue his case. Buffett's side of the argument won.

Last summer Buffett handed Sokol perhaps the biggest assignment of his career: turning around NetJets. The fractional-ownership jet company last year lost $711 million before taxes—not the kind of performance that warms Buffett's heart. Today the company is profitable, and *Fortune* got a rare, exclusive view of how Sokol did it. But more on that later.

It's not hard to understand why Buffett likes this driven Midwesterner. Sokol complements his skills. While Buffett comes off as your favorite uncle—relaxed, with a warm sense of humor—Sokol is always revving in high gear. An engineer by training, he is a tough, no-nonsense manager. He's up before 5 A.M. each day and jogs five miles and lifts weights five days a week, in part to keep his weight down but also to survive a grueling schedule. He's on the road half the year, not counting the shuttling between his homes in Omaha and in Columbus, where NetJets is based. He and his wife, Peggy, have a grown daughter, Kelly. In his rare time off he likes to fish and ski. "He gets more done in a day," says Buffett, "than probably I get done in a week, and I'm not kidding."

Sokol has been richly rewarded for his hard work. He, Walter Scott, and Greg Abel, now CEO of MidAmerican, together owned (not in equal shares) a 19% chunk of that company, worth around $300 million when Berkshire acquired the utility in 2000. On any given day Sokol might be out rubbing shoulders with his employees or spending time with customers and business partners, looking for new opportunities in China, Brazil, Germany, or elsewhere. How can he spend so much time out of the office and still run three major businesses? Sokol has a formula, one that is laid out in *Pleased but Not Satisfied*. (He hands out the self-published book to all his executives.)

The concise, 129-page treatise expounds Sokol's six laws: operational excellence, integrity, customer commitment, employee commitment, financial strength, and environmental respect. Yes, they are management bromides, but Sokol drives them so hard and so consistently into every organization he touches—ruthlessly if need be—that time and again they get him the kind of results even a Warren Buffett could like.

Another trick to running three businesses at once, Sokol says, is to hire first-class executive assistants and use them aggressively. "Too many people use assistants just to make phone calls, type letters, and file," he says. "At most, mine do that a third of time." He has two full-time assistants and one part-timer who, he says, "know how I think." They give him an update once a week on all the goals he's set for his businesses and for the executives who run them.

His assistants also know he never likes to be late for a meeting—he believes it shows disrespect. They always build in extra time in case something goes wrong, but they also make sure he has work to do if he happens to show up a half-hour early.

Sokol's childhood offered little evidence that he would one day become a big success. He grew up in Omaha, in what he calls "the wrong side of town." At the University of Nebraska he wanted to be a doctor, but the first time he saw a cadaver he fainted and hit his head on the edge of a marble table. His father gently suggested that he follow in the footsteps of his older brother and study civil engineering.

In 1982, four years after graduating, he was hired by Citicorp in New York City, where he advised clients on investing in big waste-energy projects. He was soon lured away to run a waste-energy business called Ogden Martin, which he built into a New York Stock Exchange company before joining Walter Scott at what was to become MidAmerican.

Sokol's record is not unblemished—even if you bat .406 you strike out sometimes. In what he now says was probably the biggest failure of his career, Sokol in the early 2000s decided to invest in a new method to remove zinc from one of MidAmerican's geothermal wells in California. The technology worked in the lab, but when applied in the field it flopped, leaving MidAmerican with a $200 million loss. In retrospect, Sokol should have done more pilot-testing. "The worst mistake I made," he says, "was that when I approved the project, in the pit of my stomach I knew it was a mistake. I've tried to teach this to young executives ever since. Your gut instincts are extremely important to listen to, particularly when they are telling you not to do something." When he reported the bad news to Buffett, the boss simply said, "Don't make a habit of it."

Sokol got stung again last April, when an Omaha judge issued a $32 million ruling against MidAmerican, finding that the company had "willfully and intentionally" miscalculated future profits to force out minority stockholders in a hydropower project in the Philippines in the 1990s. Sokol strongly disagrees with the ruling, and the company is appealing.

Such setbacks notwithstanding, Sokol is the Mr. Fix-It Buffett sends in when some part of the Berkshire machine breaks down. What's it like when David Sokol parachutes in? Consider the NetJets story.

In mid-August 2009, NetJets was losing money and customers. Founder and CEO Rich Santulli drafted a letter of resignation, and Buffett accepted it. The situation was painful for both men. Buffett liked Santulli as a friend, and in the 2003 Berkshire annual report he had described him as "an extraordinary CEO."

An ex-Goldman Sachs banker, Santulli had created the fractional jet ownership industry in 1986; by 2009, NetJets had 842 aircraft, 3,500 pilots, and revenue of $3.1 billion. Santulli, who signed a non-disparagement agreement, chose not to comment for this article.

Santulli came up with the notion of fractional ownership when he noticed that most owners used their jets only a couple hundred hours a year. Why not split the heavy cost of ownership, he thought, and at the same time avoid the hassles of hiring pilots and maintaining the plane? Today a NetJets customer typically buys a one-eighth share of a jet for, say, five years. He also pays around $5,000 an hour for operations. Because NetJets has a huge fleet, it can guarantee an owner a plane—not necessarily his own but an identical model—with only four hours' notice.

Buffett and his family, and many Berkshire executives, have long been happy NetJets customers. Buffett is so fond of the company he likes to peddle the service to Berkshire shareholders at his annual meetings, where he sometimes puts jets on display. In his 2001 report, Buffett, whose company also owns Fruit of the Loom, wrote, "If you buy a fraction of a plane, we might even throw in a three-pack of briefs or boxers." Yet since Buffett bought NetJets from the entrepreneur in 1998 for $725 million, it has not come close to earning back Berkshire's investment.

The fractional-jet business is like running an airline, only exponentially more complicated. Imagine having to fly a customer to a destination on four hours' notice. Not only does the jet need to be available, but the pilots, flight attendants, maintenance crew, and catering services all have to be at the right place at the right time. NetJets spends $100 million a year alone on pilot training. Headquarters in Columbus has its own staff of meteorologists to track weather that might delay flights.

And NetJets' well-heeled customers are used to getting what they want. One G-5 owner drank his coffee only out of a white Styrofoam cup, and crews would have to scramble to find the cups and put them next to his seat. A NetJets pilot recalls flying a passenger from Denver to L.A. for a haircut, and then returning him to Denver. The passenger was a poodle. The flights cost $32,000.

By August of last year, the financial meltdown had taken its toll on NetJets. Some top executives no longer wanted to be seen climbing onto a $50 million Gulfstream. (Those Detroit CEOs flying on private jets to the congressional bailout hearings didn't help.) Others couldn't afford it. The NetJets contract guarantees buying back an owner's share at a fair market price. Squeezed Wall Street titans couldn't sell their houses, their art, or their horses, but they did have a guarantee that Berkshire would buy back their jets. Owners started selling shares back at a level that was unprecedented. One NetJets executive there at the time says, "We were looking into the precipice. The charts looked like the Superman roller coaster at Six Flags." NetJets was left holding on its books a large number of unsold aircraft worth, in some cases, 40% less than had been paid for them.

As the situation worsened, Sokol replaced Santulli as CEO. When he had flown to NetJets' Columbus headquarters in early August to check things out, Sokol discovered two major problems with the company. First, it had bought too many new planes, causing its debt to skyrocket. Second, NetJets management, according to Sokol, was too informally organized to be effective. Sokol began handing out copies of his management book. Before long he realized that fixing NetJets was going to be far harder than he had imagined.

Over the last quarter of a century Santulli, a charismatic leader, had built a strong culture at NetJets. Many employees felt like family, willing to go the extra mile to make sure this complex business worked day in and day out. If you needed help, you got it. Employees filled in for one another.

Sokol's challenge was to radically change NetJets without ruining the esprit de corps that defined the company. But top management liked things just the way they were. At meetings Sokol would propose selling planes or cutting costs, and executives would push back. Before long Sokol grew frustrated. Says Bill Olsen, who at the time was running NetJets Aviation, an operating division: "It was no secret that David was not open to suggestions, critical debate, or constructive criticism. Once you challenged him in a meeting, he'd give you a look to kill and you'd fall very fast out of his favor." (Olsen left management and went back to being a NetJets pilot.) Sokol responds: "That's just not true. My management style is collaborative."

Despite the blowback, Sokol pushed ahead, canceling orders for new planes, selling off old ones, and reducing debt from $1.9 billion to $1.3 billion. He also cut some $100 million in costs, enough to make operations profitable. He started with low-hanging fruit: About $30 million of cost savings came from canceling the free use of airplanes. The old regime often let a movie star, singer, or friend of the company have free rides or upgrades for promotional purposes. Says Sokol: "We might have been getting only $2 or $3 million in value for $30 million in costs" on such promotions. Sokol also cut out an expensive Las Vegas poker tournament that the company put on each year for its clients.

Next came layoffs. Santulli had already reduced headcount by about 4%. Sokol laid off another 5% and furloughed some 500 pilots, bringing the total headcount to 6,400. He says that because NetJets was flying fewer planes, the company didn't need as many employees. Many top managers disagreed fiercely with the depth of the cuts, arguing that service would suffer. Before long about half the senior management team had been let go. The rest were reassigned or left on their own.

Sokol argues that the company was long overdue for a shakeup. "One thing that can be very nice in a dysfunctional management is that it's very hard to measure people," he says. "So you have managers who are patting themselves on the back, saying they're doing great, while the reality is that there's no way to measure what they're doing." One NetJets executive whose sales region was losing money still received multimillion-dollar bonuses.

Having purged senior management, Sokol elevated three NetJets executives from the next rung down to his new team and hired three from the outside. Says he: "NetJets was top-heavy and lacked a good organizational structure. We needed to give employees responsibilities and goals that were clear and deliverable. We needed to make clear who was doing what."

Under the old regime, service and costs had been measured to some extent, but not broadly throughout the organization. Explains Bill Noe, a longtime employee whom Sokol elevated to president of NetJets North America: "In the old regime, you got everyone in top management in a room and said, 'Here's our goal, here's what we're doing.' But did the employee on the second floor of accounts receivable know what was going on? Probably not."

Sokol has trained his team to measure every single thing the company does, from on-schedule service to bill collection to the quality of catering. "When we make a mistake," he says, "we analyze why we made the mistake, and if there's a way to fix it, we fix it by putting a system in place that solves the problem." Recently a NetJets customer who was landing at a small private airfield in Fort Lauderdale said he needed a rental car at Fort Lauderdale International. His mistake, but the NetJets service rep didn't pick it up. Sokol's team has since adjusted the software system so the service rep can't make that car reservation without the computer system pointing out that the car and airport don't match. Says he: "In less than 0.5% of our flights do we make a mistake in making a reservation. If it's a half of 1%, it's still too many."

Sokol has also brought customer service, sales, and marketing into one group, creating cross-functional teams that are much more familiar with an owner's needs. The service people, who are often in the field meeting and greeting owners, might find out that Mr. X likes caviar and Coke Zero and add that information to a master file the company keeps on each customer. Says Adam Johnson, NetJets' senior vice president: "Just knowing the owner, knowing anniversaries and birthdays, helps to build strong relationships."

The old, entrepreneurial NetJets culture, says Sokol, focused on immediate growth rather than long-term planning. He instituted a rigorous five- and 10-year planning process that looks at everything from future demand for new planes to jet fuel prices, inflation, and new markets like China. Says Jordan Hansell, NetJets' general counsel: "You lay out a whole series of explicit assumptions about the economy, business planning, regulations. That forces you to ask yourself what are the important factors that might make you change some decisions. It helps reduce surprises."

One thing that did surprise Sokol was the venom with which some ex-Net-

Jets managers have been waging a war of words against him, partly on Buffett biographer Alice Schroeder's website. Jim Jacobs, the co-founder of NetJets, is one of the harshest critics. Jacobs, who left his post as vice chairman in January, argues that Sokol's cost cutting is sacrificing service and that owners are complaining and many are leaving. He also claims that canceling orders for new planes is a big mistake. Says he: "We were protecting the franchise value and the ability of the golden goose to keep laying eggs. We didn't panic and lay off pilots who cost a fortune to bring back on. We didn't cancel new planes to let our fleet get older and thus more expensive to run. We didn't shut down our influencer network. No one at NetJets now has a clue how to run it."

Criticizing the staff cuts, Jacobs points out that most of the $711 million loss in 2009 was a noncash charge and says the company was headed toward being about $70 million cash-flow positive in 2010 even if the company didn't sell another new fractional share. The cuts, he argues, have made NetJets "a tiny shadow of what it was."

"Ludicrous," Sokol snaps back. "In all the acquisitions and business turn-arounds I've done, I've never seen senior people leave a company who then go out and try to spread rumors and call customers and try to be harmful to the business. It's a horrible thing to see, because the only people they are hurting are themselves and the employees of the company."

The judgment that matters here, of course, is Buffett's, and he is pleased and satisfied. "Dave is now making very good money, and not from selling planes," Buffett says. "It looks like NetJets will earn $200 million pretax this year. It's as remarkable a managerial achievement as I have ever seen. When aviation picks up, it could be a company that could earn $500 million a year."

Sokol feels that this turnaround is largely done. He hopes to elevate one of the six in his new management team to CEO, perhaps by the end of the year. The question now is, When the phone rings again from Omaha, where will he fly off to next?

# A New Buffett Takes Beijing

October 17, 2011

## BY BILL POWELL

*The Kids Are All Right, said a 2010 movie. The same line works for Warren Buffett's three "kids": Susie, 60; Howard, 58; and Peter, 55. Graduates of Omaha's public schools and familiar from an early age with their parents' strong opinions about not-giving-it-all-to-the-children, they long ago grew up to be solid citizens with careers of their own. True, all three today run foundations funded with their parents' money—an occupational niche reserved for the privileged. But the three attack that work seriously, knowing the job of giving away money wisely to be extraordinarily hard. Susie's foundation has primarily supported early education in Omaha, where she lives; Howard, who works a farm outside his Decatur, Illinois, home, has focused on bettering the lives of Africa's rural poor; and New Yorkers Peter and his wife, Jennifer, have sought to improve the lot of women around the world.*

*Peter Buffett became the subject of the* Fortune *article reprinted here because of the smashing Chinese success of his 2010 book,* Life Is What You Make It. *Translations of the book had sold 320,000 copies in China when this article was published, and the count in mid-2013 was more than 400,000. Warren Buffett's reputation in China clearly didn't hurt. He is known there as the "god of stocks," and his every move is catalogued. But something about Peter's dropping out of prestigious Stanford and going off, without loads of money, to pursue an uncertain career—well, that grabbed the minds of China's young people, many of them unable to imagine how he could possibly have taken that risk.*

*Howard Buffett has as well written a book,* Forty Chances, *due to be published in October 2013, about his tumbling into a farming career and later becoming an expert on Africa's agricultural challenges. Susie Buffett is not writing a book—not now, at least. From her post in Omaha, she is the family's most effective communicator with her father about all things important—say, personal security systems. Warren has no patience for their details nor even their existence. Susie takes over, and the security job gets done. —CL*

It is—and this is putting it mildly—sometimes difficult to generalize about a nation of 1.3 billion people. But let's go out on a limb and say there aren't many who would quibble with the description of China as money-obsessed. This is a nation in which arguably the most important phrase ever attributed to its transformational leader, Deng Xiaoping, was "to get rich is glorious." In China they call Warren Buffett the "god of stocks," and whenever he visits, the Chinese media cover his every move and utterance. There have been over 40 books about Warren Buffett translated into Chinese.

Which makes it very interesting that Peter Buffett, Warren's unassuming 53-year-old son, has recently become a rising star in China in his own right.

And it's not because everyone thinks Warren's investment acumen has been handed down via DNA. Peter Buffett is a successful musician and a composer, writing scores for television and film (the *Dances With Wolves* soundtrack is one of his prominent credits) and performing his New Agey music in concert. He played most recently in August at Beijing Tanglewood, a gorgeous new outdoor concert space in the shadow of the Great Wall.

But Beijing isn't exactly Marin County. In today's China, New Age music will take you only so far. The reason Buffett has piqued the interest of a lot of Chinese—students and young professionals in particular—is that he has taken to dispensing life advice along with his music. And if part of his core message—in essence, that money isn't everything—seems rather counterintuitive in China these days, that's precisely the reason he has struck a chord. Warren Buffett's rock-star status tells us something about what China is today; Peter's success might tell us something about where it's going.

Earlier this year a publisher in Beijing decided to capitalize on the Chinese demand for all things Buffett and translate a book Peter had written in 2010, titled *Life Is What You Make It: Find Your Own Path to Fulfillment.* It sold modestly in the U.S. and was released in China in March. Carrying the Chinese title *Be Yourself,* by the end of August the book had sold 320,000 copies—a huge number, even in a country of 1.3 billion. Through much of the spring and summer, says Zhang Haióu, editor-in-chief of New World Press, Buffett's Chinese publisher, they were selling 1,000 copies a day online. "We obviously had hoped for the best, but honestly, we were stunned," says Zhang.

Buffett did a four-city promotional tour this past spring in which, as he often does in the States, he paired his music with his message. ("Concert and Conversation," the events are called.) He did 25 press interviews with the electronic and print media—national and local—including a web chat on what, for students and young professionals, has become the most important media site of them all, Sina.com's microblog (the Chinese version of Twitter).

It was only his second visit to China. And though he was aware of his father's status in the country, he hadn't quite grasped the magnitude of it. Sitting in a Beijing hotel in August, a day before his Great Wall concert, Buffett says he was taken aback by the intensity of the reception. "It wasn't quite what I was expecting," he says, laughing. "It was like a presidential campaign or something. There were reporters everywhere."

You have to remember that while Peter Andrew Buffett may be the second son of the "god of stocks" and the late Susan Buffett—his mother died in 2004—he is not used to the star treatment. Far from it, in fact. He and his wife, Jennifer, have a place in New York City but spend much of their time in quiet Ulster County, N.Y., 90 miles north of the city. (The couple have no children.) In addition to pursuing his music career, he, like his two older siblings, runs his own charitable foundation, which his father has funded generously with Berkshire Hathaway stock. (His sister, Susie, still lives in Omaha and focuses on her philanthropic work; his brother, Howard, owns a farm in Decatur, Ill.) Above all, the key thing about Peter Buffett is that he appears to be absolutely and completely normal. It hardly seems possible, but there it is. Well-grounded, affable, nary a twitch of neurosis or insecurity about him. "Oh, yeah," he says, "I get that all the time. You're Warren Buffett's son, and you're soooo normal."

Audiences everywhere are, inevitably, curious as to how exactly that came to be. But in China, the curiosity is off the charts. One of the things Buffett likes to remind audiences of is that when he was growing up—long before Dad became America's economic oracle, adviser to Presidents and writer of op-eds reassuring a depressed nation that all is not lost—his father was a supremely successful but largely anonymous investor. He was a regular guy who was known and revered only by the kind of folks who go to sleep with a copy of Graham and Dodd under their pillow. And he's basically the same guy now.

The curiosity in China is fed by the fact that when Peter's father announced he was giving away his considerable wealth to a foundation run by another supremely rich guy, Bill Gates, a lot of folks there had a single thought: "Why would he do that to his kids?" Mostly lost in translation was the fact that the elder Buffett was acting in accordance with his long-articulated position that he would give his kids "enough money so that they would feel they could do anything—but not so much that they could do nothing."

But curiosity alone wouldn't have resulted in the sale of 320,000 books. Something about Buffett's message "is definitely resonating with many young Chinese," says Zhang, his editor. That message is inextricable from Peter's biography. He tells audiences that from the time he can remember he always loved music. "My mother said I sang before I spoke," he told an interviewer for CCTV last spring. (His dad has been known to play a little ukulele.) A good student, he got into Stanford University, but was not particularly career-focused or interested in Graham and Dodd. For the first year and a half of college, he says, "I took everything that ended in 101 or -ology."

Then—and here is where a young Chinese audience leans in, not quite believing what they are hearing—he dropped out. He decided that he wanted to pursue a career in music. "It was right in front of my nose my whole life," he says. So he took a "small inheritance from my grandfather, bought an apartment in San Francisco, and tried to make a go of it." And his parents, he tells mostly stunned audiences, were fine with it. "They were encouraging but also made it clear that if you blow it—well, good luck," says Buffett. Within two years he was confident he'd made the right choice: "By then I knew I could make a living in music."

The point, Buffett repeats in all his appearances in China, is that by quitting Stanford and trying to make a go of it in music, he was doing the same thing his father did. "My father knew early on what he loved to do, and he did it, and he's doing it to this day," he says. "So I tell audiences [in China] that my father and I do, in fact, do the same thing for a living. We both do what we love."

To American ears, this can sound trite. The cynic says, "Okay, c'mon, it's a lot easier to do whatever it is you want to do if Warren Buffett is your dad." But that's not how most Chinese audiences react. Most audiences in China are gob-smacked—and for reasons that are perfectly understandable. The outside world sees China as a rising economic power, a nation with seemingly irreversible economic momentum. That may be true enough. But for all its gaudy economic statistics, on the inside the country is also an economic pressure cooker. Children with aspirations for college put in 14 to 18 hours a day studying, desperate to get accepted to a good university. If they get in, they have to pick a major early. They're on an up escalator—which, true enough, is better than not being on one—and they can't get off. If a student graduates and lands a desirable job, he or she often doesn't get paid particularly well and has to put in long hours. To top it off, many of today's younger workers are children of China's one-child policy, which means that they alone are responsible for taking care of their parents when they retire. In short, says, Edward Bell, an executive at Ogilvy & Mather in Shanghai who has studied the twentysomething Chinese in depth, "this is a generation that has to sprint just to stay even. I call it Generation Stress."

It's precisely that angst that Peter Buffett taps into. That's why Tian Li Feng, like a lot of Chinese young professionals, isn't particularly surprised by its success. He graduated from business school a year ago in Beijing, a finance major who now works for the Bank of Communications in China, a large state-owned bank. A big fan of Peter's father—"I think I've read all the books about him," he says—he went to see Peter Buffett speak this past spring, not quite knowing what to expect. "I was touched," he says. "Particularly when he spoke about leaving Stanford to pursue his music." Shaking his head, he adds, "Such a prestigious school."

Buffett understands that the experiences he writes about, and the impulses that drove his career, are uniquely American. He also is self-effacing and secure enough to acknowledge that if his name were Smith or Jones, no one in China would be interested. But China novice or not, when he says that "it seems as if this place is moving at such light speed that a lot of young people don't get a chance to have a second thought," he's right.

"I don't think my parents would ever let me do [what he did]," says Tian, the banker. "But maybe someday," he adds softly, "my own child can have that choice." If so, Peter might leave as rich a legacy in China as his dad.

## A NATION GRAPPLES WITH CHARITY
## OCTOBER 17, 2011

### *A Sidebar by Bill Powell*

Last year Warren Buffett and Bill Gates visited Beijing for what they thought would be the least controversial of reasons. They had arranged to have a private dinner with a group of rich, successful Chinese businessmen, and to talk with them about a subject that seems innocuous: philanthropy. The Chinese blogosphere caught wind of the dinner and erupted in chatter. "And not all of it," acknowledges Peter Buffett, "was positive."

That's putting it mildly. The subject of rich folks giving away their money to charity might be uncontroversial in the U.S., but in China it's not. In fact, Peter says, when he comes to China to perform and speak to groups of students and young professionals, "the subject of second-generation wealth always comes up. They always want to talk about it."

There are two reasons philanthropy gets people riled up in China. First, a fair number of rich folks there believe giving it away is antithetical to Chinese values—which stress family above all. It's why some Chinese were upset when they heard (mistakenly) that Buffett and Gates were coming to tell rich Chinese how to give away their wealth. Many young Chinese were stunned when Buffett said he was giving most of his wealth to the Gates Foundation.

But the second reason wealthy Chinese haven't been racing to donate more of their money, particularly this year, is less obvious: Charitable foundations in China are dogged by the whiff—and sometimes more than that—of corruption. Management fees for charities in China are often up to 10% of donations collected, compared with around 3% in the West. Earlier this year, the mere photograph on the web of a young woman identified as a manager of the Red Cross in China sent the blogosphere into a frenzy. The reason? The photo showed her driving a fancy car and carrying a Hermès purse.

The agency insisted that the woman in question did not, in fact, work for the Red Cross in China. (She was the girlfriend of what the agency murkily called a "business partner.") The denials didn't matter. Donations to RCIC in the first half of 2011 plummeted and, according to some Chinese press reports, slowed considerably to the charitable sector as a whole.

That pointed to the lack of trust that exists in the charitable sector in China. Several prominent Chinese businessmen and philanthropists—led by Cao Dewang, owner of one of the largest glassmaking companies in China—have now publicly insisted that the domestic charities they donate to have to become more transparent and cost-effective. "This doesn't have anything to do with values, Western or Chinese," Cao has said. "To increase charity now in China is a matter of trust."

# Why Stocks Beat Gold and Bonds

February 27, 2012

*An excerpt from Buffett's letter to shareholders in the 2011 Berkshire Hathaway annual report*

*Gold is a barren asset; bonds are seldom rewarding to investors; well-chosen productive assets like common stocks and land are the logical prospects to deliver superior returns.*

Those are the messages of the article that follows, which is an excerpt (carrying a *Fortune* title) from Warren Buffett's letter in Berkshire's 2011 annual report. Those are also the principles by which Buffett has led his investing life. So this piece is a good one to encounter as we near the end of our forty-seven-year Buffett expedition—this real-time business biography as played out in the pages of *Fortune*.

We can also add up what Buffett has accomplished, both as investor and businessman, in those forty-seven years. In 1966 he was the proprietor of an unfamous hedge fund, Buffett Partnership Ltd., and the controlling shareowner and de facto CEO of a small New England textile company, Berkshire Hathaway, with $49 million in annual revenues. By 2012, Berkshire was No. 5 in the *Fortune* 500, with $162 billion in revenues. That leap, largely unrecognized—even Buffett was surprised to learn he had the distinction about to be noted—is extraordinary: No other man has within his lifetime taken a company from obscurity to the top ten of the 500.

Buffett would say that doesn't matter much—revenues not being that important. Market value is something he respects much more, and for 2012, Berkshire ranked fourth in the 500, with $257 billion. Well in front in that measurement then was another company built by one man in his lifetime, the late Steve Jobs of Apple, an enterprise whose market value at that same point was $416 billion. The two men had gotten to know each other decades ago, when both were members of the Grinnell College board. They talked rarely after that, but Buffett just happens to remember that once not too long ago Jobs called to ask about ideas for dealing with Apple's excess cash—and then went away and did nothing that Buffett had suggested.

That hedge fund in Buffett's life, Buffett Partnership Ltd., disappeared long ago, closed at the end of 1969 because Buffett could not stomach the speculation that had entered the market. But the $100 million it then had in investments was the seed, so to speak, of $103 billion in common stocks that Berkshire held in mid-2013. Buffett's biggest stakes were spread across the American economy: Berkshire then had $19.9 billion in Wells Fargo, $16 billion in Coca-Cola, $13 billion in IBM, and $11.3 billion in American Express.

In 2012, all of Berkshire's financial feats were overshadowed by two pieces of Buffett news. First, a bit earlier, in August 2011, the *New York Times* ran an op-ed Buffett had written, under the headline "Stop Coddling the Rich." Buffett compared the low tax rate he was paying (17 percent) to the rates of the twenty other people in his office (33 percent to 41 percent) and called for tax increases for anyone earning more than $1 million. In the election year of 2012, the Obama administration both embraced and expanded that proposition, backing a "Buffett Rule"—immediately and hugely controversial, of course—that would impose higher taxes on everyone with taxable income above $250,000. After Obama won, tax rates for upper-income filers were indeed raised, but the new, higher rates did not reach down to the $250,000 level.

In the second news item, Buffett announced by press release on April 17 that he had been diagnosed with stage 1 prostate cancer, a label denoting (among other specifics) a cancer that has not spread outside the prostate gland. In July, Buffett commenced two months of radiation at an Omaha hospital. During his treatment, he experienced the fatigue that normally accompanies it and consequently elected on some days to work from home. But by the end of the year he had regained all of his old vigor and was back to his office full-time.

At Berkshire's 2013 annual meeting in the spring, a non-stop five days of events for Buffett, he sailed through it all, displaying the amazing energy he brings to anything he likes. Buffett turned 83 in August 2013, and he has every expectation that he will live for many years to come and keep tap dancing to work. —CL

I nvesting is often described as the process of laying out money now in the expectation of receiving more money in the future. At Berkshire Hathaway we take a more demanding approach, defining investing as the transfer to others of purchasing power now with the reasoned expectation of receiving more purchasing power—after taxes have been paid on nominal gains—in the future. More succinctly, investing is forgoing consumption now in order to have the ability to consume more at a later date.

From our definition there flows an important corollary: The riskiness of an investment is not measured by beta (a Wall Street term encompassing volatility and often used in measuring risk) but rather by the probability—the reasoned probability—of that investment causing its owner a loss of purchasing power over his contemplated holding period. Assets can fluctuate greatly in price and not be risky as long as they are reasonably certain to deliver increased purchasing power over their holding period. And as we will see, a nonfluctuating asset can be laden with risk.

Investment possibilities are both many and varied. There are three major categories, however, and it's important to understand the characteristics of each. So let's survey the field.

Investments that are denominated in a given currency include money-market funds, bonds, mortgages, bank deposits, and other instruments. Most of these currency-based investments are thought of as "safe." In truth they are among the most dangerous of assets. Their beta may be zero, but their risk is huge.

Over the past century these instruments have destroyed the purchasing power of investors in many countries, even as these holders continued to receive timely payments of interest and principal. This ugly result, moreover, will forever recur. Governments determine the ultimate value of money, and systemic forces will sometimes cause them to gravitate to policies that produce inflation. From time to time such policies spin out of control.

Even in the U.S., where the wish for a stable currency is strong, the dollar has fallen a staggering 86% in value since 1965, when I took over management of Berkshire. It takes no less than $7 today to buy what $1 did at that time. Consequently, a tax-free institution would have needed 4.3% interest annually from bond investments over that period to simply maintain its purchasing power. Its managers would have been kidding themselves if they thought of *any* portion of that interest as "income."

For taxpaying investors like you and me, the picture has been far worse. During the same 47-year period, continuous rolling of U.S. Treasury bills produced 5.7% annually. That sounds satisfactory. But if an individual investor paid personal income taxes at a rate averaging 25%, this 5.7% return would have yielded nothing in the way of real income. This investor's visible income tax would have stripped him of 1.4 points of the stated yield, and the invisible inflation tax would have devoured the remaining 4.3 points. It's noteworthy that the implicit inflation "tax" was more than triple the explicit income tax that our investor probably thought of as his main burden. "In God We Trust" may be imprinted on our currency, but the hand that activates our government's printing press has been all too human.

High interest rates, of course, can compensate purchasers for the inflation risk they face with currency-based investments—and indeed, rates in the early 1980s did that job nicely. Current rates, however, do not come close to offsetting the purchasing-power risk that investors assume. Right now bonds should come with a warning label.

Under today's conditions, therefore, I do not like currency-based investments. Even so, Berkshire holds significant amounts of them, primarily of the short-term variety. At Berkshire the need for ample liquidity occupies center stage and will never be slighted, however inadequate rates may be. Accommodating this need, we primarily hold U.S. Treasury bills, the only investment that can be counted on for liquidity under the most chaotic of economic conditions. Our working level for liquidity is $20 billion; $10 billion is our absolute minimum.

Beyond the requirements that liquidity and regulators impose on us, we will purchase currency-related securities only if they offer the possibility of unusual gain—either because a particular credit is mispriced, as can occur in periodic junk-bond debacles, or because rates rise to a level that offers the possibility of realizing substantial capital gains on high-grade bonds when rates fall. Though we've exploited both opportunities in the past—and may do so again—we are now 180 degrees removed from such prospects. Today, a wry comment that Wall Streeter Shelby Cullom Davis made long ago seems apt: "Bonds promoted as offering risk-free returns are now priced to deliver return-free risk."

The second major category of investments involves assets that will never produce anything, but that are purchased in the buyer's hope that someone else—who also knows that the assets will be forever unproductive—will pay more for them in the future. Tulips, of all things, briefly became a favorite of such buyers in the 17th century.

This type of investment requires an expanding pool of buyers, who, in turn, are enticed because they believe the buying pool will expand still further. Owners are *not* inspired by what the asset itself can produce—it will remain lifeless forever—but rather by the belief that others will desire it even more avidly in the future.

The major asset in this category is gold, currently a huge favorite of investors who fear almost all other assets, especially paper money (of whose value, as noted, they are right to be fearful). Gold, however, has two significant shortcomings, being neither of much use nor procreative. True, gold has some industrial and decorative utility, but the demand for these purposes is both limited and incapable of soaking up new production. Meanwhile, if you own one ounce of gold for an eternity, you will still own one ounce at its end.

What motivates most gold purchasers is their belief that the ranks of the fearful will grow. During the past decade that belief has proved correct. Beyond that, the rising price has on its own generated additional buying enthusiasm, attracting purchasers who see the rise as validating an investment thesis. As "bandwagon" investors join any party, they create their own truth—*for a while*.

Over the past 15 years, both Internet stocks and houses have demonstrated the extraordinary excesses that can be created by combining an initially sensible thesis with well-publicized rising prices. In these bubbles, an army of originally skeptical investors succumbed to the "proof" delivered by the market, and the pool of buyers—for a time—expanded sufficiently to keep the bandwagon rolling. But bubbles blown large enough inevitably pop. And then the old proverb is confirmed once again: "What the wise man does in the beginning, the fool does in the end."

Today the world's gold stock is about 170,000 metric tons. If all of this gold were melded together, it would form a cube of about 68 feet per side. (Picture it fitting comfortably within a baseball infield.) At $1,750 per ounce—gold's price as I write this—its value would be about $9.6 trillion. Call this cube pile A.

Let's now create a pile B costing an equal amount. For that, we could buy *all* U.S. cropland (400 million acres with output of about $200 billion annually), plus 16 Exxon Mobils (the world's most profitable company, one earning more than $40 billion annually). After these purchases, we would have about $1 trillion left over for walking-around money (no sense feeling strapped after this buying binge). Can you imagine an investor with $9.6 trillion selecting pile A over pile B?

Beyond the staggering valuation given the existing stock of gold, current prices make today's annual production of gold command about $160 billion. Buyers—whether jewelry and industrial users, frightened individuals, or speculators—must continually absorb this additional supply to merely maintain an equilibrium at present prices.

A century from now the 400 million acres of farmland will have produced staggering amounts of corn, wheat, cotton, and other crops—and will continue to produce that valuable bounty, whatever the currency may be. Exxon Mobil will probably have delivered trillions of dollars in dividends to its owners and will also hold assets worth many more trillions (and, remember, you get 16 Exxons). The 170,000 tons of gold will be unchanged in size and still incapable of producing anything. You can fondle the cube, but it will not respond.

Admittedly, when people a century from now are fearful, it's likely many will still rush to gold. I'm confident, however, that the $9.6 trillion current valuation of pile A will compound over the century at a rate far inferior to that achieved by pile B.

Our first two categories enjoy maximum popularity at peaks of fear: Terror over economic collapse drives individuals to currency-based assets, most particularly U.S. obligations, and fear of currency collapse fosters movement to sterile assets such as gold. We heard "cash is king" in late 2008, just when cash should have been deployed rather than held. Similarly, we heard "cash is trash" in the early 1980s just when fixed-dollar investments were at their most attractive level in memory. On those occasions, investors who required a supportive crowd paid dearly for that comfort.

My own preference—and you knew this was coming—is our third category: investment in productive assets, whether businesses, farms, or real estate. Ideally, these assets should have the ability in inflationary times to deliver output that will retain its purchasing-power value while requiring a minimum of new capital investment. Farms, real estate, and many businesses such as Coca-Cola, IBM, and our own See's Candy meet that double-barreled test. Certain other companies—think of our regulated utilities, for example—fail it because inflation places heavy capital requirements on them. To earn more, their owners must invest more. Even so, these investments will remain superior to nonproductive or currency-based assets.

Whether the currency a century from now is based on gold, seashells, shark teeth, or a piece of paper (as today), people will be willing to exchange a couple of minutes of their daily labor for a Coca-Cola or some See's peanut brittle. In the future the U.S. population will move more goods, consume more food, and require more living space than it does now. People will forever exchange what they produce for what others produce.

Our country's businesses will continue to efficiently deliver goods and services wanted by our citizens. Metaphorically, these commercial "cows" will live for centuries and give ever greater quantities of "milk" to boot. Their value will be determined not by the medium of exchange but rather by their capacity to deliver milk. Proceeds from the sale of the milk will compound for the owners of the cows, just as they did during the 20th century when the Dow increased from 66 to 11,497 (and paid loads of dividends as well).

Berkshire's goal will be to increase its ownership of first-class businesses. Our first choice will be to own them in their entirety—but we will also be owners by way of holding sizable amounts of marketable stocks. I believe that over any extended period of time this category of investing will prove to be the runaway winner among the three we've examined. More important, it will be by far the safest.

# Warren Buffett Is Bullish . . . on Women

May 20, 2013

**BY WARREN BUFFETT**

*This article, as the preface noted, is new to* Tap Dancing to Work. *The article appeared in* Fortune *in early 2013, months after the hardcover edition of the book was released in late 2012. Welcoming it to the paperback, though, is a pleasure, not only because it is first-class reading but also because it provides me an opportunity to look back at Buffett's history insofar as it relates to women in the workplace.*

*He deserves, first, an unalloyed compliment: Among the many hundreds of top business executives I have known, he has always seemed to me to be the least biased about such characteristics as gender, race, and ethnicity. He simply doesn't care how intelligence and ability come packaged—though as that statement suggests, those are qualities about which he is* indeed *biased.*

*I myself am among those who have benefitted from Buffett's mind-set about gender. He could, after all, have chosen a man—but he didn't—to edit his annual shareholder letter (a thirty-six-year pro bono job I have found greatly satisfying). He has also said publicly that he would have long ago nominated me for the Berkshire Hathaway board had the rules of my company, Time Inc., not forbidden its journalists to be corporate directors.*

*To that fact, though, there is an offset. Despite Buffett's lack of prejudice about gender, he was very slow to climb on the policy train that said major corporations should be putting women on their boards. That was not entirely by accident, as an incident from the early 1990s will show. Buffett was then for a time running Salomon Inc. (on an emergency basis—see page 78 of this book), whose directors were all men. The press was meanwhile focusing increasingly on the paucity of women directors in the corporate world generally. I distinctly recall a conversation then between Buffett and me in which he criticized the press for missing the real point. "The goal," he said, "should be electing the very best possible director, regardless of whether that's a man or a woman."*

*That is totally logical, of course. But it ignores the practicalities of the time, which is that the number of credentialed business and professional women from which a company might select a board member was then greatly limited—which meant that the odds of identifying and signing up a woman who might be "the very best possible director" were not good at all.*

*Change ultimately came on the Omaha front in 2003 when Charlotte Guyman, then 46, a former Microsoft manager whom Buffett knew through Bill Gates, went on the Berkshire board. She proved herself a smart, very interested and hardworking director, and in four years she was joined on the board by Susan Decker, then 44, a former CEO of Yahoo! whom Charlie Munger knew from the Costco board. Then, just this year, Meryl Witmer, 51, who runs a New York investment partnership and was recommended to Buffett by one of his Berkshire colleagues, also joined the board.*

*The election of these three directors, along with Steve Burke of NBCUniversal and Comcast, who joined the board in 2009 at age 49, had the added advantage of significantly lowering the average age of Berkshire's directors, among them six octogenarians, including Buffett and Munger. Also reducing the average age are directors Howard Buffett, 58, and Bill Gates, 56.* —CL

I n the flood of words written recently about women and work, one related and hugely significant point seems to me to have been neglected. It has to do with America's future, about which—here's a familiar opinion from me—I'm an unqualified optimist. Now entertain another opinion of mine: Women are a major reason we will do so well.

Start with the fact that our country's progress since 1776 has been mindblowing, like nothing the world has ever seen. Our secret sauce has been a political and economic system that unleashes human potential to an extraordinary degree. As a result Americans today enjoy an abundance of goods and services that no one could have dreamed of just a few centuries ago

But that's not the half of it—or, rather, it's just about the half of it. America has forged this success while utilizing, in large part, only half of the country's talent. For most of our history, women—whatever their abilities—have been relegated to the sidelines. Only in recent years have we begun to correct that problem.

Despite the inspiring "all men are created equal" assertion in the Declaration of Independence, male supremacy quickly became enshrined in the Constitution. In Article II, dealing with the presidency, the 39 delegates who signed the document—all men, naturally—repeatedly used male pronouns. In poker, they call that a "tell."

Finally, 133 years later, in 1920, the U.S. softened its discrimination against women via the 19th Amendment, which gave them the right to vote. But that law scarcely budged attitudes and behaviors. In its wake, 33 men rose to the Supreme Court before Sandra Day O'Connor made the grade—61 years after the amendment was ratified. For those of you who like numbers, the odds against that procession of males occurring by chance are more than 8 billion to one.

When people questioned the absence of female appointees, the standard reply over those 61 years was simply "no qualified candidates." The electorate took a similar stance. When my dad was elected to Congress in 1942, only eight of his 434 colleagues were women. One lonely woman, Maine's Margaret Chase Smith, sat in the Senate.

Resistance among the powerful is natural when change clashes with their self-interest. Business, politics, and, yes, religions provide many examples of such defensive behavior. After all, who wants to double the number of competitors for top positions?

But an even greater enemy of change may well be the ingrained attitudes of those who simply can't imagine a world different from the one they've lived in. What happened in my own family provides an example. I have two sisters. The three of us were regarded, by our parents and teachers alike, as having roughly equal intelligence—and IQ tests in fact confirmed our equality. For a long time, to boot, my sisters had far greater "social" IQ than I. (No, we weren't tested for that—but, believe me, the evidence was overwhelming.)

The moment I emerged from my mother's womb, however, my possibilities dwarfed those of my siblings, for I was a boy! And my brainy, personable, and good-looking siblings were not. My parents would love us equally, and our teachers would give us similar grades. But at every turn my sisters would be told—more through signals than words—that success for them would be "marrying well." I was meanwhile hearing that the world's opportunities were there for me to seize.

So my floor became my sisters' ceiling—and nobody thought much about ripping up that pattern until a few decades ago. Now, thank heavens, the structural barriers for women are falling.

Still an obstacle remains: Too many women continue to impose limitations on themselves, talking themselves out of achieving their potential. Here, too, I have had some firsthand experience.

Among the scores of brilliant and interesting women I've known is the late Katharine Graham, long the controlling shareholder and CEO of the Washington Post Co. Kay knew she was intelligent. But she had been brainwashed—I don't like that word, but it's appropriate—by her mother, husband, and who knows who else to believe that men were superior, particularly at business.

When her husband died, it was in the self-interest of some of the men around Kay to convince her that her feelings of inadequacy were justified. The pressures they put on her were torturing. Fortunately, Kay, in addition to being smart, had an inner strength. Calling on it, she managed to ignore the baritone voices urging her to turn over her heritage to them.

I met Kay in 1973 and quickly saw that she was a person of unusual ability and character. But the gender-related self-doubt was certainly there too. Her brain knew better, but she could never quite still the voice inside her that said, "Men know more about running a business than you ever will."

I told Kay that she had to discard the fun-house mirror that others had set before her and instead view herself in a mirror that reflected reality. "Then," I said, "you will see a woman who is a match for anyone, male or female."

I wish I could claim I was successful in that campaign. Proof was certainly on my side: Washington Post stock went up more than 4,000%—that's 40 for 1—during Kay's 18 years as boss. After retiring, she won a Pulitzer Prize for her superb autobiography. But her self-doubt remained, a testament to how deeply a message of unworthiness can be implanted in even a brilliant mind.

I'm happy to say that fun-house mirrors are becoming less common among the women I meet. Try putting one in front of my daughter. She'll just laugh and smash it. Women should never forget that it is common for powerful and seemingly self-assured males to have more than a bit of the Wizard of Oz in them. Pull the curtain aside, and you'll often discover they are not supermen after all. (Just ask their wives!)

So, my fellow males, what's in this for us? Why should we care whether the remaining barriers facing women are dismantled and the fun-house mirrors junked? Never mind that I believe the ethical case in itself is compelling. Let's look instead to your self-interest.

No manager operates his or her plants at 80% efficiency when steps could be taken that would increase output. And no CEO wants male employees to be underutilized when improved training or working conditions would boost productivity. So take it one step further: If obvious benefits flow from helping the male component of the workforce achieve its potential, why in the world wouldn't you want to include its counterpart?

Fellow males, get onboard. The closer that America comes to fully employing the talents of all its citizens, the greater its output of goods and services will be. We've seen what can be accomplished when we use 50% of our human capacity. If you visualize what 100% can do, you'll join me as an unbridled optimist about America's future.

## Final Note from the Editor

*When* Fortune *first mentioned Warren Buffett, in 1966, Berkshire's stock (today's Class A) was about $22. In mid-2013, it was $168,600. Had $1,000 been invested in Berkshire at that 1966 price of $22, it would have grown by mid-2013 to $7,663,636. —CL*

# ACKNOWLEDGMENTS

I could not have done this book without . . . Warren Buffett. Thanks, Warren, for being so continuously interesting that I could orchestrate a book even when I didn't expect there to be a book.

I could not have done this book without . . . Doris Burke. She's a *Fortune* staff member, trained as a librarian but grown to be so expert about all manner of facts that she is this writer's (and many *Fortune* writers') essential aide when the going gets tough on an article—or book. Her name is on one of the articles in this book (page 286). In my mind, it is carved on the entryway into dozens of those articles.

Doris's fact-gathering colleague Marilyn Adamo was of great assistance as well (which is one reason the two never go on vacation at the same time).

And I could not forget the help of so many other *Fortune* people. The top brass, Andy Serwer and Hank Gilman (and *their* boss, Time Inc. editor-in-chief John Huey), gave me the time to complete this book after I had not come close to finishing it on several successive vacations. And what a blessing that I didn't finish it years ago, because if I had, there would have been no Giving Pledge, no long-term bet with Protégé Partners, and even no David Sokol. And then, when I went into full gear on the book and ran into both a hand operation (think of typing!) and illness in my family, they gave me more time. I am deeply indebted to all.

And besides that, when he was just a writer, not the ruler of our realm, Andy wrote three of the articles in the book (making himself the second-most prolific contributor, after me). Hank meanwhile oversaw every aspect of the book, from initial contract to final contract, and then final copy, with the great common sense he brings to everything. Both of them made it a pleasure for me to be in business with this magazine, for which I have happily worked almost fifty-nine years.

Mia Diehl, *Fortune*'s director of photography, combed our treasure trove of Warren Buffett photographs and picked out the ones we used with her usual fine eye for what's engaging and distinctive. Chad McCabe assisted with a layout that worked.

There are about ninety separate "items" in this book—full articles, excerpts, sound bites (so to speak), and letters from readers. In a *Fortune* world that is still not totally digitized (this is a hint, guys) or is sometimes digitized in a way that isn't totally helpful, just getting all that copy into an easy-to-handle form was a challenge. Cullen Wheeler, Chris Tkaczyk, and Kelly Champion each did a part of that less-than-stimulating work. And at the end, Cappy Lyons turned a steady stream of articles into Word documents I could easily deal with. Thanks to all for seeing that through.

*Fortune*'s copyroom, run by Carol Gwinn and Alfie Graham, is one of my favorite haunts, and the two as usual kept me on the grammatical, clean-English track—I hope. Their colleague, Angel Mass, delivered the charts I needed with perfect timing.

And then there was the Time Inc. lawyer assigned to this case, Amy Glickman, who thought of more details than I could possibly have imagined. Beyond that, Amy took the whole digital book home to read one weekend and reported to me both midway and at the end that she had really liked it, not only in its coverage of Buffett, but also in its sweep of business history! We should all have such lawyers.

I—who had never much wanted to do a book—was lucky enough to secure an agent, Tracy Brown, who knew the ropes and kept me relatively calm at nerve-racking moments. He was a writer's joy, because he loved the book's introductions and articles from the minute he saw them—and then loved the book's jacket, too. I could not have asked for more. Thanks, Tracy, for all the support.

And thanks also to Adrian Zackheim, president of Portfolio, the publisher of this book. He knows business books extremely well, so his vote of confidence in what came to be *Tap Dancing to Work* was very heartening to me and *Fortune*. His colleagues Will Weisser, Emily Angell, and Bria Sandford then shepherded the book along on what turned out to be a tight schedule. Kudos to all.

Running through my mind as I compiled this book were the names and faces of scores of editors, writers, and reporter associates (known as "researchers" in the days when I started as one) who worked on the articles in this book. Editors, in the *Fortune* style, are almost always anonymous. But there are three on the staff now, Tim Smith, Nick Varchaver, and Brian O'Keefe, who have been wonderful to work with on various Buffett stories. (Brian came up with—see page 267—my all-time favorite headline, "Would You Like That $11 Billion in Twenties?").

An alphabetical list of the reporter associates who worked on this book's articles does not fit the brainpower and effort they put into the job, but in the interests of practicality, I will resort to one: Maria Atanasov, Edward Baig, Kate Ballen, Suzanne Barlyn, Rosalind Klein Berlin, Julia Boorstin, Doris Burke (again), John Curran, Eric Dash, Patty de Llosa, Darienne Dennis, Jane Folpe,

Carrie Gottlieb, David Kirkpatrick, Claudine Knight, Susan Kuhn, Michael McFadden, Joe McGowan, Anthony J. Michels, Ruth Moss, Patricia Neering, Lou Richman, Ellen Schultz, Sally Shaver, Bill Sheeline, Robert Steyer, Natasha Tarpley, Carol Vinzant, Melanie Warner, and Wilton Woods.

From the start, I knew of course that my stories would be plentiful in this book. Then came the pleasant surprise: About forty other *Fortune* writers, most not now on the staff, were contributors, too. One, the late Dan Seligman, was a mentor of mine; many, like him, were close friends; almost all were writers whom I greatly respected when they were on the staff, and still do. *Fortune* has been fortunate in its writers—and all the edit people around them—over the years. Most have been class acts, and that has shown up in the quality of the magazine.

I am glad to have found an excuse for again showcasing their work. I am delighted as well to have done it while realizing once again that every member of my trade who has dealt with Warren Buffett, and with his ability to put exceptional ideas into words, was handed a great journalistic gift.

# INDEX

# JIM O'NEILL

**THE GROWTH MAP: Economic Opportunity in the BRICs and Beyond**

Ten years ago, Jim O'Neill made a startling prediction: the G-7 countries including the US, the UK and Japan would no longer be the world's economic powerhouses. With globalization, a new era would emerge in which the emerging forces of Brazil, Russia, India and China - populous, increasingly urbanized and overflowing with raw materials and ambition - would overtake the largest Western economies.

The BRICs were born.

No other economic idea has defined the 21st Century more powerfully or more accurately. In the past decade all four BRIC nations have experienced significant growth and are now among the top ten economies in the world. Jim O'Neill's single prediction has spurred economic and social change, created new political structures and challenged the thinking of business leaders, governments, and decision makers.

But what does the future hold? Can the BRICs sustain their exceptional levels of growth? Which other nations will drive economic power further south and east?

In this landmark book Jim O'Neill, chairman of Goldman Sachs Asset Management, shares his insights on how and why he developed one of the most compelling economic concepts of our time. He sets out the 'Next 11' concept for the set of fast-growing countries that could have a BRIC-like impact on the world (Bangladesh, Egypt, Indonesia, Iran, Mexico, Nigeria, Pakistan, Philippines, South Korea, Turkey and Vietnam). And he redefines those that offer the strongest potential for transformation as Growth Markets.

The world needs growth. The world needs *The Growth Map*.

'Goldman Sachs' rock star' *Business Week*

'Lively, powerful and highly accessible' Gillian Tett, *Financial Times*

'This is a book we all needed' Sir Martin Sorrell, CEO, WPP

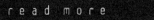
# PHILIP DELVES BROUGHTON

---

**WHAT THEY TEACH YOU AT HARVARD BUSINESS SCHOOL**

**What *do* they teach you at Harvard Business School?**

Graduates of Harvard Business School run many of the world's biggest and most influential banks, companies and countries. But what kind of person does it take to succeed at HBS? And would you want to be one of them?

For anyone who has ever wondered what goes on behind Harvard Business School's hallowed walls, Philip Delves Broughton's hilarious and enlightening account of his experiences on its prestigious MBA programme provides an extraordinary glimpse into a world of case-study conundrums, guest lectures, *Apprentice*-style tasks, booze luging, burn-outs and high flyers.

And with HBS alumni heading the very global governments, financial institutions and FTSE 500 companies whose reckless love of deregulation and debt got us into so much trouble, Delves Broughton discovers where HBS really adds value – and where it falls disturbingly short.

'Delves Broughton captures an essence of HBS that is part cult, part psychological morass, part hothouse . . . His book is invaluable. Quite brilliant'
Simon Heffer, *Literary Review*

'A funny and revealing insider's view . . . his fascination is infectious' *Sunday Times*

'A particularly absorbing and entertaining read' *Financial Times*

'Horrifying and very funny . . . An excellent book' *Wall Street Journal*

---